Masquerade in Black

by
William Torbert Leonard

The Scarecrow Press, Inc.
Metuchen, N.J., & London
1986

BOOKS BY WILLIAM TORBERT LEONARD:

Broadway Bound: A Guide to Shows That Died Aborning

Theatre: Stage to Screen to Television

The Funsters*

Hollywood Players: The Thirties*

Hollywood Players: The Forties*

Film Directors Guide: The U.S.*

---

*Co-authored with James Robert Parish.

Library of Congress Cataloging-in-Publication Data

Leonard, William T.
   Masquerade in black.

   Bibliography: p.
   Includes index.
   1. Blackface entertainers. 2. Actors--United
States--Biography. 3. Minstrel shows. 4. Shakespeare,
William, 1564-1616--Stage history. 5. Blacks in the
performing arts. 6. Afro-Americans in the performing
arts. I. Title.
PN2071.B58L46   1986   792'.028'0922 [B]   86-6597
ISBN 0-8108-1895-7

For my father,

WILLIAM CARLTON LEONARD,

who could black-up with the best of them;
and my mother,

HATTIE WILLIAMS LEONARD,

who tolerated it

CONTENTS

LIST OF ILLUSTRATIONS

ACKNOWLEDGMENTS

During the two-year period of research that resulted in this history of whites in blackface many unsuspecting people willingly contributed their services (often with straight faces) to what must have seemed to be arcane, bizarre, obscure, and persistent questioning. Among the brave ones were the efficient and helpful staffs of The Folger Shakespeare Library of Washington, D.C.; Geraldine Duclow and Elaine Ebo of The Free Library of Philadelphia Theatre Collection; David King of the Rare Book Department of The Free Library of Philadelphia; Curator Dorothy Swerdlove and her staff at the Library of the Performing Arts at Lincoln Center, New York; Frederick Kent, Linda Wood, and Cecilia Jessum of the Music Department; Bernard Pasqualini and Frank Green of the Newspaper Department and Robert Looney of the Print and Pictures Department of The Free Library of Philadelphia.

Special appreciation, too, should be given to Gerald Bordman, G. Harold Hozey, and Mimi and Ralph Rosnow, both for immediate aid and for assistance whenever it was needed.

Langston Hughes's poem "CROSS," copyright 1926 by Alfred A. Knopf, Inc. and renewed 1954 by Langston Hughes, is reprinted from Selected Poems of Langston Hughes and used by permission of the publisher, Random House.

Photographs of Walter Huston and Paul Robeson by Florence Vandamm and of Frank Tinney by White Studios are published by permission from The New York Public Library, Astor, Lenox and Tilden Foundations, Billy Rose Collection.

PREAMBLE TO BURNT CORK

Blackface, today in America, is justifiably taboo and anathema to many, heading an appreciable decline in derogatory ethnic humor. But there was a time, during a past age of innocence, when whites masquerading in blackface served to lighten and brighten the lives of millions of theatregoers. The true history of any race or nation is seldom edifying; this is equally true of some aspects of theatre history, especially when these aspects are magnified by today's long-neglected advancement in civil rights and progressive liberalism. Whether people are white, black, yellow, or purple, their emotions run high when exposing or chronicling color-oriented history.

Some time ago, Robert Guillaume (television's title character in Benson) and I had a discussion about the problems that whites today may have accepting Tobacco Road and that blacks may have accepting Porgy and Bess and Uncle Tom's Cabin. Also discussed was whether these works merited acceptance and whether they were true examples of either race. Unfortunately, they are accurate and like it or not, they are segments of history as much as the horrors of slavery are--or recurrent wars or the present threat of nuclear holocaust or even the ongoing saga of Elizabeth Taylor's love life.

Research for this brief history of whites in blackface extended to source material in numerous newspapers: Spirit of the Times, The New York Clipper, The Times of London, the New York Times, plus many others. Histories, biographies and autobiographies (included here in the Bibliography) have been studied and, wherever possible, original data were examined to clarify many of the perpetuated myths and errors published and republished throughout the years on productions, places, and performers.

Consequently, some definitive statements (such as the constant description of Edmund Kean's acting as being "like reading Shakespeare by flashes of lightning") proved not to be the dearly beloved encomia persistently quoted by critics and historians. The ever-documented 100 nights of Uncle Tom's Cabin in Troy, New York, and notices of John Barrymore's shattering of Broadway's Hamlet performance record included in many volumes are incorrect. The first performance given by The American Company in Williamsburg (clearly advertised in the <u>Virginia Gazette</u>) consistently is recorded incorrectly. Andrew Barton's 1767 character Racoon (<u>sic</u>) in <u>The Disappointment</u> being an American Negro and one of the first black roles written for the stage is absurd. Authoritative "firsts," and other exacting documentations that continue to find their way into print as being "historically accurate" were unearthed as apocryphal emissions.

Imaginative first and last names of performers continue to be recorded. The first name of D. W. Griffith's close friend, black actress Madame Sul-te-wan has been elusive for years, even to Lillian Gish. Pinpointing the origins of "Jim Crow" would challenge any bureaucratic birth registry, and the academic hullabaloo over Othello's color would perplex the most dedicated dermatologist. Prolix psychoanalytical examination of Shakespeare's protagonists in <u>Othello</u> resulted in more psychodrama than the Bard of Avon would have ever imagined possible. Published accounts of Harriet Beecher Stowe's writing of <u>Uncle Tom's Cabin</u> and her relationship to the supposed prototype of Uncle Tom are highly fictionalized. Theatrical legends will always persist and are frequently based on self-dramatized, elaborately embroidered fiction, contributed either by the performer or imaginatively improvised by dedicated admirers or press agents.

A performance record sampling 380 years of Shakespeare's <u>Othello</u> and nearly a century of Verdi's <u>Otello</u> is published for the first time in Appendix "A" of this volume. A sampling of whites in blackface in motion pictures (now known as "films") is given in Appendix "B." Attempting to clarify the myths and errors of the past has undoubtedly created further contributions to the canon of theatrical misinformation. Should you discover these new erroneous contributions, carefully compile them and write your own history.

William Torbert Leonard
Radnor, Pa.   1985

PART I:

GENESIS

The Commedia dell'Arte established in 1560 gained fame with the black half-masked character Harlequin. But the first masquerade in black on the English-speaking stage was satanic, black Aaron, the Moor beloved by Tamora, white Queen of the Goths, in William Shakespeare's play Titus Andronicus. Shakespeare's cataclysmic gothic tale of horror found a few isolated defenders over the years, but generally the tragedy has been anathema and vigorously despised from its first performance by Philip Henslowe's company on January 23, 1594, and in its repeat performances on June 7th and 14th of that year by the Chamberlain's company. Compounded by its necrological mayhem, convoluted plot, and construction, Titus Andronicus has been called the worst play in the Shakespeare canon.

Barbaric and macabre Titus Andronicus has been compared to the excessively gory and grotesque melodramas produced by Oscar Metenier's Grand Giugnol Theatre in Paris during the latter part of the nineteenth century. Shakespeare's Titus describes the climate of Rome as "but a wilderness of tigers." Tigers are probably less ferocious. The scenes of multiple murders, mutilations, dismemberments, vicious rape, necrophagia and wholesale bloodletting and slaughter would have tested the depraved imagination of the Marquis de Sade. Certainly, they exceeded any incest, lunacy, and rape scenes devised by Eugene O'Neill and overshadowed the manic sexual aberrations and Southern suppressions of the psychotic characters created by Tennessee Williams.

T. S. Eliot viewed Titus Andronicus as "one of the stupidest and most uninspiring plays ever written." William Archer, reflecting on his desire to see all of Shakespeare's plays wrote, "My ambition stops short of Troilus and Cressida, which is not intended for the stage; and of Titus Andronicus, which is absurd." Critic Kenneth Tynan saw the play as "A Chamber of Horrors;--this is tragedy, naked, godless, and unredeemed, a carnival of carnage in which pity is the first man down."

London's Stationers' Register on February 6, 1594, recorded the publication in quarto form of THE MOST LA-mentable Romaine Tragedie of Titus Andronicus: "As it was Plaide by the Right Honourable the Earle of Darbie, Earle of Pembrooke and Earle of Suffex, their Seruants. London, Printed by John Danter, and are

to be fold by Edward White & Thomas Millington, at the little North
doors of Paules at the figne of the Gunne."

Shakespeare's original source for Titus Andronicus theoretical-
ly had roots in Euripides' Hecuba and Seneca's Thyestes, and was
influenced by Ovid's Metamorphoses. The tragedy--allegedly,
Shakespeare's apocrypha--is presumed to have been based on an
earlier lost play Titus and Vespasian. (A 1620 German play Trago-
edia von Tito Andronico and Jan Vos's 1641 Dutch play Aran en
Titus are also assumed to have originated from this lost play.)

Edward Ravenscroft revised Shakespeare's tragedy in 1678
(under the title of Titus Andronicus, or the Rape of Lavinia: A
Tragedy Alter'd from Mr. Shakespeare's Works) and made a lofty
claim that he would refine the language, add new scenes, and
heighten most of the principal characters. Instead, he increased
the violence described in Shakespeare's original script (e.g., he
burned Aaron to death on-stage). Ravenscroft's "improved" version was prefaced with a statement of his conviction that the play
was not Shakespeare's. Shakespeare, wrote Ravenscroft, merely
"gave some Master-strokes to one or two of the Principal Parts or
Characters" to a play by another author. English author Francis
Meres, however, included the play in his Palladis Tamia (1598) as
being authored by William Shakespeare.

Dr. Samuel Johnson in The Plays of William Shakespeare (1765)
wrote:

> All the editors and criticks agree with Mr. Theobald in sup-
> posing this play spurious. I see no reason for differing
> from them; for the colour of the stile is wholly different
> from that of the other plays, and there is an attempt at
> regular versification, and artificial closes, not always in-
> elegant, yet seldom pleasing. The barbarity of the spec-
> tacles, and the general massacre which are here exhibited,
> can scarcely be conceived tolerable to any audience....
> That Shakespeare wrote any part, though Theobald declares
> it incontestable, I see no reason for believing.... I do not
> find Shakespeare's touches very discernible.

On August 21, 1955, nearly two hundred years later, Kenneth
Tynan wrote in the London Observer: "Whoever wrote it, whether
a member of the Shakespeare syndicate or the chairman himself, he
deserves our thanks for having shown us, at the dawn of our drama,
just how far drama could go."

Frederick Gard Fleahy advanced his revolutionary theory in
his A Chronicle History of the Life and Work of William Shakespeare,
Player, Poet and Play-Maker (London, 1886). "I think the opinion
that Kyd wrote the play of Andronicus worth the examination; although with such evidence as has yet been adduced, Marlowe has

certainly the better claim. Shakespeare probably never touched the play."

Ravenscroft's five-act revision of Titus Andronicus was first performed after several years on August 23, 1704, and repeated on September 16th and November 17th of that year. Drury Lane Theatre revived the tragedy for four performances on August 13, 1717, with James Quin as Aaron, the Moor. Bickerstaff was Aaron at Drury Lane on July 8, 1718, and Quin repeated his performance as the Moor on December 21 and 30, 1720; on February 12, 1721; and on March 19, 1724, at Lincoln's Inn Fields Theatre. Thomas Walker was Drury Lane's Aaron on June 27, 1721, and he reenacted his performance on August 1, 1722, at Lincoln's Inn Fields Theatre.

In 1839, Titus Andronicus was produced in America for four performances at Philadelphia's Walnut Street Theatre. Advertised as "altered by N. H. Bannister into a beautiful play," this version of Titus had to have been the greatest piece of writing in the City of Brotherly Love since Thomas Jefferson composed "The Declaration of Independence." The Bannister Titus was presented on January 30th with an afterpiece, A Lesson for Ladies; on January 31st it was followed by Charming Polly; on February 1st it was accompanied by Maidens Beware and Mischief Makers; and on February 2, 1839; it was followed by The Lady and the Devil. Alexander L. Pickering was Aaron, and Bannister played the title role.

It was also in 1839 when American-born black actor Ira Aldridge collaborated with C. A. Somerset, author of Shakespeare's Early Days, to drastically rewrite untidy Titus. The arcane Aldridge-Somerset adaptation expurgated the horror of Shakespeare's tale as being "repugnant to good taste and modern refinements." In the adaptation the role of demonic, unrelentingly, evil black Aaron was elevated from villain to stalwart, noble hero. Interpolated into the cleansed Shakespearean text was a scene from a play, Zaraffa, the Slave King, written especially for Aldridge.

Aldridge appeared as Aaron, the Moor, in Ireland in 1849 and 1850, and at Edinburgh, Scotland's Adelphi Theatre on July 24, 1850. He opened at Sara Lane's Hoxton Britannia Theatre, London, on March 15, 1852, acting his purified concept of Titus Andronicus for six performances. Aldridge mitigated the bowdlerized tragedy by appearing as Ginger Blue in an afterpiece, Virginian Mummy, which included several American Negro-type songs, such as "Opossum up a Gum Tree."

During Aldridge's last engagement as Aaron at the Britannia Theatre, the London Era reported on April 26, 1857,

> Titus Andronicus is not a favorite play and is utterly unfit
> for presentation, for a more dreadful catalogue of horrors
> and atrocities than it consists of would be impossible to

conceive.... In fact, there are numerous internal evidences
that the play is not written by Shakespeare, and we are
strongly inclined to agree with Malone, Johnson and others
that it is spurious. The Titus Andronicus produced under
Mr. Aldridge's direction is a wholly different affair.

The Era also praised Aldridge's performance in "a part he has made
completely and emphatically his own." The Brighton Herald on October 6, 1860, reviewed Aldridge's revision of Shakespeare's play
as "Beyond the title, a few incidents and some scraps of language,
his Titus has nothing in common with Shakespeare."

Nearly seventy-five years later The MOST LA-mentable Romaine
Tragedie was unearthed by London's Old Vic Theatre's creative and
dedicated manager Lilian Baylis at the Royal Victoria Hall, Waterloo
Road (originally, in 1818, called the Royal Coburg Theatre), where
Ira Aldridge made his London stage debut on October 10, 1825, as
Oroonoko in an altered version of Thomas Southerne's melodrama.
In the late nineteenth century, the theatre became the Royal Vic-
toria Coffee and Music Hall under the management of Miss Baylis'
aunt Emma Cons.

Produced by Robert Atkins for the Old Vic on October 8,
1923,* Titus Andronicus was played for nine performances with
George Hayes as Aaron, the Moor, and Wilfrid Walters as Titus.
The cavalcade of deaths upon deaths at the play's end produced
uncontrolled laughter from the audience. The Morning Post crypti-
cally reported, "It is very repulsive, but workmanlike." But London's critics dismissed Titus as "impossibly bad."

Writer-actor Robert Speaight described Peter Brooks's stunning production of Titus Andronicus at the Shakespeare Memorial
Theatre in Stratford-upon-Avon on August 16, 1955 as "All in all,
the greatest Shakespearean production of our time." The Brooks-
Stratford presentation of the tragedy benefited from a magnificently
defined performance by Laurence Olivier as Titus and a superbly
corrupt, demonic black Aaron by Anthony Quayle as well as by the
casting of Maxine Audley as Tamora and of Vivien Leigh as Lavinia.

The London Times reported, "If the horrors in Titus Andronicus are not merely horrific, they may as easily seem ludicrous. Mr.
Peter Brooks has sought to prevent us from finding them so by
plunging the play into a Websterian world of nightmare." Stanley
Godfrey added, "Twelve persons were carried unconscious from one
performance. Others left the theatre because of grisly torture
scenes." The Brooks-Stratford Titus toured Europe extensively
during May and June of 1957. During the tour Titus became the

---

*A production of Titus Andronicus appeared in Munich, Germany,
on October 15, 1924. The Prinzregententheatre text of the tragedy
was translated by Nicolaus Delius.

first English play to be seen behind the Iron Curtain in Warsaw.
On July 1, 1957, it returned to London where it played at the Stoll
Theatre.

The Old Vic Theatre celebrated the anniversary of Shakespeare's birth on April 23, 1957, with a double bill of The Comedy
of Errors and Titus Andronicus. The plays were staged without
intervals and included only one intermission between the comedy
and the tragedy. Director John Barton edited the text of Titus
Andronicus to an acting time of ninety-five minutes. "Aaron, the
half-Iago in Othello's skin was lustily done by Keith Michell," according to W. A. Darlington of London's Daily Telegraph. Barbara
Jefford played Tamora.

Joseph Papp's New York Shakespeare Theatre Workshop's experiment with Titus in November 1956 began with Eric Burroughs
as Aaron; he was replaced by black actor Roscoe Lee Browne who
played opposite Colleen Dewhurst's Tamora. The Off-Broadway
Titus was eulogized as "If Shakespeare managed to live down Titus
Andronicus, they probably can too." England's prestigious Birmingham Repertory Theatre celebrated its golden anniversary in 1963
with Ronald Eyre's production of Titus Andronicus; Derek Jacobi
was Aaron, the Moor. Douglas Seale's production of Titus was seen
at Baltimore's Center Stage from February 9 to March 12, 1967, with
Graham Brown as Aaron. The Baltimore Sun found it "surpassing
the Grand Guignol" and Richard L. Coe (Washington Post) saw the
play emerging as "sheer modern Theatre of Cruelty."

Called "a powerful, disturbing evening of theatre," the New
York Shakespeare Festival production of Titus Andronicus staged by
Gerald Freedman was a rather arty, highly stylized concept with
overtones of Oriental theatre via Greece; the cast wore half-masks
designed by Theoni V. Aldridge. Black actor Moses Gunn played
Aaron, the Moor, for twenty-two performances in the Festival's
production at New York's Delacorte Theatre, which opened on August 2, 1967. London's Roundhouse Theatre staged Titus on July
13, 1971, with Barry Bennen as the evil black Moor.

Trevor Nunn's Stratford-upon-Avon production of the tragedy
on October 12, 1972, featured Colin Blakely in the title role, Janet
Suzman (Lavinia), Margaret Tyzack (Tamora), and English black
actor Calvin Lockhart (Aaron). Nunn's production was criticized
for extravagant concentration on details of blood and gore at the
expense of Shakespeare's verse. Trevor Nunn reproduced Titus
at London's Aldwych Theatre on August 4, 1973, with Patrick Stewart as the black villain.

Paul Barry, designating Titus as "a Roman black mass," directed the tragedy for the Madison, New Jersey Shakespeare Festival
in July 1977. Much of the gory bloodletting was reduced to symbolism, and the play was mounted as a Roman ritual without intermission. Eric Tavoris played Aaron.

Stratford, Ontario's Shakespearean Festival produced <u>Titus Andronicus</u> on August 26, 1978, with Alan Scarfe as Aaron. In 1980 their repertoire again included <u>Titus</u>, directed by Brian Bedford. Mel Gussow of <u>The New York Times</u> wrote,

> <u>Titus Andronicus</u> is Shakespeare's most savage pit--a caldron of rape, maiming, killings and cannibalism. It is tragedy without catharsis--Vengeance follows vengeance until the stage is blighted with corpses--a record of 35 by the count of the Polish critic Jan Kott. Errol Slue is a suitably reptilian Moor.

Directed by John Barton, The Royal Shakespeare Company presented <u>Titus Andronicus</u> on a double bill with <u>The Two Gentlemen of Verona</u> at Stratford's Royal Shakespeare Theatre on August 26, 1981. London <u>Observer</u>'s Robert Cushman admired Hugh Quarshie's interpretation of Aaron but admitted, "There are inevitably laughs when at the concluding banquet three characters fall dead in as many lines."

The Shakespeare Recording Society, Inc. of New York released their recording of <u>Titus Andronicus</u> in 1966. It featured Anthony Quayle as Aaron, Maxine Audley as Tamora, with Colin Blakely, Michael Hordern, and others.

Various regional theatres now adventurously include <u>Titus Andronicus</u> in their repertoires. The mercurial public taste having been sated with the violence, blood, and mayhem that have been glorified in countless Hollywood films and television series may find untidy <u>Titus</u> tedious and dull by comparison. It is not unreasonable to suspect that Mr. Shakespeare's damned and beleaguered tragedy could yet become grist for the musical stage. Given the current mania for adaptations and public fascination with explicitly detailed gore (e.g., 1979's <u>Sweeney Todd, the Demon Barber of Fleet Street</u> that the Drama Critics Circle and "Tony" Awards selected as "the best musical of the year"), <u>Titus Andronicus</u> could be waiting in the wings for the overture; or, as Shakespeare closed his tragedy,

> And, being so, shall have like want of pity.
> See justice done on Aaron, that damn'd Moor,
> By whom our heavy haps had their beginning....

THE MOOR

"That damn'd Moor" Aaron was Shakespeare's beginning in
writing tragedy. But the most enduring black masquerade--which
became the longest performed blackface role in theatrical history--
was The Moor in William Shakespeare's Othello.

Shakespeare's 1604 tragedy Othello: The Moor of Venice was
based on a story Il Moro de Venezia written in 1565 by Giovanni
Battista Giraldi, surnamed Cinthio. Giraldi was a nobleman of Fer-
rara and a professor of philosophy at that city's university. Giraldi's tale of lethal jealousy is included in a collection of contes called
Gli Degli Hecatommithi as story seven of the third decade under the
general heading, The Unfaithfulness of Husbands and Wives.

In 1584, Gabriel Chappuys made a French translation of the
Hecatommithi in Paris. Twenty years later William Shakespeare's
dramatization of Il Moro de Venezia mitigated the macabre story.
The original Italian version was translated into English by John Edward Taylor for his treatise Cinthio's Tale of the Moor of Venice,
published by Chapman-Hall in London in 1855. Taylor examined the
close parallels between Giraldi's story and Shakespeare's dramatization, noting:

> The simple elements of the Story were precisely calculated
> to seize upon Shakespear's attention--the opposition and
> contrast of characters, the deep play of passion, the sug-
> gestive motives, thoughts, and springs of action, the capa-
> bilities of the plot--were all materials as if created for his
> genius to mould, work upon, and fashion.

Giraldi's story relates the tragedy of a handsome and valiant
black Moor who resides in Venice with his white Italian wife, Disdemona. The Moor is given command of troops in Cyprus where
his deceptively devoted Ensign, convinced Disdemona prefers the
Captain of the Troop after repelling his passionate pursuit, seeks
revenge by accusing her of unfaithfulness to her black husband.
Disdemona's innocent defense of the Captain after the Moor has demoted him for striking a soldier supports the malicious Ensign's
accusation and arouses doubt and jealousy in the Moor. During
Disdemona's visit to his wife, the Ensign steals her wedding handkerchief and leaves it in the Captain's bedroom.

When the bewildered officer attempts to return the handkerchief, the Moor accuses his faithful wife of arranging a rendezvous.
The Moor observes a craftily arranged meeting by the Ensign with
the Captain and, although their conversation is of little conse-
quence, the Ensign tells the Moor that the Captain has confessed
his affair with Disdemona and that she gave him the beloved handkerchief as a souvenir. The Moor pays the fiendish Ensign to kill
the Captain, but he only succeeds in severing the Captain's leg.

With the encouragement and help of the Moor, the Ensign ar-
ranges Disdemona's murder by beating her to death with stockings
filled with sand and pulling down the ancient bedroom ceiling to
make her death seem accidental. The Ensign tells the Captain that
the Moor was responsible for his lost leg and that he has also murdered Disdemona. After being tortured and resolutely denying the
charges against him before the Signori of Venice, the Moor is pursued and killed by Disdemona's family. The Ensign is later tortured
until his body erupts.

> Thus did Heaven avenge the innocence of Disdemona, and
> all these events were narrated by the Ensign's wife, who
> was privy to the whole, after his death, as I have told them
> here.

Shakespeare's adaptation improved and enlarged the scope of
Giraldi's story and altered the names of the principals to Othello
and Desdemona. The Ensign Alfiero was rechristened Iago. For
other prototrophic characters, the Captain became Lieutenant
Michael Cassio, the Ensign's wife, Emilia, and the soldier, Roderigo.
Unnamed minor characters in the story were given proper names.
Shakespeare elevated Giraldi's Cristophoro Moro to "Othello, a noble
Moor in the service of the Venetian State," while retaining the dia-
bolical intrigue built on the black General's malevolent Ensign Alfiero's false evidence of Desdemona's purloined handkerchief as proof
of her unfaithfulness. Emilia exposes her husband's treachery and
is killed by Iago who, in turn, is wounded by Othello and taken
prisoner by Desdemona's kinsmen. Giraldi's Moor was unrelenting,
but Shakespeare's emotionally tortured Othello pleads for understanding with "...then must you speak of one that loved not wisely
but too well" before committing suicide after strangling and stabbing
his faithful wife, as Iago has suggested he should.

Unlike Titus Andronicus, Shakespeare's tragedy of Othello inspired praise over the centuries. Dr. Samuel Johnson enthused,
"Othello is the vigorous and vivacious off-spring of observation im-
pregnated by genius." English historian Thomas Babington Macaulay
declared in 1824 that Othello was "perhaps, the greatest work in the
world." And English poet Algernon Charles Swinburne wrote, "As
surely as Othello is the noblest of man's making, Iago is the most
perfect evil-doer, the most potent demi-devil." August Wilhelm von
Schlegel saw Othello as "a strongly shaded picture: we might call it

a tragical Rembrandt. No eloquence is capable of painting the overwhelming force of a catastrophe in Othello--the pressure of feelings
which measure out in a moment the abysses of eternity." George
Bernard Shaw (no devotee of Shakespeare) concluded that Othello
"Tested by the brain, it is ridiculous; tested by the ear, it is sub-
lime [and] remains magnificent by the volume of its passion."

Biographer F. W. Hawkins classified Othello as "by far the
most difficult character in the whole range of English literature to
represent with any degree of success on the stage." But Othello
has been performed on the world's stages for nearly four hundred
years and "as a work of art is is perfect--being in construction the
best of Shakespeare's plays," according to New York Tribune's
drama critic William Winter. In 1908, however, Bernard Spewack in
Shakespeare and the Allegory of Evil, described Cinthio's and
Shakespeare's Ensign as "depraved, lustful, deceitful and a Machiavel
--an artisan of intrigue."

The demanding and controversial role of the black Moor has,
with varying degrees of success, challenged the talents of many actors; some played the role neither wisely nor too well, and some
played it wisely and very well. Several actors gained more fame
or notoriety in their private lives and performances than they did
in agonizing over the trials and tribulations depicted in Othello.

One actor's daughter married the son of the tenth President
of the United States, and another actor assassinated the sixteenth
President of the United States. An eccentric, sharp-tongued
tragedian killed two men and wounded a third. An alcoholic, but
legendary, great actor literally lost his head; another lost a leg but
gained a theatre. Two players were murdered, and two other performers killed men in a duel: one with a sword and the other with
a cane. A famous tragedian collapsed on-stage while playing Othello.
He later died and an American-born Negro became the first black
actor to reach stardom on the London stage. A prestigious performer became the first actor to be knighted in England but not,
however, for his interpretation of Othello.

One despondent Othello committed suicide on his honeymoon,
and another on-stage Moor drowned himself. A famous tragedian
sired ten children out of wedlock, and two famous Othellos were declared adulterers. The animosity and feud existing between two
actors who gained prominence and fame portraying the Moor of
Venice erupted into the bloodiest theatre riot ever recorded in
theatre history. One fine tragedian had his ravings and dreadful
death from paresis (the final stage of syphilis) dramatized on the
stage and immortalized on phonograph records. In performance,
several Othellos strangled their off-stage wives playing Desdemona
on-stage. An acclaimed Iago drowned in the St. Lawrence River.
An Othello went down in a blazing ship on Long Island Sound and
a philandering Iago was killed by a Hudson River railroad train.

The first Desdemona was a lady of easy virtue who became the mistress of royalty; a black Othello married his white Desdemona.

Several Othellos received awards, knighthood and accolades; they also reaped prestigious historical acclamation. Others reaped rotten eggs, deceased vegetables, abuse, and vitriolic ridicule. This almost idolatrous reverence each generation accorded their "greatest" Othellos would inevitably militate against "the greatest" of succeeding generations and cloud their fame and lustre. One decade's "star" became the next decade's "ham," and the ambiguous and often ambivalent judgment of the Moor continued throughout the centuries.

The first production of Othello was given before the Court of James I in the Banqueting House in Whitehall, London on Hallowmas Day, November 1, 1604, with Richard Burbage as Othello supported by the King's Men--a group of actors appointed by the son of Mary, Queen of Scots, ten days after his arrival in London on May 16, 1603, a little more than two months before he was crowned James I of England on July 25, 1603. The original King's Men Company included William Shakespeare, Richard Burbage, Lawrence Fletcher, John Heminges, Augustine Phillips, Henry Condell, William Sly, Richard Cowley, and Robert Armin.

Six years later, Othello was performed at London's Globe Theatre (April 30, 1610) and at Oxford (September 1610). The Blackfriars presented Shakespeare's tragedy in 1629 and on May 6, 1635; on December 8, 1636, Othello was performed at Hampton Court. The Earl of Southampton praised Burbage's Othello: "He is a man famous as our English Roscius; one who fitteth the action to the word, and the word to the action, most admirably."

The play was entered in London's Stationers' Register on October 6, 1621, and published in London in 1622 by Thomas Walkley as The Tragoedy of Othello: The Moore of Venice, "As it hath beene diuerfe times acted by the Globe and at the Black-Friers, by his Maiefties Seruants. Written by VVilliam Shakefpeare, London."

Nathaniel Burt and Walter Clun, previously assigned female characters, were Othello and Iago, respectively, in The Moore of Venice at the Cockpit Theatre in Drury Lane on October 11, 1660. Clun, who had gained fame for his playing of the evil Ensign, was murdered on Kentish Town Road while returning to his home on August 3, 1664. London's Drury Lane Theatre presented The Moore of Venice on February 6, 1669, with Burt as the Moor and Michael Mohun as Iago. Mohun's Iago, considered inferior to Charles Hart's interpretation, was observed by Samuel Pepys (who spelled the actor's name Moone) as less effective than Walter Clun's. Desdemona was played by Mistress Margaret Hughes in this production. She is presumed to have been the first woman to appear on the English stage.

Although Margaret Hughes is credited with being the Eve of London's theatrical Eden, an unknown woman appeared on the London stage in Thomas Killigrew's Vere Street Theatre production of the tragedy on December 8, 1660. For this revolutionary female debut, Thomas Jordan wrote "A Prologue to introduce the first woman that came to act on the stage in the tragedy call'd The Moor of Venice."

> I come, known to any of the rest
> To tell you news, I saw the lady drest!
> The woman plays today, mistake me not
> No man in gown, or page in petticoat
> A woman to my knowledge, yet I can't
> If I should die, make affidavit on't
> Do you not twitter, Gentlemen? I know
> You will be censuring; do it fairly though.
> T'is possible a virtuous woman may
> Abhor all sorts of looseness, and yet play;
> Play on the stage--where all eyes are upon her;
> Shall we count that a crime France counts an honour?
> In other kingdoms husbands safely trust 'em;
> The difference lies only in the custom.
> And let it be our custom, I advise
> I'm sure this custom's better than Th'excise,
> And may procure us custom; hearts of flint
> Will melt in passion, when a woman's in't.
> But, gentlemen, you that as judges sit
> In the Star Chamber of the house--the pit
> Have modest thoughts of her; pray do not run
> To give her visits when the play is done,
> With "Damn me, your most humble servant, lady"--
> She knows those things as well as you, it may be,
> Not a bit there, dear gallants, she doth know
> Her own deserts--and your temptations, too.
> But to the point;--in this reforming age
> We have intents to civilize the stage.
> Our women are defective and so sized
> You'd think they were some of the Guard disguised;
> For to speak truth, men act, that are between
> Forty and fifty, wenches of fifteen;
> With bone so large and nerve so incompliant
> When you call Desdemona, enter giant.
> We shall purge everything thus is unclean,
> Lascivious, scurrilous, impious or obscene;
> And when we've put all things in this fair way
> Barebones himself may come to see a play.

According to Dr. Doran, the woman was assumed to have been either Anne Marshall or Margaret Hughes. Margaret Hughes, who died on October 1, 1719, became the mistress of Prince Rupert, who set her up in Brandenburg House with their illegitimate daughter,

Ruperta.   Jordan's Epilogue probably pleased Margaret, Mistress of
Rupert:

> And how do you like her?   Come, what is't ye drive at?
> She's the same thing in public as in private,
> As far from being what you call a whore
> As Desdemona injured by the Moor;
> Then he that censures her in such a case
> Hath a soul blacker than Othello's face.

The celebrated voluptuous and beautiful Eleanor (Nell) Gwyn graduated from selling oranges at the Theatre Royal, Drury Lane to become London's favorite, if most notorious, actress. Beloved by
Charles Hart and schooled by him in theatre techniques and acting,
Nell made her acting debut in 1665 at Drury Lane as Cydaria in
John Dryden's play The Indian Emperor. Four years later she as-
cended to her greatest role as the mistress of King Charles II, for
whom she bore two sons. Nell was a far more talented actress than
was Margaret Hughes, yet both women became more famous off-stage
than on, as mistresses to royalty. Their friendship became strained,
not because of rivalry from their theatre days, but because of mis-
understandings and misconceptions regarding their royal concubin-
age.

In a letter to "Sister Peg," Nell took Margaret to task for
squandering Prince Rupert's estate.

> Of all the concubines in christendom, that ever were happy
> in so kind a keeper, none sure ever squandered away the
> fruits of her labour so indiscreetly as yourself; whoring
> and gaming I acknowledge are two very serviceable vices
> in a commonwealth, because they make money circulate;
> but for a woman that has enriched herself by the one, to
> impoverish herself by the other, is so great a fault, that
> a harlot deserves correction for it.
> In a few years you have gamed away the large estate
> given you by the good old gentleman; fie upon't, I am
> ashamed to think that a woman who had wit enough to tickle
> a prince out of so fine an estate, should at last prove such
> a fool as to be bubbled of it by a little spotted ivory and
> painted paper.

Sister Peg replied to Nell's letter:

> Madam: I am sorry a mistress of a king should degener-
> ate so much from that generosity which was always applauded
> as a virtue in us ladies. Should I have plac'd an esteem
> upon the riches that was left me, the world might have
> suppos'd it was for the greediness of gain, that made me
> yield my favours; had I expos'd my honour for the lucre of
> base coin, and sinned on for the sake only of advantage.

Beauty's the reward of great actions, and I generously be-
stow'd mine upon a prince that deserv'd it, abstractly from
the thoughts of interest, but rather to shew my gratitude,
in return of his noble passion for me; and since he had
made me the object of his affections. I resolved thro' the
true principle of love to surrender the ultimate of my
charms to make him happy; my embraces was all he wanted,
and the utmost I could give, and if a prince would submit
to take up with a player, I think on my side there was
honour enough, without interest, to induce me to a compli-
ance. I am so far from repenting the loss of my estate,
that I look upon't my glory, and the only place of careless-
ness I ever committed worthy my boasting. When I have
lost all, perhaps I may take care to save myself, which will
be much better, than like you to be damn'd with a full
pocket.

Margaret's brother William was killed by one of Charles II's
men during an argument over the physical attributes of Nell and
Peg; the two disagreed about which of the women was the most
beautiful mistress then in residence at Windsor. William's insistence
that dark and sultry Sister Peg was infinitely more beautiful than
sexy and blonde Sweet Nell cost him his life.

A cousin to King Charles II, Prince Rupert had led the Royal-
ists against Oliver Cromwell. Later he became a noted chemist,
but he died in poverty. Margaret Hughes's profligate living and
addiction to tossing the dice forced her to sell the fabulous jewels
given to her by Rupert. Nell Gwyn vindictively purchased "Sister
Peg's" exquisite pearl necklace (once owned by Elizabeth, Queen of
Bavaria) for the sum of L4520. Ironically, after Charles II's death,
"Sweet Nell of Old Drury" was forced to sell Peg's necklace to settle
her own debts.

Illegitimate daughter, Ruperta, married General Emmanuel
Scroope Howe and gained great wealth and respectability before her
death in 1740 at Somerset House. Samuel Pepys had observed that
Margaret Hughes, one-time mistress of Charles Sedley, was "a
mighty pretty woman and seems--but is not--modest." Despite adverse criticism, Margaret firmly maintained that she and Prince
Rupert "were as constant to each other as any man and his wife
were in England." W. Macqueen-Pope in his fascinating book Ladies
First wrote that Margaret Hughes "played many good parts and
played them well. If she was the not best actress of her time, at
least she was the literal leading lady of the Stage." Margaret's extended performance at Brandenburgh House was obviously superior
to any role she performed at Drury Lane or with Davenant's Duke's
Theatre.

After being closed for three years, Dublin's Smock Alley
Theatre reopened during the Yuletide (1690) with a free performance

of Othello, featuring Robert Wilks in the title role. Wilks's success
as Othello was repeated at Dublin's Theatre Royal on March 31,
1691; but in his first London appearance as the Moor he failed.
The foremost actor of the seventeenth century was Thomas Betterton, the son of an under-cook to Charles I, presumably born on
Tothill Street in the City of Westminster, London, in 1635.

Thomas Betterton was considered "the first great actor of the
Restoration." He played without extravagant gesture or bombast
and was called by Pepys "the best actor in the world." In 1748,
Anthony Ashton described Betterton as a superb actor whose figure
left a good deal to be desired but who possessed a well-governed if
low and grumbling voice. Colley Cibber, in his Apology for the
Life of Colley Cibber, Comedian: Views of the Stage during his own
time wrote, "Betterton was an actor, as Shakespeare was an author,
both without competitors! form'd for the mutual assistance and illustration of each other's genius." Cibber also stated that Betterton
"had a voice of that kind which gave more Spirit to Terror than to
the softer Passions, of more Strength than Melody. The rage and
Jealousy of Othello became him better than the Sighs and Tender-
ness of Castalio."*

After watching Betterton's performance as Othello, with Anne
Bracegirdle as Desdemona and John Baptista Verbruggen as Iago,
Isaac Bicker wrote in The Tatler, "Such an actor as Mr. Betterton
ought to be recorded with the same respect as Roscius among the
Romans." Richard Steele in The Tatler of May 4, 1710, felt that no
earlier performer could surpass Betterton's interpretation of the Moor
and that he "betrayed in his gestures such a variety and vicissitude
of passion as would admonish a man to be afraid of his own heart,
and perfectly convince him that it is to stab it to admit that worst
of daggers, jealousy." Betterton was later described as "a well dis-
ciplined, sober actor with a melodious voice of great range." He
excelled as Othello from 1683 to March 24, 1709, when Colley Cibber
was his Iago at Drury Lane.

Betterton's marriage on December 24, 1662, to Mary Saunder-
son was as blissful and career-rewarding as was the twentieth-
century Lunts's marriage. Mrs. Betterton was frequently her husband's leading lady (alternating with Mrs. Elizabeth Barry and comedienne Mrs. Anne Bracegirdle). Betterton's final stage appearance
was at his benefit at the Haymarket on April 25, 1719; he played
Melantius in Francis Beaumont, and John Fletcher's 1619 play The
Maid's Tragedy. Thomas Betterton, "the pride of the English Theatre," died three days later on Monday, April 28, 1710, and was
buried on May 2, 1710, in Westminster Abbey, next to St. Margaret's
Church, where he had been baptized on August 11, 1635.

---

*The character Castalio in Thomas Otway's 1680 tragedy The Orphan;
or The Unhappy Marriage.

In 1862, <u>Cornbill</u> magazine eulogized Betterton:

> He was not a greater actor than he was a true and honour-
> able gentleman. He enriched himself and them, and as long
> as he lived, gave dignity to his profession--he was the king
> of an art which had well-nigh perished in the commonwealth
> times, and he was a monarch who probably has never since
> had, altogether, his equal.

Trained by Betterton, Lancashire-born Barton Booth made his
stage debut in blackface in <u>Oroonoko</u> in Dublin; later he became a
notable Othello. In London on January 21, 1710, with Theophilus
Keene as Iago, Booth played his first Othello. He was deeply blackface and wore a long, white gown embroidered with flowers. For
twelve years Colley Cibber played Booth's subordinate nemesis, his
last performance occurring on September 7, 1727. Although Betterton had better control and variation in his playing, Benjamin Victor
said of Booth's performance, "His articulation was so exceedingly
distinct and clear that he could be heard to the farthest part of
the house, even in a whisper." Thomas Davies called Booth "an actor of genius and an amiable man." Barton Booth retired from the
stage on April 1, 1728, and died on May 10, 1733. He is buried in
Westminster Abbey.

Iconoclastic James Quin was born on King Street in the Covent
Garden area of London on February 24, 1693. From his first performance on January 10, 1722, at Lincoln's Inn Fields Theatre until
his last appearance as the Moor on February 9, 1751, at Covent
Garden, he was a popular Othello. Quin's singsong oratory and
exaggerated acting style often garnered critical comment that he
bellowed like a bull. He became a great favorite with the public
despite Henry Barton Baker's classification of Quin as "the despot
of the stage."

In <u>The Dramatic Censor</u>, Francis Gentleman described Quin's
Othello as follows:

> His declamation was as heavy as his person, his tone, monot-
> onous, his passions bellowing, his emphasis affected and his
> under-strokes growling. I remember once to see this es-
> teemed performer play the Moor in a large powdered major
> wig, which, with the black face, made such a magpye ap-
> pearance of his head, as tended greatly to laughter; one
> stroke, however, was not amiss, coming on in white gloves,
> by pulling off which the black hands became more realised.

Frederick, Prince of Wales, later to become King George III, was
taught elocution by Quin. Glowing comments on the King's speeches
always prompted Quin's reply, "Ah, it was I who taught the boy to
speak!"

During an extended drinking bout at Pope's Head Tavern on
April 17, 1718, fiery, acerbic Quin raised his sword in a duel with
a drunken actor named Bowen, who was described as "a low comedian of some talent and more conceit." The argument began when
Quin extolled Ben Jonson's performance as Facomo in The Libertine
and caustically condemned Bowen's poor performance in the same
role. The duel ended when Bowen accidentally fell against Quin's
sword. But before dying on April 20, 1718, Bowen magnanimously
forgave Quin both for the brawl and for his mortal wound. Quin
was found guilty of manslaughter but acquitted on July 10, 1718;
he returned to the stage.

Lacy Ryan who was Iago to Quin's Othello for several years
killed a drunken, belligerent Mr. Kelley in a sword-duel at Longacre two months later on June 20, 1718.

Frequently described as "rough, coarse and caustic," Quin
floored Prompter critic Aaron Hill with one blow for the writer's
"adverse comments" on his talent. Quin's vivid description of Welsh
actor Williams' poor performance in Cato resulted in a duel beneath
the arches of Covent Garden Piazza. Quin killed Williams but again,
was acquitted. Theophilus Cibber, the son of Colley Cibber and
husband of Susannah Maria Cibber, resented the sarcastic barbs
Quin made on March 9, 1739. The remarks led to a third duel,
which took place in Inigo Jones's beautifully designed Covent Garden Piazza. Passersby separated the two sword-wielding thespians
but not before Quin had slightly wounded Cibber in the arm.

Quin reluctantly acknowledged David Garrick's new naturalistic
acting style. "If this young fellow is right, then we have all been
wrong." Aware that the public favored Garrick in London and
Sheridan in Dublin, Quin retired from the stage on March 19, 1753.
The irascible but talented Quin died at his home in Bath on Tuesday, January 21, 1766, and is buried in Bath Abbey. On his monument in the Abbey is a tablet that is located beneath the sculptured
face of Quin. Written on the tablet is his old rival David Garrick's
ten-line epitaph ending with "The scene is chang'd. I am no more.
Death's is the last Act. Now all is O'er."

England's great actor David Garrick, born in Hereford, England on Friday, February 19, 1717, first appeared in blackface as
Alboan in Thomas Southerne's play Oroonoko at Ipswich in 1741.
Garrick used the fictitious name of Lyddal, which was the maiden
name of his actor-friend Henry Giffard's wife. He repeated his
performance on January 23, 1742, at London's Goodman's Fields
Theatre with Henry Giffard as Oroonoko. Three years later Garrick began studying the role of Othello, hoping to supersede James
Quin's popular, if portentious, concept of the Moor. Garrick was
convinced his characterization of Othello would be of "great service" to his fledgling career. It wasn't.

Garrick first played <u>Othello</u> on March 7, 1745, at Drury Lane, doing the play again for a Royal Command Performance on March 9th, with Charles Macklin as Iago and Mrs. Susannah Maria Cibber as Desdemona. Garrick restored the original epileptic-trance scene to Shakespeare's text of <u>Othello</u> but in later years vigorously hacked and emasculated several of Shakespeare's plays into more "modern" refinements.

Despite Quin's all-white costume, complete with white gloves and with a white wig topping his blackened face, the costume that short-statured Garrick wore was outlandish, and his strenuously prepared performance failed to out-finesse Quin. The Garrick regalia as the Moor included a large, plumed oriental turban. This was worn to increase his height and was greeted by laughter from the audience. Garrick was compared to the little Negro boy Pompey in William Hogarth's famous etching <u>A Harlot's Progress</u>. From the audience, and loud enough to be heard on-stage, James Quin scathingly bellowed, "Here's Pompey, by God! Where's the lamp and kettle?" and "Othello!--Psha! no such thing! There was a little black boy, like Pompey attending with a teakettle, fretting and fuming about the stage; but I saw no Othello!"

John Galt explained Garrick's mangled Moor by saying "he failed in the expression of the countenance alone, and that this default and short-coming to expectation was entirely owing to the black disguise he was obliged to assume." During February 1746 at Dublin's Smock Alley Theatre, Garrick again played Othello, this time opposite the declamatory Iago of overly pompous Thomas Sheridan, father of the famous playwright of <u>The Rivals</u> and <u>The School for Scandal</u>, Richard Brinsley Sheridan. It was to Richard Sheridan that Garrick, after nearly thirty years as manager and partner of the Drury Lane Theatre, would sell his interest in the theatre in 1776. On February 26, 1746, Garrick and Sheridan alternated in the roles of Othello and Iago. After playing Iago opposite Henry Mossop's Othello with George Anne Bellamy as Desdemona on April 12, 1753, Garrick abandoned further Shakespearean adventures in Venice and Cyprus as either Moor or Ensign.

Favoring a more natural acting style, Garrick discarded the pretentious, rhetorical style of acting in tragedy perfected by Quin and others. At Drury Lane he founded a co-operative company of performers adept at ensemble playing. The actors opposed the star performer school, in which a star is supported by minor players. Later, James Quin sarcastically acknowledged that "Garrick was a new religion." Prior to his death, Garrick contemplated, but wisely discarded, the idea of once again attempting Othello.

Edmund Burke wrote that Garrick had raised "the character of his profession to the rank of a liberal art" and that he considered Garrick "the greatest actor of his century." Sheldon Cheney said of Garrick, "In the Age of Great Acting in England, all other names

pale beside him." David Garrick
died in London on Wednesday,
January 20, 1779, and is buried
in Westminster Abbey.

Spranger Barry, born in
Skinner Row, Dublin, on Monday,
November 20, 1719, was a tall,
graceful Irishman described as
"handsome as a god" and, by
Thomas Gray, as "upwards of
six feet in height, well and
proportionately made, treads
well and knows what to do with
his limbs, in short, a noble
figure." Barry made his stage
debut as Othello on February
15, 1744, at Dublin's Aungier
Street Theatre. Clad in a scarlet suit trimmed in gold lace with
knee breeches and silk stockings and using a cocked hat
to top his blackened face, he
became London's favorite Moor,
enchanting London with the
"silver cadence" of his voice.

Spranger Barry as Othello

Barry's first London performance as Othello was on October
4, 1746, with Garrick's Drury Lane company, opposite Charles Macklin's memorable Iago and Mrs. Ridout's Desdemona. In his Dramatic
Miscellanies, Thomas Davies recalled Barry's London debut in
Othello: "Every word which Barry spoke, in this greatest character
of the greatest poet, seemed to come from the heart--but indeed the
same heart-rending feelings which charmed his audience in Othello
diffused themselves through all Barry's acting when the softer passions predominate." The London Chronicle reported, "His first ten-
dencies to jealousy are beautifully expressed, and are finely smothered, till at length they burst out into an amazing wildness of rage."

Francis Gentleman wrote, in The Dramatic Censor:

> If we may venture to say that any performer ever was born
> for one part in particular, it must have been Mr. Barry for
> the Moor ... there is a length of periods and an extrava-
> gance of passion in this part, not to be found in any other,
> for so many successive scenes, to which Mr. Barry appeared
> peculiarly suitable.

David Garrick played Iago to Barry's Othello five times during

the 1749-1750 season; James Quin was Barry's Iago on March 8th
and 11th in 1751. Barry's characterization stressed the passion
and nobility of the Moor; during his era he was judged the finest
Othello on the English stage. Before his death on Friday, January
10, 1777, Barry continued to play Othello for nearly thirty years--
to February 9, 1775--often opposite his second wife, famous tragedi-
enne Anne Street Barry.

Charles Macklin, whose real name was MacLaughlin, was a wild,
intemperate Irishman who had been born in May, 1690. In 1741, he
became the "greatest Shylock of his day." For his benefit at the
age of ninety-eight on May 7, 1789, Macklin attempted to reenact his
famous interpretation of Shylock (which had been documented by
Pope "This is the Jew, that Shakespeare drew") but the infirmities
of old age robbed his memory--for which lapse Macklin humbly apol-
ogized to his audience. John Ryder finished the play in Macklin's
greatest role. Charles Macklin died on Tuesday, July 11, 1797, at
the age of 107!

On February 14, 1741, Macklin daringly had altered the prescribed interpretation of Shakespeare's Jew in The Merchant of
Venice from comedy to tragedy. Six years before, he had killed
another actor. During a performance of The Merry Cobbler in 1735,
Macklin became enraged when he discovered actor Thomas Hallam,
the brother of William and Lewis Hallam, had stolen one of his wigs.
Hallam returned the wigs with a chorus of suggestive profanity,
and Macklin's violent Irish temper erupted. He jabbed Hallam in
the left eye with his cane, piercing Hallam's brain and killing him.
Macklin was found guilty of "manslaughter without malice afore-
thought" and permitted to return to the stage.

Macklin produced Othello on February 6, 1744, at London's
Haymarket Theatre. Charging no admission, he had the price of
tickets paid directly to him to sidestep the rigid London Licensing
Act. Macklin played Iago to the Othello of a twenty-four-year-old
ill-tempered, unlovable, and devastating raconteur named Samuel
Foote. Foote was billed as "A young gentleman making his first appearance on any stage." When he returned to the Haymarket as
Othello on April 26, 1744, he was listed as "Othello, being played
by a Citizen for his Diversions."

Foote's interpretation of the Moor was described by Charles
Lee Lewes in his 1804 Comic Sketches: "His performance of Othello
was such that it never yet has been forgotten by those who saw it";
and it was labeled "a masterpiece of burlesque." Foote excelled in
mimicry and satirical farce on-stage and off. W. MacQueen-Pope
later wrote, "a less suitable Moor could not have been found" but
added, "He was perhaps the greatest mimic who ever lived." The
Macklin production of Othello was a failure, but Samuel Foote became
one of London's theatrical legends.

Foote's devastatingly accurate, if ruthless, caricature of
eminent Englishmen extended to an advanced state of braggadocio
that included an elaborate fiction regarding his expert horseman-
ship. Encouraged by Lord Mexborough, Sir Francis Delaval, and
the King's brother (the Duke of York), short and portly Foote was
quickly thrown from a horse, the accident resulting in the loss of
his right leg on February 13, 1766. Egocentric opportunist Foote
made light of becoming a one-legged actor but seized the moment to
persuade the Duke of York to intercede with his brother King
George III to grant Foote a patent for his rented theatre, The Haymarket.

King George III approved Foote's request, and the patent was
granted by the Lord Chamberlain on July 5, 1766. In 1767, Foote
purchased the theatre from the estate of its builder, John Potter,
and established the Theatre Royal Haymarket. As owner-patentee
of the Theatre Royal, Foote's arrogance became more pronounced
against his presumed enemies and rivals: the Drury Lane's David
Garrick and the Covent Garden's John Rich.

Foote's initial disappointment over his failure with Macklin
faded with his success as a "one-legged actor" and playwright.*
His satirical plays ridiculed London's elite, and, in The Lame Lover
of 1770, he ridiculed himself and used his stage and "everyday"
wooden leg as a comedy prop. Another prosthesis was maintained
for formal wear. It was equipped with a silk stocking and a highly
polished shoe that had a gold buckle. Foote, who died on October
21, 1777, at the age of fifty-seven, was an expert showman. He
had resurrected a declining theatre and turned it into one of London's finest houses--just as Samuel Phelps later would transform
Sadler's Wells.

Samuel Foote, baptized in Truro, England on January 27,
1721, was unceremoniously buried at night by torchlight in the
cloisters of Westminster Abbey (November 3, 1777).

A group of socialites became pupils trained in the art of acting by Charles Macklin. They appeared under his direction in
Othello on March 7, 1751, at Drury Lane. The performance was
attended by the Prince and Princess of Wales and by London's elite.
It featured Sir Francis Blake Delaval as Othello, Mrs. Quon as
Desdemona, and John Delaval as Iago. Critical comment on the elegant amateur production said "The performance was very decent and
met with great applause. Mr. Macklin got great honour and de-
servedly, by his pupils on this occasion."

---

*Foote's popular plays are long forgotten and included, among oth-
ers, The Knights (1749); The Englishman in Paris (1753); The Author (1757); The Minor (1760); The Orators (1762); The Commis-
sary (1765); The Devil on Two Sticks (1768); The Mayor of Garratt
(1770); The Maid of Bath (1771) and The Nabob; The Bankrupt; and
A Trip to Calais; or the Capuchin (1772).

Walter Murray and Thomas Kent's Company of Comedians had performed in America at the Virginia Colony and in Philadelphia in 1749. On March 5, 1750, they appeared in an improvised theatre on Nassau Street in New York City; the play--Shakespeare's Richard III. The first production of Othello given in America was presented at the Nassau Street Theatre on December 23, 1751. It featured Robert Upton as the Moor. Upton had been sent to the colonies from England as an advance man for British producer William Hallam. But he had abandoned his mission and joined the Murray and Kean Company. When Hallam's company of players arrived in Virginia, Robert Upton scurried back to England.

English producer and financially depleted manager of London's Goodman's Fields Theatre, William Hallam, organized a group of English performers. The group was led by his brother Lewis Hallam who had arrived at America's Virginia colony in 1752. Known as the American Company, the group became the first "stock company" in America whose members received shares entitling them to a proportionate distribution of the receipts according to position in the company. The company was advertised in the Virginia Gazette as "A Company of COMEDIANS from LONDON AT the THEATRE in WILLIAMSBURG on Friday next, being the 15th of September, will be prefented A PLAY call'd THE MERCHANT OF VENICE." Shakespeare's play was followed by Edward Ravenscroft's farce The Anatomist; or Sham Doctor. Their repertoire also included Othello.

The American Company's honored guests at Williamsburg on November 19, 1752, were the Emperor and Empress of the Cherokee Indian Nation. According to the Maryland Gazette, the "Empress" halted a performance of Othello during a dueling scene to prevent what she assumed would be unnecessary bloodshed, sending "some about her to go and prevent them killing one another."

After the elder Lewis Hallam's death in Jamaica in 1756, the American Company was led by David Douglass, an Englishman recruited by Hallam in Jamaica, the place where he had started his theatrical career with John Moody's company of players. Douglass married Hallam's widow and built Cruger's Wharf Theatre in New York City in 1758. He also built Philadelphia's historic Southwark Theatre in 1766 where, on Friday, April 24, 1767, the American Company produced the first play written by an American: The Prince of Parthia by Thomas Godfrey, Jr. (1736-1763) of Philadelphia. Douglass' John Street Theatre in New York opened on December 7, 1767, with George Farquhar's play The Beaux' Stratagem.

Douglass, considered a mediocre actor, played the title role in Othello at Cruger's Wharf Theatre on January 10, 1759. Lewis Hallam, Jr. was Iago and Miss Cheer (Margaret Cheer Cameron) was Desdemona to Douglass' Othello at New York's John Street Theatre (April 11, 1768). Douglass played Iago to Lewis Hallam, Jr.'s ranting Othello at Philadelphia's Southwark Theatre on January 27, 1773.

Returning to Jamaica, Douglass was appointed King's Printer. Before he died at Spanish Town in Jamaica, on August 9, 1789, he had founded several newspapers.

Lewis Hallam, Jr. (1740-1808) attained less prominence for his role as the Moor of Venice than for his lauded performance as the drunken West Indian slave, Mungo, in Isaac Bickerstaffe and Charles Dibdin's comic opera The Padlock. Hallam performed Mungo in The Padlock at New York's John Street Theatre on May 29, 1769. William Dunlap, in his History of the American Theatre, recorded that Lewis Hallam was "unrivaled to his death giving the Mungo with a truth derived from study of the Negro slave character, which Dibdin the author could not have conceived."

George Odell (Annals of the New York Stage) wrote, "Hallam's acting as Mungo, the Negro servant, became famous and stands at the head of every chapter of the subject of Negro Minstrelsy in America. It is said that he modeled his performance on what he observed of negro theatre in Jamaica." Charles Dibdin, composer of the music to Isaac Bickerstaffe's two-act comic opera, was the original Mungo at London's Drury Lane Theatre on October 3, 1768. Black actor Ira Aldridge paced his classical roles in Shakespeare's Othello and Titus Andronicus and other dramas with an expert comic performance as Mungo in The Padlock. The Morning Advertiser extolled Aldridge's versatility, "In the farce of The Padlock, his performance of the part of Mungo was equal to anything we ever witnessed." Aldridge also accompanied himself expertly on a guitar when singing Dibdin's merry songs.

Bickerstaffe's The Padlock was based on a story, "The Jealous Husband" (El Celoso Estremeño) written by Don Quixote's creator, Miguel de Cervantes. The comedy reveals trusting, aged Don Diego leaving his Negro servant, Mungo, in charge of his home during his absence. Mungo's job is to protect Don Diego's young fiancée, Leonara. Mungo admits young student Leander to the house. Leander woos Leonara and plies the black servant with wine. Don Diego returns and reluctantly accepts the reality of youthful passion. He gives his blessing to the young lovers, Leonara and Leander, while quelling his astonishment at the drunken, outspoken Mungo.

Stately, tall, and handsome John Philip Kemble, was born at Prescot, Lancashire, England on Tuesday, February 1, 1757. He gave his final stage performance as Coriolanus--his best role--on June 25, 1817 and died at the age of sixty-six in Lausanne, Switzerland on Wednesday, February 26, 1823. In 1775, John Philip abandoned his six-year education for the Roman Catholic priesthood in Douai, France so that he could join his famous family in the theatre. His grandfather John Ward had portrayed Othello at Stratford-upon-Avon on September 9, 1746, and, on March 8, 1785, John Philip Kemble was a commercially successful Othello at Drury Lane, where

his famous sister Sarah Kemble
Siddons played Desdemona and
Robert Bensley played Iago.

Kemble's gentlemanly con-
cept of Othello was played in
the grand manner. Due to his
habitual cough, Kemble was
given to long pauses. His
Othello was described by Washington Irving: "When wit-
nessing the exertion of his
powers, though my head is
satisfied and even astonished,
yet my heart is seldom affected. I am not led to forget
that it is Kemble the actor,
not Othello, the Moor." William Dunlap described Kemble's appearance as Othello
clad in a scarlet military uniform offset by gold lace, with
waistcoat and breeches and
white silk stockings; "his
face was black and his long,

Robert Bensley as Iago

black hair, queued." The Public Advertiser reported on October
29, 1787, that Kemble was "more anxious to do justice to the text of
his author than the feelings of Othello. We much approve his
dressing Othello in the Moorish habit [but] is it necessary the Moor
should be as black as a native of Guiney?"

In an 1831 Tatler article, critic Leigh Hunt said that Kemble
was the antithesis of London's new star Edmund Kean and that he
found it difficult to compare Kean's dynamic, passionate Othello to
Kemble's "systematical, despotical style," which he classified as "all
external and artificial." Hunt added: "His voice is hollow and monot-
onous from the malformation, as it is said, of his organs of utterance
--he seems reckoning how many lines he has learnt by heart." Kemble's contemporary and rival, George Frederick Cooke, often laboring
under what he called "my old complaint" (meaning that he was frequently drunk), added his powerful, projecting harsh voice to his
unconcealed hostility of Kemble by comparing the pristine, aristocratic actor's intonations to "an emasculated French Horn." Kemble's
devoted biographer, Boaden, felt it was impossible for John Philip to
identify with the role of Othello, "Mr. Kemble was grand and awful
and pathetic. But he was European; there seemed to be philosophy
in his bearing; there was reason in his rage--It was, at most, only
a part very finely played."

For eight years, beginning on September 23, 1788, Kemble was
manager of London's Drury Lane Theatre; he became manager of

John Philip Kemble, painted by Sully from an earlier portrait by
Stuart.

Covent Garden in the autumn of 1803. In 1804, Kemble and his
sister Mrs. Siddons were invited by the Royal Family to read
Othello at Buckingham Palace. Acclaimed as the greatest actress
of the English stage, Sarah Kemble Siddons, at Covent Garden on
January 21, 1804, gave her last performance as Desdemona opposite
her brother's Othello and George Frederick Cooke's Iago.

Handsome, Ireland-born (1738) John Henry had played Othello
in Dublin and London before making his American debut in Philadelphia in October 1776 at the age of thirty-eight. In 1790 and
1791, Henry was praised for his Othello (Lewis Hallam, Jr. played
Iago). William Dunlap wrote, "Mr. John Henry was full six feet in
height, and had been uncommonly handsome. He played Othello,
we believe, better than any man had done before him in America;
it is recorded that he wore the uniform of a British general officer,
his face black and hair wooly." Henry became the leading stage
idol of his day. Off-stage, he was a leading Lothario to various
sisters of the acting Storer family. He first married Helen Storer,
who later perished by fire in a shipwreck off Fire Island. He then
allied himself, without benefit of clergy, with Helen's younger sister, Ann, who bore his child and was illegally known as Mrs. Ann
Henry. Ann later wed actor John Hogg; Henry returned to the
Storer nest to marry the youngest daughter, Maria. While en route
by ship to Rhode Island, John Henry died on Thursday, October
16, 1794, and hastily was buried ashore; his remains were later
transferred to Bristol's St. James's Church. Henry's bereaved
wife, Maria, lost her mind and, on April 28, 1795, died at her modest home behind Philadelphia's Southwark Theatre.

John Hodgkinson (real name Meadowcroft) was a five-foot ten-
inch, corpulent, versatile actor who died of yellow fever in Wilming-
ton, Delaware on Thursday, September 12, 1805, at the age of
thirty-eight. In England, Hodgkinson had been called "the provincial Garrick," and he had successfully appeared in Bath as Othello.
After giving elaborate fictions of his theatrical accomplishments to
Lewis Hallam, Jr. and John Henry, he joined their American Company at Philadelphia's Southwark Theatre on September 6, 1792.
Following his performance there as Othello, on October 29, 1792,
with Hallam as Iago, Hodgkinson was dubbed "The American Kemble" by the Federal Gazette. Despite his fine acting, Hodgkinson
was ruthlessly ambitious. He forced John Henry from the management of The American Company. Later he brushed aside Lewis
Hallam. Hodgkinson became co-manager of The American Company
with Lewis Hallam and William Dunlap, who in 1833 with his History
of the American Theatre, would become America's first theatre
historian.

James Fennell, born in London on December 11, 1766, was im-
ported from England by Thomas Wignell, manager of Philadelphia's
New Chestnut Street Theatre where, on May 2 and 10 in 1794,
Fennell appeared in the title role of Othello. Fennell had played

Othello at Edinburgh, Scotland under the fictitious name of Cambray. On October 12, 1787 (still as Cambray), he was the Moor at
London's Covent Garden, with Thomas Ryder as Iago and Mrs. Pope
as Desdemona. Returning to Edinburgh as Othello on February 3,
1788, Fennell discarded the mask of Cambray and used his own
name. He was billed as James Fennell for his title role performance
in Othello at Covent Garden on October 16th and 26th. The Moor
became Fennell's best effort on the stage.

        Capricious and adventurously speculative in an assortment of
constantly failed business ventures (e.g., a desalination process),
Fennell returned to the stage to recoup his business losses; for
more than a decade he blacked-up as Othello. He was praised for
his performance as Zanga, the Moor, in Young's drama The Revenge, which was presented in 1800 at New York's Park Theatre.
It was in this theatre that, on November 2, 1810, he gave his last
performance as Othello. William Dunlap recorded of Fennell, "He
was a remarkably handsome figure--his appearance as the Moors,
Othello and Zanga, was noble; his face appeared better and more
expressive, and his towering figure superb." Joseph Cowell wrote,
"He excels as the more weighty characters of the drama. His masterpiece is Othello, the Moor of Venice."

        Fennell was elegantly fastidious. His talent and popularity
were overshadowed by the arrival from England of Thomas Cooper,
who played Iago to Fennell's Othello in Boston in 1808. Thomas
Abthorpe Cooper described six-foot-two-inch Fennell as "Two yards
of a very proper man." The mercurial James Fennell died in Philadelphia on Thursday, June 13, 1816.

        Thomas Wignell, a former member of the American Company
and a cousin of Lewis Hallam, was reportedly George Washington's
favorite comedian. On October 18, 1796, Wignell imported Thomas
Abthorpe Cooper, born at Harrow-on-the-Hill, England on Monday,
December 16, 1776, to head his company of players at his New
Theatre on Chestnut Street in Philadelphia. Cooper was said to
have added "Abthorpe" to his name in America. He made his debut
with Wignell's company at Baltimore, Maryland on November 11, 1796.
Historian George Freedley described Cooper as "the first really fine
English actor to settle in this country."

        Cooper's Othello was acclaimed in New York on April 23, 1799,
and he continued to play the Moor until his retirement from the
stage. He returned to England to a less than rewarding engagement
at Drury Lane and, in March 1803, alternated Othello and Iago with
the brilliant, eccentric, heavy-drinking tragedian George Frederick
Cooke. Debauched and besotted Cooke, having reneged on contracts
and managing to stay a mere skip ahead of debtor's prison, accepted
Cooper's offer to leave England for America. Cooper, though unsuccessful in maintaining Cooke's sobriety, managed to get him aboard
the ship Columbia on October 4, 1810, to join Cooper's company at
New York's Park Theatre.

FOR THE BENEFIT OF

Mr. COOPER.

Theatre Royal, Drury Lane.

This prefent FRIDAY, JUNE 10, 1803.

Their Majefties Servants will perform a Tragedy called

OTHELLO.

Duke of Venice, Mr. MADDOCKS,
Brabantio, Mr. POWELL,
Gratiano, Mr. CAULFIELD,
Lodovico, Mr. PACKER,
Othello, Mr. COOPER,
From the PHILADELPHIA. and NEW YORK Theatres
(Being His Fifth Appearance on this Stage.)
Caffio, Mr. C. KEMBLE,
Iago, Mr. COOKE,
By permission of the PROPRIETORS of the THEATRE ROYAL,
COVENT GARDEN.
(Being his First Appearance on this Stage.)
Roderigo, Mr. RUSSELL,
Montano, Mr. HOLLAND,
Officers, Mr. EVANS, Mr. GIBBONS,
Julio, Mr. RHODES, Antonio, Mr. COOKE,
Meffenger, Mr. FISHER, Sailor, Mr. WEBB,
Defdemona, Mrs. POPE,
Emilia, Mrs. ANSELL,
(Being her Firft Appearance in that Character.)
To which will be added a Mufical Farce called

OF AGE TO-MORROW,

Baron Willinghurft, Mr. BANNISTER, Jun.
Baron Piffleberg, (Firft Time) Mr. PURSER,
Hans Molkus, Mr. WEWITZER,
Hair Dreffer, Mr. HOLLINGSWORTH,
Servant, Mr. EVANS,
Lady Brumback, Mrs. SPARKS,
Sophia, Mifs STEPHENS,
Maria, Mifs DE CAMP,

VIVANT REX ET REGINA! C. LOWNDES, Printer,(66) Drury-Lane

Program: Drury Lane Theatre Othello (1803).

In London, on January 25, 1832, Cooper replaced the suddenly ill Edmund Kean in the role of Othello. He then returned to the
United States where his career continued to flourish. His daughter
Elizabeth Priscilla Cooper appeared onstage with her father in Virginius and in other plays, gaining an enviable reputation as an
actress, prior to her marriage to Robert Tyler on, September 12,
1839. Robert was the son of John Tyler (who became vice-president
to William Henry Harrison in 1840 and later, on April 4, 1841, became the tenth President of the United States after Harrison died
from pneumonia, which struck one month after his inauguration as
President).

Joseph R. Chandler, editor of the United States Gazette, composed a verse expressing hope that the rising young tragedian Edwin Forrest would become Cooper's successor:

"Cooper's our Sun, his orbit is our stage,
Long may he shine, by sense and taste approved,
By fancy reverenced, and by genius loved!
And when retiring, mourned by every grace,
May Forrest rise to fill his envied place!"

Edwin Forrest had been disappointed in his interview with the older
actor in 1821. But seven years later Cooper and Forrest co-starred
in Othello, alternating the roles of Moor and Ensign for a profitable
tour that closed at New York's Bowery Theatre on May 21, 1828.
Cooper, who became the father of six daughters and three sons by
his second marriage, retired from the stage in October 1837 after
making his last New York stage appearance as Mark Antony in Julius
Caesar (November 24, 1835). Through the influence of ex-President
Tyler, Cooper was appointed to the position of Inspector of the New
York Customs House by President James Knox Polk. On Saturday,
April 21, 1849, the renowned actor died at the age of seventy-two
at his daughter's home in Bristol, Pennsylvania.

Biographers disagree regarding the birthdate of England's
consummate tragedian, Edmund Kean. Presumably, he was born il-
legitimately either on Sunday, November 4, 1787, or on Tuesday,
March 17, 1789. Though historians are confused over his birthdate,
they do agree that Kean was one of the historically exemplary por-
trayers of Othello.

Samuel Taylor Coleridge's frequently misquoted acclamation of
Kean's acting ("like reading Shakespeare by flashes of lightning")
was not the paean perpetually recorded. Coleridge's full statement
was "Kean is original; but he copies himself. His rapid descents
from the hyper-tragic to the infra-colloquial, though sometimes pro-
ductive of great effect, are often unreasonable. To see him act,
is like reading Shakespeare by flashes of lightning. I do not think
him thorough-bred gentleman enough to play Othello." On May 5,
1814, Kean's Othello was praised by William Hazlitt as "the finest

Edmund Kean as Othello, "drawn and engraved by J. W. Gear."

piece of acting in the world--a masterpiece of passion" with "repeated burst of feeling and energy which we have never seen sur-
passed--the character never stands still, there is no vacant pause
in the action; the eye is never silent."

The Tatler's critic James Henry Leigh Hunt wrote, "We never
witnessed a performance that struck us so forcibly--we never saw
anything that so completely held us suspended and heart stricken as
Mr. Kean's Othello. Mr. Kean's Othello is the masterpiece of the
living stage." Kean's contemporary and rival, John Philip Kemble,
described Kean's interpretation of the Moor as inferior. Kean
carped, "If the justness of Kean's conception had been equal to the

brilliancy of its execution it would have been perfect. But the
whole thing is a mistake, the fact being that the Moor was a <u>slow</u>
man."

A year later Hazlitt reappraised Kean's Othello in the <u>Examiner</u>,
"Mr. Kean is in general all passion, all energy, all relentless will.
He wants imagination, that faculty which contemplates events, and
brooks over feelings with a certain calmness and grandeur; his feelings almost always hurry on to action, and hardly ever repose upon
themselves. He is too often in the highest key of passion, too uni-
formly on the verge of extravagance."

Kean further astonished London on Saturday, May 7, 1814,
with his vicious portrayal of Iago opposite Sowerby's dismal depiction
of Othello. William Hazlitt wrote, "It was the most faultless of his
performances, the most consistent and entire. Perhaps the accomplished hypocrite was never so finely, so adroitly portrayed--a gay,
lightheaded monster, a careless, cordial, comfortable villain." Lord
Byron proclaimed of Kean: "This is a man of Genius!" On May 9,
1814, London's <u>Morning Herald</u> reported, "The character of Iago is
so much more consonant to the capabilities of Mr. Kean than that of
Othello; cold and designing and unvaried in its nature, it demands
none of those powers which are absolutely necessary to depict those
bursts of feeling or passion with which the latter abounds." But
the <u>Herald</u> caustically added, "there was a total absence of anything
that could be fairly called excellence--there was nothing that might
not be found in any tolerable provincial theatre in the kingdom."

In the provinces, Kean had played the role of black Zanga in
<u>The Revenge</u>. When, on May 24, 1815, he appeared as the black
Iago at Drury Lane, he invited comparison in one of John Philip
Kemble's favorite roles. Dr. Edward Young's 1721 five-act tragedy
reflected Shakespeare's <u>Othello</u> and had characteristics of Alpha
Behn's <u>Abdelazar</u>.

For the love of Lenore, lawyer Young's anti-hero Zanga--the
captured heir to the Moorish throne--maliciously instills jealousy in
the mind of his kind and liberal master Don Alonzo, thus poisoning
Don Alonzo's mind against the Don's good friend, Carlos. Black
Zanga revels in his vindictiveness and confesses his villainy to Don
Alonzo, taunting the distraught man with "Know then, T'was I!
Groan on, and with the sound refresh my soul." Zanga fulfills his
revenge for his capture by killing his master.

<u>The Revenge</u> was first performed at Drury Lane on April 18,
1721, with Mr. Milk as Zanga and Barton Booth as Alonzo. Dr.
Doran depreciated the drama: The "story of love, jealousy, and
murder is, however, a little marred by the puling lines of the black
Iago--Zanga--at the close." The blackface role of Zanga attracted
and tested the talents of many actors (e.g., Thomas Sheridan, Henry
Mossop, John Philip Kemble, Thomas Abthorpe Cooper, William Charles

Macready, and others). Edmund Kean found in Zanga a
role equal to Iago. It was designed for his frenetically passionate performance opposite
Alexander Rae, who was Alonzo.

In the Examiner, William
Hazlitt described Kean's Zanga:
He had all the wild
impetuosity of bar-
barous revenge, the
glowing energy of the
untamed children of
the sun.... He was
like a man stung with
rage, and bursting
with stifled passions.
His hurried motions
had the restlessness
of the panther's; his
wily caution, his cruel
eye, his quivering
visage, his violent ges-
tures, his hollow pauses,
his abrupt transitions,
were all in character.

Edmund Kean as Iago

The Theatrical Inquisitor reviewers were not impressed by
what they considered a waste of Kean's talent as the black Iago,
"The very excellence of his system destroyed the part, for it
showed, in glaring lights, its absurdity; his action and utterance
were those of a human being; but Zanga is not a human being, and
no better mode could have been devised to make that fact evident
to common comprehension than that of natural acting." Another
dissenter reported Kean, as Zanga, "rushed on the stage as a wild
beast may be supposed to enter a new den."

Otis Skinner's essay "Three Madmen of the Theatre" included
Edmund Kean, George Frederick Cooke, and Junius Brutus Booth
who, the grandson of a Jewish Portuguese silversmith, was born in
London on Sunday, May 1, 1796, the son of Richard Booth and
Welsh-woman Elizabeth Game. Ambitious young Booth had created
a sensation in Richard III at Covent Garden, although his triumph
in the title role was rumored to have been based on Edmund Kean's
brilliant interpretation of the part. Not believing imitation to be
the purest form of flattery, Kean invited the acclaimed twenty-one-
year-old performing parvenu to play Iago to his Othello at Drury
Lane.

Kean and Booth were both small men (Kean was five feet four; Booth, slightly shorter). They were compared to pygmies acting like giants when, on February 20, 1817, at London's Drury Lane Theatre with Mrs. Bartley as Desdemona, Booth was a nervous, fiery Iago to Kean's overpowering Othello. London's Morning Post reported, "As the play advances Mr. Booth lost the high ground on which he had stood at its commencement, and the comparison which the audience were increasingly called upon to make, was not very favorable to him. His Iago on the whole was a creditable performance but it was nothing like what a sanguine public had fondly anticipated it would prove--With another actor as that character, the Iago of the evening might have been thought great, but by the side of KEAN we could discover in him nothing strikingly original in thought, vivid in conception, or brilliant in execution."

Although advertised to reappear on February 22 for a second performance of Othello, Booth declined to repeat the contest and defected with a letter expressing his regrets that he "was too unnerved to play." Alexander Rae appeared before the Drury Lane curtain to inform the sold-out house that he would play the role of Iago at that performance, due to Booth's recalcitrance and decampment. On July 7, 1817, Junius Brutus Booth did return to play Iago--but opposite the Othello of Charles Mayne Young and the Desdemona of Eliza O'Neill.

Charles Mayne Young, born in London on January 10, 1777, had played Othello in London for over a decade. His performance was highlighted by his bursting into a deluge of tears after smothering and stabbing Desdemona. Young gave an expert interpretation of Iago both in Kean's Othello (November 27, 1822) and in Charles Kemble's Covent Garden production of Othello (December 21, 1827). Kean's later mitigated observation of Young (who retired from the stage on May 30, 1832, and died at Brighton on July 28, 1856) was "He is an actor, and though I flatter myself that he could not act Othello as I do, yet what chance should I have in Iago after him, with his personal advantages and his damned musical voice? An actor such as I did not dream him to have been, but he was also a gentleman." Yet, in 1822, egocentric Kean--then experiencing rare days of sobriety--was raked with jealousy greater than Othello's at Young's critical and public success at Drury Lane in Hamlet and Macbeth, title roles Kean felt were solely his property. Believing he had been crowned as England's "first actor," Kean demanded that Drury Lane's hard-drinking manager, Robert William Elliston, dismiss Young and rightfully restore the leads in Hamlet and Macbeth to him. But Kean's riotous private life soon clouded his limelight and unsettled his hollow crown.

Kean had met Frances Charlotte Cox while he was appearing in Othello at Taunton, England in 1817, and three years later she became his mistress. Well aware, for several years, of the affair between Kean and his wife, the far from innocent Alderman Robert

Albion Cox, on January 17, 1825, charged Kean with adultery with
his wife Charlotte. The trial was staged with an explosion of publicity and public furor, and the court found Kean guilty as charged.
Kean returned to Drury Lane on January 28, 1825, as Othello. He
played to an audience composed largely of prostitutes and their
pimps bolstered by the dregs of London and all rallying in sympathetic support of a fellow traveler. Kean closed his season at
Drury Lane on March 26, 1825, pacing the five acts of Othello, off-
stage, with brandy and three accommodating whores.

Kean's second American tour in 1825 was not a repetition of
his initial success in 1821, his rebuff due to his highly publicized
love affairs, eccentricities, and bacchanalian revels, which had become the talk of two continents. Kean's misjudgement in Boston on
May 24, 1821 (when he refused to perform Richard III because of
a sparse audience) added to his growing decline in American favor.
Opening in Richard III at New York's Park Theatre on November 14,
1825, Kean played to a caustic and boisterous assembly, but, on
November 16th, his Othello was received by a relatively calm, at-
tentive house.

William Charles Macready was hailed as Kean's successor in
Macready's acclaimed Manhattan debut at the Park Theatre on October 2, 1826. Macready was editorialized as having "talents of un-
common eminence and an unspotted private character"--an obvious
condemnation of Kean. Outraged Bostonians forced Kean from the
stage on December 21, 1825 in retaliation for his ill-judged temperamental 1821 defection. After a tour of America's East Coast cities
and a triumphant engagement in Canada, Kean returned to England
on December 8, 1826, where he was unenthusiastically received in
the theatre. He continued his declining career while blatantly living with an attractive, hell-raising, red-headed Irish prostitute,
Ophelia Benjamin.

William Charles Macready's warm reception in Paris encouraged
Kean to visit France in the spring of 1828. He appeared at the
Salle Favart Theatre in Paris on May 12th in Richard III followed
by an appearance in Othello, with Irish actress Harriet Smithson of
the resident English company (who married composer Hector Berlioz
in 1833) as Desdemona. Macready, who had played Othello at Covent
Garden in October, 1816, alternating Iago with Charles Mayne Young
as the Moor, was Iago to Kean's Othello on November 26, 1832.
Macready privately recorded Kean as "that low man" but played the
crafty Ensign to Kean's Moor ten times until February 8, 1833.

Writer Leigh Hunt described Kean's Othello in the Tatler in
1831: "[H]is little person absolutely becomes tall, and rises to the
height of moral grandeur in such characters as that of Othello."
Lewes recalled in 1832, "how puny he appeared beside Macready";
then he "seems to swell into a stature which made Macready appear
small." A hundred years later petite Helen Hayes, playing the title

role in Maxwell Anderon's play <u>Mary of Scotland</u>, was asked how she appeared to tower over stately Helen Mencken as Queen Elizabeth. Miss Hayes modestly replied, "I thought tall."

Kean realized that his personal hedonistic excesses were taking their toll in his performances. In a letter to his friend W. H. Halpin, editor of the London <u>Star</u>, Kean wrote: "Fight for me. I have no resources in myself; mind is gone, and body is hopeless. God knows my heart. I would do, but cannot. Memory, the first of goddesses, has forsaken me, and I am left without a hope but from those old resources that the public and myself are tired of. Damn, God-damn ambition! The soul leaps, the body fails."

On February 19, 1833, Kean collapsed on-stage at Brighton. Nonetheless, on Monday, March 25, 1833, he returned to London's Covent Garden Theatre playing the title role in <u>Othello</u> with his son Charles John Kean as Iago and Ellen Tree as Desdemona. During act 3, scene 3, Edmund Kean collapsed on-stage after speaking the line, "Villain, be sure thou prove my love a whore...." Falling into his son's arms, Kean gasped, "Oh, God, I'm dying ... speak to them for me."

Edmund Kean died at his home in Richmond on Wednesday morning, May 15, 1833, at the age of forty-five. The Dean of Westminster Abbey refused Kean's burial in the Abbey, and Kean was interred in Richmond Parish Cemetery without fanfare and without a historically dedicated monument such as he had erected to George Frederick Cooke in New York, in 1821.

Three years after Kean's death, playwright Emmanuel Théaulon wrote a five-act play specifically for the celebrated French actor Frédérick Lemaitre called <u>Kean, ou Désordre et Génie</u>. Dissatisfied with Theaulon's work, play-doctor Courcy was asked to reconstruct the play. Courcy's treatment produced little improvement, and the play was submitted to Alexandre Dumas who rewrote Théaulon's script into an acceptable working play. Frédérick Lemaître was acclaimed in the title role of <u>Kean, ou Désordre et Génie</u> at Paris' Variétés Théâtre on August 31, 1836.

Critic Théophile Gautier wrote, "Never has a better role been written for Frédérick Lemaître. Kean himself could not have played his own part any better. At this moment Frédérick is undoubtedly the greatest actor in the world; no one has ever had a wider range." Heinrich Heine enthused,

> The whole production is wonderfully true to life--I really thought I was watching the late Edmund Kean again--the illusion was doubtless largely due to the actor who played the leading role, although Frédérick Lemaître is a tall, imposing figure and Kean was short and stocky. But there was something in the latter's personality and acting which is also to be found in Frédérick Lemaître.

Kean and Lemaître were kindred souls. Their tempestuous lifestyles were as compatible as was their acting genius. Like Junius Brutus Booth and George Frederick Cooke before him, Lemaître arrived at the theatre so drunk he could barely find the footlights. Despite his advanced state of inebriation, he gave a brilliant interpretation of the English tragedian in an early performance of Kean.

Sarah Bernhardt's first great success in Paris was as Kean's fictitious mistress, Anna Damby, in a revival of Dumas's comedy produced by Félix Duquesnel and Charles-Marie de Chilly at their Odeon Theatre in 1868; the comedy featured Pierre Berton as Kean. Alexandre Dumas and his current mistress were in the audience. Lucien Guitry appeared as the passionate English tragedian in Kean, ou Désordre et Génie at Paris' Odeon Theatre in October 1891.

London's Holborn Theatre presented Kean with Swinbourne in the title role on September 25, 1871. P. A. Fitzgerald wrote a highly imaginative melodrama, Edmund Kean; or Life Among the Gypsies, for a young tragedian George M. Ciprico. The Fitzgerald fable, which opened at New York's Wood Museum on January 11, 1875, had Ciprico as Gale Rolfe, a wild gypsy who became England's famous actor Edmund Kean! Haddington Templin's play Edmund Kean was seen in England on November 20, 1893, and J. Edgar Pemberton's English translation of Dumas's comedy, retitled Edmund Kean, Tragedian, was produced on October 23, 1896. Gladys Unger's one-act play, Edmund Kean, starred Seymour Hicks in the title role at London's Vaudeville Theatre in 1903.

Dumas's Kean became a popular attraction for the German Theatre in New York where Adolf Sonnenthal portrayed the English tragedian on March 14, 1885; Friedrich Mitterwurzer, on November 30, 1885; Ludwig Barnay, on March 15, 1888; Maurice Morrison, on October 20, 1890; and Ferdinand Bohn, on April 9, 1902. Schneider's German translation of Dumas's Kean, ou Désordre et Génie exchanged Dumas's play-within-the-play of Romeo and Juliet for Hamlet. Ludwig Barnay made a German translation of the play called Genie und Leidenschaft.

Two years before his mysterious death, actor Charles Francis Coghlan, in 1897, adapted Dumas's Kean; ou Désordre et Génie under the title of The Royal Box. Coghlan directed his adaptation and appeared in the leading role of James Clarence (Edmund Kean) at New York's Fifth Avenue Theatre on December 21, 1897. The successful play moved to the Garden Theatre on January 10, 1898. It completed sixty-three performances and added thirty-two more when the play was revived on September 10, 1898. Salvini's countryman Ernesto Rossi appeared in Dumas's Kean on Broadway in November, 1875, and Italian actor Ermente Novelli included The Royal Box and Othello in his repertoire of plays on Broadway in 1907.

The Royal Theatre of Copenhagen, Denmark filmed Kean; or
the Prince and the Actor, which was released in the United States
on November 6, 1910. The Royal Box was filmed by Selig and released on May 27, 1914. The film featured Thomas J. Carrigan as
the flamboyant Kean, with Charles Coghlan's daughter Gertrude as
Kean's mistress. Herbert Brenon directed Paul H. Sloane's screen
adaptation of Dumas's Kean. Retitled A Stage Romance, the adaptation was released by Fox Films on March 5, 1922; William Farnum
starred as Edmund. Ivan Mosjoukine starred in a 1924 French film
version of Dumas's play called Kean--The Madness of Genius, which
was released in America in 1927 as Edmund Kean, Prince Among
Lovers. Paraphrasing Shakespeare's Othello, a critic noted that
Mosjoukine (in his performance as Kean) was "acting too much and
not so well."

Walker Whiteside revived The Royal Box on Broadway and
played the leading role at the Belmont Theatre on November 20, 1928,
for a run of thirty-nine performances. The following year Warner
Bros.-Vitaphone produced America's first German language film in
their screen version of Coghlan's play, which starred Alexander
Moissi as Kean. Die Köenigsloge was directed by Bryan Foy and
released in the United States as The Royal Box on December 24,
1929.

Jean-Paul Sartre rewrote Dumas's comedy in 1951 for French
actor Pierre Brasseur and intelligently substituted Dumas's inclusion
of Kean's less noted role of Romeo in Romeo and Juliet for his triumphant portrayal of the Moor in Othello. Sartre's Othello segment
included a ribald scene in which Kean's mistress Anna, as an inept
Desdemona, forgets her lines and longs for quick strangulation.
Kitty Black's English translation of Sartre's reconstruction of Dumas's
Kean, or Disorder and Genius was published in 1954. Marianne
Wentzel's German translation of the Dumas-Sartre comedy Kean, oder
Unordnung und Genie, starring Paul Hoffmann in the title role, de-
lighted audiences in Vienna.

Vittorio Gassman and Luciano Lucignani adapted the Dumas-
Sartre Kean as Genio e Sregolatezza. The Italian Kean was co-
directed by Gassman and Lucignani and became a huge success for
Vittorio as the English tragedian. He played at the Teatro d'Arte
Italiano during the 1954-1955 season in Rome and went on tour of
the major Italian cities with Anna Maria Ferrero as Kean's mistress,
Anna Damby. Twenty years later, in 1975, Gassman and Lucignani
collaborated on an Edmund Kean satire called Either Caesar or No
One, which became a showcase for Vittorio Gassman, who, under
the guise of Edmund Kean, expounded his personal and often con-
troversial views on the state of the theatre and the art of acting.
Gassman's 1957 film version of Kean won him Italy's Silver Riband.

Alfred Drake (born Alfredo Capurro in the Bronx, New York,
on Wednesday, October 7, 1914) starred in Peter Stone's musical

version of the Dumas-Sartre play, Kean (music and lyrics by Robert
Wright and George Forrest). The elaborately staged Kean opened
at the Broadway Theatre on November 2, 1961. Some of Manhattan's
appraisers applauded and praised Kean, but Time magazine saw the
three-hour cantata more clearly and reported, "This lavishly mounted,
richly costumed wide-stage dramarama is the most elaborate fiasco
of the new theatre season." Despite Alfred Drake's bravura performance and the show's expensive mounting, Kean was an elaborate
failure and closed on January 20, 1962, after ninety-two performances.

Frank Hauser made another English translation of Jean-Paul
Sartre's play and directed it at London's Globe Theatre on January
28, 1971; the play starred Alan Badel in the title role of Kean.
Alan Badel, as the vain, temperamental, bragging genius that was
Edmund Kean, gave a virtuoso performance, personifying Sartre's
description of Kean as a fabulous egoist and as an "actor who never
ceases acting." The Hartford (Connecticut) Stage Company revived
Dumas-Sartre-Hauser's Kean in December 1981 with Keith Baxter,
in an exemplary performance, embellishing the leading role.

Yorkshireman Krishna Bhanji became actor Ben Kingsley and
a Motion Picture Academy Award winner for his brilliant portrayal
of Gandhi. Kingsley also won acclaim in the title role in Hamlet, in
1975, at London's Round House Theatre. He extended his talent in
Edmund Kean, a two hour one-man play by Raymond Fitzsimons
(based on his 1976 biography Edmund Kean: Fire From Heaven)
performed at England's Harrogate Theatre in August 1981 and at
London's Haymarket Theatre and on Broadway in 1983. Directed by
his wife, Alison Sutcliffe, Kingsley repeated his interpretation of
Kean in the summer of 1984, during a compressed one hour television version of Fitzsimon's monodrama.

Theatrical legends are myriad but none so convoluted and
bizarre as the one based on the life of George Frederick Cooke. It
is assumed that Cooke was born in Westminster, London, on Saturday, April 17, 1756, but other sources claim Dublin to be Cooke's
birthplace, or Scotland--the birthplace of his mother. Cooke re-
peatedly claimed Westminster as his place of birth, but his alcoholic
musings and frequent delusory rhetoric clouded many facts of his
life.

Otis Skinner called Cooke a "Madman of the Theatre" but "the
first actor of real power who has ever faced the American public"
and who "created a new era in American theatrical annals." Cooke
gave a masterful performance as Othello on July 13, 1801. The
same year, his brilliant Iago outshone the Othellos of Alexander
Pope, Robert William Elliston, and Henry Siddons, Jr. Cooke's
thespian genius was acknowledged in his portrayal of sinister characters; he was both a towering Othello and viciously malevolent Iago.

George Frederick Cooke as Iago (painted by J. Green, engraved by
J. Ward, 1801).

On January 21, 1804, Cooke's treacherous Iago was appraised
as overcoming with naturalness the lilting recitation of John Philip
Kemble's Othello. James E. Murdoch compared the two actors in his
book The Stage:

> In marked contrast to the dignified, unimpassioned, and
> coldly-impressive manner of John Philip Kemble was the
> acting of George Frederick Cooke, an actor who divided
> honors with that gentleman, and by some was even pre-
> ferred to him. Mr. Cooke's voice was powerful and well
> sustained throughout--rather hard and sharp, but remark-
> able for compass--while the actor's entire command over it
> gave it a special effect in ease and rapidity of movement....

Cooke's wonderful performance of Iago, of which it has been said of all the impersonators of that character he was the only one who never took the audience into his special consideration, or evinced a desire to make them "chuckle over" his successful villainy.

Washington Irving described Cooke's acting as having "a simplicity in his performance that throws all rant, stage-trickery and stage-effect completely in the background." But Cooke's brilliant career in England was dissipated by his unquenchable thirst and eccentric behavior. In 1780, he literally disappeared for the entire year. Cooke frequently appeared on-stage in an advanced state of inebriation, apologizing to his audience for his "old complaint." Often the curtain was rung down or the performance canceled due to "Mr. Cooke's inability to perform."

Thomas Abthorpe Cooper brought Cooke to America where the great actor made his American stage debut on November 21, 1810, at New York's Park Theatre in one of his finest roles, Shakespeare's Richard III. Although occasionally slipping into dark debauch and bacchanalian miasma, rotund five-feet-ten-inch Cooke became a brilliant and respected star on the American stage. His last appearance at New York's Park Theatre was on June 22, 1812 as Sir Pertinax Macsycophant in Charles Macklin's 1780 play, The Man of the World. After 160 performances in America over a period of one year and ten months, Cooke, on July 31, 1812, at Providence, Rhode Island Theatre, made his last stage appearance as Sir Giles Overreach, in Philip Massinger's 1625 play A New Way to Pay Old Debts.

Cooke died in his attic apartment in New York's Mechanics Hall on Saturday, September 26, 1812. A cortege, which included Governor David D. Tompkins of New York and New York City's Mayor De Witt Clinton--in additon to many other dignitaries and representatives of the arts--escorted Cooke's body to St. Paul's Churchyard, Broadway and Vesey Street (the area of New York's present-day financial district), where it was buried in the Stranger's Vault. On June 7, 1821, before returning to England, Edmund Kean--a great admirer of Cooke--and Cooke's personal physician, Dr. John Wakefield Francis, received permission from Bishop John Henry Hobart to disinter the remains of Cooke's body to rebury them in the center of St. Paul's Churchyard, and to grace Cooke's grave with an appropriate monument.

The two-step, dolomite marble monument is topped by an urn from which a marble flame points toward the original site of the Park Theatre. The monument was the first monument to an actor in America and was completed and erected before Kean's return to England in 1821. Edmund Kean, proudly showing the stone to Dr. J. W. Francis, is depicted in I. R. Smith's 1822 painting and lithograph "The Actor's Monument":

"Erected to the Memory of George Frederick Cooke
by Edmund Kean of the Theatre Royal, Drury Lane, 1821"

At the base of the memorial is a verse written by Fitz-Green Hallick:

"Three Kingdoms claim his birth,
Both hemispheres pronounce his worth."

The inscriptions on the soft marble stone have been recut six times
by: Charles Kean (1846); E. A. Sothern (1874); Edwin Booth
(1890); The Players' Club (1898); and Percy S. Bullen (1912).
Members of the Edmund Kean Club of New York placed a bronze
plaque on the monument in 1948. Over the years, Cooke's monument became a shrine for visiting actors.

Legend persists that Kean extracted the forefinger bone from
the right hand of Cooke's remains and kept it in England as a highly
revered and sacred remembrance of the actor. Dr. Francis already
possessed Cooke's skull, which had been removed at the time of re-
interment and was originally offered to the physician by Cooke in
lieu of payment for his medical expenses. Dr. John Wakefield Francis once loaned Cooke's skull to the Park Theatre for their production of Hamlet. Consequently, after his death Cooke represented
Yorick, the King's Jester, in the grave digger's scene in act 5 of
Hamlet. "Alas, poor Yorick--a fellow of infinite jest, of most excellent fancy."

As late as 1930, Dr. John Wakefield Francis and Dr. David
Hosack were being attacked in the press for the unethical decapitation of Cooke. Neither physician was charged with illegally dese-
crating the body. But the case of Cooke's Wandering Skull became
a cause célèbre for over a century. A more detailed and fascinating
account of Cooke's Wandering Skull is given in Don B. Wilmoth's
excellent and definitive biography, George Frederick Cooke:
Machiavel of the Stage, published by Greenwood Press in 1980.
The biography painstakingly clarifies "one of the strangest legends
in the history of the theatre."

Dr. Valentine Mott Francis, the son of Cooke's Dr. Francis,
inherited the actor's skull and gave it to Dr. George McClellan,
dean of Philadelphia's Jefferson Medical College, in gratitude for
Dr. McClellan's professional services. After Dr. McClellan's death,
the skull was bequeathed to Dr. Ross V. Patterson, McClellan's
successor at the college who in turn willed Cooke's skull to the
Jefferson Medical College, where today it has come to rest in a
display case in the college's library.

A molar from Cooke's skull was given by Dr. V. Mott Francis
to actor Edwin Booth who in turn donated the relic to The Players'
Club where it was assembled as a tie-pin and exhibited. The tooth
is now in the City Museum of New York. (The origin of the Harvard

Theatre Collection's death mask made of George Frederick Cooke remains another mystery.)

The first Black Theatre in America was established in 1821 by James Brown on the corner of Mercer and Bleecker Streets in New York City. Known as The African Theatre, "the Ladies and Gentlemen of Colour" produced Shakespeare's Richard III on September 22, 1821, and Othello in 1822. Both plays featured a West Indies-born, light-colored mulatto James Hewlett, who was a talented singer, dancer, and actor.

Othello was so badly performed that the audience strewed the stage with apple cores and debris until the cast resorted to a minstrel-type variety show, which they played against the backdrop of Othello's Venetian scenery. Ill-prepared Desdemona, who had frantically referred to the script for her lines, danced a quick hornpipe; other deposed Venetians broke into song. Othello, in flowing white robes, and Iago, in blue satin pantaloons, sang a duet, "The Rival Beauties."

Advertised as "Vocalist and Shakespeare's proud Representative," James Hewlett continued performing in theatres in England and America, giving imitations of Thomas Abthorpe Cooper, John Philip Kemble, Edmund Kean, and Charles Mathews. On December 22, 1825, the Star reported that Hewlett's "songs were excellent, and his style, taste, voice and action such as would have done credit to any stage. His imitations of Kean, Mathews, and others were recognized as correct, and evinced a nice discrimination of tact." Hewlett gave a farewell concert performance at New York's Columbian Hall on September 22, 1831. Following a performance of Mr. Brown's play The Drama of King Shotaway on June 21, 1823, which featured James Hewlett in the title role, The African Theatre --except for Charles Mathews--passed into history.

Versatile English dialect comedian, quick-change artist, and satirical monologist Charles Mathews (1776-1835) made an art of mimicking all nationalities. Mathews appeared in several plays at New York's Park Theatre (e.g., The Heir at Law and The Road to Ruin) and, on May 16, 1823, he was foolishly persuaded to appear as the Moor in Othello. Mathews paced the stage and spoke the text in an accurate imitation of John Philip Kemble. His duplication of Kemble's precisely orated Moor was called by actor-manager Joseph Cowell "the most melancholy limping negro I ever beheld." Cowell further suggested the audience would have gladly smothered Mathews "long before he smothered Desdemona!"

Based on observations made during his 1822-1823 American tour, Mathews wrote his one-man, three and a half-hour satire A Trip to America, which he performed at London's English Opera House on March 25, 1824. He brilliantly portrayed a variety of "American Characters," including Boston Yankee Jonathan W.

Ira Aldridge as Othello

Doubikin and two American Negroes, Maxmillan and Agamemnon,
later using these caricatures in his equally successful satire,
Jonathan in England, co-authored with England's expert farce writer Richard B. Peake. Mathew's most amusing segment in A Trip to
America was based on his visit to the African Theatre's performance
of Hamlet during which the audience interrupted the Prince of Denmark's debate "To Be, or Not to Be" by demanding that he sing
"Oppossum up a Gum Tree."

According to his autobiographical Memoir, American-born black
actor Ira Aldridge (New York City, Friday, July 24, 1807) made his
stage debut at the African Theatre as Rolla, in Richard Brinsley
Sheridan's play Pizarro. Aldridge's fame, however, was attained in
England where he became the first black man to reach stardom on
the London stage (though he had not been the first black man to
appear there). Ignatius Sancho, an ex-slave and former servant of
the fourth Earl of Montague, was the first black man to appear on
the English stage in the 1760s. Sancho appeared in the title roles
of Oroonoko and Othello.

Aldridge made his London stage debut on Monday, October 10,
1825, billed as "Mr. Keene, Tragedian of Colour, from the African
Theatre, New York." His first London appearance was at the Royal
Coburg Theatre as Oroonoko, the Royal Slave, in an altered version
of Thomas Southerne's play Oroonoko, retitled Revolt of Surinam; or
A Slave's Revenge.

Thomas Southerne was born February 12, 1659, at Oxmantown
near Dublin, Ireland, and died on Monday, May 26, 1746, in London.
Southerne's play Oroonoko, the Royal Slave was first published in
London on December 16, 1695, following its premiere performance
during November 1695 at London's Theatre Royal, Drury Lane, with
John Verbruggen as Oroonoko, Jane Rogers as Imoinda, and George
Powell as Aboan. Southerne based his play on Aphra Behn's novel,
Oroonoko; or The Royal Slave, A True Story, which was published
in London in 1688. England's first female writer Aphra Behn used
her childhood in Surinam (then a British Colony and later to become
Dutch Guiana) as background for her novel, claiming, "I was an
eyewitness to a great part of what you will find here set down."

Behn's saga of Oroonoko related the horrifying tale of an African prince of Coromantien, educated by European tutors, who is
tricked into slavery by an English sea captain. Aphra described
Oroonoko as "pretty tall, but of a Shape the most exact than can
be fancy'd--His face was not of that brown rusty Black which most
of that Nation are, but a perfect Ebony, or polished Jet." The
Prince is reunited with his lost love, slave Imoinda, in Surinam.
Goaded by Aboan to rebel, Oroonoko leads the slaves in a revolt
against their owners. Surinam's lieutenant governor passionately
lusts after pregnant Imoinda and is killed by Oroonoko. Rather
than have his wife and unborn child returned to slavery, Oroonoko

stabs Imoinda to death and is tortured and killed by the lieutenant governor's men.

Thomas Southerne's adaptation of Behn's novel portrayed Oroonoko (a prince of Angola) as a noble, dignified, intelligent, and passionate black man reminiscent of Othello. Imoinda was recreated from Behn's "beautiful black venus" into a beautiful white girl. Southerne altered and extended other characters in the novel and strongly mitigated Behn's catastasis of the violent and barbaric death of Oroonoko in which Oroonoko is brutally dismembered and his body hacked into quarters. As counterpoint to the tragedy, Southerne wrote a comedic subplot, which Sullen in his 1702 Comparison Between the Two Stages felt fell "below that Author's usual Genius." The incongruous inclusion of a cuckolding comedy was considered detrimental to the play, and the Gentleman's Magazine found the discordant combination of tragedy and farce "absurd and most unnatural."

William Walsh's 1698 play, Victorious Love, was an adaptation of Behn's Oroonoko; and, in 1759, James Hawkesworth altered Southerne's play deleting the comedy subplot. David Garrick made a successful appearance in the Hawkesworth version. Francis Gentleman wrote another excised version of the play in 1760, and, in 1788, John Ferriar rewrote Oroonoko "rejecting the absurd and insufferable underplot of the Old Play as grovelling apology for slave-holders"; he stressed the antislavery theme in his version (called The Prince of Angola). Southerne's comedic subplot was typical of Restoration drama and catered to the public taste.

Aphra Behn was controversial and a member of the avant-garde. Her biographer, Vita Sackville-West, wrote, "The importance of Aphra Behn is that she was the first woman in England to earn her living by her pen." George Freedley and James A. Reeves, in their massive 1941 History of the Theatre, more fully described the authoress: "Being of a generous mind and naturally of a loving disposition, she was called a harlot among other unpleasant names, but she seems merely to have lived a full life. She was attacked by the critics because she dared to be the first woman to earn her living by writing instead of the more usual courses of marriage or a less regular relationship."

Aphra married a Dutch merchant named Behn. But she maintained her independence--and promiscuity, which flourished as much as her literary accomplishments. Her 1676 play, Abdelazar, or the Moor's Revenge was based on Marlowe's 1657 work, Lust's Dominion, or the Lascivious Queen. Her play had an Othellian theme of obsessional passion and jealousy and, in the love of the white Queen of Spain for Abdelazar, the Black Moor, echoed Titus Andronicus. Thomas Betterton originated the role of Abdelazar on July 3, 1676. Born Aphra Amis in Canterbury (or Wye) on July 12, 1640, England's first authoress and female playwright died a syphilitic on April 16, 1689. She is buried in Westminster Abbey.

Over three hundred performances of <u>Oroonoko</u> were given during the seventeenth and eighteenth centuries. Barton Booth's 1698 stage debut in Dublin as Oroonoko produced unscheduled laughter in the audience when Booth wiped his perspiring face and suddenly was half-black, half-white. Booth played the Royal Savage through 1717, with George Powell as Aboan and Jane Rogers as Imoinda. Dennis Delane acted <u>Oroonoko</u> for ten years, until 1744. On January 23, 1742, at London's Goodman's Fields Theatre, David Garrick was Aboan to Henry Giffard's Oroonoko. Four years later on February 24, 1746, Spranger Barry played Oroonoko in Dublin, with George Anne Bellamy as Imoinda and Lacy Ryan as Aboan. James Quin was the Royal Slave in London's <u>Oroonoko</u> on November 28, 1746, and Thomas Sheridan made his first appearance as Oroonoko in Dublin on February 16, 1749, with Francis Gentleman as Aboan.

Two songs had been featured in the original 1695 production of <u>Oroonoko</u>, and in 1774 the drama was paced with a dance by the slaves. Mr. Gaupher, a blackface banjoist singing "The Gay Negro Boy," was featured in Boston on December 30, 1799. Fifteen-year-old Master Betty (William Henry West Betty) portrayed Oroonoko at Covent Garden on March 22, 1806, with Charles Kemble as Aboan. Edmund Kean's nine performances as Oroonoko (beginning December 20, 1816 at London's Drury Lane Theatre, with Alexander Rae as Aboan) was criticized for unnecessarily and unartistically elaborating the violence and horror. Junius Brutus Booth appeared in the title role of <u>Oroonoko</u> at New York's Bowery Theatre on November 29, 1832, and again on December 5, 1832, with Matilda Flynn as Imoinda and the fatuous George Jones ("Count Joannes") as Aboan. This was the first American production of <u>Oroonoko</u> since the late eighteenth century. The play had been produced on February 21, 1794 at Charleston, South Carolina, with Mr. Edgar in the title role and Mr. Lewis as Aboan. And, in December, 1796, it had been performed in Bsoton, with Mr. Cleveland as Oroonoko and Mr. Williamson as Aboan. Charles Kean played the title role in <u>Oroonoko</u> in Ireland, with Ira Aldridge as Aboan on July 9, 1829. Ralph Richardson revived the ancient play at the Malvern Festival in England on August 3, 1932.

Ira Aldridge, using the name of "Mr. Keene," appeared in the title role of <u>Oroonoko</u> on Friday, December 16, 1825, at Brighton's Theatre Royal. On Saturday, December 17, 1825, he made his first appearance in the title role of <u>Othello</u>. The London <u>Morning Post</u> reported that as Othello, "He was not as much at home in the character, however, as he had previously been in that of Oroonoko." Aldridge was dubbed "The Celebrated Mr. Keene, the <u>African</u> Roscius," in 1826, after the famous Roman actor Roscius (126-62 B.C.) who was born a slave but, with his great fame and fortune as an actor, purchased his freedom and, adopting the name of Quintas Roscius Gallas, later became an instructor to Cicero.

Edmund Kean was greatly impressed with Aldridge's performances in Othello and Oroonoko and said of Aldridge: "He possesses
wonderous versatility." The American-born black actor's repertoire
was versatile and included not only Othello and Oroonoko and, later,
Titus Andronicus but outstanding performances as Zanga in The Revenge; Gambia in the Slave; Mungo in the Padlock; Friday in Po-
cock's stage version of Robinson Crusoe called the Bold Buccaneer;
the title role in Anicet-Bourgeois and Dumanoir's Le Docteur Noir
(The Black Doctor) and in John Fawcett's Obi; or Three-Fingered
Jack. Additionally, Aldridge acted white roles in Bertram, Macbeth, King Lear, Guy Mannering, Richard III, The Merchant of
Venice and other dramas.

The Theatre Royal, Covent Garden, on Wednesday, April 10,
1833, billed Aldridge as "A Native of Senegal, Known by the Appellation of The African Roscius, who has been received with great
applause at the Theatres Royal, Dublin,* Edinburgh, Bath and most
of the principal provincial Theatres as Othello." Ira appeared at
Covent Garden as Othello, on April 10 and 12, with basically the
same cast that had supported Edmund Kean in the tragedy two weeks
before, on the night of Kean's last stage appearance. Frederick
Warde, who was Kean's standby on that fatal night, replaced Kean's
son Charles as Iago in Aldridge's company.

The London Times called Aldridge's Othello "An experiment,
and not a remarkably successful one.... Mr. Aldridge's Othello,
with all the advantages of hic niger est, wanted spirit and feeling."
London's Standard reported, "...notwithstanding the impression
which the inimitable Kean had created in this character, and the
genius by which he has made it peculiarly his own, the result showed
the African Roscius was fully justified in making the bold attempt."

London's weekly Spectator found a similarity in Aldridge's
Othello to William Charles Macready's interpretation but felt Aldridge demonstrated greater projection:

> His person is tall and well-formed, and his action free, flow-
> ing and graceful--His voice is rich and melodious, and son-
> orous withal--His deportment is manly, and occasionally dig-
> nified; he moves and speaks with deliberation and self-
> possession. He has no genius but is not without talent;
> and he has two great requisites--a good voice and a good
> figure.

The Theatrical Observer (April 11, 1833) reported that "Mr. Aldridge looked the part well, and his acting was more than respectable, though it fell short of excellence."

---

*Aldridge performed Othello at Dublin's Theatre Royal on December
7, 1831, with John Vandenhoff as Iago. Vandenhoff first played
that part with Aldridge in Liverpool in 1827.

The high-minded, academic London Athenaeum, while proclaiming and defending their racial liberalism and dedication to literary and theatrical genius, raged in self-righteous indignation that Aldridge, "comedian Henry Wallack's black servant" (Aldridge had served both Henry Wallack and his brother James as a goffer and dresser when he first arrived in England), should presume to appear as Othello at Covent Gardens, pawing a decent white actress such as Ellen Tree as Desdemona.

Aldridge gave one performance in the title role of Othello at Stratford-upon-Avon on April 28, 1851. On July 14, 1852, he left England for an extensive European tour. He first appeared at the Theatre Royal in Brussels, opening his continental tour with Othello; Mr. and Mrs. Stanton played Iago and Desdemona. Aldridge was acclaimed in Berlin at the Italian Opera House on January 3, 1853, where he played Othello in English with a German-speaking cast.

The Preussische Zeitung critic wrote:

> The acting and miming are clear interpreters of the artist who speaks in a foreign language. His face is the mirror of his soul. After this Othello it would be anticlimax to have to see an ordinary Othello again! A Negro from Africa's Western Coast had to come to show me the real Othello, the great one and only, the most beautiful male artist that one can imagine. If Shakespeare were to present this play himself, as he had written it, he could not have presented it better even to the tiniest detail.... If he were Hamlet, as he is Othello, then the Negro Ira Aldridge would, in my eyes, be not only the African Roscius, but the greatest of all actors.

King Frederick William IV of Prussia awarded Aldridge the Golden Medal for Art and Sciences on February 1, 1853, and Emperor Franz Josef of Austria presented him with the Medal of Ferdinand. Duke Bernhard of Saxe-Meiningen bestowed the Golden Order of Service on Aldridge on January 31, 1858, making him a Chevalier, Knight of Saxony. During his engagement in Dresden, Aldridge became a friend of composer Otto Goldschmidt and his more-world-famous wife, Jenny Lind. The renowned "Swedish Nightingale" always referred to Aldridge as "the greatest Othello of them all."

A Viennese critic wrote about Aldridge's portrayal of the Moor, "It may well be doubted whether Shakespeare himself had ever dreamed for his masterpiece, Othello, an interpretation so masterly, so truly perfect." Aldridge's success continued in France and in Russia, where Othello is the most revered and revived of all of Shakespeare's plays. Aldridge appeared as an English-speaking Moor in Schlegel's German translation of Othello with

a German-speaking cast at the Imperial Alexandrinski Theatre in
St. Petersburg (now the Academic Pushkin Theatre, Leningrad).

Famous French author and drama critic for Paris' La Presse,
Théophile Gautier recalled (in his Voyage en Russie) seeing Aldridge's St. Petersburg performance: "His first entry was magnificent, he was Othello himself as created by Shakespeare, his eyes
half closed as though dazzled by an Afric sun, his manner orient-
ally carefree with that Negroid grace of movement which no European can imitate." Gautier praised Aldridge's acting as "a majes-
tically classical style much resembling that of Macready." The
French critic's admiration of Aldridge's Othello extended to his
praise of Russian actor Samoilov who had also played Othello at the
Alexandrinski Theatre in St. Petersburg. "His impersonations were
popular, but not as popular as those of Ira Aldridge--for, to be
frank, Samoilov could not make himself into a Negro."

Returning to England, Aldridge appeared as Othello at London's Lyceum Theatre on July 31, 1858, with Stuart as Iago and
Annie Ness as Desdemona. During an 1859-1860 seasonal tour of
the British provinces, Aldridge played Aaron, the Moor, in his reconstructed version of Shakespeare's Titus Andronicus. He performed Macbeth and Othello (with actress Nikulin-Kositzkaya as
Desdemona) at Moscow's Malyi Theatre in 1862 and became a natur-
alized British citizen on November 7, 1863. Aldridge's last appearance on the London stage was at the Haymarket Theatre in August,
1865 in the title role of Othello, with seventeen-year-old Madge
Robertson as Desdemona and Walter Montgomery as Iago.

Margaret Shafto Robertson was born on March 15, 1849, her
parents' twenty-second child. She eventually married William Hunter
Grimston, whose stage name was Kendal. In 1926, Madge Robertson
--at the age of seventy-seven--became Dame Madge Kendal. In her
autobiography, Dame Madge Kendal by Herself (published in 1933
two years before her death on September 14, 1935 at the age of
eighty-six) she recalled playing Desdemona to Aldridge's Othello.
Dame Kendal remembered that Aldridge made her wear

> toed stockings to suggest being undressed and in the last
> act he used to take Desdemona out of the bed by her hair
> and drag her around the stage before he smothered her.
> I remember very distinctly this dragging Desdemona about
> by the hair was considered so brutal that he was loudly
> hissed.... He had some species of well I will not say
> genius, because I dislike that word as used nowadays--but
> gleams of real intelligence....

The once deprecating Athenaeum reported on Aldridge's final
London Othello: "He plays with feeling, intelligence, and finish.
We were glad that he was well received--the tragedy was remarkably
well performed--Madge Robertson excellent as Desdemona--altogether

we have seldom witnessed a representation of this great tragedy
which pleases us more." J. Edgar Pemberton, the Kendals' biographer, demurred: "I remember seeing Mr. Ira Aldridge as Othello
and I could not get it out of my mind that he was playing the part
because he happened to be black, and not because he had any special aptitude for Shakespeare's grandly drawn character."

Walter Montgomery of "the superb physique" was a popular
actor in the British provinces but less than a favorite in London.
Madge Robertson made her adult London stage debut at the Haymarket Theatre on July 29, 1853. She played Ophelia to the Hamlet
of Montgomery, who was Aldridge's Iago three weeks later. Ellen
Terry was Desdemona to Montgomery's Othello on June 20, 1863.
In 1870, during his American tour, Montgomery was described by
the New York Times as "one of the most agreeable, as well as one
of the best-studied young tragedians, we have seen for some time."
But, on December 6, 1870, the Times reported that Montgomery's
Othello at Niblo's Garden" lacks dignity for the part, whether as
expressed by the barbaric loftiness of Mr. Forrest, or the Oriental
suppleness of Mr. Booth. He lacks the prodigious power of the
first-named actor and the ferocious intensity of the other. Mr.
Montgomery's Othello yet deserves to be praised as a deeply pon-
dered and elaborate piece of art."

After a season in America (primarily with Lawrence Barrett's
company), Montgomery returned to England. He was breathlessly
followed by an American actress Winnetta (Bigelow) Montague Taylor. Montgomery married Mrs. Taylor on Wednesday, August 30,
1871, and three days later, on Friday, September 1, 1871, at the
age of forty-four, committed suicide by shooting himself in the
head. Winnetta Taylor had capriciously neglected to tell Montgomery
that her husband, Dr. Taylor, was alive and well and living in Boston. The passionate bigamist Winnetta died in New York City in
May 1887.

Ira Aldridge, the theatre's first black actor to gain recognition and stardom on the English stage, died on Wednesday, August
7, 1867, in Lodz, Poland, where he is buried in the Evangelical
Cemetery. Henry Perronet Briggs' mid-nineteenth-century oil portrait of Ira Aldridge as Othello hangs in the National Portrait Gallery
of the Smithsonian Institution in Washington, D.C. (the portrait is
on loan from London's Garrick Club).

On July 16, 1869, two years after Aldridge's death, Morgan
Smith, advertised as "The Coloured Tragedian," appeared as Othello
at the Royal Alfred Theatre, with his wife as Desdemona and H. S.
Hayner as Iago. The prestige, talent, and fame of Ira Aldridge
were not threatened. "The Coloured Tragedian" Smith's appearance
had no more impact on England's theatre history than did the debut
of a mulatto ship's steward (from an American packet) in the character of Tom Tug. On April 8, 1833, two days before Ira Aldridge's

appearance in Othello at Covent Garden, the opportunistic City
Theatre, Cripplegate, presented "Tom Tug" in The Waterman. The
City Theatre's conscripted amateur was booed and hissed off the
stage.

The celebrated American tragedian Edwin Forrest had a tower-
ing talent that was equal to his temperament. He first appeared in
blackface as the Negro "Cuff" in Sol Smith's comedy The Tailor in
Distress; or A Yankee Trick (Cincinnati, Ohio's Globe Theatre on
July 17, 1823) and first attempted Othello at the age of seventeen
(November 4, 1823, at Lexington, Kentucky). Two years later,
Edmund Kean praised the young actor's playing of Iago to his
Othello in Albany, New York as one of the finest interpretations of
the Ensign he had witnessed, publicly announcing later, "I have met
one actor in this country, a young man named Edwin Forrest, who
gave proofs of a decided genius for his profession and will, I believe, rise to great eminence." Kean was perceptive.

On June 23, 1826, at the Park Theatre, Forrest made his
Broadway debut in the title role in Othello, with Jacob Woodhull
as Iago. The Mirror considered young Forrest's selection of Othello
for his New York debut "somewhat rash" in view of the acclaim
showered on Edmund Kean's performance as the Moor,

> but the event proved our miscalculation, and our disappoint-
> ment was most agreeable. Mr. Forrest, we understand, is
> not yet twenty-three years of age; and the rapid advance-
> ment he has made towards professional eminence in so young
> an actor, is little less than astonishing--Mr. Forrest's Othel-
> lo is superior to any in this country except Kean's.

Critical praise for his portrayal of the Moor continued on November
6, 1826, when he appeared (with William Augustus Conway as Iago)
at the New Bowery Theatre, which had opened on October 23, 1826.

England-born (1789) William Augustus Conway stood six feet,
four inches and made his American stage debut in the title role in
Hamlet in 1824. Later, he played Othello to Thomas Abthorpe
Cooper's Iago. Forrest had played the Ensign to Conway's Moor in
New Orleans and at Albany's Pearl Street Theatre in 1825. "Handsome Conway" assumed "holy orders" the following year and seques-
tered himself throughout 1827. Off Charleston harbor in 1828, while
his fellow passengers were at dinner aboard the S.S. Niagara, Conway committed suicide by leaping from the ship.

Forrest's first appearance on the London stage at Drury Lane
on October 17, 1836, as "the principal tragedian of the United
States" included nine appearances as Othello from October 17 to
December 19 with Frederick Warde as Iago and Miss Taylor as Des-
demona. Junius Brutus Booth played Iago to Forrest's Othello on
November 25, 1836. Forrest was well received by public and press.

London's Morning Post described the American actor as "powerful
and original" and the Sun called him "the first tragedian of the
age," while other scribes extolled "the dignity, quiet power and
poetic grandeur of his Othello." The lone dissenter was London's
Examiner's vitriolic drama critic John Forster, a close, personal
friend of England's popular actor William Charles Macready (who
had appeared at Covent Garden on October 21 and 25 in 1836 to
mild reviews as Othello, with John Vandenhoff as Iago and Helen
Faucit as Desdemona).

John Forster wrote in the Examiner on October 30, 1836,

> There is a vicious style in art which the public taste should
> be carefully guarded against, and Mr. Forrest is one of its
> professors.... The performance was made up of an infinite
> variety of parts, through which there was no unity.... Mr.
> Forrest had no intellectual comprehension of what he was
> about. All he showed was that he very closely watched the
> celebrated performance of Mr. Kean, that he brought away
> from it only the more vulgar and obvious points.

Macready declined producer Edward Fitzball's invitation to
play Iago opposite Forrest's Othello, insisting, "By no means, but
I must play my own parts." Ironically, Iago was probably Macready's finest Shakespearean role, despite the constant "excessive
tendency to impersonation" in which he excelled. Forrest retaliated
by refusing to play Iago to the Othello of England's eminent tragedian, and a mounting, bitter rivalry developed between the two actors that would ultimately lead to death and destruction. Rankled
by Forrest's glowing notices as Othello on February 6, 1837, at
Drury Lane, Macready presented a less glowing Othello at the Haymarket Theatre on June 23, 1837.

A conviction that Macready had influenced his friends in
France not to permit the American actor to perform in Paris (where
Macready had successfully appeared as Othello at the Ventadour-
Salle Favart on December 16, 1844, with Helen Faucit as Desdemona),
plus Forrest's poor reception in Othello at London's Princess's
Theatre on February 17, 1845 (augmented by loud hissing in the
audience), was credited both to Macready and to the actor's devoted
friend and adviser, London's Examiner drama critic, John Forster.
Mrs. Edward Stirling (Mary Anne Hehl) performing her first Desdemona, Graham performing as Iago, and American actress Charlotte
Cushman (who had refused Macready's invitation to become his leading, and subservient, lady) performing as Emilia, were neither
publicly nor critically attacked.

Although Macready had urged Forster to "deal liberally and
kindly by Forrest" in his reviews, the elegantly egotistical actor
had confided to his diary on October 24, 1836, "It would be stupid
and shallow hypocrisy to say that I am indifferent to the result--

careless whether he is likely to be esteemed less or more than myself; it is of great importance to me to retain my superiority, and
my wishes for his success follow the desire I have to be considered
above him!"

Forrest retaliated for what he believed to be Macready's malicious interference and machinations. He loudly hissed William
Charles' prancing, effeminate Hamlet at Edinburgh's Theatre Royal
on March 2, 1846--an act he later publicly acknowledged in a letter
to the London Times on April 4, 1846. Macready referred to Forrest in his diary as "a thick-headed, thick-legged brute," and, on
September 26, 1848, Macready described Forrest in his diary as "an
ignorant, uneducated man, burning with envy and rancour at my
success."

Macready's paranoia about the American actor reached frantic
proportions during his American tour in 1848. The English actor
opened in Macbeth at Philadelphia's Arch Street Theatre on Monday,
November 20, 1848, and Edwin Forrest arranged to appear in Macbeth the same night at the Walnut Street Theatre. Macready rashly
belabored the escalating feud by telling an American audience, for
the third time, that he was innocent of any hostility to any American
actor playing in England but deplored "an American actor's outrageous act" in Edinburgh.

Forrest exacerbated the vendetta. On November 21, 1848, he
fired back an article that was published in the Philadelphia Public
Ledger on November 22:

> Mr. Macready, in his speech last night, to the audience as-
> sembled at the Arch Street Theatre, made allusion, I under-
> stand, to "an American actor" who had the temerity, on
> one occasion, "openly to hiss him." This is true and, by
> the way, the only truth which I have been enabled to gath-
> er from the whole scope of his address. But why say "an
> American actor"? Why not openly charge me with the act?
> for I did it, and publicly avowed it in the Times newspaper
> of London, and at the same time asserted my right to do so.

Forrest continued his rebuttal to Macready's charges by exposing
the machinations of Forster, calling Forster "a toady of the eminent
tragedian--one who is ever ready to do his dirty work" and continuing his scathing salvo at Macready with:

> I assert also, and solemnly believe that Mr. Macready con-
> nived when his friends went to the theatre in London to
> hiss me, and did hiss me with the purpose of driving me
> from the stage--and all this happened many months before
> the affair in Edinburgh, to which Mr. Macready refers, and
> in relation to which he jesuitically remarks that "until that
> act he never entertained towards me a feeling of unkindness."

Pah! Mr. Macready has not feeling of kindness for any actor who is likely, by his talent, to stand in his way. His
whole course as manager and actor proves this--there is
nothing in him but self! self! self! and his own countrymen, the English actors, know this well.

The following night Macready appeared as Othello at the Arch
Street Theatre and enlisted support of his American friends to de-
fend himself against Forrest's charges.

Dour, priggish but impressively talented, William Charles Macready was born on Mary Street, Euston Road, London on Sunday,
March 3, 1973 (he later altered his family name of McCready to
Macready). He first played Othello on October 10, 1816, and five
nights later alternated Othello and Iago with Charles Mayne Young.
William Hazlitt wrote, "Young in Othello was like a great humming
top and Macready in Iago like a mischievous boy whipping him."
Hazlitt's appraisal of Macready's Othello, however, was that "He
whined and whimpered in his attempt to effect the audience by affecting a pitiful sensibility." The London News called Macready's
Othello "stilted and studiously eloquent. On November 16, 1816,
a month after playing black Othello, Macready blacked-up again as
Gambia in Thomas Morton's play the Slave, with Kitty Stephens as
the quadroon, Zelinda.

Ignoring the brilliance of Edmund Kean's acclaimed Othello,
Macready enacted the Moor at Covent Garden on May 30, 1822, to
generally good notices. Ten years later, despite his dislike for
Kean, he played Iago to Kean's Othello. George Henry Lewes, in
his On Actors and the Art of Acting, in 1875 appraised Macready
as lacking in Shakespearean parts but said that Macready was a far
more versatile actor in modern plays in which Kean inevitably failed.
Lewes wrote about Macready, "He was irritable when he should have
been passionate, querulous where he should have been terrible. In
Othello, again, his passion was irritability and his agony had no
grandeur." However, Lewes added, "He was a thorough artist,
very conscientious, very much in earnest, and very careful about
all the resources of his art."

Beginning August 19, 1838, at the Haymarket Theatre, Macready alternated Othello and Iago with Samuel Phelps; Helen Faucit
played Desdemona. The Weekly Dispatch reported that Phelps's
performance "was of all things that which we have never witnessed
since the death of Kean--natural--Mr. Phelps is as much superior
to Macready's Othello as Macready is superior to Cooper's Iago."
The temperamental and tyrannical Macready refused to take a curtain call after Phelps's ovation on September 2, 1838, claiming he
was "undressed."

Macready recorded his opinion of Phelps and actor Wallack in
his diary "as persons who think themselves great actors and imagine

one great evidence of their own talent is to frustrate or weaken the effects of their superiors." The eminent tragedian could not tolerate the threat of rivalry in others (as Forrest had noted). Neither could he abide criticism and demanded that Haymarket manager Ben Webster remove Othello from the repertoire.

Macready was contemptuous of his fellow players, considering them to be subordinates or inferiors; many of them wholeheartedly hated him. In 1890, William Archer wrote the following: "His own part was everything, the opportunities of his fellow actors, and even the poet's text, must all give place to the complete development of his effects." Charles James Mathews and his wife Madame Vestris (née Lucia Elizabeth Bartolozzi) had known the full force of Macready's vitriolic nature while employed by the eminent tragedian at Drury Lane. Mathews later recorded his outrage and humiliation in a letter to Macready in which he described the eminent tragedian's entire theatrical career as "tyrannical and oppressive, especially to those you supposed were beneath you." Mathews noted Macready's imperative insistence in prescribing an acting style completely opposed to Shakespeare's advice to the Players, which engendered "a school in tragedy of gutteral and spasmodic enunciation joined with exaggerated and melodramatic action." Henry Irving's son, Laurence, later observed that "Macready was disdainful of his fellow players and contemptuous of his managers."

With Samuel Phelps again as Iago, Macready appeared as Othello on October 20, 1842, attired in a long, black and white flecked gown with white piping. Parisian critic Théophile Gautier described Macready's appearance as "grotesque" and said that he looked like "an elderly negress, of evil repute, going to a fancy ball." Edinburgh critic John Colman compared Macready's strange costume to that of a Christy Minstrel.

Samuel Phelps, born at Devonport, Plymouth, England on Friday, February 3, 1804, became the prestigious manager and savior of a derelict theatre when he converted Sadler's Wells Theatre into a reputable showplace. Phelps opened Sadler's Wells on May 27, 1844, playing the title role in Macbeth. His second production, on June 3, 1844, was Othello, in which he played the title role, with Henry Marston as Iago and Miss Cooper as Desdemona. During Phelps's eighteen-year management of Sadler's Wells, Othello was performed ninety-nine times.

Phelps was an excellent Othello. He died on Wednesday, November 6, 1878, at Anson's Farm, Coopersdale, England, at the age of seventy-four. In May, 1860, London's Examiner described Phelps's playing of the Moor as lacking the emotional power of Edmund Kean but intelligently depending

> little on those flashes of expressive power which are the
> highest gift of nature to the actor, relies chiefly on study,

taste and a right sense of poetry.--One of the chief merits of Mr. Phelps as an actor of Shakespeare is that he studies each play as a poem, avoids all temptation to mere personal display, and directs attention to the poet whom he is illustrating rather than to himself as illustrator.

During the 1850-1851 season at London's Haymarket Theatre, E. L. Davenport alternated Othello and Iago with Macready. Macready loathed Davenport's performances, especially since they were praised by the London press for their "force and intelligence." Boston-born Edward Loomis Davenport is probably more famous as the father of the celebrated actress Fanny Davenport. Nevertheless, he successfully starred on the American stage and appeared on the London stage for seven years. On September 11, 1854, the New York Herald described Davenport's portrayal of Othello as "a natural and truthful rendering with an absence of exaggerated gestures." Edwin Booth was Iago to Davenport's Othello on April 12, 1858.

Fanned by explosive editorials in the New York newspapers and using the well-publicized feud between Forrest and Macready, a rabble of Bowery B'hoys and rabid anti-English rebels provoked a class-war at Niblo and Hackett's 1,800-seat Astor Place Opera House on May 7, 1849, where Macready was appearing as Macbeth. That night, Forrest was playing the same role at the Broadway Theatre, as was Thomas S. Hamblin at the Bowery Theatre.

Macready attempted to placate the unruly audience, but they ignored him. According to his diary on May 7, 1849,

> Macbeth proceeded in dumb show. I hurrying the players on. Copper cents were thrown, some struck me, four or five eggs, a great many apples, nearly--if not quite--a peck of potatoes, lemons, pieces of wood, a bottle of asafoetida which splashed my own dress, smelling, of course, most horribly.

Ignoring the counseling of friends or even Shakespeare's Witches in Macbeth, "Double, double toil and trouble; Fire burn and cauldron bubble," Macready bravely resumed his attempt to play Macbeth on May 10 at the Astor Place Opera House while Forrest was appearing as Spartacus in The Gladiator at the Broadway Theatre.

Despite constant interruption and Macready's being pelted with large quantities of various food of questionable purity from the gallery by the Bowery B'hoys, the performance of Macbeth was completed. Macready recorded in his diary,

> Stones were hurled against the windows in Eighth Street, smashing many; the work of destruction became then more systematic; the volleys of stones flew without intermission,

battering and smashing all before them; the Gallery and
Upper Gallery still kept up the din within, aided by the
crashing of glass and boarding without.

A full-scale riot erupted inside and outside the theatre where
a tremendous, uncontrollable mob threw stones and stormed two hundred members of the Seventh Regiment holding fixed bayonets, 325
policemen, two troops of Cavalry, and one unit of Hussars. Unlike
Shakespeare's Macbeth's "signifying nothing," when this sound and
fury had cleared thirty-one persons were dead and forty-eight were
seriously wounded. Macready's friend Robert Emmett spirited the
actor away from the theatre to his home where, before dawn of the
next day, the eminent British tragedian was taken safely out of Manhattan. Edwin Forrest, however, was not implicated either in the
Macready attack or in the Astor Place riot. On July 9, 1834, at
the Bowery Theatre, Forrest was performing Metamora for the benefit of George F. Farren when a riot erupted against Englishman
Farren, which theatre manager, actor Thomas Sowerby Hamblin,
was unable to quell. Forrest was not implicated in the Farren riot,
but his involvement in the Astor Place riots was less than silent.
Ten rioters were convicted after a fifteen-day trial before Judge
Daly of New York's Court of General Sessions.

Riots in the theatrical world were not new. Early on, Shakespearean actors were targets for vituperative victuals when six-
teenth-century audiences vented their displeasure with a performance. A rebellious audience forced John Hodgkinson to leave the
stage of New York's John Street Theatre on March 29, 1797, during
a performance of The Conscious Lovers. The opening of London's
new Covent Garden Theatre in September 1809 fermented one of the
longest riots in theatrical history; the insurrection was due to increased admission prices, the redesigning of the third tier into
private boxes, and the conversion of the upper gallery into separate units. The Old Price riot began on opening night and continued
for three months. Oddly, the opening play was Macbeth; and John
Philip Kemble and Sarah Siddons carried on a mute performance
against the constant uproar in the theatre. Kemble's home was
stoned and constantly threatened. The Covent Garden management
and manager Kemble finally capitulated by reducing the number of
private boxes and reinstating the old admission prices.

Junius Brutus Booth, after his escape from Drury Lane and
contractural constrictions placing him under the dominance of Edmund
Kean, was hissed, booed, and bombarded with oranges when he returned to Covent Garden in Richard III on February 25, 1817. The
play was constantly interrupted by outraged Kean supporters. London's Morning Post accused Kean of instigating the riot--a charge
Kean vehemently denied in a letter published by the Morning Post
on February 27th.

Edmund Kean had been pelted with rotten apples and forced to

perform Richard III in pantomime at New York's Park Theatre on
November 14, 1825, but the first major American theatre riot occurred in Boston at Kean's scheduled opening in the same play on
December 21, 1825. Aware of Bostonians' outrage for his refusing
to act before a sparse audience in 1821, Kean attempted to atone for
his past indiscretion in a letter written from Boston's Exchange Coffee House to the editors of the morning papers on Wednesday, December 21, 1825.

> That I have suffered for my errors, my loss of fame and
> fortune is too melancholy an illustration. Acting from the
> impulse of irritation, I certainly was disrespectful to the
> Boston public; calm deliberation convinces me I was wrong.
> The first step toward the Throne of Mercy is confession--
> the hope we are taught, forgiveness. Man must not expect
> more than those attributes which we offer to God.

Kean's bulletin of atonement was met with contempt, and, when
he appeared on-stage to further apologize, the unappeasable, af-
fronted Boston audience refused to hear him speak and tossed at
him an astonishing arsenal of debris. Theatre manager, Henry James
Finn, who had played Othello to Thomas Abthorpe Cooper's Iago in
1822, placed a placard on-stage announcing "Mr. Kean declines
playing--replaced by Mr. Finn." Finn's announcement that Kean
had left the theatre incited the audience to a frenzy of wanton destruction. Kean quickly left the city he had once called "the literary Emporium of the New World." On January 13, 1840, Henry
James Finn drowned when a burning ship, The Lexington, sank in
Long Island Sound.

Edwin Forrest scored tremendous hits in a variety of parts.
He appeared in John Stone's 1829 prizewinning play Metamora, or
the Last of the Wampanoags, for twenty-five years. In the role of
Spartacus, he also performed in the 1831 five-act tragedy The
Gladiator written by Pennsylvania Medical College professor of medicine, Dr. Robert Montgomery Bird. At New York's Park Theatre,
on May 24, 1841, Forrest first played the title role in Robert Taylor Conrad's drama Jack Cade, also known as Aylmere; or The
Kentich Rebellion, which was based on the life of the fifteenth-
century rebel. Publisher, judge, and former mayor of Philadelphia
Robert T. Conrad wrote Jack Cade under the title of The Noble
Yeoman for actor Augustus A. Addams, a notable Othello whose
slavery to alcohol destroyed his career.

Augustus A. Addams portrayed the Moor in New York on
April 4, 1835, and the Knickerbocker Magazine reported, "This
young American actor bids fair to attain distinguished rank as a
native tragedian--His personation of Othello was the best we have
witnessed since we saw Forrest--whom Mr. Addams as an actor
greatly resembles." Physically, Addams did resemble Forrest and
copied his stage delivery in deep, resonant tones while cloning

Forrest's Othello. But Addams was so drunk the night of the December 7, 1835, premiere of Jack Cade at Philadelphia's Walnut Street Theatre that he was quickly replaced by David Ingersoll. T. Allston Brown later observed: "Had he let drink alone he would have become the greatest actor ever seen in this country."

Dr. Robert Montgomery Bird and Judge Conrad survived Forrest's persistent parsimony. But John Augustus Stone, on June 1, 1834, at the age of thirty-four, despondent over the acclaim and fortune Forrest had accumulated from his role in Metamora, leaped from Philadelphia's Spruce Street Bridge into the Schuylkill River and drowned. Forrest paid Stone's hotel bills and the expenses of his funeral and burial. He also paid for a stone marker for the young playwright's grave inscribed, "In Memory of the Author of Metamora by His Friend Edwin Forrest."

Forrest married Catherine Sinclair on June 23, 1837, in London's St. Paul's Covent Garden Church; twelve years later, he angrily separated from his wife, calling her a "dysgenic female." Returning unexpectedly to a Cincinnati hotel, Forrest discovered his wife standing between actor George Jamieson's legs while his hands explored her body. Catherine casually explained that Jamieson was merely pointing out her phrenological developments. This statement clearly indicated that neither Catherine nor Jamieson was too well versed in anatomy; phrenology is a study of the skull. Later Forrest found a passionate love letter; it had been written by Jamieson, who addressed Forrest's wife as "Sweet Consuelo." The letter was sprinkled with such lyrics as "Have we not known real bliss?" and "Think of the time when we shall meet again--I shall do the utmost to be worthy of your love."

George Jamieson had played Iago to Forrest's Othello several times, but Edwin now saw Jamieson through Othello's eyes as Cassio. Jamieson was the original old Negro Pete in Dion Boucicault's 1859 melodrama The Octoroon, and he portrayed Uncle Tom in 1860 in his own stage adaptation of Uncle Tom's Cabin (called The Old Plantation; or The Real Uncle Tom). During the summer of 1850, Forrest started divorce proceedings against his wife and, on November 19, 1850, Catherine countered by filing for divorce in New York Supreme Court.

Forrest's former housekeeper testified that eight men had "called on Catherine" during Forrest's absence. Mrs. Forrest's personal maid related juicier tales such as discovering Captain William H. Howard in bed with Mrs. Forrest. Catherine's clever lawyer presented evidence of Edwin's frequent visits to Madam Caroline Ingersoll's bordello and said also that Edwin had "carnal knowledge" of the late actress Josephine Clifton. Edwin's former dresser and designer of his stage costumes was one-time blackface singer Andrew Jackson Allen, then owner and proprietor of the Bowery's Rialto Saloon (who died at the age of sixty-five on Saturday, October 29,

1853); Allen, too, testified against his former employer, thus confirming Edwin's affair with his leading lady Josephine Clifton. Despite aspersions cast on Catherine's casual chastity, it was Forrest
who was ultimately charged with adultery! After a lurid six-week
trial on January 26, 1852, Forrest was branded as an "adulterer"
and forced to pay Catherine $3,000 annual alimony. For a period
of eighteen years Forrest appealed the decision; but he never won.

Coached by actor George Vandenhoff, Catherine went on the
stage billed as Mrs. C. N. Sinclair, THE LATE MRS. FORREST.
She appeared in New York and other cities in five plays for which
she received little acclamation: The School for Scandal; The Patrician's Daughter; Love's Sacrifice; Lady of Lyons; and Much Ado
about Nothing. Playing a month's engagement at London's Haymarket Theatre in 1857, she garnered fairly pleasant notices and
retired from the stage in 1858. Catherine died in her brother-in-
law's (actor Henry Sedley) 84th Street home in New York on Tuesday, June 9, 1891. George Jamieson was killed by a railroad train
near Yonkers, New York on Monday, October 5, 1868. Forrest joy-
ously observed, "God is great and Justice, though slow, is sure--
another scoundrel has gone to Hell, I trust forever!"

Edwin Forrest's last appearance on the stage was on December
7, 1872, at Boston's Tremont Temple where he gave a solo reading of
Othello. He died at his home in Philadelphia on Thursday, December
12, 1872. William Charles Macready, having made his last stage appearance at London's Drury Lane Theatre on February 26, 1851, as
Macbeth, died the following year on Sunday, April 27, 1873, in
Cheltenham, England.

Frank Barrie's monodrama Macready!, based on the Diaries of
William Charles Macready (1793-1873), was produced by New York's
Circle Repertory Theatre on July 29, 1980. Barrie portrayed the
eminent tragedian in his one-man "celebration" of the actor, stress-
ing Macready's duality in the theatre and in his private life. After
thirty-four performances in New York, Barrie opened Macready! in
London during September 1981, where Charles Spencer (London
Standard) called the event "a curiously poignant evening," and
Rosemary Say (Sunday Telegram) applauded Barrie's interpretation
of the famous tragedian, correctly observing "To do a 'Macready' is
to pause long on stage." William Charles would have excelled in
Harold Pinter's latter-day plays.

Edwin Forrest's friend and protégé John McCullough was a
handsome, highly personable actor with a rich, resonant voice. His
most impressive performance was considered to be the title role in
James Sheridan Knowles's 1820 drama Virginius, but he was especially fine as Shakespeare's Othello. Critic William Winter described
McCullough's Othello as being "like a grand tower bathed in sun-
shine--played with great nobility through an intensified passionate
climax." McCullough presented a lightly tanned Othello. He was

clad in a suit of armor that featured a skirt of mail and wore a
close-fitting round metal helmet unlike the crescent-shaped crown
favored by Kean, Forrest, and other tragedians.

New York Evening Post critic John Ranken Towse wrote that
McCullough's

> Othello was an imposing and martial figure, with authority
> in voice and mien and all the external indications of the
> "frank and noble nature" with which Iago credited him.
> And his "waked wrath" was terrible. This was the best of
> his Shakespearean embodiments, and in respect of adequate
> passion was superior to that of any other contemporary Eng-
> lish-speaking actor. But it was only in storm and stress
> that it was remarkable. In detail it was crude, unimagina-
> tive, unfinished, a bold freehand sketch rather than a com-
> pleted study.

McCullough was frequently accused of copying the histrionics of his
mentor Edwin Forrest but congratulated on refining and mitigating
the vivid violence of Forrest's performance.

John Edward McCullough, born on Wednesday, November 14,
1832, at Blakes near Coleraine, Londonderry, Ireland, migrated to
America in 1847. Illiterate McCullough learned to read and write in
Philadelphia and graduated from Lemuel R. Shewell's Boothenian
Dramatic Association of Philadelphia where manager William T. Fredericks saw the neophyte actor perform as Othello. Fredericks engaged McCullough at four dollars per week at his Arch Street Theatre where John Edward made his first professional stage appearance
in a subminor role in The Belle's Stratagem on August 15, 1857.
Following an apprenticeship with E. L. Davenport's Boston Howard
Athenaeum Company during the 1860-1861 season, McCullough was
contracted by Edwin Forrest to be a second lead and supporting
player. McCullough played Iago to Forrest's Othello in 1861 and
alternated Iago and the Moor with the great tragedian on September
18, 1862, at New York's Niblo's Garden.

San Francisco had seen its first Othello on February 4, 1850,
with Mr. Carleton as the Moor and John Hambleton as Iago. It was
in San Francisco that McCullough attained his greatest recognition
and stardom as an actor and, in partnership with Lawrence Barrett,
became extremely successful as the theatre manager of San Francisco's California Theatre. There, McCullough played Othello and
continued his masquerade in black by appearing in the title role of
Uncle Tom's Cabin.

McCullough was playing Iago to Forrest's Othello at Niblo's
Garden on Friday, April 14, 1865, when John Wilkes Booth assassinated President Abraham Lincoln. Three weeks before, McCullough
had shared a room with John Wilkes at Washington, D.C.'s National

Hotel; he was stunned by the news of the tragedy. The following
morning, McCullough, unable to comprehend or believe his one-time
friend's lunatic act, related the tragedy to Forrest. Forrest, re-
affirming the family's reputation as "The Mad Booths of Maryland"
and that all the American Booths were born bastards, countered
McCullough's disbelief of John Wilkes's homicide with "well, I do!
All those god-damned Booths are crazy!"

The ninth child sired out of wedlock by Junius Brutus Booth
was the most handsome of his sons and named after a distant family
ancestor John Wilkes, England's parliamentary reformer. John
Wilkes Booth was born on the Booth farm in Harford County outside
of Bel Air, Maryland, on Thursday, May 10, 1838. On August 14,
1855, at the age of seventeen, he quakingly made his stage debut
as Richmond in Richard III at Baltimore's St. Charles Theatre.

Using the name of J. B. Wilks, Booth became a stock player
at Wheatley's Arch Street Theatre in Philadelphia. There he formed
a close friendship with John McCullough, another fledgling actor making his debut as the servant Thomas in The Belle's Stratagem in
which John Wilkes was a supernumerary. As Wilks he played a minor
role in Othello on September 28, 1857, with Mr. and Mrs. E. L.
Davenport as the Moor and Desdemona, and John Dolman as Iago.

John Wilkes Booth appeared as the Moor in Othello on October
7, 1858, at Richmond, Virginia and there, on May 2, 1859, his
brother Edwin played Iago to his younger brother's Othello. John
played Othello for seven years in the South, in the Midwest and in
New England, but not in New York City. Wearing tight, black, silk
tights trimmed with white velvet, John played Iago at Nashville,
Tennessee and Cincinnati, Ohio in 1864. John Wilkes's Othello at
the Boston Museum on May 2 and 10 in 1864, with L. R. Shewell as
Iago (a part Shewell would play opposite Salvini's Othello at Booth's
Theatre in New York on December 13, 1881), had terrified Kate
Reignolds as Desdemona.

Praise for his playing of Othello continued in Detroit at Perry's
Metropolitan Theatre on November 13 and 14 in 1861, with J. W. Al-
baugh as Iago and Mrs. H. A. Perry as Desdemona. The Detroit
Free Press likened Booth's talent as "bidding fair to be almost
equalled by that of his father.... The genius of Booth the senior
has already descended in no small measure to the son." the Baltimore Sun once dubbed John Wilkes as "The Gymnastic Actor" due
to his athletic and agile performing. Others discerned in John all
the "fire, the dash, the touch of strangeness of his father." It is
possible young John could have inherited Junius B.'s aberration of
genius masking latent insanity. Critic William Winter, a devoted
friend of Edwin Booth, however, appraised John Wilkes's acting as
"raw, crude, and much given to boisterous declamation."

John Wilkes Booth's dark, handsome features and magnetic

personality had "an almost aphrodisiac effect upon women," and
men admired his dashing theatrical charm and verve. Actress Clara
Mooris in her 1901 autobiography, Life on the Stage, recalled:

> He was, like his great elder brother, rather lacking in
> height, but his head and throat, and the manner of its ris-
> ing from the shoulders, were truly beautiful. His coloring
> was unusual, the ivory pallor of his skin, the inky black-
> ness of his densely thick hair, the heavy lids of his glowing
> eyes, were all Oriental, and they gave a touch of mystery
> to his face when it fell into gravity; but there was gener-
> ally a flash of white teeth behind his silky mustouche [sic],
> and a laugh in his eyes.... Now it is scarcely an exagger-
> ation to say the [female] sex was in love with John Booth,
> the name Wilkes being apparently unknown to his family and
> close friends.

President Abraham Lincoln vigorously applauded John Wilkes
Booth's November 9, 1863, performance in The Marble Heart, and
there is evidence the President attended the Ford Theatre for John
Wilkes's last professional appearance. John Wilkes Booth made his
last appearance on the legitimate stage on Saturday evening March
18, 1865, at Ford's Theatre, Tenth Street above E Street in Washington, D.C., for his friend John McCullough's benefit. Booth
starred in his father's old role of Pescara in Richard Laler Shiel's
drama The Apostate, with John McCullough as Hemeya and W. H.
Hamblin as Malec. McCullough left Washington the following day
for an engagement in Canada.

Three weeks later, President Lincoln returned to Ford's Theatre on Good Friday, April 14, 1865, for a performance of Tom Taylor's comedy Our American Cousin, starring Laura Keene in her
original role of Florence Trenchard. E. E. Emerson played Lord
Dundreary, a role that made Edward A. Sothern famous and established a career for him, but which he did not perform that evening
as has been widely reported. Joseph Jefferson's famous role of
Yankee Asa Trenchard was played by Harry Hawk. John Wilkes,
having appeared several times in Our American Cousin, was familiar
with the comedy and awaited his cue for murder which Hawk, alone
on-stage, unknowingly gave to him with the line, "Well, I guess I
know enough to turn you inside out, old gal, you sockdologizing old
man-trap!" The laugh-provoking line was followed by a pistol shot
and Shakespeare's Brutus's cry to Caesar, "Sic semper tyrannis!"

Twenty-six-year-old John Wilkes Booth had assassinated
President Abraham Lincoln.

Pursued by twenty-five men of the Sixteenth New York Caval-
ry led out of Washington, D.C., by Colonel Everton J. Conger,
Booth was trapped in a burning tobacco barn on the farm of Richard
Henry Garrett, which was located three miles south of Port Royal,

Virginia. He shot himself in the back of the neck and was removed
to the porch of Garrett's farmhouse. Looking at his limp hands,
the hands he had used to kill the sixteenth President of the United
States, Booth muttered his last words, "Useless, Useless!" and died
on Wednesday, April 26, 1865.

In the pocket of Booth's diary pictures of four actresses were
found, including one of Effie Germon, the daughter of Greene C.
Germon who created the role of Uncle Tom in George L. Aiken's
dramatization of Uncle Tom's Cabin. Effie Germon, the great-grand-
daughter of Joseph Jefferson, had played Ophelia to John Wilkes's
Hamlet at Grover's Theatre in Washington, D.C. in 1863. Although
he later played the Prince of Denmark, John had shied away from
Hamlet, explaining: "No!, No!, No! there's but one Hamlet to my
mind, that's my brother Edwin. You see, between ourselves, he is
Hamlet, melancholy and all."

Four years later, President Andrew Jackson who had officially
pardoned all secessionists on Christmas Day, 1868, approved Edwin's request for John Wilkes's body to be exhumed from a store-
room grave in Washington's Arsenal and reinterred in the Booth
family burial plot in Baltimore, Maryland's Greenmount Cemetery.
John Wilkes Booth was buried in Greenmount on June 26, 1869, his
name added to those of Junius Brutus Booth's other deceased children on the memorial shaft Edwin had erected in 1858.

Edwin Booth later came into possession of John Wilkes's theatrical trunk. In Manhattan, during the early morning hours some
time in March 1873, Edwin burned all of John's costumes (including
a beautifully designed gown made of fine Indian shawl material
created for his infamous brother's Othello) in the furnace of Booth's
Theatre. Edwin would not discuss his brother and recoiled at the
mere mention of the Civil War. But on July 28, 1881, Edwin wrote
to his friend Nahum Capen about John,

> He was of a gentle, loving disposition, very boyish and full
> of fun--his mother's darling--and his deed and death crushed
> her spirit. He possessed rare dramatic talent, and would
> have made a brilliant mark in the theatrical world. All his
> theatrical friends speak of him as a poor, crazy boy, and
> such his family think of him.

Until his death in his bedroom at the Players' Club, Edwin
Booth retained a photograph of John Wilkes. The photograph is still
there.

Shakespeare's Othello was accepted in the South until the
tremblings of Civil War reverberated throughout the nation. Southerners saw Othello as an antimiscegenation drama. Junius Brutus
Booth had been commended in 1822 for playing the Moor in blackface rather than as the prevalent, lighter-skinned mulatto. Then,
in August 1822, a report (possibly apocryphal) circulated that a

soldier on guard at a Baltimore theatre fired his gun at an actor
playing Othello, breaking the actor's arm. (The soldier justified
his poor aim but righteous indignation as "It will never be said that
in my presence a confounded Negro has killed a white woman!")

Edwin Forrest played Othello in New Orleans on January 28,
1839, and received critical and public compliments on his blackface
role. In addition his payment for the performance was the largest
he had received in his career. Actor Harry Watkins, however, discovered in 1852 that presenting a blackface Othello in Macon, Georgia, would militate against his performance and personal health.
Watkins wisely appeared as near white as a Blackamoor can get minus
burnt cork. James Wallack, Jr. dogmatically refused to play a
scheduled blackface performance of Othello in Alabama on December
24, 1860, the evening of that State's Secession Convention. After
the Civil War, attitudes changed; Othello became anathema in the
South.

The sixth President of the United States, an ersatz Shakespearean scholar and staunch Unitarian, John Quincy Adams, rose
in high literary self-righteousness and wrote: "The great moral
lesson of the tragedy of Othello is that black and white blood cannot be intermingled in marriage without a gross outrage upon the
law of Nature, and that, in such violations, Nature will vindicate
her laws!"

Edwin Booth played Iago to John McCullough's Othello at New
York's Academy of Music on September 10, 1869; during 1877 Mc-
Cullough starred as Othello in New York at Booth's Theatre, where
he was awarded a silver laurel wreath for his interpretation of the
Moor on April 27, 1877. McCullough appeared at London's Drury
Lane Theatre on May 2, 1881, as Othello, with Hermann Vezin as
Iago and Isabel Bateman as Desdemona. But the great excitement
in London's West End that night was at the Lyceum Theatre where
Henry Irving and Edwin Booth were starring in Othello, an event
which eclipsed McCullough's Venetian adventures.

The London Era reported on McCullough's performing:

> After Salvini the Othellos of the stage are inevitably disap-
> pointing. The Othello of John McCullough cannot satisfy
> such as these. He is an actor of the people, rough, it is
> true, unequal, old-fashioned, as we now express it, but
> there is a boldness of treatment, a firmness of grasp, and
> a hold upon the multitude that can be distinguished from
> trickiness, claptrap and rant ... he is an actor for a large
> stage and a large audience, and he paints his effects broad-
> ly with a coarse brush. This is no doubt why the Drury
> Lane audience warmed instantly to the actor, liked his firm
> stride, listened to his deep tones, and detected a terrible
> meaning in his savage passion. An artist of polish, precision,

and fantastic fastidiousness might have failed on the very
scene where McCullough succeeded.

London Theatre added: "From John McCullough we have the Othello
of the camp and field. He is a soldier, every inch of him."

Edwin Booth expressed his 1881 appraisal of John McCullough's talent in this way: "I was impressed by his repose and
freedom from the fault we tragedy-boys indulge so freely in--over
gesticulation, both qualities are most difficult to acquire--but I
think they are natural with him."

McCullough's last stage appearance was at Chicago's McVicker
Theatre on September 28, 1884, as Spartacus in The Gladiator. During the performance, McCullough's failing health and mental break-
down caused him to forget his lines and leave the stage. Returning
to the stage, McCullough rebuked his laughing and derisive audience: "You are the most ill-mannered audience I ever saw. If you
had suffered tonight as I have suffered, you would never have done
this. Good night!"

The newspapers blatantly exposed McCullough's downfall after
his commitment to Bloomingdale Asylum on June 27, 1885. On October 25, 1885, McCullough was transferred to his home in Philadelphia where, on Sunday, November 8, 1885, he died from paresis,
the final stage of syphilis. Three years later a forty-foot granite
monument topped by a stone eternal flame above a bronze bust of
McCullough as Virginius was erected above his grave. It was unveiled on November 28, 1888, in Philadelphia's Mount Moriah Cemetery.

Following McCullough's death, a macabre but popular attraction
at variety halls was a sordid sketch, "The Ravings of John McCullough." Laurence Hutton in an October 1894 Century magazine
article recalled putting a nickel in a public slot-phonograph mounted
with a picture of the late actor. The phonograph played a recording of "The Ravings of John McCullough" and included passionately
quoted excerpts from his roles of Brutus, Spartacus, and Virginius,
each excerpt ending with maniacal, violent laughter.

Junius Brutus Booth had been Iago to Kean's Othello at Covent
Garden in 1817. He portrayed Othello in America, frequently alternating in the roles of Othello and Iago with Edwin Forrest, Thomas
Abthorpe Cooper, Thomas Sowerby Hamblin, and others. Booth's
son Edwin was less notable as Othello than he was renowned as Iago
(especially as Iago to the historically greatest Othello of all time:
Tommaso Salvini).

It was paraodoxical that critical and public acclaim were accorded Salvini on the English-speaking stage (he spoke Shakespeare's text in a foreign tongue). Not the understanding of

Tommaso Salvini as Othello (courtesy of The Free Library of Philadelphia Theatre Collection)

Othello's lines but the consummate power of the Italian tragedian's acting was the spur to his fame. Boston critic Charles Townsend Copeland, aware of Coleridge's often misquoted appraisal of Kean's acting as "like reading Shakespeare by flashes of lightning" wrote this about the tragedian: "When Salvini played Othello and Booth Iago there were no flashes because there were not periods of darkness. It was like reading Shakespeare by a mighty fire that rose and fell with the passions of the scene."

Tommaso Salvini, born in Milan, Italy, on Saturday, January 10, 1829, has been historically celebrated in theatre annals as the greatest Othello. Having attained a glowing reputation with his portrayal of Orosmane, the Moor in Voltaire's Zaire, Salvini won even greater acclaim at the age of twenty-seven at Vicenza, Italy in June 1856, when he played Othello, with Clemtina Cazzola as Desdemona and Lorenzo Piccinini as Iago. Salvini terrified actresses playing Desdemona and stunned audiences with the passionate power of his sensual, vibrant acting.

Salvini made a triumphant Broadway debut as the Moor at the Academy of Music on September 16, 1873, in Giulio Carcano's Italian translation of Othello. The production was acted by an all Italian-speaking cast, which included Isolina Piamonti as Desdemona and Salvini's brother Alessandro Salvini as Iago. The New York Times reported: "His conception of Othello is notable for its simplicity and its strength--It was stupendous, and yet--meaning no derogation of its greatness--it was all very animal." Historian George Odell's appraisal was this: "Salvini's Othello was large and passionate and fiery, and made all other Othellos seem pale, however dark their complexion."

Henry James wrote in the Atlantic Monthly (March 1883) that Salvini's Othello was played

> with the dusky brilliancy that is in the tone of the part--at every point. No more complete picture of passion can have been given to the stage in our day--passion beginning in noble repose and spending itself in black insanity--there is at least not a weak spot in it from beginning to end. It has from the first the quality that thrills and excites, and this quality deepens with great strides to the magnificent climax. The last two acts constitute the finest piece of tragic acting that I know.

Salvini's fame increased in 1875 (despite his playing Othello in his native Italian opposite English-speaking casts) when, from April 1st to June 16th of that year, he appeared thirty times at London's Drury Lane Theatre, with Edwin Booth as Iago. Booth had played Iago in English at New York's Winter Garden Theatre on December 9, 1866, opposite German-speaking Bogumil Dawison's Othello and Marie Mathus-Scheller's Desdemona. Although Salvini

spoke his roles in Italian, George Henry Lewes described his voice
as follows: "In the three great elements of musical expression, tone,
timbre and rhythm, Salvini is the greatest speaker I have ever
heard."

Richard Dickins reviewed Salvini's Drury Lane performance as
the Moor in the London Era,

> His splendid voice was capable of expressing every emotion
> without apparent exertion--In the later scenes, the veneer
> of civilisation had disappeared, and he was merely a mad-
> dened wild animal completely mastered by frenzied jealousy.
> Such an exhibition of overwhelming passion had probably
> not been seen since the days of Edmund Kean.

Salvini's countryman and contemporary, Ernesto Fortunato
Giovanni Rossi, also played Othello, but was judged by Maybury
Flemming in the New York Evening Mail as never to be compared
with Salvini. "His performance of the part, however, was extremely sensual and coarse, unabashed lewdness being on many occasions
its salient feature." The New York Times reviewed Rossi's first appearance at Booth's Theatre on October 31, 1881, by saying "He
never rises to the rare height of Salvini's genius; nor has the sustaining power, the steady poise, and the perfect self-mastery of
his countryman" but added he did have "the fire, brutality, primitive savagery which plainly belong to the Othello of Shakespeare."

Tommaso Salvini, acclaimed "the world's greatest actor," and
whose Othello became the model of excellence against which all future interpreters of the Moor would be judged, died on Saturday,
January 1, 1916, at Florence, Italy, nine days before his eighty-
seventh birthday. England's lovely, charming, and brilliant actress
Ellen Terry recalled no actor as Othello diminishing the glory of
Salvini, including her beloved co-star Henry Irving.

Henry Irving was born John Henry Brodribb at Keinton,
Mandeville, Somerset, England, on Tuesday, February 6, 1838.
He became the first actor to be knighted in England, on Thursday,
July 18, 1895, by Queen Victoria at Windsor Castle, but not for his
interpretation of the Moor of Venice.* Irving had played Cassio
opposite T. C. King's Othello in Dublin on March 5, 1860, and in-
advertently first attempted the role of Othello later that year in
Manchester when he quickly replaced vanished Gustavus Vasa
Brooke in the last act of the tragedy. Brooke, who made his first
London appearance as Othello at the Olympic Theatre on January 3,
1848, was later discovered backstage where, in full costume and

---

*England's actor-producer William D'Avenant was knighted for his
service at the Siege of Gloucester in 1643 (not for his theatrical accomplishments), despite gossip that he was the illegitimate son (or
godson) of William Shakespeare.

makeup, he was peacefully sleeping off an alcoholic binge. Following an unsuccessful engagement in London, Edwin Booth toured the provinces, and in Manchester in 1861, young Henry Irving played Cassio to Booth's Othello.

Discarding the traditional long gown and turban for an elaborate Venetian uniform, Henry Irving played Othello in a pale, bronze makeup. Irving opened on February 14, 1876, at London's Lyceum Theatre and acted forty-nine performances, with Isabel Bateman as Desdemona and Henry Forrester as an unconventional, but acclaimed, Iago. Forrester was seen the following season as Othello at London's St. James's Theatre. Although Edwin Booth derided Forrester's characterization of the Moor as "about as direful as you'll find in Ypsilanti or Oskosh," the actor's performance as Othello met with considerable success.

Booth had opened at London's Princess Theatre on November 6, 1880, in manager Walter Gooch's series of cheaply produced and poorly cast productions. Though admiring Booth's versatility on January 17, 1881, the London critics dismissed his Othello (with Henry Forrester as Iago) as "over-elaborate and artificial." But when Booth and Forrester exchanged roles, they called Booth's Iago "a masterpiece."

The great theatrical event of London's 1880-1881 season was the first performance of Othello starring Henry Irving and Edwin Booth at the Lyceum Theatre on May 2, 1881. Irving's inventive and malignantly riveting Iago was clad in a crimson and gold jacket with a mantle of dull green. He leaned against an archway, deliberately plucking a bunch of grapes and insolently spewing seeds; his swift transitions of mood outstripped Booth's Othello. The critics found Booth's Othello "More sustained, riper and more mature than before" according to the Globe, while Charles Dunphie discovered in the Morning Post that Booth "presented more concentration, more force, and more balance" than he had presented in his Princess Theatre performance.

Everyone agreed "Irving's Iago was one of his finest performances." Irving's controlled furtiveness produced a brilliant, Machiavellian portrait of Iago "full of fresh and ingenious interpretation" and "his most definitive performance of a Shakespearean role." William Archer described Irving's Iago as coming "as near to perfection as anything he has ever done." But Irving's Othello was judged a good deal less than perfection and described as "artistically suicidal." Frank Benson defined Irving's Moor by saying "the towering rage of Othello was beyond his physical strength."

On May 5, 1881, London's Daily Telegraph reported that Booth's Othello

does not have the imaginative mind. He can create excitement,

but he cannot touch the heart. Mr. Booth moves in the
path chalked out for him by his father and the traditions
his father inherited; Mr. Irving, like the elder Kean, trans-
lates his characters with great freedom and ingenuity into
a language of his own. So unlike are the two actors in
manner and method, they read the characters of Othello
and Iago so distinctly from opposing bases, that it would
be a bold man who could afford to be dogmatic as to the
correctness of either principle.

Beginning May 10, Irving and Booth alternated in the roles of
Othello and Iago, three performances a week for seven weeks, with
the inestimable Ellen Terry as their Desdemona and William Terriss
as Cassio. William Terriss (né Lewin) arriving at London's Adelphi
Theatre to play the leading role in William Gillette's play Secret
Service, was murdered outside the stage door on December 16, 1897.
An unbalanced, previously discharged bit player, Richard Arthur
Prince (known as "Mad Arthur"), stabbed Terriss twice in the back
and once in the chest with a butcher's knife. Terriss was taken
into the theatre where he died in the arms of his mistress, actress
Jessie Millward. Henry Irving's astute prediction that Prince would
not be executed since "he only killed an actor" was unfortunately
true. "Mad Arthur" was committed to Broadmoor where he became
the respected conductor of the Insane Asylum's band.

London's World critic Dutton Cook accurately appraised Booth
and Irving as follows: "We have here, two simply masterly Iagos,
two insufficient Othellos." Ellen Terry, in her amusing and informative autobiography, The Story of My Life, wrote, "Booth was a
melancholy, dignified Othello but not great as Salvini was great."
Miss Terry felt Irving's failure as Othello represented

> one of the unspoken bitternesses of his life. Henry Irving's
> Othello was condemned almost as universally as his Iago was
> praised. For once I found myself with the majority. He
> screamed, he ranted, and he raved--lost his voice, was slow
> where he should have been swift--incoherent where he should
> have been strong.

But Miss Terry also felt that Irving's speech to the Senate in
Othello was "one of the most superb and beautiful bits of acting in
his life."

On the last night of the twenty-one performance engagement
of Othello, Ellen Terry recalled Henry Irving rolling up the clothes
he had worn as the Moor "one by one, carefully laying one garment
on top of the other, and then, half humorously and very deliberately, [he] said 'Never again! ... and gave a great sigh of relief."

Three years before her death on Saturday, July 21, 1928,
Ellen Terry, at the age of seventy-eight, went to Buckingham

Palace in February 1925 where King George V conferred upon her the title of Dame of the Most Excellent Order of the British Empire.

The great Sir Henry Irving died on Friday, October 13, 1905, following a performance of Alfred Lord Tennyson's play Becket, in Bradford, England. The celebrated actor died penniless. His body was cremated and his ashes buried in Westminster Abbey. The first statue erected in London to an actor was that of Sir Henry Irving. Donated by members of his profession, the statue can be seen behind the National Portrait Gallery on St. Martin's Place.

Edwin Booth made his first appearance as Iago in 1852 in Nevada City, California. The following year Booth first applied burnt cork to his face at Tom Maguire's Hall in San Francisco; he was playing a little Negro boy, Dandy Cox, in a comedy sketch. Throughout his career small-statured (five-feet-seven-inch), gentle Booth preferred portraying sinister villains to playing romantic or comedic leads; he played Iago more frequently than Othello, Othello not being one of his finer achievements. Booth's demonic, masterful portrayal of Iago was called by MacMillan's Magazine, "the finest interpretation of the villain in his time" and "a performance of marvelous balance and regularity, polished to the finger-nails." Booth later admitted, "My Iago is clever; my Othello is feeble."

Former New York Evening Post drama critic J. Rankin Towse, writing in the Saturday Review of Literature, on October 22, 1932, called Booth "The Last Tragedian of His Era--His Iago, probably his masterpiece, has rarely been equaled, never excelled. It was a triumph of subtle deviltry masked beneath an outward garb of brisk geniality." Richard Lockridge in his biography of Edwin Booth, Darling of Misfortune, wrote, "He was a famous Iago, but never a satisfactory Othello. Booth knew well enough he was not fitted to play Othello." The New York Times on November 24, 1873, criticized Booth's performance as Othello, with James Wheelock as Iago, for "knowing, as he must, that he cannot personate Othello thoroughly, should never take the role, seeing he is actually the finest Iago not only of the present, but even of the past."

Booth was well aware of the accuracy of all of the above. He made copious notes about how to perform Iago, but he did not write constructive methods of interpreting Othello. His promptbook for Othello does outline details of his costume for the Moor:

(1) A long gown of cashmere, wraught with gold and various colours, this is looped up to the hip, on the left side with jewels. A Moorish burnoose, striped with purple and gold. Purple velvet shoes, embroidered with gold and pearl. A sash of green and gold. A jewelled chain.

(2) Steel plate Armour with white burnoose made of African goat's hair.

(3)   A long, white gown, Moorish with hood and with scarlet
       trimmings. A white sash made of goat's hair. Scarlet
       velvet shoes. Pearl ear-rings.

But there is no profound, illuminating entry for the concept or construction of the physical or emotional delineation of the character
of the Moor of Venice. Shakespeare's contemporary Vicillo described
Othello's original costume as a "Gown of crimson velvet, with loose
sleeves, over which a mantle cloth of gold, buttoned over the shoulder, with massive gold buttons. His cap of crimson velvet, and he
bore a silver baton."

Booth omitted the epileptic scene in act 4 of Othello, and, in
1878, he defended his editing of Shakespeare's text of scene 1,
in the same act of Iago's deceptive and misleading conversation with
Cassio about Bianca which was overheard by Othello and presumed
by him to relate to Desdemona. Booth said, "My long and varied
experience has taught me that the closer and the quicker tragedy
can be acted the better the audience is pleased." He had seen
Charles Albert Fechter play the scene and "considered it a bore."

Charles Fechter, born of French parents at Hanway Yard,
Oxford Street, London, England on Saturday, October 23, 1824,
was the original Armand Duval in Dumas' La Dame aux Camelias, opposite Mme. Eugenie Doche's Marguerite Gautier at the Vaudeville
Theatre in Paris on February 2, 1852. Fechter was more a glamor-
ous, romantic actor than he was a tragedian, and his Othello was
condemned by most critics. Critic Edmund Yates described Fechter's
Moor as "a desperately poor performance full of French tricks and
nonsense." George Henry Lewes wrote, "His Hamlet was one of the
very best, and his Othello one of the very worst I have ever seen--
His physique wholly incapacitated him from representing Othello;
and his naturalism, being mainly determined by his personality, became utter feebleness." George Eliot added, "We went to see Fechter's Othello the other night. It is lamentably bad. He has not
weight and passion enough for deep tragedy." Playwright Dion
Boucicault labeled Fechter with damned praise as "a very good
Boulevard actor."

Considering the negative appraisals written at a later date,
Fechter's forty performances as Othello (which began October 23,
1861, at London's Princess's Theatre), with John Ryder as Iago
and Carlotta Leclercq as Desdemona, received good reviews from
contemporary scribes. Charles Albert Fechter died at Rockland
Center in Bucks County, Pennsylvania on Tuesday, August 5, 1879;
he is buried in Philadelphia's Mount Vernon Cemetery.

Junius Brutus Booth's three sons--Edwin, John Wilkes, and
Junius Brutus, Jr.--appeared on stage together for the first time
on Friday, November 25, 1864, at New York's Winter Garden Theatre.
Their one-time-only benefit performance of Julius Caesar was

The Booths (left to right): Junius Brutus, Jr., Edwin, and John
Wilkes (courtesy of The Free Library of Philadelphia Theatre Collection).

designed to raise funds for a proposed statue of William Shakespeare
to be erected in Central Park. The following night Edwin began
his extensive engagement in Hamlet, which became the longest running production of a Shakespeare play at that time and lasted 100
nights until March 22, 1865.

Edwin Booth's record-breaking 100 performances of Hamlet at
New York's Winter Garden Theatre was erroneously reported to have
been shattered by John Barrymore, who opened in the Arthur Hopkins production of Hamlet at the Sam H. Harris Theatre on November
16, 1922, for 101 performances. Barrymore's highly publicized, headlined record-shattering event, however, had been surpassed ten
years earlier by John E. Kellard's Hamlet, which opened at New
York's Garden Theatre on November 18, 1912, for 102 performances.
John Gielgud remained on Broadway as the Prince of Denmark at the
Empire Theatre in 1936 for 132 performances, winning the Hamlet re-
lay by one performance over Maurice Evan's Hamlet, which closed on
Broadway on April 6, 1946, after 131 showings. Richard Burton,
surprisingly, won the Denmark sweepstakes as the longest resident
of Elsinore on Broadway; he appeared from April 9 until August 8
in 1964 with 137 recitations of "To be, or not to be."

Three weeks after Booth's record-breaking 100 nights of Hamlet, his younger brother John Wilkes assassinated President Abraham
Lincoln at John T. Ford's Theatre in Washington, D.C. Thirteen
years later Edwin barely escaped assassination. Two shots were
fired at him from the gallery of Chicago's McVicker's Theatre (owned
by his father-in-law James McVicker) during a performance of
Richard III. The badly aimed shots were fired by a mentally deranged clerk called Mark Gray. Gray (whose real name was Walter
Lyons) was captured then confined in a mental institution at Elgin,
Illinois. Following Lincoln's assassination, Edwin was reluctant to
return to the stage. But, with great apprehension, on January 3,
1866, he reappeared at the Winter Garden Theatre in Hamlet and was
received by a wildly cheering audience.

Edwin Forrest, stung by his dethroning as the country's leading tragedian by his namesake Booth and smarting under a critic's
proclamation "They have crowned a new king, before whom they
bow, and 'the old man eloquent' is cheered by few voices," frigidly
refused Booth's invitation to play Othello to his Iago for the inauguration of Booth's handsome, one-million-dollar-plus theatre.

Forrest, who was born in Philadelphia on Sunday, March 9,
1806, was then sixty-three-years old and bedeviled with poor health
and a sharply declining career, which he still pursued on-the-road
away from Manhattan where Booth had become the public's favorite
tragedian. Despite being rheumatic and suffering from gout and
partial paralysis, Forrest dogmatically continued performing. The
once-great tragedian was reduced to accepting his last New York
engagement at the second-rate Fourteenth Street Theatre in

February, 1871. He made his final New York poorly-attended appearance on November 22, 1872 at Steinway Hall where he gave
a reading of Othello. Forrest's intense dislike for Booth and his
refusal to share the stage with the younger actor robbed the theatre of riches that their appearing together in Othello would have
provided.

Instead of opening his theatre with Othello (with Forrest as
the Moor and Booth as Iago), Edwin opened on a rainy Wednesday
evening (February 3, 1869) with a ten-week run of Romeo and
Juliet, in which he played young Montague to Mary McVicker's
Juliet Capulet--on April 12 he appeared as Othello. Edwin Adams
played Othello in tandem with Booth's Iago. Commencing April 26,
the tragedy ran forty-two performances, with Mary McVicker as
Desdemona.

Booth's depiction of tragedy on-stage was mirrored by the
tragic mask in his personal life. The insanity and drunkenness
of his famous father was followed by the early death of his beloved
first wife, actress Mary Devlin, on February 21, 1863. Booth had
married Mary Devlin on July 7, 1860, and, on December 9, 1861,
their daughter Edwina was born in London. Edwin never recovered
from the agony and disgrace of his younger brother's assassination
of President Lincoln. Mary McVicker, who became Edwin's second
wife on June 7, 1869, died hopelessly insane on Edwin's forty-eighth
birthday, November 13, 1881; Edwin was viciously attacked by the
press.

Booth's magnificent theatre was built of granite on the south-
east corner of Twenty-third Street and Sixth Avenue in New York.
The costly, posh theatre seated over eighteen-hundred people in its
horseshoe-shaped auditorium. There were six proscenium boxes and
three balconies. Over the center of the proscenium arch hovered a
statue of William Shakespeare. Portraits of Garrick, Kean, Cooke,
Betterton, and French actor Talma, were set around the proscenium
arch in white ovals. Thomas Ridgeway Gould's bust of Edwin's
father, Junius Brutus Booth, occupied a niche on the wall of the
balcony staircase.

The New York Tribune drama critic, and Booth's close friend,
William Winter, described Booth's "Temple of Dramatic Art" as "the
stateliest, the handsomest, and the best appointed structure of its
class than can be found on the American continent." Less pro-
phetically he added, "It has been built to endure." Booth's Theatre
eventually forced the actor-owner into bankruptcy and was sold at
auction for $500,000. Later it was converted into James T. McCreery
and Company's Department Store.

Sarah Bernhardt first appeared in America at Booth's Theatre
on November 8, 1880, in Eugène Scribe and Gabriel Legouvé's 1849
play Adrianne Lecouvreur. A week later, she starred there in her

greatest role, Marguerite Gautier in Dumas' La Dame aux Camélias
(erroneously known as Camille). Tommaso Salvini appeared as
Othello with Lewis Morrison at Booth's Theatre on April 28, 1883.
The final performance at Edwin's luxurious, lost theatre on April
30, 1883, was Romeo and Juliet, with Herbert Arthur Chamberlayne
Blyth--better known as Maurice Barrymore, and Polish Countess
Bozenta Chlapowski--the renowned actress Helena Modjeska.

During the final days of the demise of his New York theatre,
Booth was completing a successful tour of Europe. He opened at
Berlin's Residenz Theatre on January 11, 1883, playing his roles in
English with a German-speaking cast, as Ira Aldridge had done
thirty years before; he closed his Berlin engagement on February 11
as Othello. Booth ended his tour in Vienna on April 11, 1883, as
Iago. The Viennese critics admired his Iago but on April 4 disdain-
fully categorized his Othello as "more of a Cat than a Lion."

Booth purchased a charming property in Manhattan at Sixteen
Gramercy Park (East Twentieth Street between Park Avenue South
and Third Avenue). After architect Stanford White completed reno-
vations, Booth opened the building as The Players' Club, reserving
the third floor for his home. With fifteen other professionals (Lawrence Barrett, William Bispham, Samuel L. Clemens [Mark Twain],
Augustin Daly, Joseph F. Daly, John Drew, Henry Edwards, Laurence Hutton, Joseph Jefferson, John A. Lane, James Lewis, Brander
Matthews, Stephen H. Olin, A. M. Palmer, and General William
Tecumseh Sherman), Booth incorporated The Players' Club on January 7, 1888, following a grand inauguration on New Year's Eve.

Commemorating the event with a satin souvenir program, Booth
announced his "farewell" performance as Iago on November 20, 1875,
at New York's Daly's Fifth Avenue Theatre, with D. H. Harkins as
Othello and Jeffreys Lewis as Desdemona. But he continued to play
the scarlet-cloaked despicable Ensign for several years. He played
Iago opposite the Othellos of Frederic Robinson, Joseph Wheelock,
Charles Barron and Henry Forrester, Tommaso Salvini, and Henry
Irving and others. During a performance of Othello, in Rochester,
New York on April 3, 1889, with Lawrence Barrett as the Moor,
Booth, as Iago, was suddenly stricken with a slight stroke. He
recovered and continued to act but clearly apparent in his less
than glowing performances, was the deterioration of his physical
strength. He was mercilessly attacked by a once-devoted New York
press as "the tottering Mr. Booth."

For many seasons Booth alternated Iago and Othello with Lawrence Barrett. The long partnership between Booth and Barrett
ended on Wednesday, March 18, 1891 at the Broadway Theatre when
Barrett collapsed on-stage while playing De Mauprat in Edward
Bulwer-Lytton's 1839 play Richelieu. Lawrence Patrick Barrett,
born in Paterson, New Jersey on Saturday, April 14, 1838, died
on Friday, March 20, 1891. Booth gave his last performance in

Othello at New York's Broadway Theatre on March 25, 1891, and, after a matinee of Hamlet at Brooklyn's Academy of Music (April 4, 1891), he retired from the stage.

In Chicago on March 19, 1890, at the North American Phonograph Company, Booth made two recordings on Edison wax-cylinders for his daughter Edwina Booth Grossmann: Hamlet's "To be, or not to be" soliloquy and Othello's speech to the Senators in act 1, scene 3, beginning with "Most potent, grave and reverend Signoirs." Booth's grandson Edwin Booth Grossmann donated the cylinders to Harvard University in Cambridge, Massachusetts, where Professor Frederick Clifton Packard, Jr. made a more modern re-pressing of the Edison cylinders; they are now in the Harvard Theatre Collection. Still later, Booth's voice as Hamlet and Othello was transferred to three long-playing records by Ariel, Delta, and Summit.

Edwin Thomas Booth, hailed as America's greatest actor, was born on Wednesday, November 13, 1833, outside of Bel Air, Maryland, the seventh of ten children, all sired out-of-wedlock by Junius Brutus Booth. The elder Booth migrated to America in 1821 with Mary Ann Holmes (a former Bow Street-Covent Garden flower girl), leaving in London a son Richard Junius and his legal wife Adelaide, to whom he was married on May 8, 1815. Finally aware that Booth had produced another family in the colonies, Marie Christine Adelaide Delancy Booth sailed to America. She filed suit for adultery on March 26, 1851, and divorced Junius Brutus in Baltimore, Maryland, on April 18, 1851. After begetting ten children during thirty years of unmarried life, Junius Brutus Booth married Mary Ann Holmes on May 10, 1851, a year before his death. Junius Brutus died aboard the Mississippi River steamship J. S. Chenoweth on Tuesday, November 30, 1852, at the age of fifty-six.

Years later Edwin Booth would write about his famous father,

> To see my father act, when in the acting mood, was not "like reading Shakespeare by flashes of lightning" which could give but fitful glimpses of the author's meaning; but the full sunlight of his genius shone on every character he portrayed, and so illuminated the obscurities of the text that Shakespearians wondered with delight as his lurid interpretations of passages which to them had previously been unintelligible.

On the twenty-foot high Italian marble monument Edwin had erected in Baltimore's Greenmount Cemetery is carved:

> "Behold the spot where genius lies
> O drop a tear when talent dies!
> Of tragedy the mighty chief,
> His power to please beyond belief.
> Hic tacet matchless Booth."

Eleanor Ruggles' well-researched biography of Edwin Booth,
The Prince of Players, was adapted to the screen by Moss Hart in
a simplistic scenario overlaid with inaccuracies; the film was designed to create a theatrical Hollywood impact. The screen version
had Edwin being pelted with vegetables on his return to the stage
after Lincoln's assassination; the truth is that he was received with
great warmth and enthusiasm by the New York audience. Included
among other fictions was the legend of his father's drunken denouncement to an impatient audience to "Shut up and I'll give you
the damndest Richard III you ever saw!"--an action attributed to
gentle, mild-mannered Edwin. The 1955 Twentieth Century-Fox film
included excerpts from Richard III and Hamlet but not Booth's superlative interpretation of Iago in Othello. Richard Burton portrayed
Edwin Booth, with Raymond Massey as Junius Brutus Booth and
John Derek as John Wilkes. Time magazine acknowledged that Burton displayed talent "though not exactly for Shakespeare." However, Burton's closet scene from Hamlet with Eva LeGallienne as
Queen Gertrude, was excellent.

José Ferrer and the Playwrights Company produced Milton
Geiger's play Edwin Booth on Broadway at the Forty-sixth Street
Theatre on November 24, 1958. The play was directed by José
Ferrer and starred him in the title role. Ian Keith appeared as
father Junius; Richard Waring was John Wilkes; and Sydney Smith
was Junius Brutus Booth, Jr.; Lorne Greene was writer, critic,
and Booth's devoted friend William Winter. The play covered a
forty-two year span of Booth's life, and Ferrer appeared in excerpts from Edwin's roles in Richard III, Romeo and Juliet, Macbeth,
and Othello. Geiger's play was called "flat and colorless" and faded
away after twenty-four performances.

Edwin Booth died at his Players' Club home in Gramercy Park
on Wednesday, June 7, 1893. Following a massive funeral at New
York's Little Church Around the Corner, he was buried in Mount
Auburn Cemetery in Cambridge, Massachusetts. George Odell observed, "The passing of Booth and Barrett closed an epoch in American theatrical history and with them the art of tragedy."

Edmond T. Quinn's statue of Edwin Booth as Hamlet stands in
Gramercy Park on a pedestal designed by Edwin Sherill Dodge. It
is a mute reminder of the passing of an inestimable actor accurately
called, by Otis Skinner in his biography of Booth The Last Tragedian.

Jean Mounet-Sully (1841-1916), described as "a Jupiter of a
man with a voice of distant thunder and eyes of lightning" and "the
handsomest actor in France and its greatest tragedian since Talma,"
played the Moor in the fifth act of Othello on March 4, 1878, in
Jean Aicard's French translation of the tragedy. For the three performances of Mounet-Sully's Othello, Sarah Bernhardt was his Desdemona at the Comédie-Française in Paris. Mounet-Sully was reluctant

to perform Aicard's full version of the play without Bernhardt but
finally agreed to appear in Aicard's complete translation of <u>Othello</u>
on March 23, 1899, with French actress Lara as Desdemona. The
tragedy's failure was accredited to Aicard's depiction of black
Othello as a regal descendant of kings rather than as a reformed
savage. Mounet-Sully did gain added prestige in France with his
portrayal of the Moor of Venice.

Surpassing master-mimic Samuel Foote's 1744 determinedly
dramatic, but unintentional, burlesque as Othello was a presumptuous popinjay and untalented actor, George Jones, who possessed an
astonishing repertoire of classical roles and who used the flamboyant
stage name of "Count Joannes." Prior to his royal ascension, Jones
appeared on the English stage with minor success, gaining, however, surprising popularity in Boston. George "Count Joannes"
Jones, born in London on Thursday, May 10, 1810, was to the
legitimate theatre what The Cherry Sisters (Effie and Addie) were
to vaudeville: "Perfectly terrible."

Jones hyperbolically announced he had been made a Count of
Sertorii of the Holy Roman Empire in 1857 by the Prussian ambas-
sador to England. He was also a lawyer and a member of the New
York Bar. But, in his execrable exploits as a tragedian, he was
more than kindly described as "absurd and tiresome." Performances
by George "The Count Joannes" at New York's Bowery Theatre in
1876, vastly increased the economy of local hucksters; patrons arrived at the theatre well-armed with an arsenal of eggs and vegetables. The Bowery Theatre management installed a wire netting
across the stage as a barricade against the inevitable barrage.

Jones's ludicrous playing of Othello at New York's Theatre on
February 13, 1878, with his "pupil" Lydia Avonia Fairbanks as an
unperturbed Desdemona and Frank Noyes as Iago, was greeted with
great howls and jeers. The "Count" had anticipated the response
and announced prior to the performance that fifty New York policemen had been stationed in the theatre to preserve the peace. The
fifty of New York's finest would have been useful preserving the
flying array of vegetables. Several well-aimed eggs and vegetables
bespattered the Moor of Venice and his brave entourage but did not
disturb the unflappable Miss Fairbanks. One critic tersely observed
"Shakespeare may be dead but he has been murdered here tonight,"
and cartoonists delighted in creating drawings that depicted Jones
murdering the Bard of Avon.

"Count Joannes" Jones indulged "more and more in self-
exploitation, eccentric behaviour and apparent evidence of deranged
character, if not intellect," observed Historian George Odell, and
gave "an exhibition almost inconceivable in a civilised community."
Odell added, "Some cynics believed that Jones kept on because of
the financial returns that accrued from his large, if jeering audiences." "Count Joannes" personified Goethe's dictum that "Men are

so constructed that everybody undertakes what he sees another
successful in, whether he has aptitudes for it or not." Shakespeare would probably have excused Jones with "Sweet are the
uses of adversity."

Edward A. Sothern based his characterization and makeup for
the role of DeLacy Fitzaltamont in H. J. Bryon's play The Crushed
Tragedian; or The Prompter's Box (New York's Park Theatre on
September 3, 1877) on the fatuously famous "Count Joannes."
Sothern's expert duplication of Jones did not escape the count,
who brought a court injunction against Sothern for "public ridicule"
--a charge he could have launched against any of his audiences.
The libel suit was dropped, but minstrel Neil Bryant quickly bur-
lesqued both Joannes' and Sothern's DeLacy Fitzaltamont character
(November 12, 1877). The financial returns that George "Count
Joannes" received from his besieged performing soon dissipated; he
died penniless on Tuesday, September 30, 1879.

Equally bizarre, perhaps, but possibly more creditable than
the histrionics of George "The Count Joannes" Jones were the English actresses who took on both the Moor and his Ensign. Mrs.
Charles Whitley blacked-up as Othello at London's Avenue Theatre
in February, 1897. Rebecca Deering and Emilie Burke became
blackamoors in Shakespeare's tragedy in 1883, and they had been
preceded by Charlotte Crampton flouncing on-stage as Iago in 1857.
Marie Prescott played Iago to R. D. MacLean's Othello in America
in 1891. Mrs. Henry Lewis made a career in America portraying
Othello and Richard III.

The first performance of Othello at Stratford-upon-Avon's
Shakespeare Memorial Theatre (which had opened on April 23, 1879)
was produced on May 1, 1880, with Irish tragedian Barry Sullivan
in the title role and W. H. Hallatt as Iago. William Charles Macready, who had played Iago to Sullivan's Othello at London's Drury
Lane on January 30, 1850, snidely confided in his diary that Sullivan's performance was "really indifferent." Thomas Barry Sullivan,
who was born in Birmingham, England in 1821 and died on Sunday,
May 3, 1891, had few equals in bravura acting and expert swords-
manship in on-stage dueling; but he held his command over audiences more by his dynamic personality than by his art of acting.

During his prime years Barry Sullivan was the favorite actor
of George Bernard Shaw, who called Sullivan "the last British ex-
ponent of superhuman acting--Barry Sullivan was a splendidly monstrous performer in his prime; there was hardly any part sufficiently
heroic for him to be natural in it." The Irish dramatist, then critic,
felt however that Othello was a part Sullivan "could not play at all--
through which he walked as if the only line in the play that con-
veyed any idea to him was the description of Othello as 'perplexed
in the extreme'." Sullivan retained his old-school style of acting
through his declining years but maintained his popularity in England
and in the United States.

A performance of Othello was given by The Astor Place Shake-spearean Colored Tragedians at New York's Cosmopolitan Theatre on July 18, 1884, with Benjamin G. Ford as the Moor, J. A. Arneaux as Iago, and Alice Brooks as Desdemona. The New York Times dismissed their effort as a "dull recitation" and reported that "The appearance of these worthies and their speeches, gestures and exits, provoked roars of laughter." Two years later Benjamin G. Ford and J. A. Arneaux repeated their performances as Othello and Iago at New York's Steinway Hall (November 10, 1886); Eloise Molineau was Desdemona. Equally bizarre was the portrayal of the Moor by Lillian Russell's former Indian coachman, Tacatanee (with Charles Fletcher as Iago) in a scene from Othello at New York's Herrmann's Theatre on May 25, 1893.

George Bernard Shaw's appraisal of Wilson Barrett as the Moor, with Franklin McLeay as Iago and Maud Jeffries as Desdemona (at London's Lyric Theatre on May 22, 1897) was that he lacked the tone of Othello. Shaw described Barrett's Moor by saying "he has not this special musical and vocal gift. Mr. Wilson Barrett is an unmusical speaker except when he is talking Manx. It is a pity he is not built to fit Othello; for he produces the play, as usual, very well." G. B. Shaw also was neither impressed nor enthralled with Mr. Shakespeare's play and called the tragedy "pure melodrama--there is not a touch of character in it that goes below the skin, and the fitful attempts to make Iago something better than a melodramatic villain only makes a hopeless mess of him and his motives." Shaw, who wrote Caesar and Cleopatra in 1899 to correct and illuminate Shakespeare's evaluation of the middle-aged Roman Emperor and Egypt's sixteen-year-old Queen, also doubted that Shakespeare "ever made up his mind as to the character and motives of a single person" in Othello.

Russia's famous actor-director Constantin Stanislavsky (1863-1938) unsuccessfully portrayed Othello on April 16, 1896, at Moscow's Solodovnikov Theatre. Petrossyan, a bad actor with a resonant voice, was a poor Iago. Stanislavsky, aware of his Iago's flawed talent, kept the actor physically darkened on-stage while permitting his fine voice to offset the dim lighting. Additionally, a neophyte, untested actress was cast as Desdemona; all three leads in Othello floundered in Venice, Cyprus, and Moscow.

Stanislavsky in his autobiography, My Life in Art (translated into English by J. J. Robbins in 1924), wrote, "What role fitted me least at that time? What role was most harmful to me at that time? Othello. But it was of Othello I dreamed, especially since the time I visited Venice." Stanislavsky was ill-suited for interpreting Othello. His performance was capsulized by a critic who said that "Stanislavsky has been to Venice and brought back a bit of a gon-dola." Leon Leonidov's Othello (at the Moscow Art Theatre on March 14, 1930, directed by Stanislavsky from his later published flawed text of the play) was also a failure.

Constantin Stanislavsky as Othello (April 16, 1896)

The tragedy of <u>Othello, the Moor of Venice</u> continued into the twentieth century with many of the same controversies and variances that had prevailed and flamed in the past. Traditional styles of acting, passed down like folklore from earlier interpreters of the Moor, were altered as much as the metamorphic life-styles, morals, and mores of succeeding generations. What grandfather thought was the apex of excellence, grandson would find old-fashioned, dreadfully "hammy," and the nadir of nonsense. Garrick and Kean first attempted "natural acting" while others continued to spout Othello's lines in declamatory oratory augmented with extravagant gestures and elaborate posturing. The genius of an actor remained within his era; for future generations, the actor became a revered and nostalgic historical tradition. Iago's deviltry was clothed in the same sinister benevolence, and Desdemona continued to be smothered and stabbed. Critical classifications of "great" and "greatest" related to each era, with little definition.

Brooks Atkinson once observed "Nothing vanishes into nothingness so completely as a stage performance. Performances in the past were appraised and judged according to the standard of excellence prescribed for that period reflected by mirroring the past. Critical effusion, encomiums, epitaphs, or savage assaults flowered or staggered in adjectives of the moment. But without the reports of earlier auditors of drama and theatre, we would have scant knowledge of past performance or the passing parade of players"--this despite French writer Gustave Flaubert's didactic that "A man is a critic when he cannot be an artist" or Mark Twain's later caustic comment, "The trade of critic is the most degraded of all trades."

Shakespeare made a critic of Hamlet in his instruction to the Players in act 3, scene 2, "O, there be players that I have seen play, and heard others praise, and that highly, not to speak it profanely, that, neither having the accent of Christians nor the gait of Christians, pagan, nor man, have so strutted and bellowed that I have thought some of nature's journeymen had made men and made them well, they imitated humanity so abominably."

The constant cultural change and climate of the theatre within its time often reflects the fickle, unpredictable taste and collective behavior of audiences. For centuries audiences awarded performances and performers with hearty applause (and on occasion less hearty vegetation) or infrequent silence that sometimes was broken by catcalls and often echoing "bravos." Today, as if on cue, a standing ovation is accorded everyone and everything brave enough to stand under a proscenium, confront an audience, or mumble through a microphone. No longer is projection by actors required. Performers in musicals need not be well trained in voice or musical talent. The theatre is wired for sound. The audience is wired for standing.

In 1894, Laurence Hutton capably described theatrical tradition as follows:

If it be traced through pure channels and to the fountain-
head, leads one as near to Nature as can be followed by her
servant Art. Whatever Quin, Barton Booth, Garrick and
Cooke gave to stage-craft, or, as we now term it "business,"
they received from their predecessors; from Betterton, and
perhaps from Shakespeare himself, who, though not distinguished as an actor, well knew what acting should be; and
what they inherited in this way bequeathed, in turn, to
their art, and we should not despise it. Kean knew without
seeing Cooke, who in turn knew from Macklin, and so back
to Betterton, just what to do and how to do it. Their great
mother Nature, who reiterates her teachings and preserves
her monotone in motion, form, and sound, taught them.
There must be some similitude in all things that are True!

Tommaso Salvini clarified the fleeting fame of legendary performers and performances, their greatness and their failures in 1886.
Salvini described the ephemeral appraisal of acting and actors as
"La vita dello artista é come il fumo del sigaro--si vede, si gusta,
é si dilegua!" ("An actor's life is like cigar smoke--so obvious,
so pungent, and so vanishing!") Yesterday's magic becomes tomorrow's memory. Edmund Kean expressed it this way: "My fame
is a mere ephemeron, at the command of caprice. The same breath
that nourishes the flame today, puts it out tomorrow."

The early years of the twentieth century produced another
generation of Othellos. These actors demonstrated varying degrees
of accomplishment and artistry and failure and folly. Some heeded
Shakespeare's direction while others ignored it:

> Speak the speech, I pray you, as I pronounced it to you,
> trippingly on the tongue; but if you mouth it, as many of
> your players do, I had as lief the town-crier spoke my lines.
> Nor do not saw the air too much with your hand, thus, but
> use all gently; for in the very torrent, tempest, and, as I
> may say, the whirlwind of passion, you must acquire and
> beget a temperance that may give it smoothness. O, it of-
> fends me to the soul to hear a robustious periwig-pated fel-
> low tear a passion to tatters, to very rages, to split the
> ears of the groundlings, who for the most part as capable
> of nothing but inexplicable dumb-show and noise--suit the
> action to the word, the word to the action; with this special
> observance, that you o'erstep not the modesty of nature;
> for any thing so overdone is from the purpose of playing,
> whose end, both at the first and now, was and is, to hold
> as 'twere, the mirror up to nature. [Hamlet's instructions
> to The Players; Hamlet, act 3, scene 2]

Thomas Strange Heiss Oscar Asche, born in Geleong, Victoria,
Australia on Thursday, January 26, 1871, gained theatrical fame
under the name of Oscar Asche. He was lauded as the librettist of

the spectacular musical production Chu-Chin-Chow, which remained
on the London stage from 1916 to 1921 for a run of 2,238 performances. Asche, who died on Monday, March 23, 1936, at the age of
sixty-five, considered the Moor of Venice his favorite part and was
recorded as one of the best Othellos of his time. His highly physical interpretation of the Moor was merciless to Herbert Grimwood's
Iago (London's His Majesty's Theatre on November 7, 1907, with
Asche's wife Lily Brayton as Desdemona), but his ferocity and histrionics were also seen as obscuring the text.

The most violent Moor was created by Sicilian actor Giovanni
Grasso at London's Lyric Theatre on March 21, 1910. Grasso's
savage Othello bellowed, howled, stalked the stage and nearly killed
his Iago, while terrifying Marinella Bragoglia as Desdemona. J. C.
Trewin in Shakespeare on the English Stage described the Sicilian
actor's Othello as "Bearded and brown rather than black, Grasso
generated a terrifying fury. He caught Iago by the throat and
flung him to the floor; he collapsed in a convulsion of rage; he had
a frantic outburst before the epilepsy; and he died with a hideous
death-rattle! "

Described by Sir Cedric Hardwicke as "tall, willowy, resplend-
ent, with sandy hair, striking blue eyes and an absent-minded manner," Herbert Raper Beerbohm (1852-1917), having been knighted
in 1909, was known to the theatre as Sir Herbert Beerbohm-Tree.
In the spring of 1897, Tree failed to persuade Edmund Tearle to
play Iago to his Othello. It was fifteen years later before Sir Herbert produced his sumptuously staged Othello at His Majesty's Theatre on April 9, 1912, with Phyllis Nielson-Terry as Desdemona and
Laurence Irving as Iago. The Beerbohm-Tree concept of Othello
was subdued and diminished by his overpowering production. Tree
appeared as a light-colored Moor and was costumed in an excessively elaborate armor, worthy of a Wagnerian opus and capable of striking awe in Attila the Hun.

The Illustrated London News reported, "Picturesque is the
epithet which should, and will, be applied to Sir Herbert Tree's
production of Othello and his performance in the title role. Sir
Herbert Tree's Moor never takes you by storm, never carries you
away, as did Grasso's by dint of passion and animal ferocity ...
more of a scenic than acting triumph." The Evening Telegraph
deplored Tree's Venetian adventure, "Sir Herbert Tree has tried
to make an Othello who is a noble, and, needless to say he has
failed ... the effect was as though Sir Herbert was playing the part
of Sir Herbert Tree and not the part of the Moor. Right through
the play one could only discover Sir Herbert Tree--Othello had
vanished, and with him the genius of Shakespeare." London's
Daily Express faintly praised Tree's Othello as "a dreamer, interesting always, and always dignified." J. C. Trewin's summation was
precise, "As for Othello of 1912--Tree, as so many actors have been--
was a victim to his ambition."

The New York Times correspondent found Henry Irving's
darkly handsome son Laurence's Iago "An extraordinary study in
devilish grotesque, an uncanny thing that haunts you like a nightmare after you left the theatre." Laurence Sidney (Brodribb) Irving, the second son born to Sir Henry Irving and his wife Lady
Irving (Florence O'Callaghan) on Thursday, December 21, 1871, in
London, was a talented actor and playwright who translated Victor-
ien Sardou's French play, Robespierre (written for his father Henry)
and Sardou and Emile Moreau's play Dante. Laurence also translated and adapted Dostoyevski's Crime and Punishment for the English stage as The Fool Hath Said in His Heart: There Is No God,
which was later reduced to A Fool Hath Said. Young Laurence also
planned to become the husband of Ethel Barrymore.

Eighteen-year-old Ethel Barrymore became engaged to Laurence
Irving following her London stage debut, on May 13, 1897, in the
small part of Miss Kittridge, with William Gillette in his play Secret
Service and while she was playing the role of Annette, with Henry
Irving and Ellen Terry, in The Bells. After playing Euphrosine in
Laurence Irving's ponderous Tolstoyian play, Peter the Great, which
opened on January 1, 1898, Miss Barrymore broke the engagement.
By June of 1898, young Ethel had found romance with twenty-five-
year-old Gerald Du Maurier, but, as plans for their wedding progressed, she had second thoughts and returned to America.

Du Maurier married actress Muriel Beaumont on April 11, 1903,
and, on May 16, 1904, co-starred with Ethel Barrymore at London's
Wyndham Theatre, in Hubert Henry Davies's play Cynthia. Roman-
tically pursued by an impressive list of young men, including Win-
ston Churchill, the much engaged Miss Barrymore finally married
(on Sunday, March 14, 1909) her one and only husband, millionaire's son Russell Griswold Colt.

Two years after his acclaimed performance in Tree's Othello,
Laurence Sidney Irving and his actress wife Mabel Hackney, on
Friday, May 29, 1914, drowned in Canada's St. Lawrence River in
the wreck of the ship Empress of Ireland.

America's famous Shakespearean actor, Robert Bruce Mantell,
born in Irvine, Scotland on Tuesday, February 7, 1854, for nearly
three decades included Othello in his repertory company's schedule.
Mantell alternated the role of the Moor with various Iagos, including
Russ Whytal, Fritz Leiber, and Francis McGinn. According to the
season of his marital status, he cast three of his four wives--
Charlotte Berhans, Marie Booth Russell and Genevieve Hamper--as
Desdemona. Mantell's Othello was audited as being vocally superb
but lacking in action. On Thursday, June 27, 1928, Mantell died
at the age of seventy-four in Atlantic Highlands, New Jersey.

Johnston Forbes-Robertson, born in London on Sunday, January 16, 1853, was considered the greatest and most celebrated Hamlet

of his time; Forbes-Robertson spoke Shakespearean verse with a
perfection seldom equaled. George Bernard Shaw compared Forbes-
Robertson's golden voice to the chalumeau register of the clarinet
and more sardonically as "an organ with only one stop on it."
Forbes-Robertson's presentation of a gentle, subdued and rigidly
dignified Othello was not one of his greatest accomplishments. He
excised the epileptic scene and bowdlerized Shakespeare's text of
Othello to orchestrate the dignity of his performance and escape
offending theatre audiences with passages he felt "distasteful to a
modern audience" (e.g., he substituted the word strumpet for
whore: an editorial practice previously employed to laughable proportions by Frank Benson).

Forbes-Robertson first appeared as Othello at Manchester,
England, on April 30, 1897, and unsuccessfully at London's Lyric
Theatre on December 15, 1902, with Herbert Waring as Iago and
Gertrude Elliott (Mrs. Forbes-Robertson) as Desdemona. The highly esteemed actor appeared as Othello on both sides of the Atlantic
costumed in a white turban with bright silver armor over a velvet
blouse and wearing small, gold earrings and a light, suntanned
makeup. On December 16, 1902, the London Times reported, "His
Othello is interesting rather than great, because it is somewhat
lacking in volcanic force."

Johnston Forbes-Robertson was knighted in June, 1913. He
gave a series of "farewell" performances at London's Drury Lane
Theatre from March 22 until June 3, 1912, including Othello on
May 19, 1913. His last Broadway appearance was at the Shubert
Theatre from September 29, 1913, to December 29, 1913, in a reper-
toire that included Othello. The New York Times classified his
Othello as "gentlemanly--an artistic accomplishment, if not a wholly
satisfying one." Alan Dale, the insolent, irreverent drama critic
for William Randolph Hearst's newspaper The American, snidely asked,
"Was it Othello or was it Pink Tea that was played by Forbes-
Robertson and his company at the Shubert Theatre last night?"

After an extensive six-month tour of 122 American cities and
towns in 1915, Sir Johnston, in 1916, made his last appearance as
Hamlet at Harvard University's Sheldon Lecture Theatre. Sir
Johnston Forbes-Robertson died at the age of eighty-four at St.
Margaret's Bay, Dover, England, on Saturday, November 6, 1937.
In his autobiography, A Player Under Three Reigns, published in
1925, Sir Johnston Forbes-Robertson strangely revealed, "I am persuaded, as I look back upon my career, that I was not temperamentally suited for my calling"--a strange admission for an actor considered the greatest Hamlet of his era (though not a notable Othello).

Francis Robert Benson was born at Tunbridge Wells, Kent,
England, on Thursday, November 4, 1858; he spent his childhood
in Alresford, Hants, England. Benson portrayed Othello at
Stratford-upon-Avon on April 28, 1886, and in London on April 17,

1890.   The Stratford Shakespeare Memorial Theatre (founded by
Charles Flower) opened on April 23, 1879, with Barry Sullivan's
Company.   Sir Frank Benson was the director of the theatre from
April 26, 1886, until 1919.

Although accused of "upholstering Shakespeare with pageants
processions and dances," Benson, during his extensive career
throughout the British Empire, produced all of Shakespeare's plays
except Measure for Measure, Troilus and Cressida, and Titus Andronicus.   For Shakespeare's tercentenary, Benson played the title
role in Julius Caesar and was knighted by His Majesty King George
V with a property sword in the Royal Box of the Drury Lane Theatre, following the performance on May 2, 1916.

Benson's Shakespearean performances were much admired, but,
as Othello, he reportedly spoke in an affected theatrical declamatory
tone after the mannered elegance of another era.   He also altered
the running time of Othello by discarding "unnecessary speeches,"
and he carefully excised Shakespeare's "offensive" sexual references.
Benson reduced Shakespeare's tragedy to Victorian melodrama, ending the play with a flamboyant, center-stage, star-performer, spotlighted death scene for the Moor.   Othello's raging accusations to
Desdemona in act 4, scene 2 "Impudent strumpet!"; "Are you not a
strumpet?"; "What not a whore?"; and "I took you for that cunning
whore of Venice that married with Othello" were cleansed and purified to "wanton"; "that cunning one"; and simply, "What not a...?"
Benson's pristine "improvements" became hilariously known as his
"what notta" scene.

Every age has its self-appointed arbiters of taste, culture,
and censorship.   These minor, meddling self-righteous oracles im-
pose their irrational demands and condemn literary classics, films,
or religions other than their own until a more rational and intelligent age restores them.   Shakespeare's Othello had been submitted
to various "refinements" throughout the centures (e.g., Francis
Gentleman's 1773 revisions) and also had been cut, unmercifully,
to reduce playing time, but Thomas Bowdler's 1818 twenty-play
Family Edition of Shakespeare purified all previous careless cleans-
ings; hence, the word "bowdlerizing."   The British Critic lashed
out at Bowdler's presumptive and pristine versions, "They have
purged and castrated Shakespeare, tattooed and beplaistered him
and cauterized and phlebotomized him."

Thomas Bowdler, mirroring the approaching Victorian age,
prefaced his purification of Shakespeare in part, "If any word or
expression is of such a nature, that the first impression which it
excites is an impression of obscenity, that word ought not to be
spoken or written or printed: and if printed, it ought to be
erased" and "words which are in themselves indecent, but those
which, though naturally innocent, are rendered otherwise by context."   Othello must have driven poor Bowdler bonkers with its

emphasis on adultery and specific references to prostitution and elaborations of sex.

Bowdler, while advising that the play was unsuitable to "family reading," carefully stated in his preface to Othello,

> This tragedy is justly considered as one of the noblest efforts of dramatic genius--The arguments which are urged and the facts which are abduced as proofs of adultery are necessarily of such a nature as cannot be expressed in terms of perfect delicacy; yet neither the argument nor the facts can be omitted. From the multitude of indecent expressions which abound in the speeches of the inferior characters, I have endeavored to clear the play; but I cannot erase all the bitter terms of reproach and execration with which the transports of jealousy and revenge are expressed by the Moor, without altering his character, losing sight of the horror of those passions, and, in fact, destroying the tragedy. I find myself therefore, reduced to the alternative of either departing from the principle on which this is undertaken, or materially injuring a most valuable exertion of the genius of Shakespeare. I have adopted the former alternative.

Bowdler's sanctification of Shakespeare was minor when compared to the prior presumptuous and preposterous nineteenth-century meddling of the Reverend James Plumpre. Reverend Plumpre (as had Jean Francois Ducis before him in France in 1792) gave Othello a happy ending by discarding Shakespeare's deaths of Desdemona, Emilia, and Othello. Sanctimonious Plumpre prefaced his farcical rewriting of Othello with, "The object has been to do away with the prodigality of death--and to clear injured virtue in preserving the life of Desdemona and, with that, the life of Othello, and to expose and punish the villany of Iago." Reverend Plumpre expressed surprise that his joyous alterations to Othello had not occurred to others before him. Apparently he had never heard of Monsieur Ducis.

In 1930, at the age of seventy-one, Sir Frank wrote his autobiography, My Memoirs. At the age of eighty-one, he died (Sunday, December 31, 1939). In accordance with his wishes his ashes were scattered on the South Downs. A massive memorial service was held for Sir Frank Robert Benson at London's St. Martin's-in-the-Fields Church, in London, on January 12, 1940.

Sir Frank Benson's ever-performing Shakespearean repertorial company became an excellent training ground for young actors. Former Bensonian actors, Cedric Hardwicke, Henry Ainley, Leslie Faber, Harcourt Williams, Basil Rathbone, Matheson Lang, and others proudly maintained their loyalty to their mentor Benson.

William Faversham, born William Jones in London (Wednesday, February 12, 1868), produced and directed Othello at Broadway's Lyric Theatre (on February 9, 1916) for a brief engagement of sixteen performances. Confirming Edwin Booth's theory that Iago should be played by a comedian, Faversham enacted a humorous Iago, with R. D. MacLean acting a perfect straight-man as Othello, Cecilia Loftus struggling as Desdemona and Constance Collier playing a definitive Emilia. Faversham told writer Walter Pritchard Eaton, "I have always seen Iago as a humorist. I have never been able to conceive of him in any other way." The New York Times called Faversham's Iago "superb, a distinct and interesting creation --an event of more than ordinary impact and an occasion to be remembered."

Faversham patterned his interpretation on a Cellini-type Renaissance man, lacking in conscience, who succeeded in his treacherous deception because he was "gay, humorous, light-hearted, you might say dashing there by embellishing his image as 'honest Iago' and capable of deceiving everyone including 'the stupid Moor'." Walter P. Eaton observed, "This Iago engages us, wins our interest, almost charms us, as he must have Othello, or the plot falls through ... R. D. MacLean plays Othello and plays him with a certain slow-witted dignity which is an excellent foil to Iago's sprightliness." William Faversham died destitute at the age of seventy-three in Bayshore, Long Island, New York, on Sunday, April 7, 1940. R. D. MacLean's Iago in 1891 had been Marie Prescott.

Produced by Edward Sterling Wright and directed by A. C. Winn, an all-black production of Othello was presented at Harlem's Lafayette Theatre on April 25, 1916, with Edward Sterling Wright as the Moor, John H. Ramsey as Iago, and Marion Teney as Desdemona. Wright, a lecturer for the New York Board of Education, had given a twelve-minute reading of Othello (before a large black audience and his illustrious English guests, Sir Herbert Beerbohm-Tree, Mrs. Patrick Campbell, Iris Tree, and others, at Harlem's Lafayette Theatre) on April 8, 1916.

Sir Herbert Beerbohm-Tree was appearing on Broadway at the New Amsterdam Theatre as Cardinal Wolsey in Shakespeare's Henry VIII. Wright invited Sir Herbert on-stage where the English actor expounded on the virtues of the congregation's fellow-man apotheosizing the Moor of Venice as "being one of the most lovable characters created by Shakespeare and instead of being passionate and jealous he was not only a gentleman but a gentle man." Small wonder that Sir Herbert's Othello was less than a beacon in his career! Wright's Othello played Harlem's York Theatre on May 15, 1916, and toured the East in the spring of 1916, playing Boston's Grand Opera House and Philadelphia's Walnut Street Theatre.

During the 1907-1908 season, Maurice Morrison was a Yiddish Moor at Thomashevsky's Philadelphia Theatre, with Maurice Schwartz

as Iago. Morrison, who died on August 29, 1917, last played
Othello in Yiddish at New York's Thomashefsky's Theatre, Houston
Street and Second Avenue, on June 4, 1917, with E. Rothstein as
Iago and Mrs. Laxer as Desdemona. Fritz Kortner successfully ap-
peared as Othello in Der Mohr von Venedig at Berlin, Germany's
Staats Theatre, on October 17, 1922, in Leopold Jessner's trans-
lation of the play with Rudolf Forster as Iago and Johanna Hofer as
Desdemona. Paul Wegener's 1922 portrayal of Othello on the German
stage was described as "a negro who stands with both feet in the
animal world." (Jessner's production of Othello in 1932 at Berlin's
Schauspielhaus, with Heinrich George as the Moor and Werner Klaus
as Iago, was called "almost a burlesque of the play.")

Walter Hampden, born Walter Hampden Dougherty in Brooklyn,
New York, on Monday, June 30, 1879, made his stage debut in England with Frank R. Benson's Company in 1901 and first appeared in
the United States in 1907 where he played many classical roles and
seemingly made a career of the title role of Edmond Rostand's Cyrano
de Bergerac. Hampden brought a strikingly theatrical three and
one-half hour Othello to Broadway at the Shubert Theatre, on January 10, 1925, with Baliol Holloway as Iago and Jeanette Sherwin as
Desdemona.

Arthur Hornblow reported in Theatre magazine, "With memories
of Salvini, Booth and McCullough in the role, the newcomers' interpretation cannot but prove a disappointment--always intelligent,
earnest and sincere, Mr. Hampden moderately, by his elocution and
authority, gives a sound but uninspired rendering of the role.
Baliol Holloway's Iago is Shakespeare to the finger tips." Time
magazine's summation of Walter Hampden's record fifty-seven performances of Othello was "The interpretation of Mr. Hampden, schol-
arly and earnest as it is, seems somehow to fail the Moor. He
plays Othello resonantly and with determination. Always he plays
it; never does he bring the suffering soldier to life."

A Christian Science Monitor writer stated that "The American
theatre owes a debt of gratitude to Walter Hampden, as the first
outstanding figure in what will be known as the years in which revival of interest in Shakespeare took place in the United States."
But he appraised Hampden's Othello as follows: "He gives a fine,
restrained presentation, until the scene where Iago emplants [sic]
the seed of jealousy; then Mr. Hampden begins to lose his actor
poise and with it his audience. The part seems to run away with
him, and then he begins to pound and vocalize."

Ten years later Walter Hampden returned to Broadway in blackface in Achilles Had a Heel, a deplorable drama which found both no
audience and no praise from the press. Walter Hampden died in Los
Angeles on Saturday, June 11, 1955. He succeeded Edwin Booth
and John Drew as president of The Players' Club in 1928 and held
the position until his retirement in 1954.

Baliol Holloway, born at Brentwood, Essex, England, on
Wednesday, February 28, 1883, had played the Moor at Stratford-
upon-Avon, on April 22, 1924, with Eric Maxon as Iago and Ethel Carrington as Desdemona. On March 7, 1927, he was Othello at London's Old Vic Theatre, with Neil Porter as Iago and Dorothy Mas-
singham as Desdemona. Baliol Holloway, who died at the age of
eighty-four on April 15, 1967, returned to Stratford on April 20,
1943, alternating Othello and Iago with Abraham Sofaer, whose melo-
dic silver-toned voice clouded the text. In London on January 21,
1935, Sofaer played Othello clad in cloth-of-gold. The play was
seen by Charles Morgan as "masterly in its unsurpassed use of language and the flowing urgency of its thought." Maurice Evans as
Iago caught the quicksilver essence of evil but created a much too
likable villain; Vivienne Bennett was enchanting as Desdemona.

The Lyceum Club Stage Society performed Othello at London's
Apollo Theatre on April 3, 1927, for the benefit of Stratford's
Shakespeare Memorial Theatre, with Robert Loraine (the Moor), Ion
Swinley (Iago), Elissa Landi (Desdemona), Gertrude Elliott (Emilia),
and John Gielgud (Cassio). Leopold Biberti played the title role
in Richard Weichart's translation of the tragedy at Frankfurt, Ger-
many's Schauspielhaus Theatre on May 5, 1928, and New York's
Yiddish Art Theatre presented on January 31, 1929, Mark Schweid's
Yiddish translation of Othello with Ben Zvi Baratoff as the Moor,
Celia Adler as Desdemona, and Maurice Schwartz as Iago. England's
Birmingham Repertory Theatre experimented with Shakespeare's plays
in modern dress and on February 23, 1929, costumed Othello in cur-
rent fashion. Scott Sunderland was featured as the noble Moor,
Julian D'Albie was his Ensign--or Ancient--and Daphne Heard was
Desdemona.

The gifted black singer and actor Paul Robeson, born on Saturday, April 9, 1898, at Princeton, New Jersey, appeared, on May
19, 1930, at London's Savoy Theatre as the Moor in Maurice Browne's
"murky, offbeat" production of Othello, directed by Ellen Van Volk-
enburg (Mrs. Maurice Browne). Robeson was supported by Peggy
Ashcroft as Desdemona, Maurice Browne as Iago, Sybil Thorndyke
as Emilia, and Ralph Richardson as Roderigo. The arty, dimly
lighted production was called "pretentious and ill-judged," but
Robeson's performance commanded twenty curtain calls, and Othello
remained at the Savoy Theatre until July.

London's Morning Post reported, "There has been no Othello
on our stage, certainly for forty years, to compare with his dignity,
simplicity and true passion." London's Sphere added, "the quality
of his voice was superb ranging from tender whisper to a resonant
scream of outraged fury." Robeson did possess what Laurence
Olivier feared he lacked when he was first contemplating playing the
Moor, "a dark, black, violet, velvet, bass voice." The Spectator
did not consider Robeson's Othello as Shakespeare's, "He might be
the son of Uncle Tom being taught a cruel lesson by Simon Legree."

Critic Herbert Farjeon, establishing that Shakespeare wrote the part for a white man, slashed away for tradition, "He was the underdog from the start. The cares of 'Old Man River' were still upon him. He was a member of a subject race, still dragging the chains of his ancestors. He was not noble enough. He was not stark enough. He seemed to me a very depressed Othello. The fact that he was a Negro did not assist him."

Paul Robeson had appeared in April 1922 on Broadway (with Margaret Wycherly in Mary Hoy Wyborg's play Taboo) and made his first appearance on the English stage at the Opera House, Blackpool, on July 20, 1922, in Wyborg's play, retitled The Voodoo, which starred Mrs. Patrick Campbell. Mrs. "Pat" urged Robeson to attempt Othello, and Sir Frank Benson offered instruction and encouragement in Robeson's Shakespearean pursuit. For his debut as the Moor, Robeson was coached by the daughter of Ira Aldridge, Amanda Christina Elizabeth Aldridge, who as a student of Jenny Lind at London's Royal College of Music had been advised by "The Swedish Nightingale" to always retain her father's name; she was known thereafter as Amanda Ira Aldridge.

Being aware of the deviation of Shakespeare's description of Othello's color by Edmund Kean and others over the years, Robeson said, "I intend to play him as a man whose tragedy lay in the fact that he was 'sooty black': a concept later brought to controversial perfection by Laurence Olivier. But Robeson's Othello did not produce unanimous praise. John Gielgud later recalled in his book, Gielgud, an Actor and His Time, written with John Miller and John Powell in 1979,

> It was a great failure, Robeson, who should have been superb was not helped by an Elizabethean costume of padded trunks, square shoes and a ruff. It was not until the last scene, when he came on in a white kaftan, that he looked really magnificent. He had a fine singing voice, uniquely gentle and deep, but somehow not suited to blank verse.

Othello was performed in its original setting in Venice, in August 1933, at the Palazzo Ducale. Camillo Pilotto was the Moor; Filippe Scelzo was Iago; and Kiki Palmer was Desdemona. On September 27, 1935, Philip Merivale and Gladys Cooper starred in Othello on Broadway at the Ethel Barrymore Theatre, with Kenneth MacKenna as Iago. Philip Merivale, who had played Cassio in Sir Herbert Beerbohm-Tree's 1912 production of Othello at London's His Majesty's Theatre, presented--for eleven performances--a respectable, cocoa-colored "finely tempered and poorly planned" Othello. Critic John Mason Brown in his epithet reluctantly admitted, "There can be no question about it. Othello was a tragedy last night."

During the summer layoff of his hugely successful Broadway play Dodsworth, Walter Huston (né Houghston, born in Toronto,

GLADYS COOPER
And
PHILIP MERIVALE

in William Shakespeare's

OTHELLO
And
MACBETH
With
KENNETH M^cKENNA
And
ALEXANDRA CARLISLE

A CROSBY GAIGE *inc Production*

Program: Gladys Cooper and Philip Merivale in <u>Othello</u>

Canada, on Sunday, April 6, 1884) was acclaimed on July 31, 1934, for his performance in the title role of Othello at the refurbished 1878 Central City, Colorado Opera House. Produced and directed by Robert Edmond Jones, the two-week Central City Othello featured Kenneth MacKenna as Iago and Nan Sunderland as Desdemona. On November 26, 1936, Huston ventured to Broadway at the New Amsterdam Theatre in Robert Edmond Jones's handsome production of Othello. Brian Aherne gave an exceptionally exciting, finely etched interpretation of Iago, and Huston's third wife, Nan Sunderland, was pleasing as Desdemona. Huston's Othello, however, was lynched by the critics.

Brooks Atkison (the New York Times) referring to Philip Merivale's misadventure with the Moor, wrote "Put this Othello down as the second proof of the season that good will and personal candor are not potent enough to transform a modern actor into a hero of Elizabethan drama." Huston's fine performance on Broadway in 1934 (reprised on the screen in 1936) in the genial, affable title role of Sidney Howard's adaptation of Sinclair Lewis's novel Dodsworth (played by Philip Merivale in London) was critically acclaimed, but John Mason Brown labeled Huston's Moor of Venice "Dodsworth in cork" and unfavorably compared his interpretation to the failed, humdrum Othello portrayed in the past by Charles Fechter.

Huston, in an article for Stage magazine in March 1937 wrote,

> I went forth with a mighty breath in my lungs and tore through the performance like a madman, I hammed the part within an inch of burlesque; I ate all the scenery I had time and digestion for; I frightened the other actors, none of whom knew I had changed my characterization. And upon my soul, the audience seemed to enjoy it. But please accept it from me--that performance was no good, on the contrary, it was terrible. Any twenty-year-old schoolboy could have played it that way. It was ten-twenty-thirty melodrama of the very lowest sort, so far as my actions were concerned, in beautiful costumes and against magnificent settings.

Walter Huston died in Beverly Hills, California, on Friday, April 7, 1950, one day after his sixty-sixth birthday. Huston's Othello was the last legitimate show housed in the New Amsterdam Theatre (once the home of Ziegfeld's Follies). The famous theatre, which had opened on November 2, 1903, with twenty-four performances of Nat C. Goodwin's production of Shakespeare's A Midsummer Night's Dream, ended its reign with twenty-one performances of Shakespeare's Othello to join other former legitimate theatres on Forty-second Street as a motion-picture grind house.

Established Freudian gladiators in the arena of psychoanalysis had an Olympian holiday with Othello. Their interpretations would

Walter Huston as Othello in 1936 (courtesy of The Free Library of
Philadelphia Theatre Collection and the Billy Rose Theatre Collection,
The New York Public Library at Lincoln Center, Astor, Lenox and
Tilden Foundations)

have astonished William Shakespeare and bedazzled and tested the
comprehension of generations past, present, and future. Dr. Martin Waugh discovered that Desdemona's white handkerchief "spotted
with strawberries" symbolized a woman's breast--a hypothesis sec-
onded by Dr. Robert Fliess. Professor Gordon Ross Smith determined that the embroidered strawberries on Desdemona's busy handkerchief were indicative of the glans penis, which, in turn, was
representative of "Iago's homosexual fantasies."

Dr. Theodore Reik theorized that Othello's jealousy stemmed
from his "permanent and ineradicable doubt of himself" rather than
from an awareness of his race and color. Dr. Enrique Racker concluded that Othello's jealousy was wrought with "an oedipal element." Dr. A. Bronson Feldman analyzed the Moor's jealousy as
"castration paranoia," creating doubts of his virility. Feldman
agreed with Dr. Theodore Reik that Iago is really Othello's base
and evil alter ego. L. A. G. Strong explained that the genesis of
Othello's jealousy originated in his birth as a Negro and was compounded by an instinctive disbelief that a white woman could not be
faithful to a black man. Professor John V. Hagopian established
the basis for Othello's problem as Othello's being unable to sexually
satisfy Desdemona because of his age.

Sigmund Freud's biographer and associate for thirty years,
the eminent Welsh psychiatrist Dr. Ernest Jones, was interviewed
by Laurence Olivier and director Tyrone Guthrie in 1937. Dr.
Jones gave an analysis of the character of Iago correlative to previous psychoanalytical concepts of Hamlet's oedipus complex that
he had interpreted in his 1923 book Essays in Applied Psycho-
Analysis, which was republished in 1949 as Hamlet and Oedipus.

Dr. Jones's interpretation was based on Iago's latent homo-
sexuality and subconscious love for the black Moor that resulted in
his hatred for Othello. Jones theorized, "the clue to the play was
not Iago's hatred for Othello's position but his deep affection for
him. His jealousy was not because he envied Othello's position, not
because he was in love with Desdemona, but because he himself
possessed a subconscious affection for the Moor, the homosexual
foundation of which he did not understand."

Armed with this revealing Freudian insight, Olivier and Guthrie devised a new, revolutionary concept; they portrayed Iago as
a repressed homosexual who, unknowingly, was in love with Othello.
Virulently inculcated with the Freudian Iagoan neurosis theory,
Olivier, during a rehearsal of the play, impulsively threw his arms
around unsuspecting Ralph Richardson (who was playing the Moor)
and kissed him passionately on the lips. Richardson, blissfully
ignorant of the startlingly new pathological revelation, was justifiably
horrified.

Guthrie's disastrous production of Othello for the Old Vic's

twenty-fourth consecutive season opened on February 8, 1938.
During the performance, Olivier--still in hot pursuit of Iago's suggested psychiatric aberration--fell beside Richardson in the epileptic
scene and simulated an orgasm. Olivier's psychological dallying with
Dr. Jones's Hamlet-Oedipus complex escaped audiences completely;
no one other than Guthrie, Olivier, and one Dr. James Bridie, understood the sudden, gasping, writhing collapse of Iago.

Dr. James Bridie, a Scottish physician whose real name was
Osborne Henry Mavor, was also the author of more than twenty
plays including: The Anatomist; Tobias and the Angel (1930);
Susannah and the Elders (1937); The King of Nowhere (1938). Dr.
Bridie dramatically rose to the defense of Guthrie's critically damned
and confused 1938 Othello. In a letter to the New Statesman,
Bridie wrote that he believed the relationship between Iago and
Othello to be "perfectly clear." Dr. Bridie's letter of March 12,
1938, read as follows:

> We are shown a vital and intelligent man with a diseased
> and perverted sexual "make-up." His mental and physical
> forces were at odds and drove him into sadistic mischief
> and on to the edge of mania. His pathetic rationalizations
> and uncontrolled bursts of smutty talk were the expressions
> of his conflict. It is not necessary to accept the doctrines
> of neo-psychology to recognize the type. It was drawn
> from a real man and the picture is horrifyingly accurate.

The reality of Iago's subordinate position to Othello became
manifestly clear to Olivier during his World War II service in the
Fleet Air Arm of the Royal Navy. Later, Olivier said, "When you
are in a service, then you understand Iago--And Iago, like a
gnarled NCO soldier, would hope to Christ he was going to get into
the officer class, and when he failed he was going to react like
everybody I've seen in any service I've been in, which was only
one, The Navy." Olivier realized that the Freudian approach to
Iago just "couldn't work, because you couldn't express it--I made
a most miserable flop. I think we played it completely wrong. I
played it as a young charmer--I think that the NCO Iago is right."
Sir Laurence would later write, "Iago just hated Othello because he
was black and his superior officer. It was also obvious that Othello
preferred Cassio as his Lieutenant because he was a gentleman and
Iago was not."

Charles Morgan (the New York Times) reported from London,
"The outcome is an unquestionable failure--the play ceased to be a
tragedy--There was no horror in it, no sense of storm intolerably
gathering, no emotional depth." London's Sphere added, "Mr.
Ralph Richardson--his Othello, for all its good moments, was far
from being outstanding and sometimes not even adequate. I expected
Mr. Laurence Olivier's Iago to be much better." James Agate headed
his apologetic but devastating review of Guthrie's Freudian frolic,

"Othello without the Moor; Iago takes a Holiday." Tyrone Guthrie
was more realistic and called his production "a ghastly, boring
hash!"

England's protean performer Ralph David Richardson was born
in a dwelling (Langsyne) on Tivioli Road, Cheltenham, Gloucester-
shire, England (Friday, December 19, 1902). On January 10, 1921,
he made his stage debut at Brighton as a Gendarme in Jean Valjean,
an adaptation of Hugo's Les Miserables. His London stage debut
took place at the Scala Theatre on July 10, 1926 where the actor
played the Stranger in William Butler Yeats's translation of Sopho-
cles's Oedipus at Coloneus. Richardson headed the Malvern Festival
of "400 years of English Drama" in August 1932. The play was
produced by Sir Barry Jackson under whose management Richardson received exceptional early acting training with the Birmingham
Repertory Theatre. The festival included England's first comedy,
Nicholas Udall's Ralph Roister Doister (1550). It also included:
Ben Jonson's The Alchemist (1610); Henry Fielding's Tom Thumb the
Great (1730); Dion Boucicault's London Assurance (1841); George
Bernard Shaw's Too True to Be Good (1931). Dipping into the
burnt cork, Richardson played the title role in Thomas Southerne's
Oroonoko.

On December 23, 1935, Ralph Richardson made his Broadway
stage debut at the Martin Beck Theatre where he played Mercutio
and Chorus in Katharine Cornell's production of Romeo and Juliet.
The play was directed by Guthrie McClintic, with Cornell as Juliet,
Maurice Evans as Romeo, Florence Reed as Nurse, and a neophyte
young actor--Tyrone Power, Jr.--as Benvolio. Katharine Cornell
had produced and starred in Romeo and Juliet at the Martin Beck
Theatre on December 20, 1934, with Basil Rathbone as Romeo, Brian
Aherne as Mercutio, Edith Evans as Nurse, and Orson Welles as
Tybalt and Chorus.

After the death of his first wife, Muriel Hewitt, on October 4,
1942, Richardson (on Wednesday, January 26, 1944) married, Meriel
Forbes, the grandniece of Sir Johnston Forbes-Robertson. During
World War II Richardson had served in the Fleet Air Arm of the
Royal Naval Volunteer Reserve with Olivier. While playing the title
role in Rostand's Cyrano de Bergerac, the esteemed, highly praised
actor was knighted in 1947 and became Sir Ralph Richardson, an
elevation in rank he gleefully accepted with "Sir Ralph--fancy that!
I shall have to buy new stationery."

For sixty-three years in England and America, Ralph Richardson enriched the stage and screen with superlative performances in
a wide variety of both classical and modern roles. Richardson's
Shakespearean roles included, among others: Sir Toby Belch,
Petruchio, Bottom, Caliban, Sir John Falstaff, Lear, Prospero, and
Shylock. Richardson also excelled in more contemporary characterizations: Chekhov's Uncle Vanya and Three Sisters; Shaw's Arms and

the Man; Rattigan's Separate Tables; Anouilh's The Waltz of the
Toreadors; and Rostand's Cyrano de Bergerac, to name but a few.

Following his fine performance as Dr. Austin Sloper in The
Heiress (a part in which he was succeeded by Godfrey Tearle),
which opened at London's Haymarket Theatre on February 1, 1949,
Richardson unprophetically commented, "That was, I think, the
summit. Not that the rest was downhill. But really good roles
are not easy to find--especially as the years pass." (Richardson
played Sloper in the screen version of the play.) The passing
years only reflected Sir Ralph Richardson's enduring talent in
meticulously, persistently perfected parts on stage and screen.

Unfortunately his 1938 Othello was not one of his acclaimed
achievements in the theatre. During an interview in 1938, Richardson said,

> I know the play so well, I've played Roderigo, and Iago
> to Wilfrid Walter's Othello at the Old Vic. All Shakespeare's
> tragedies deal with greatness misdirected or destroyed
> through a frailty. Mr. Gielgud, who, of course, has a
> great understanding of Shakespeare, suggested to me that
> Othello is a saint overcome by villainy. But I don't think
> Othello was a saint. Despite his greatness I think that
> jealousy was in him all the time.

Richardson's Othello was neither saint nor tragedy; clearly, the
actor was misdirected.

England's greatest thespian triumvirate--Olivier, Gielgud, and
Richardson--lost one third of the trinity on Monday, October 10,
1983, when Sir Ralph Richardson died at the age of eighty-two at
London's King Edward VII Hospital.

Although Ira Aldridge had played Othello opposite a white
cast in England in the early 1800s, director Margaret Webster was
convinced that Paul Robeson performing as the Moor would be of
equal historic importance.. Robeson, as the first black man to play
Othello with a white supporting cast in America would, Webster believed, establish "a landmark in the American theatre and in the
history of American consciousness." Miss Webster had initially not
been overcome with Robeson's Moor. She later wrote, "Paradoxical-
ly, it wasn't an especially fine piece of acting. Robeson was never
a born player and he had not acquired much acting skill. I had
seen him play in London in 1930 and thought him very bad."

Margaret Webster, however, followed up her prediction that
Robeson in Othello would establish history in America; on August
10, 1942, she tested her expertly directed production of Othello
at John Huntington's 400-seat Brattle Theatre in Cambridge, Massachusetts, with Robeson as the Moor of Venice, Uta Hagen as

Paul Robeson as Othello in 1943 (courtesy of The Free Public Library of Philadelphia Theatre Collection and the Billy Rose Theatre Collection, The New York Public Library at Lincoln Center, Astor, Lenox and Tilden Foundations)

Desdemona, José Ferrer as Iago, and Margaret Webster as Emilia.
The following week another tryout was given at Richard Skinner
and Day Tuttle's McCarter Theatre in Princeton, New Jersey. One
critic wrote about Robeson's performance, "Physically he is perfectly fitted to the part, massive, austere and with a deep, resonant
voice capable of infinite inflection."

At Broadway's Shubert Theatre, on October 19, 1943, the
Theatre Guild presented Margaret Webster's superbly directed production of Othello (opulently designed by Robert Edmond Jones).
Paul Robeson starred. The curtain fell to ten curtain calls and a
twenty-minute ovation. Lewis Nichols (the New York Times)
praised the Webster-Robeson effort as "excellently done both in
the production and in the acting, it is the best interpretation of
Othello to be seen here in a good many years." His commentary on
Robeson's performance as Othello was close to oblation, "He looks
the part--his voice--reverberates through the house--His final
speech about being a man 'who loved not wisely but too well' is
magnificent." Nicholas also stressed José Ferrer's excellence as
Iago and described Uta Hagen's Desdemona as "a very pretty, soft-
spoken heroine and victim, whose death scene is the most moving
of the play."

Howard Barnes (Herald Tribune) averred that it was

> Robeson's color as much as his fine acting skill which brings
> a rather tricky melodrama into sharp and memorable focus.
> Lines which meant nothing when a white man played the part
> of the Moorish soldier of fortune--led into a homicidal frenzy,
> loom impressively in the Shubert Theatre offering, giving a
> motivation for murder which has been obscure to most of us
> in the past.

There were dissenters. Stark Young felt Robeson "lacked the fine
tragic style," and Brooks Atkinson later recalled Robeson's portrayal
as "a slack and ponderous Othello."

Robeson's Othello established the longest consecutive run for
any Shakespearean production. The 296 performances demolished
Walter Hampden's 1925 record of 57 performances for Othello. Robeson toured forty-five cities across America in Othello and after completing a month's engagement (beginning April 10, 1945) at Chicago's
Erlanger Theatre, the show closed. Robeson as Othello won the
1944 Donaldson Award for the year's best performance. The American Academy of Arts and Sciences awarded him their Gold Medal for
the best diction in the American Theatre--an award won by only
nine others since 1924.

Margaret Webster, in her delightfully informative autobiography, Don't Put Your Daughter on the Stage (1972), recalled that
Robeson "though he understood Othello, he could never play him"

and "was apt to get sonorous and preachy" but that he "matched
the part and the hour ... he endowed the play with a stature and
perspective which I have not seen before or since--The Robeson
Othello became more than just a successful revival, it was a declaration and its success an event in which the performance itself was
of less importance than the public response."

Paul Robeson, in an interview with Robert Van Gelder of the
New York Times on January 14, 1944, said, "When I set up as an
actor, I didn't know how to get from one side of the stage to the
other. When I started playing Othello--in London--that is--I was
almost as bad." Robeson admitted facing the role of the Moor with
great trepidation because of the color barrier, "For the first two
weeks in every scene I played with Desdemona that girl couldn't
get near me. I was backin' away from her all the time. I was like
a plantation hand in the parlor, that clumsy. But the notices were
good. I got over it."

Acerbic George Jean Nathan's polemical comments on the virtues and sins of the Webster-Robeson Othello were,

> Black or white, the whole question rests in whether the
> actor can act the role. Robeson acts it poorly. It is sure-
> ly no more out of place for a Negro to depict the Moor than
> it is for, say, a Canadian like Walter Huston--Mr. Robeson
> has the physical exterior for the role; it is the artistic in-
> terior that is lacking; and that alone is what counts--Robe-
> son's performance suggests mainly a Walter Hampden in
> blackface, overly rhetorical, monotonous, rigid and given
> to barely concealed consciousness of its vocal organ tones.

Goddard Lieberson produced Othello in 1944 for Columbia
Records. Robeson, Ferrer and Hagen performed in their original
roles, but Edith King (who played the part of Bianca on Broadway)
replaced Margaret Webster as Emilia.

The New York Herald Tribune editorialized in 1944,

> The run of the play is a tribute to the art which transcends
> racial boundaries--a sign of hope for the future--when a
> Negro actor of the quality of Mr. Robeson is so enthusiastic-
> ally welcomed into the great traditions of the English-speaking
> stage in a part of such power and nobility as Othello....
> Although Will Shakespeare would doubtless be extremely
> surprised to learn of the social significance his tragedy has
> acquired in a new world, it is, as it happens, uniquely
> adapted to serve as a vehicle for conveying mutual under-
> standing and mutual respect.

On April 7, 1959, prior to his sixty-first birthday, Paul Robeson again played Othello at Stratford-upon-Avon, with Sam Wanamaker

as Iago, Mary Ure as Desdemona, and Albert Finney as Cassio.
Critical and public comment varied regarding the merits of Tony
Richardson's fancy, fussy, insensitive direction and collided with
occasional carping on the rumbling monotony of Robeson's voice.
Kenneth Tynan did not admire Wanamaker's Iago nor Mary Ure's
ill-equipped Desdemona. He reported, "In more appropriate company, I am sure, Mr. Robeson would rise to greater heights than
he does. As things are, he seems to be murdering a butterfly on
the advice of a gossip columnist. His voice, of course, is incom-
parable--a foundation-shaking boom...."

Paul Leroy Robeson died at Philadelphia's Presbyterian Hospital on Friday, January 23, 1976, at the age of seventy-seven.
Betsy Graves Reyneau's oil portrait of Paul Robeson costumed as
Othello can be seen in the National Portrait Gallery of the Smithsonian Institution.

If Paul Robeson's Moor was found wanting by some for lack
of power and ferocity, an accomplished Czech actor Frederick Valk,
who died at the age of fifty-five on Monday, July 23, 1956, was
hailed as Othello in Prague and in London. Valk's powerful portrayal of the Moor was a sharply defined interpretation, although
his heavy Slavic accent frequently garbled the verse. Valk gave
a forceful performance as Othello at London's Old Vic Theatre on
July 22, 1942. He played opposite Bernard Miles's eerily devilish
Iago. Miles's "whiff of Cockney gave an unexpected aroma to his
performance"; he was highly praised. The Czech actor's Othello
garnered added kudos at London's Savoy Theatre on April 24,
1947, opposite Donald Wolfit's slyly brilliant Iago and Rosalind
Iden's beautifully played Desdemona.

At London's Piccadilly Theatre an opposing Othello had opened
on March 26, 1947. Jack Hawkins played the Moor. His pathos
was described by Theatre World as "rather more effective than his
passion." Hawkins performed opposite Anthony Quayle's fascinatingly
wicked Iago and Elizabeth Kentish's Desdemona. The Comedie-
Française in Paris presented Othello on January 11, 1950, with Almé
Clariond as the Moor, Jean Debucourt as Iago, and Line Noro as
Desdemona.

Laurence Olivier produced Othello at London's St. James's
Theatre on October 18, 1951. The production featured Orson Welles
in his London stage debut as the Moor of Venice. Welles increased
his imposing six-foot presence by adding heel lifts until he towered
over Peter Finch (Iago) and Gudrun Ure (Desdemona). The beautifully staged production directed by Welles was not matched by
Welles's performance and mangled "improvements" to Shakespeare's
text. Ivor Brown (the Observer) found Welles "treated the text
as a script to work on rather than as a document to be revered"
while Stephen Williams (Evening Mail) felt "he missed tremendous
chances, misquoted or threw away some of the most sonorous lines
in the language."

ST. JAMES's THEATRE

KING STREET, S.W.1

Lessees: S. J. & L. Ltd.
Joint Managing Directors: GILBERT MILLER and PRINCE LITTLER

Licensed by the Lord Chamberlain to PRINCE LITTLER
Under the direction of SIR LAURENCE OLIVIER

In association with S. A. GORLINSKY
and on behalf of MERCURY ARTS SOCIETY, LTD.

LAURENCE OLIVIER

presents

ORSON WELLES

in

"OTHELLO"

by

WILLIAM SHAKESPEARE

First Performance Thursday, October 18th, 1951

Program: Orson Welles in Othello

Alas, the critics ignored Othello's advice to "Keep up your
bright swords" and slashed away at Welles's conception of General
Othello of Venice. Critic Kenneth Tynan, allowing that Welles "has
the courage of his restrictions" described the actor's interpretation
of Othello as "a performance of a magnificent amateur--What we saw
was a tightly limited acting performance in a bound-bursting production.... Welles's Othello is the lordly and mannered performance
we saw in Citizen Kane, slightly adapted to read 'Citizen Coon.'"

Cecil Wilson (Daily Mail) reported, "His was a performance
which appealed as much to the mind as to the emotions." New
Statesman's critic T. C. Worsley wrote, "The great lumbering dazed
bull which Mr. Welles gives us for Othello may have its shortcomings
in detail; but the fact remains that it imposes itself on us so power-
fully and terrifyingly that we hardly notice them." J. C. Trewin
called the Wellesian version of Othello, "a subdued, inexpressive
affair in which speech after speech flickered away, passion was
never released, and one was appropriately unmoved."

The London Times added,

> Mr. Welles gives us an impressive but an unexciting Othello.
> He smoulders purposefully, but the repression holds to the
> end: the expected flame never once flashes out. So in-
> sistently quiet is Mr. Welles that almost we are made to feel
> that it was somehow improper to expect flame; almost, for
> the spell he casts soon ceases to work, and we come away
> muttering rebelliously that the part the actor has chosen to
> play is, after all, that of Othello--Othello has been given
> the cue for passion, but the cue is not taken up.

The Spectator slashed Welles's concept of the Moor. "Very large,
very black, very sonorous, he is nevertheless insufficiently volcanic. He does not sweep us away, he arouses sympathy rather
than pity and we cannot help wondering why a man who appears to
be both shrewd and self-controlled should suddenly start behaving
very unreasonably."

Orson Welles's stimulating and provocative observation, "It
would be so much better if the critics would come not on first nights
but on last nights, when they could exercise their undoubted flair
for funeral orations" was not bloody likely!

The talented and unpredictable Mr. Welles, pride of Kenosha,
Wisconsin, where he was born on Thursday, May 6, 1915, agreed
to perform Othello on Broadway, in January 1953. S. A. Gorlinsky
was Olivier's co-producer of Welles's London Othello. Anticipating
that he would recover losses from the London production, Gorlinsky
took to heart Orson's gossamer promise, which, of course, never
materialized.

Rosemary Harris with John Neville (left) and Richard Burton (right) in London's Old Vic production of Othello, 1956 (courtesy of The Free Library of Philadelphia Theatre Collection).

George Orson Welles died in Los Angeles, California, at the age of seventy on Thursday, October 10, 1985. The great promise of continued genius displayed in his youth was never fulfilled in later years in which ambitious projects were left unfinished or aborted.

"Even in prospect, the double Othello of John Neville and Richard Burton looked fairly black" announced Kenneth Tynan. But beginning February 21, 1956, after six weeks of rehearsal, Richard Burton and John Neville alternated Othello and Iago (opposite Rosemary Harris' Desdemona) in Michael Benthall's Old Vic production of Othello. Their Iagos won. Their Othellos lost. Tynan ably described both actors as "born Cassios" and compared Burton's Othello to Neville's Iago as "a drab squabble between the Chocolate Soldier and the Vagabond King."

Burton gave a finely etched Janus-like portrait of Iago to elegantly dignified Neville's fluctuating gentle Othello; Neville's shrewdly cunning smoothness as Iago, however, could not counterbalance the bombast and oratory of Burton's Moor. Burton had never appeared more handsome on-stage than when costumed as

Othello, wearing his floor-length flowing white robe with large
epaulets. His chocolate makeup covered his poor complexion and
was set off with mustache and beard and a black curly wig. Eleven
years later, on September 20, 1967, at England's Nottingham Playhouse, John Neville (born Saturday, May 2, 1925, at Willesden,
London, England) played Iago to American actor Robert Ryan's
Othello, with Ann Bell as Desdemona.

On Tuesday, November 10, 1925, the paradox known as Richard Burton was born Richard Walter Jenkins--the twelfth of thirteen
children of a Welsh coal-miner--in Pontrhydyfen, South Wales. In
1943, Burton adopted the surname of his teacher and mentor Philip
Burton. Ronald Bryden made the observation that "no one who saw
Burton at Stratford-upon-Avon and The Old Vic in the early fifties
can have much doubt that here was--the next wearer of the mantle
of Edmund Kean"; the observation became a shattered truth. Burton
was accused of "wallowing in public vulgarity," debasing a brilliant
acting career, and becoming famous for all the wrong reasons.
Richard's widely exposed private life was reminiscent of the late,
great John Barrymore and echoed the uninhibited and debilitating
lifestyle of literature's F. Scott Fitzgerald.

Eventually, the great promise of Burton's acting career became less celebrated than did his internationally headlined private
life, which spotlighted in minute detail his five marriages and proudly proclaimed marathon drinking. Actor-producer-director Bryan
Forbes in his informative and delightful delineation of the acting
profession, That Despicable Race, well described Burton's digres-
sion, "When Olivier's crown and Gielgud's orb were his for the
claiming he embarked upon a period of self-destruction, or so it
seemed to most."

Richard Burton was the recipient of Broadway's 1960 "Tony"
Award for his appearance as King Arthur in Lerner and Loewe's
Camelot, his first musical. He exceed all prior productions records
on Broadway with 137 performances in Hamlet, directed by John
Gielgud in 1964. Peter Shaffer's brilliant play Equus opened on
Broadway on October 24, 1974, with Anthony Hopkins as psychiatrist Martin Dysart. Hopkins was succeeded by Anthony Perkins,
and, in March 1976, Richard Burton took over the role of Dysart,
for which part he received a special "Tony" Award. He contributed
several fine performances on the stage, although his screen appearances were mainly poorly conceived--often walk-through performances in dismal films. Despite his squandering his talent for money,
Burton was nominated for six Academy Awards as Best Actor of the
Year: The Robe (1953); Becket (1964); The Spy Who Came In From
the Cold (1965); Who's Afraid of Virginia Woolf? (1966); Anne of the
Thousand Days (1969); and Equus (1977). His final screen appearance in Orwell's 1984, released in March 1985, was a superb piece
of acting.

Burton had a sonorous, powerful, ponderous voice. But his frequently prostituted talent and lost promise of attaining Kean's, Olivier's, and Gielgud's fame and prestige resulted in his battling--self-destructively, it seems--with his troubled spirit. The battle ended on Sunday, August 5, 1984, when, at the age of fifty-eight, Burton died of a cerebral hemorrhage in Geneva, Switzerland. Richard Burton was awarded the C.B.E. (Commander of the Order of the British Empire) by Queen Elizabeth II in 1970 and last appeared on the Broadway stage at the Lunt-Fontanne Theatre on May 8, 1983, in an ill-advised, disastrous revival of Noel Coward's brittle comedy Private Lives, co-starring with his twice-wedded former wife Elizabeth Taylor. Burton's career and life has been compared to Faust's and Burton once observed to Roderick Mann, "People keep saying I sold my soul to the devil--but one thing you've got to admit, I've had a hell of an interesting life!"

Glen Byam Shaw's production of Othello at the Shakespeare Memorial Theatre at Stratford-upon-Avon (May 29, 1956) gave former supporting actor Harry Andrews the opportunity to play a difficult leading role as Othello, paced by Emlyn Williams's Iago and Margaret Johnston's Desdemona. Andrews's Othello started strong but faded away in a weak finish. Henry Alleyn (Plays and Players) wrote, "If Mr. Andrews' failure is puzzling, then that of Emlyn Williams remains an unsolvable mystery. His villainy is never credible because he does not believe in it enough." Other judges, however, found Andrews's Othello intriguing and Williams's Iago "the complete villain." J. C. Trewin described Emlyn Williams's Iago as "a stocky, black-bearded devil, with enunciation like the print of a branding iron, and the face of a Judas from a Renaissance painting."

Vittorio Gassman was born in Genoa, Italy on Friday, September 1, 1922. He is known in the United States and England as a motion-picture actor who appeared in a few dreary Hollywood films in the late 1900s and was the more-publicized former husband of actress Shelley Winters. In Italy, Gassman is a leading film star. He has also been called the finest actor of the contemporary Italian theatre. With his well-trained acting company, Teatro Popolare Italiano, he has produced and starred in many classical plays. In December 1956 at Rome's Teatro d'Arte Italiano, Gassman alternated in the role of Othello with Salvo Randone; Osvaldo Ruggieri was Iago, and Anna Maria Ferrero played Desdemona. Five years later, Gassman's countryman--thirty-eight-year-old Franco Zeffirelli--invaded Shakespeare's hometown with an overpowering and underwhelming Othello.

Franco Zeffirelli's handsome, but complicatedly staged, four and a half hour Othello had two long intervals. The play opened on October 10, 1961, at Stratford-upon-Avon's Royal Shakespeare Theatre. The massive Zeffirelli production, designed more for grand opera than for Shakespeare's tragedy, was a technical

disaster exposed to critical clawing and slashing. Felix Barker
(Evening News) headlined his review of the production: Gielgud
Could Not Save Othello From Disaster. "Disappointments are not
unusual in the theatre, but rarely are they so devastating as the
one which struck like a thunderbolt at Stratford-upon-Avon last
night."

John Gielgud, great-nephew of Ellen Terry, was born on
Wednesday, April 13, 1904, at Gladhow Gardens and Old Brompton
Road, London. Gielgud had one of his rare theatrical disasters
with director-designer Franco Zeffirelli's Othello. An exceptionally
fine actor, Ian Bannen, garnered no laurels as Iago; Dorothy Tutin's
Desdemona was deprecatingly compared to the nice-girl-next-door
and Dame Peggy Ashcroft was considered a much too-well-bred
Emilia. Temperamentally unsuited for playing the jealous Moor,
Gielgud was further beset by Zeffirelli's badly lit, dark, massive
settings that nearly engulfed his heavy, dark costumes and black
makeup. Compared with these settings, Rembrandt lighting seems
as bright as the noon-day sun. Gielgud's lost combat with Othello
was generally damned by the critics, and he wisely refused to head
the proposed transfer of the production to London's Aldwych Theatre after the Stratford closing on November 28, 1961. Interestingly, in his 1979 memoirs, Gielgud, an Actor and His Time, reference
to Zeffirelli's debacle and his maligned Othello is noticeably omitted.

Felix Barker felt that the abundant opulence of Zeffirelli's
production boded disaster,

> Towering Corinthian columns swayed like punchballs at the
> slightest touch, and more than once Gielgud seemed in im-
> mediate danger of doubling Othello with the role of Samson--
> He is too sensitive a person, too great an actor not to know
> that last night he did not come within striking distance of
> Othello. At his first entrance he looked superb--head,
> costume, all moulded in bronze--but he never found the
> heart of the Moor.... Sir John's mind is (as I believe he
> feared) too keen and his figure too spare for Othello.

W. A. Darlington (Daily Telegraph) properly determined the part of
Othello was unsuited to Gielgud, "He has, of course, three qualities
that the part needs--a fine voice, a poetical sense and a power of
authority. Nevertheless it is not his part. Othello should be played
by a bass and he is a tenor. The part is meant for a big man and
he is still a slender lightweight."

Caryl Brahms headlined a Plays and Players review of the Gielgud Othello "Oh, The Pity of It, Zeffirelli!" and wondered, "How
would the foremost Hamlet of his time acquit himself in the heat and
breath and writhing guts of foaming Othello?" Allowing for technical mishaps, Gielgud's beard became detached; Iago forgot and
hastily reconstructed his lines, and the stage was blackened by the

darkness of flickering candles until Zeffirelli's Othello really disappeared and died. "But as to stature, how is one to measure Gielgud, seeing him only on one disastrous first night, against the
rock of ages that was lion-hearted Valk (which was why his disin-
tegration was the more fearful to watch) or the full diapason of
Wolfit?" asked Brahms.

    J. C. Trewin (Shakespeare on the English Stage 1900-1964)
wrote,

> Gielgud could not uncover the primitive side; he seldom
> got us to credit the racial division, the racial inflammability.
> We could not believe he had been caught (as it was put
> once) at the disastrous meeting point of two cultural and
> spiritual traditions. Maybe the true Othello would be a
> Gielgud crossed with a Valk.

For all his problems under the proscenium with Othello, John
Gielgud (who had become Sir John Gielgud in 1953) made a fine recording of the play in 1962 for Living Shakespeare, Inc. Records,
reading the title role with Ralph Richardson as Iago, Barbara Jefford as Desdemona, and Coral Browne as Emilia. The recording
script was adapted by Fiona Bentley and Morys Aberdare and directed by Michael Benthall. Peter Brook's observation of the Gielgud magic would apply to his Othello-on-disc, "There is no joy like
hearing John Gielgud speak."

Caspar Wrede's production of Othello at the Old Vic Theatre
on January 31, 1963 (with black actor Errol John stripped to a loin
cloth as the Moor, Leo McKern as Iago and Adrienne Corri as Desdemona) was compared to a "Gypsy Operetta" and labeled as a
"misbegotten interpretation."

The greatest classical actor of this century was born at Dork-
ing, England on Wednesday, May 22, 1907. He was knighted by
King George VI in July 1947 as Sir Laurence Olivier, and in 1970
would be installed as a Baron (Life Peer) by Queen Elizabeth II for
his services to the theatre. The only major Shakespearean role
Laurence Olivier had not played was Othello, the actor arguing
that "no English actor in this century had succeeded in the part
and that the play's focus was on Iago." Olivier shunned portraying
the Moor, reasoning, "I have done everything but Othello and I
have no burning desire to go into blackface and have the stage
stolen from me by some young and brilliant Iago. If I take it on,
I don't want a witty, Machiavellian Iago. I want a solid, honest-
to-God NCO." He also considered the part "a monstrous, monstrous
burden for the actor" and slyly fantasized that by writing Othello,
Shakespeare might have quelled Richard Burbage's imagined boast
of being capable of playing anything Shakespeare wrote.

At the age of fifty-seven the inestimably talented Laurence

Laurence Olivier as Othello in England's National Theatre Production,
1964 (courtesy of the Doug McClelland Collection).

Olivier shed his reluctance to attempt <u>Othello</u>. It took six months of exhaustive training, which included vigorous exercise, to attain his vision of Othello's rhythm in movement, "like a soft, black leopard"; Paul Robeson had studied the sleek pacing of a leopard in the zoo for the same purpose. Undoubtedly aware of George Bernard Shaw's requisite for the Moor, "If Othello cannot turn his voice into thunder and surge of passion, he will achieve nothing but a ludicrously misplaced bit of geography," Olivier's schedule included intense vocal training to deepen his voice almost a full octave lower to the "dark, black, violet, velvet, bass voice" of the Moor. He further embellished his uninhibited Negroid portrait of Othello with two and one-half hours of coal-black makeup meticulously applied from head to toe. His pale blue fingernails and incarnadined palms, a black moustache above reddened, thickened lips topped by a close-fitting wooly wig, all strongly stressed the vital aspect of Othello's color as central to the tragedy. Olivier noted, "the whole play seeps through with it."

Following nine weeks of rehearsals, Olivier's <u>Othello</u> opened at Birmingham's Alexandra Theatre on April 6, 1964, and, during Shakespeare's Quartercentenary on April 23, 1964, Olivier made his entrance on the stage of London's Old Vic Theatre to perform his barefooted Othello three-times-weekly. "This Othello compels you to accept him, not merely as a coloured man, but as a Negro, with a negroid speech and easy, generous, frank and easily articulated gait and physically imposed authority," wrote Philip Hope-Wallace in <u>The Guardian</u>.

London's <u>Sunday Times</u> called Olivier's Othello "The only completely successful performance of that impossibly difficult part which this age has seen." Herbert Kretzner (<u>Daily Express</u>) wrote, "Sir Laurence has managed, by heaven knows what witchcraft, to capture the very essence of what it must mean to be born with a dark skin.... It is a performance full of grace, terror and insolence. I shall dream of its mysteries for years to come." Bernard Levin (<u>Daily Mail</u>) proclaimed, "Sir Laurence's Othello is great acting of the kind that we see more and more rarely today, larger than life, bloodier than death, more piteous than pity. He is stupendous."

Praise for Olivier's virtuosity was tinged by a few xenophobic critical cries in the wilderness carping that his fecund performance was not Shakespeare's Othello. Some critics said his performance was "overtrained" and "extravagant," seen both as genius and caricature geared more to the external image of the man and less to the emotional concept. Director John Dexter had envisioned this interpretation as "a pompous, word-spinning, arrogant, black general" and Olivier's Othello was based on T. S. Eliot's and Dr. F. R. Leavis's disputed definition of Othello's downfall due to his being a "narcissistic, self-dramatizing egoist."

For all the controversy and theorization, Olivier's astonishing

impersonation of the Moor became the greatest Shakespearean success in London's Old Vic Theatre's long history and a seminar for
audiences (based on Olivier's ambitious if unlikely theory) "to lead
the public toward an appreciation of acting--to watch acting for acting's sake." In an interview for _Life_ magazine, Olivier expanded
his thinking by saying: "In Shakespeare I always try to reassure
the audience initially that they are not going to see some grotesque,
outsized dimension of something which they can't understand or
sympathize with--then I think there's no end to where you can lead
them in size of acting. God knows, you have to be enormously big
as Othello."

Olivier's fear that "a young and brilliant Iago" might steal the
stage did not materialize. The actor's overpowering portrayal of the
Moor completely overshadowed Frank Finlay's performance as the
Ensign. Nor was Olivier's performance eclipsed by Maggie Smith's
graceful portrayal of Desdemona. The Old Vic had originally proposed casting Michael Redgrave as Iago and Rosemary Harris as
Desdemona. Michael Redgrave, only one year younger than Olivier,
at the age of fifty-six was twice the given age of Iago, but his
Ensign could have strongly diffused the spotlight from even Olivier's
Moor. Actor-writer Robert Speaight, who in America had been
caught in the tangled web of the 1939 Theatre Guild calamity (Orson Welles's corruption of Shakespeare called _Five Kings_), wrote,
"There was no risk of anyone stealing the stage from this Othello,
but an added dimension would have been given to the play if Michael
Redgrave had been asked to share it."

Kenneth Tynan saw Olivier's Othello as "a triumphant black
despot, aflame with unadmitted self-regard. So far from letting Iago
manipulate him he seemed to manipulate Iago, treating him as a kind
of court jester." In 1966, Tynan wrote a brief but comprehensive
history of The National Theatre's Old Vic production, _Othello, The
Actor and the Moor_. The book is illustrated with splendid photographs by Roddy McDowall and Angus McBean; it features a stunning
photo-portrait by Anthony Armstrong Jones (Lord Snowden) of Olivier as Othello.

The National Theatre Company went to Russia in September
1965, opening _Othello_ at Moscow's Kremlevsky Theatre. The historical Russian devotion to the play and Laurence Olivier's curtain
speech in impeccable Russian were given a tremendous ovation.
Felix Barker, reporting from Russia on September 8, 1965, to London's _Evening News_, wrote, "As the curtain fell on the tragic figures of Desdemona and the Moor entwined in death's agony on the
bed, the audience from the back of the theatre swept down the
central gangway in a great human tide. They stood three-deep in
the front of the stage, hurling flowers and clapping, many with
their hands above their heads."

Years later, Robert Cushman wrote in _Plays and Players_ (November 1971),

I saw Olivier play Othello several times and I was never
quite sure whether I liked it. But I felt then and I know
now that liking hardly mattered; there is little point in arguing with a historical fact. Sir Laurence himself once said
that there is no such thing as over-acting; "you can go as
high as Everest if you can fill in the space." There are
spaces, plenty of them in Othello that are never likely to be
filled as amply again, and it will be difficult in the future
to view the play without nostalgia creeping in and breeding
dissatisfaction.

Olivier, with Maggie Smith, Frank Finlay, and the original
cast directed by John Dexter, recorded the complete performance of
Othello for RCA Victor, "given in the Decca Studios in London by
the National Company of Great Britain exactly as it was performed
by them at the Old Vic. The stage setting was made exactly as at
the Old Vic, all the props were used from the theatre, the performance was given complete, as in the theatre, and the piece was recorded strictly in sequence."

John Barton's production of Othello, staged in a nineteenth-
century setting, opened at Stratford-upon-Avon on September 9,
1971. Robert Cushman (Plays and Players) called Barton's staging
"a spacious three-dimensional Shakespeare, the kind you walk around
and explore" in which Othello's request to Brabantio and his officers to "Keep up your bright swords" in act 1, scene 2 was prefaced
by the firing of a pistol. Cushman described the principal performances as "exceedingly interesting." Brewster Mason played "a very
gentle, noble Moor--his voice has thunder but no lightning by comparison with Olivier--his performance is placid." Lisa Harrow performed well as Desdemona but Emrys James as Iago was seen as "a
Kiplingesque raker, hearty and sentimental to the point of being the
mess bore."

Darkly contrasting with John Barton's Othello was London's
Mermaid Theatre's erotic experiment with the play a week later on
September 16, 1971. Bruce Purchase ranted and roared as the
Moor against a less than sustaining performance by Bernard Miles
as Iago; Sarah Stephenson enlivened the tragedy as a nude Desdemona. Robert Cushman in Plays and Players termed the Mermaid
Othello "a melancholy affair" but viewed the eroticism of the production as clarifying Shakespeare's text in act 4, scene 2. Othello's
berating of Desdemona, "Had it pleased heaven to try me with af-
fliction" was spoken with

looking Desdemona straight in the crotch which makes unusual sense of the lines about "the fountain from which my
current runs" and particularly of the instruction "Turn
thy complexion there." No other Othello I've seen has
shown much interest in where there might be, and one has
had charitably to assume that the Moor, perhaps on the

verge of another fit, was just not expressing himself clearly. This sexual interpretation of course is precisely what
Sir Bernard [Miles] was arguing in his long drawn-out
publicity campaign for his nude Desdemona.

Obviously requiring all the fresh air possible, another bas-
tardized version of Shakespeare's tragedy appeared at London's
avant-garde Open Space Theatre. Opening on June 8, 1972, and
called An Othello, this "reconstruction" was written in two weeks
by Charles Marowitz and included interpolated selected writings of
Malcolm X, James Baldwin, and Stokely Carmichael--to improve the
heretofore weak prose of Mr. Shakespeare. An Othello featured
black actor Rudolph Walker as a black liberal Moor, Anton Phillips
as Iago, a member of the Black Panthers; Judy Greeson, as Desdemona, patiently awaited death. Charles Marowitz in an interview
with Plays and Players explained that An Othello was "An attempt
to put the black power cliche into a more interest context." He
said: "What interested me most in the production was isolating the
characters from their original Shakespearean context. Othello, Iago
and Desdemona were separated and forced to operate according to
contemporary pressures." The critical consensus not surprisingly
was "Shakespeare needed protection from Charles Marowitz."

Directed by Peter Dews, the Chichester Festival Theatre's
July 29, 1975, production of Othello, set in a nineteenth-century
military barracks, cast Israeli actor Chaim Topol as a "pompous and
posturing" Moor. Producer Keith Michell played Iago, and Hannah
Gordon was Desdemona. Topol had performed well in London as
Sholom Aleicheim's Tevye in the long-running musical success Fiddler
on the Roof and in the screen version of the musical, but he was a
poor choice and no match for the Moor of Venice. Topol's cartoon
of Othello was virtually acted off the stage by Keith Michell's fascinatingly vulgar but honest interpretation of Iago. Harold Hobson,
on August 3, 1975, in the London Times, delicately found Topol's
Othello "less noble, less poetic, and less elegant than Olivier's in
the production that has hitherto dominated our time." Ivan Howlett
found Topol "out of joint with the rest of the action."

Peter Hall, former director of the Shakespeare Memorial Theatre
at Stratford-upon-Avon where he created the Royal Shakespeare Company, succeeded Sir Laurence Olivier as director of the National
Theatre in October 1973. Hall approached actor Paul Scofield in
1974 about the prospect of his playing Othello at the National.
Paul Scofield, born in Sussex, England on Saturday, January 21,
1922, is memorable for many fine performances, especially his playing
of Sir Thomas More in both the stage and film versions of Robert
Bolt's prize-winning play A Man for All Seasons. Scofield cautiously
considered the proposal and six years later decided to test his considerable talent with the Moor.

The Paul Scofield Othello opened at the National's Olivier

Theatre on March 20, 1980, with Michael Bryant as Iago and Felicity
Kendall as Desdemona. Benedict Nightingale reported from London
that Scofield's performance was "Daring, but flawed--he becomes
external and operatic, substituting vocal and physical bravura for
intensity of feeling--Since he is a great actor, his tricks are not
without fascination. It's an audacious performance but one likely
to leave even its admirers somewhat cold."

In London's Observer, Robert Cushman noted, "He is sonor-
ously somnolent, no fires, no torment. Pride of a quiet kind, there
is though what with his studied gestures--which include the trying
on for size the imaginary cuckold's horns--it often seems more like
self-approbation." James Fenton (London Sun) found "this performance is largely narcissistic--I found the performance quite incompre-
hensible--What sets Mr. Scofield apart is not his blackness but his
acting."

Robert Eyre's production of Othello, which had been seen at
Stratford-upon-Avon in 1979, opened at London's Aldwych Theatre
in August 1980. The Sunday Telegram claimed that Donald Sinden
as Othello "was fooling nobody by blacking up. Quite true, and
what other than impeccably patrician delivery did Mr. Eyre expect
in casting Mr. Sinden in the first place?" The Young Vic's October
1982 tussle with Othello (featuring Kenneth Haigh as the Moor,
George Sewell as Iago, and Amanda Boxer as Desdemona) was dismissed as "a sadly damp evening."

Margaret Webster and Paul Robeson had pioneered the emergence and acceptance in America of exceptionally talented black
actors laying claim to the role of Othello. Robeson's last appearance in America as Othello was on May 22, 1945, at New York's City
Center Theatre in Margaret Webster's production of the tragedy,
with José Ferrer and Uta Hagen reenacting their roles of Iago and
Desdemona.

Black actor Canada Lee experimented with the Moor in John
Gassner's production of act 3, scene 3 of Othello. The production
took place in 1944 at Erwin Piscator's Dramatic Workshop of the
New York School for Social Research; it featured John Ireland as
Iago and Elena Karam as Desdemona. Wilella Waldorf (New York
Post) wrote, "Canada Lee lacks the towering stature and organ-
like tones of Mr. Robeson, and he has a good deal to learn about
speaking blank verse, but there was a dignity, a sympathetic understanding of the dramatic aspects of the role." Historian-critic
George Freedley felt that Lee "seems to feel and act the part with
more conviction than does Paul Robeson."

Canada Lee, born Leonard Lionel Cornelius Canegata in New
York City on Sunday, March 3, 1907, became the first black actor
to appear on Broadway in whiteface. Black actor Frederick O'Neal
later appeared in whiteface at Harlem's Playhouse on February 27,

1947 in Walter Carroll's play <u>Tin Top Valley</u>. During the tryout of
<u>The Duchess of Malfi</u> in Providence, Rhode Island, Lee replaced
white actor McKay Morris as Daniel De Bosola. W. H. Auden's
adaptation of John Webster's 1613 horror drama, starring Elizabeth
Bergner and featuring John Carradine in his Broadway debut,
opened at the Ethel Barrymore Theatre on October 15, 1946, for
thirty-nine performances.

The talent Canada Lee exhibited in many plays achieved special recognition for his performance as Caliban in Margaret Webster's production of Shakespeare's <u>The Tempest</u> (Broadway's Alvin
Theatre on January 25, 1945). He later played Othello opposite
Claire Luce's Desdemona at Boston's Summer Theatre. The great
promise of Canada Lee's flourishing career came to an end, however, when on Friday, May 9, 1952, he died at the age of forty-
five of a heart attack.

The Shakespeare Guild Festival Company produced <u>Othello</u> at
New York's Jan Hus Auditorium on October 29, 1953, with a talented
black actor Earle Hyman as the Moor, William Thornton as Iago, and
Blanche Cholet as Desdemona. Twenty-seven-year-old Earle Hyman,
born at Rocky Mount, North Carolina on Monday, October 11, 1926,
had played the Prince of Morocco at New York's City Center Theatre
in <u>The Merchant of Venice</u> in March 1953; the production featured
Luther Adler as Shylock.

Hyman repeated the role of the Moroccan Prince opposite Morris Carnovsky's Shylock and Katharine Hepburn's Portia on July 10,
1957, at the American Shakespeare Festival in Stratford, Connecticut where their third season had opened on Saturday, June 22, 1957,
with <u>Othello</u> directed by John Houseman. Brooks Atkinson (the <u>New
York Times</u>) called the production and costumes by Rouben Ter-
Arutunian and lighting by Jean Rosenthal "shining" but said that
the performance was "thin, listless and attenuated--For this is an
<u>Othello</u> without depth--Mr. Hyman, whose speech is woefully thin,
is hardly the 'noble Moor'." Atkinson compared Alfred Drake's performance as Iago to an "extension of his suave performance in <u>Kis-
met</u>" that missed the target of Iago's demonic character. Jacqueline
Brooks's Desdemona was considered less than resourceful and the
dean of American critics concluded, "The performance does not go
much below the surface."

In April 1963, Earle Hyman portrayed the Moor in Norwegian
at Bergen, Norway's Den National Scene, with Per Theodor Haugen
as Iago and Anne Gullestad as Desdemona. Herbert Lavik, reviewing the production in Norway's oldest theatre, wrote, "Here is a
stage talent with power and musicality. His appearance is magnificent. It would be difficult to find an actor with such exterior
qualities for the part of Othello. It is a hypnotizing portrait."
Hyman toured the Scandinavian countries in 1964 with the Norwegian
State Travelling Theatre playing <u>Othello</u> and the title role in Eugene

O'Neill's The Emperor Jones, for which he received Norway's Best
Actor of the Year Award. Three years later Earle returned to
Norway and reenacted his Norwegian Othello, with Folke Hjort as
Iago and Birgitta Pettersson as Desdemona.

Twenty-five years after his first appearance as Othello, Hyman played the role for seventy-six performances at New York's
Roundabout Theatre. The performances began January 26, 1978,
with Nicholas Kepros as Iago and Mary Carney as Desdemona.
Richard Eder (the New York Times), while unmoved by Hyman's
interpretation of Othello, reported that the actor gave "a finely
measured performance." Eder emphasized the Moor's foreignness
in Venice at the expense of his appointed powerful position and felt
the final scene of rage tended toward overacting.

William Marshall had produced, directed, and played the title
role in Othello in 1953 at New York City schools and at the Mother
Zion Church. On September 7, 1955, the Brattle Shakespeare Players of Cambridge, Massachusetts, transferred their summer production of Othello (which was directed by John Stix) to New York's
City Center Theatre for sixteen performances. Marshall played
the Moor, James Kilty played Iago, and Jan Ferrand played Desdemona. Brooks Atkinson (the New York Times) called the production "an excellent performance." Although admiring Marshall's
towering physique and resonant baritone voice, Atkinson felt "he
seems to have little capacity for articulatory words or syllables--no
music in his speech--worse than that there are only occasional sentences or phrases."

William Horace Marshall, born on Tuesday, August 19, 1924,
at Gary, Indiana, had given a beautiful rendition of God (De
Lawd) for forty-four performances in the Broadway revival of Marc
Connelly's 1930 Pulitzer Prize play The Green Pastures, which
opened on March 15, 1951. Marshall repeated his performance of
Othello on July 2, 1958, in Joseph Papp's Central Park Amphitheatre
production, with Robert Geiringer as Iago and Ellen Holly as Desdemona. Again, Marshall's interpretation of the Moor was disqualified
as "prosy and rigid" and described as demonstrating no noticeable
improvement in his delivery of Shakespeare's verse.

During the summer of 1959, Queen Elizabeth II saw the Stratford, Ontario, Canada, production of Othello, which featured Douglas Campbell as the Moor. No stranger to the role of Othello, Campbell had played the part in Scotland and at London's Old Vic Theatre
on October 31, 1951, with Paul Rogers as Iago and Irene Worth as
Desdemona. Campbell's lauded portrayal of the Moor was described
by Brooks Atkinson as "the most engrossing Othello this playgoer
has seen anywhere." Douglas Rain made an attractively clever Iago
while France Hyland's Desdemona "lacked force" against Kate Reid's
"superb" Emilia.

The American Shakespeare Festival Theatre of Stratford, Connecticut produced Othello in the summer of 1970, with Lee Richardson as Iago, Roberta Maxwell as Desdemona, and a capable and talented black actor Moses Gunn as Othello. Gunn, born on Wednesday, October 2, 1929, in St. Louis, Missouri, had portrayed Aaron, the Moor in Titus Andronicus (1967) for the New York Shakespeare Festival. Walter Kerr's rapturous review published June 28, 1970, in the New York Times extolled Gunn's musical voice; Kerr singled out the "Put out the light" and "Soft you" passages. These, "as Mr. Gunn is reading them, are the two most beautiful moments to be savored anywhere on the American stage just now. We aren't able to use the word 'beautiful' often these days. The tools that might force us to it are allowed to be idle. Mr. Gunn is a master of them."

On September 14, 1970, the Stratford production of Othello, directed by Michael Kahn, was transferred to Broadway's ANTA theatre for a limited engagement of sixteen performances. Between summer and autumn a different perspective of the Stratford production and of Moses Gunn's Othello was seen by Howard Thompson of the New York Times. Thompson viewed Gunn's interpretation of Othello as that of a martyr racked with self-pity. He wrote, "Facially and with an exotic accent and a quivering voice that he uses like a tuning fork, Mr. Gunn conveys the despair and frustration of an explosive poet, not a strong man in hell."

Nachum Buchman, a fine actor from Israel's Habima Theatre, bravely struggled with the English language and lost, in his performance as the Moor (June 7, 1973, in Canada's Stratford production of Othello). Douglas Rain, who was an excellent Iago to thirty-seven-year-old Glasgow, Scotland-born Douglas Campbell's Othello in 1959, again glowed as the cleverly deceitful Iago; and Martha Henry was a placidly dignified Desdemona. But their effective supporting performances could not offset the unintelligible dialogue of Mr. Buchman. Five years later at Canada's Stratford Theatre (with Domini Blythe as Desdemona), Alan Scarfe gave, according to one critic, "a profoundly anguished characterization of the jealous, maddened Moor--fueled by Nicholas Pennell in a virtuoso performance as Iago."

Raul Julia, a versatile actor shuttling with ease from comedy to musicals to drama, was born in San Juan, Puerto Rico on Saturday, March 9, 1940. Julia had played the part of Demetrius in the New York Shakespeare Festival's 1967 production of Titus Andronicus, in which Moses Gunn was Aaron, the Moor. In 1971, he delighted Broadway as Proteus, in the musical version of Two Gentlemen of Verona and in 1979 succeeded Frank Langella in the title role of Dracula on Broadway. On August 7, 1979, at New York's Delacorte Theatre, Julia blacked up as the Moor of Venice for the New York Shakespeare Festival revival of Othello, directed by Wilford Leach.

Raul Julia's Moor was seen as "the most romantic Othello" the New York Times critic Mel Gussow could remember. Gussow reported "The actor has the power and the range to encompass tragedy, and his lilting voice is a mellifluous accompaniment to Shakespeare's verse." Richard Dreyfuss, who had played Iago to Paul Winfield's Othello in Atlanta, Georgia the same season, created a skillful portrait of Iago brushed with witty wickedness. The two actors complemented one another in their expert portrayals; Frances Conroy was "an enchanting Desdemona." As described by Gussow, here was an Othello who "renewed proof that an American company can be at one with Shakespeare."

Some Shakespearean scholars and professional pundits have denounced what they consider the dangerous precedent set by Paul Robeson, a precedent that now makes it axiomatic to cast a black actor in any revival of Othello. Their cavil that this presumed postulation cannot support the lack of talent among black actors who are neither schooled in reciting blank verse nor have, at best, a nodding acquaintance with Shakespearean tragedy plus the substitution of a racially conscious concept for the original Elizabethan Shakespearean context admittedly does find support for their accusations in past performances by blacks as Othello. Their hypothesis has been denounced as racism and academic when confronted with the past history of many whites masquerading as black Othellos who could not recite blank verse and for whom the tragedy was well beyond their minimal talents. But, then, there is James Earl Jones.

James Earl Jones, son of actor Robert Earl Jones, born at Arkabutla, Mississippi on Saturday, January 17, 1931, graduated from the University of Michigan in 1953. Jones married and divorced white actress Julienne Marie (Hendricks) who played Desdemona to his Othello in the New York Shakespeare Festival production at the Delacorte Theatre on July 8, 1964; Mitchell Ryan was Iago and Sada Thompson was Emilia. After 25 performances and a tour of the summer theatre circuit, Othello reopened at New York's Martinique Theatre on October 12, 1964, with Mitchell Ryan as Iago and Flora Elkins as Desdemona. In repertory with Bertolt Brecht's Baal, Shakespeare's Othello completed 216 performances.

Jones's greatest success in the American theatre was in Howard Sackler's Pulitzer Prize-winning play, The Great White Hope which opened on Broadway on October 3, 1968, for 546 performances. For his bravura performance as the heavyweight black boxing champion, Jack Johnson, Jones received both a "Tony" Award as Best Actor of the Year and an "Oscar" nomination for his performance in the screen version of the play. On January 19, 1978, Jones opened, for 77 performances, in the title role of Philip Hayes Dean's one-man show Paul Robeson (with Burt Williams at the piano). Despite James Earl Jones's growing fame, British Equity refused BBC's request to cast him in their September 1979 telecast

BARRY and FRAN WEISSLER

in association with CBS VIDEO ENTERPRISES

by special arrangement with DON GREGORY

present

James Earl

Jones and **Plummer**

Christopher

in William Shakespeare's

Othello

an American Shakespeare Theatre Production

with

In alphabetical order

ROBERT BURR — GRAEME CAMPBELL — KELSEY GRAMMER

AIDEEN O'KELLY — DAVID SABIN — RAYMOND SKIPP

and

KIM BEMIS — RICHARD DIX — RANDY KOVITZ

PATRICIA MAUCERI — HARRY S. MURPHY — ELLEN NEWMAN

ROBERT OUSLEY — BERN SUNDSTEDT — MEL WINKLER

DIANNE WIEST

Sets Designed by	*Hair Design by*
DAVID CHAPMAN	PATRIK D. MORETON
Costumes Designed by	*Fights Staged by*
ROBERT FLETCHER	B.H. BARRY
Lighting by	*Music by*
MARC B. WEISS	STANLEY SILVERMAN
Casting by	*Production Stage Manager*
MEG SIMON/FRAN KUMIN	THOMAS KELLY

Directed by

PETER COE

Program: James Earl Jones and Christopher Plummer in <u>Othello</u>

of Othello (The Shakespeare Plays series). BBC's accurate appraisal that Great Britain had no black British actor of Jones's talent
and stature was answered by British Equity's hiring a white actor
to perform in blackface.

Prior to his compelling performance as Othello during the 1981-
1982 season, James Earl Jones had appeared in a variety of Shakespearean roles for twenty-two years. Stratford, Connecticut's
American Shakespeare Theatre alternated Henry V with Peter Coe's
production of Othello, featuring James Earl Jones as the Moor,
Christopher Plummer as Iago, and Shannon John as an inadequate
Desdemona (July 7 to September 5 in 1981). On February 3, 1982,
Othello was remounted on Broadway at the Winter Garden Theatre
and became the most outstanding production of the tragedy in this
decade.

No stranger to the Moor, James Earl Jones gave an impressive
and deeply moving performance, stressing the agonizing jealousy of
the man but, unlike other interpretations of the role, strongly em-
phasizing the black Moor's love for his accused white wife. Christopher Plummer, an actor of incredible range, gave an awesome
characterization of Iago, superbly wielding his double-edged sword
of honesty and deceit--an approach that would have been admired
by Edwin Booth. Plummer's stunning performance was ably described by Walter Kerr: "The concept is brilliant, the execution
perfect." This splendid Othello was marred only by the miscasting
of Dianne Wiest (who later was succeeded by Cecilia Hart) as Desdemona. The Jones-Plummer Othello completed 122 performances
and received a "Tony" Award for the "Outstanding Reproduction of
a Play."

Periodic presumptive psychological and learned theorization
expounded on the raison d'être, of Shakespeare's characters, but
this became secondary to the academic debate on the degree of
Othello's color. The color controversy has raged throughout the
years. Shakespeare and his colleagues considered "blackamoor"
descriptive of Ethiopians, Gold Coast Negroes, and other black Africans. "Blackamoor," as defined in the Oxford Dictionary in 1548,
was "Ethiope, a blake More, and a man of Ethiope." The term
"Ethiope" had been frequently used to describe Satan. Also familiar
were the Roman and Grecian superstitions that black translated to
anything malevolent, condemned, or terminal. Reginald Scott's
1584 The Discovery of Witchcraft described a damned soul taking
the shape of a "blackemoore." The black Spanish-Moorish dancer
Morisco had performed in Shakespeare's time and blacks from the
Gulf of Guinea and the River Niger had also been seen.

Iconography, from the Middle Ages through the sixteenth century, represented wickedness and evil as blackfaced men. Giraldi
Cinthio established the Moor as black in his 1565 tale, Il Moro di
Venezia, from which Shakespeare derived his play Othello. Ban-
dello's Novelle (based on a tale by Pontanus which had been included in Belleforest's Histoires Tragiques) appeared in an English
translation in 1569; according to this translation, a black Moor
vengefully rapes his master's wife and murders her and their children.

On January 6, 1605, Inigo Jones and Ben Jonson produced
their first Court Masque at Whitehall's Banqueting Hall. The court
entertainment was called The Masque of Blackness and featured
Queen Anne and her ladies-in-waiting as Negresses (or Moors) in
deep, coal-black makeup. Queen Anne was aware of the concept of
the Moor; she had seen Othello performed the previous year. Ben
Jonson described Queen Anne's wish to appear in the Masque with
the ladies of her court as "Black-mores, daughters of the River
Niger" (then known as a region inhabited by the blackest people
on earth).

Shakespeare's Titus Andronicus, performed in 1594 ten years
before Othello, followed the Greek and Roman superstition of black
as evil. Scott's damned soul took the shape of a "blackemoore" in

the character of satanic black Aaron, the Moor. Aaron refers to
his soul as black like his face and "Coal-black is better than another
hue, in that it scorns to bear another hue." The white Queen
Tamora's son sired by Aaron is described as "A joyless, dismal,
black and sorrowful issue." Aaron challenges this by saying, "is
black so base a hue?" and proudly proclaims "Look how the black
slave smiles upon his father" (act 4, scene 2).

Negro and Moor are equated in the sentence spoken by Lorenzo to Launcelot in act 3, scene 5 of The Merchant of Venice. In
the same play, the Prince of Morocco is described as a "tawny Moor,"
although Portia refers to him as having "the complexion of a devil"
(which to Elizabethans meant black). In Love's Labour's Lost,
Shakespeare wrote "Black is the badge of hell, the hue of dungeons
and the suit of night" (act 4, scene 3). Additionally, the Moor was
seen as being predominantly black in George Peele's character Mully
Hamet. Hamet is called "the negro" in Peele's 1589 play, The Battle
of Alcazar, and in Marlowe's Lust's Dominion; or the Lascivious Queen.
Aphra Behn's Abdelazar, or the Moor's Revenge is clearly black, and
her vivid description of the hero in her novel Oroonoko leaves no
doubt as to his color. Edward Young's Zanga, the Moor in his play
The Revenge, firmly confirms the supposed blackness of the Moor.
The Conquest of Granada in 1670 included several black Moors:
Almanzor (Charles Hart); Abdelmelech (Michael Mohun); Boabdelin
(Edward Kynaston).

Michael Udall's play Ezechias (performed in 1564) included
very black Assyrians. Shakespeare left little doubt as to Othello's
color and registered no dissent when, in 1604, Richard Burbage
portrayed Othello as a coal-black man. No standard makeup formula was described by Shakespeare, but he was specific and deliber-
ate about Othello's color throughout the text. Iago (act 1, scene 1)
speaks to Desdemona's father Senator Brabantio, "Even now, now,
very now, an old black ram is tupping your white ewe" and to Lieutenant Michael Cassion (act 2, scene 2), "have a messure to the
health of black Othello." Othello in act 3, scene 2 states, "now
begrimed and black as mine own face"; "Arise black vengeance
from thy hollow cell" and "Haply, for I am black!" Emilia in act 5,
scene 2 calls Othello, "you the blacker devil!"

G. K. Hunter in his 1978 Dramatic Identities and Cultural
Tradition perceptively noted that although altering Cinthio's tale
and elevating Othello's cultural status, Shakespeare did not change
his color,

> and so produced a daring theatrical novelty--a black hero
> for a white community--a novelty that remains too daring
> for many recent theatrical audiences. Shakespeare cannot
> merely have carried over the colour of Othello by being too
> lazy or too uninterested to meddle with it; for no actor,
> spending his time in "blacking up," and hence no producer,

could be indifferent to such an innovation, especially in
that age, devoted to "imitation" and hostile to "originality."
In fact, the repeated reference to Othello's colour in the
play and the wider set of images of dark and light spread
across the diction, show that Shakespeare was not only
aware of his hero's colour, but was indeed intensely aware
of it as one of the primary factors in his play.

Lecturing on Shakespearean Tragedy, A. C. Bradley stated,

> What appears to me nearly certain is that he imagined Othel-
> lo as a black man and not as a light-brown one. In the
> first place, we must remember that the brown or bronze to
> which we are now accustomed in the Othellos of our theatres
> is a recent innovation. Down to Edmund Kean's time, so
> far as is known, Othello was always quite black. This stage-
> tradition goes back to the Restoration, and it almost settles
> the question. For it is impossible that the colour of the
> original Othello should have been forgotten so soon after
> Shakespeare's time, and most improbable that it should have
> been changed from black to brown. If we turn to the play
> itself, we find many references to Othello's colour and ap-
> pearance.

Philip Burton (the Sole Voice, 1970) theorized that "Moor" was
not descriptive of the concept of Negro or Black. "To the Eliza-
betheans to be fair was to be beautiful, so that 'fair' came to mean
'beautiful.' All ladies shunned the sun, for sunburn was the sign
of a peasant. And the opposite to 'fair' was 'black.'" In support
of his definition, Burton cited Shakespeare's Dark Lady of the
Sonnets:

> "Then will I swear beauty herself is black,
> And all they foul that thy complexion lack."

Over the centuries the actors' selection of makeup for Othello
was as varied as their performances and often contrary to the description given by Shakespeare in the text. Beyond Shakespeare's
aesthetic element, Othello's color is central to the tragedy or, as
Shakespearean scholar, director and actress Margaret Webster wisely explained it, "The difference in race between Othello and every
other character in the play is, indeed, the heart of the matter."
Writer James Rees noted, "All the saponaceous compounds that ever
emanated from a 'Critic's Brain' cannot wash that color out." John
Edward Taylor wrote, "Shakespeare placed a Negro-head upon the
shoulders of one of the most noble and accomplished of the proud
children of Ommiades and the Abassides."

Although his predecessors--Burbage, Quin, Garrick, Kemble,
and others--had presented an unmistakably black Othello, Edmund
Kean's appearance as a café-au-lait Moor was found by Shakespearean

scholar, critic and poet Samuel Taylor Coleridge to be "a pleasing possibility." Kean's rationale for the lighter makeup was that it gave greater awareness and appreciation to his facial expressions. Tommaso Salvini later wrote in his 1893 Leaves from the Autobiography of Tommaso Salvini, "I spent my time in Gibraltar studying the Moors" and modeled his image of Othello after one who was "between copper and coffee, not very dark and he had a slender moustacho and scanty curled hair on his chin. I sought to copy his gestures, movements and carriage."

Constantin Stanislavsky in his autobiographical My Life in Art (translated by J. J. Robbins, 1924) felt he had found "Othello himself. In one of the summer restaurants of Paris I met a handsome Arab in his national costume--I learned several bodily poses which seemed to me to characteristic...." Stanislavsky copied the skin tone of the light-colored Arab for his unsuccessful experiment in Othello. Edwin Booth appeared as a copper-toned Othello while Edwin Forrest was accused of painting his Othello to more closely resemble an American Indian. Charles Fechter envisioned Othello as a half caste.

Edwin Forrest recorded his makeup formula in 1827 as "Burnt terra de sienna, unburnt terra de sienna, ivory black number one quality; the above colors must be ground with almond oil on a glass stone--to be ground to the utmost then placed in a bladder and tied up." Laurence Olivier, as would be expected, closely followed Shakespeare's description of the Moor in the text and devised one of the blackest Othellos ever seen. Olivier justified his emphasis on color as follows:

> We hear towards the end of the play that he came from Mauretania, which was right on the blackest east coast of Africa. And some people have it that he's a Berber Moor. A blackamoor doesn't mean a Moorish Moor at all. A black man was a blackamoor. He was a black man. And all Shakespeare cared about was the idea of a black man strangling a white girl.

Paul Robeson theorized that Othello is

> a tragedy of racial conflict, a tragedy of honor rather than jealousy--The fact that he is an alien among white people makes his mind work more quickly. He feels dishonor more deeply. His color heightens the tragedy.... In Shakespeare's time, I feel, there was no great distinction between the Moor and the brown or black--In Shakespeare's own time and throughout the Restoration, notably by Garrick, the part was played as a black man. This was not changed until the time of Edmund Kean, about the middle of the nineteenth century, when he [Othello] became brown. I feel that had to do with the fact that at that time Africa was the slave

center of the world and people wanted to forget the ancient glory of the Ethiopians. Surely, most of the Moors have Ethiopian blood and come from Africa, and to Shakespeare's mind he was called a blackamoor.

G. K. Hunter, in his essay on Othello and color prejudice included in his book Dramatic Identities and Cultural Traditions (1978), perceptively wrote "assuming that soul is reality and body is appearance, we may say that Iago is the white man with the black soul while Othello is the black man with the white soul."

The New York Times review (September 17, 1873) of Tommaso Salvini's Broadway debut as Othello was an apotheosis to his acting genius. But the critic also pontificated on the eternal controversial color enigma taking exception to Salvini's less than black makeup in contradictory verbiage:

> He makes him a negro—this, we may be sure, was not Shakespeare's conception of Othello whom all the circumstances and allusions of the play point out as a Moor, one of a race whose characteristic traits, physical, intellectual and moral, are quite unlike those of the negro—In the whole play there is but one passage regarding Othello as a negro —that in which Iago says "Why, what a fortune shall the thick lips owe"—it is to be remembered that the notions of Englishmen as to the appearance of the inhabitants of Africa were very vague and confused in Shakespeare's time.

Ignoring the intelligence that no one can improve a master-piece posed no determent for several eager dramatists including translators, in their egotistical pursuit toward the "reconstruction" and "improvements" of Shakespeare's plays. Translations of Shakespeare's Othello met with as many variations and interpretations as did the performances of the play. Jean François Ducis (1733-1816) substituted Alexandrine couplets for Elizabethan blank verse in his mangled translations of Shakespeare's plays. His final effort in 1792 was a radical French adaptation of Othello, which featured a double denouement--one with a happy ending to the tragedy.

Ducis's ingenious reworking of Othello had Héldemone (Desdemona) rejecting the Doge's son Lorédan's (Captain Michael Cassio) proposal of marriage in favor of the black Moor. Héldemone sends a necklace to Lorédan that had been given to her by the Moor. She also sends a letter unwittingly renouncing her vows to Othello; this she does to save her father from political disgrace. Lorédan's devious friend Pézare (Iago) takes the letter and necklace to Othello, falsely claiming he has killed the Doge's son. The Doge and Lorédan convince the Moor that his false friend has lied about the entire affair, but the jealous and enraged Othello has already stabbed Héldemone to death. The despondent Moor dies of disgrace and remorse for his lost love.

Although France was awash in the world's bloodiest revolution, Ducis's first dramatic ending offended the fragile sensibilities of the opening-night French audience. The playwright appeased the outraged onlookers by altering his epitasis of Othello to the Moor's forgiveness of Pézare and the blissful reconciliation of the prospective black bridegroom with white Héldemone. Ducis also softened and modified the Moor's character and color, explaining, "I thought that a yellow, copperlike complexion, which is, in fact, suitable also for an African, would have the advantage of not revolting the public, especially the ladies."

Author Carbon de Flins des Oliviers saw no reason why the newly liberated French Revolutionists should be disturbed by Othello but would

find it quite acceptable that a white woman loves a man of a

color somewhat different from her own, if that man is young,
handsome and passionate. They will not be scandalized to
see a bed upon the stage, for the republicans, who have
more manners than the subjects of a monarchy are not, as
the latter, slaves of a false modesty, which is the hypocritical affection of decency.

Ducis's inventive version of Othello was performed at Paris's
Richelieu Theatre on November 26, 1792, with the great French
tragedian François-Joseph Talma as the Moor, Jacques-Marie Monuel
as Pézare (Iago), and Mlle. Simon as Héldemone (Desdemona). According to his biographer, Herbert F. Collins, Talma appeared
"ochre-coloured lest a blackamoor should outrage the feelings of the
French audience."

Talma, amid the French Revolution, revolted against the bombastic, stilted artificiality of the overly elegant French style of acting. The critics, those keepers-of-the-flame of tradition, retaliated. Countering the lethal rhythm of the guillotine and wholesale
decapitation, critic Abbe Geoffroy deplored Talma's Othello.

> His triumph lies in the portrayal of passion worked up to
> delirium, to insanity. The gloomy genre is bad in itself,
> because plays of horror are not suited to French audi-
> ences; they should be left to the population of London.
> Talma hits upon extraordinary intonations, that produced
> a shudder of fear; but these happy hits are so infrequent
> and their effect so transitory, that he would do well to re-
> turn again within the boundaries of art.

François-Joseph Talma, whose birth was registered in Paris on
Saturday, January 15, 1763, became one of the French theatre's
greatest Othellos and was the founder of the Théâtre de la Repub-
lique. Talma was Napoleon Bonaparte's favorite actor and, with the
Empress Josephine, he attended Talma's performance in Othello on
March 6, 1809 (the actor's wife, Caroline Vanhove, was Héldemone).
Talma wore a turban devised from a scarf that had been given to
him, personally, by the Empress Josephine. Six years before his
death on Thursday, October 19, 1826, Talma reinstated Shakespeare's tragic ending to Ducis's sophistic translation of Othello.

England's eminent tragedian William Charles Macready wrote,

> The genius of Talma rose above all the conventionality of
> schools. Every turn and movement as he trod the stage
> might have given a model for the sculptor's art, and yet
> all was effected with such apparent absence of preparation
> as made him seem utterly unconscious of the dignified and
> graceful attitudes he presented. His voice was flexible and
> powerful, and his delivery articulate to the finest point
> without a trace of pedantry. There was an ease and

freedom, whether in familiar coloquy, in lofty declamation, or burst of passion, that gave an air of unpremeditation to every sentence, one of the highest achievements of the histrionic art.... To my judgement, he was the most finished artist of his time, not below Kean in his most energetic displays....

Known as Frédérick Lemaître, Antoine-Louis-Prosper Lemaître was born at Le Harve on Monday, July 28, 1800. He made his first appearance in Othello in a minor (and interpolated) role, as gondolier, in Antoine Cuvelier de Trye's crude 1818 translation, Le More de Venise. Lemaître's fame increased when he burlesqued an overly melodramatic pastiche (L'Auberge des Adrets by Benjamin Antier, Locoste Saint-Amand and Paulyante) into a successful farce on July 2, 1823, at the Ambigu-Comique Theatre on Le Boulevard du Temple (which, in 1823, the Almanach des Spectacles in 1823 proposed renaming Le Boulevard du Crime, as it was known to Parisians because of the bloodcurdling, thunderous, murderous melodramas presented on the stage of the Ambigu-Comique).

Using the leading character of L'Auberge des Adrets, in 1834 Lemaitre wrote a play called Robert Macaire after receiving permission from the original author, Maurice Alboy, and playwrights Antier and Saint-Armand. Playing the leading role in the premiere of Robert Macaire for seventy-nine performances (the play had opened on June 14, 1834, at the Folies-Dramatique Theatre) established Lemaître as the premier actor on the French stage; he was dubbed "the Talma of the Boulevards." His play Robert Macaire became the famous musical comedy Erminie, adapted by Harry Paulton and Edward Jakobowski; Erminie premiered at London's Comedy Theatre on November 9, 1855, and opened at New York's Casino Theatre on May 10, 1886, for 571 performances, assuring stardom for the first president of Actors' Equity, Francis Wilson.

Alexandre Dumas specifically rewrote Kean, ou Désorde ou Génie for Lemaitre, a role that the actor performed at the Variétés Theatre in 1836. Lemaitre also created the title roles in Victor Hugo's play Ruy Blas at the Théâtre de la Renaissance on November 8, 1838, and in Phillippe-François Pinel Dumanoir and Adolph Eugène Phillipe D'Ennery's play Don César de Bazan in 1844. Frédérick gave a fine performance in the title role of Ducis's Le More de Venise with Marie Dorval (née Delaunay) as Heldemone at the Odeon Theatre in Paris in 1830. In 1835 Lemaitre bravely appeared at London's Lyceum Theatre in Ducis's glamorized version of Othello.

On August 17, 1835, the Comédie-Française prevented Frédérick's opening in Othello at the Théâtre Porte-Saint-Martin, claiming Ducis's Le More de Venise was exclusively part of their repertoire. Frédérick returned to blackface in the title role of Anicet-Bourgeois' and Dumanoir's play Le Docteur Noir (The Black Doctor) in 1846 at the Théâtre Porte-Saint-Martin. He applied the burnt

cork again at the same theatre on April 6, 1850 in the title role of
Alphonse de Lamartine's play Toussaint Louverture. Paul Robeson
re-created Toussaint Louverture in Peter Godfrey's production of
C. L. R. James's English translation of Lamartine's drama (London's
Westminster Theatre, March 15, 1936). The celebrated Frédérick
Lemaître died in Paris on Wednesday, January 26, 1876.

Preceding Ducis's there were ten translations of Shakespeare's
plays (1746 to 1749) by Pierre Antoine de la Place; Othello was one
of them. Unsuccessful adaptations were made by Douin in 1773,
Pierre La Tourneur in 1776, Butini in 1785, and Cuvelier in 1818.
A reworking of Othello called La Vengeance failed at Paris's Théâtre
de la Nation in 1791. The best and most frequently produced
translation of Othello was made in 1829 by poet Comte Alfred Victor
de Vigny (1799-1863). The translation was called Le More de Venise. It closely followed the original text and was the first translation to be done in blank verse.

De Vigny's Le More de Venise was produced on October 24,
1829, at the Théâtre Française. It ran for sixteen performances
with Joanny (Jean-Baptiste Bernard Brissebarre) as the Moor and
Mlle. Mars as Desdemona. Mlle. Mars was Anne Françoise Hippolyte
Boutet, the illegitimate daughter of French actor Jacques-Marie
Boutet, who was known on the stage as Monvel. During a visit to
Paris, William Charles Macready described Mlle. Mars's performance
as Desdemona. He said it was "a luxury to the ear to drink in the
dulcet and harmonious breath that her utterance of the poet gave
forth. Nor was her voice her only charm: in person she was most
lovely, and in grace and elegance of deportment and action unap-
proached by her contemporaries." Macready might have added that,
as Desdemona, Mlle. Mars exposed a good deal more to the audience
than merely her "grace and elegance."

In Italy, where Cinthio's saga had originated, Alessandro
Verri translated Othello into Italian about 1778. Ten years later
a Venetian socialite Giustina Renier-Michiel made another translation.
Giacomo Sernani, Virginio Sencini, and Ignazio Valletta all made
Italian adaptations of the tragedy in 1830. Tommaso Salvini's drama-
tic teacher actor Gustavo Modena translated the play in 1843, but
Modena's performance and his translation at Milan's Teatro Re were
both disastrous. Giulio Carcano's adaptation of Othello in 1843 be-
came the standard, and most frequently produced, Italian version.
It was in Giulio Carcano's Italian translation that Salvini made his
Broadway debut as the Moor on September 16, 1873.

Christian Martin Wieland made the first German translation of
Othello in the late 1700s. In addition, he adapted twenty-one of
Shakespeare's plays. Johann Heinrich Voss's German translation of
Othello in 1805 was edited by Johann von Schiller. August Wilhelm
von Schlegel published sixteen of his German Shakespearean trans-
lations (including one of Othello) from 1797 to 1810. Germany's

brilliant actor-director Friedrich Ludwig Schroeder was the first to present Shakespeare's plays in Germany in the late 1700s; his production of Othello failed.

A Russian translation of Ducis's reconstruction of Othello appeared in Moscow in 1806, with N. J. Iakovlev as the Moor. L. L. Leonidov was more successful as the Moor on November 23, 1859, in P. I. Weinberg's Russian translation of Othello. Michael Iourievitch Lermontov's 1835 play Masquerade was Othello transferred to Russia. Masquerade gained fame in Karl Theodor Kasimir Meyerhold's February 25, 1917, production at St. Petersburg's Alexandrinski Theatre.

The Othello jealousy motif was continued throughout many plays. Edward Young's 1721 drama The Revenge is a composite of Othello and Aphra Behn's 1676 Abdelazar; or the Moor's Revenge with overtones of Marlowe's Lust's Dominion (featuring Zanga, the Moor, or Young's creation of a black Iago). François Marie Arouet (known as Voltaire) modeled his 1732 play Zaire on Othello; Pedro Calderon de la Barca's seventeenth-century drama El Medico de su honra also mirrored the Moor. Carlo Marenco's drama Pia dei Tolomei was a resetting of the Othello saga, and Chief Forester Urich in Otto Ludwig's 1853 drama Der Erbforster was a Deutschland composite of Othello. Manuel Tamayo y Baus's 1867 Un drama Nuevo also found its inspiration in The Moor of Venice.

Shakespeare's dramas inspired librettists and composers of the Opera world; one of the first of Shakespeare's tragedies to be adapted to the operatic stage was Othello. The theatre voice of Othello was determined to be baritone or basso profundo. As Orson Welles explained to Kenneth Tynan in reference to Laurence Olivier's reluctance to take on the Moor, "Larry's a natural tenor and Othello is a natural baritone." But on the operatic stage Othello became a tenor.

Gioacchino Antonio Rossini (1792-1868) composed his nineteenth opera Otello, ossia Il Moro di Venezia with a libretto written by Marchese Francesco Berio di Salsa. Rossini's Otello was first heard at the Teatro del Fondo in Naples on December 4, 1816, with Andrea Nozzari in the title role, Giuseppe Ciccimarra as Jago (Iago), and Isabella Colbran as Desdemona. Tenor Enrico Tamberlik later gained international fame as Rossini's Otello. Two decades later Giuditta Pasta and Maria Malibran became bored with the placid role of Desdemona and appeared in blackface as Otello. Tenor Manuel de Popolo Vincente Garcia and his company first performed Rossini's Otello in New York at the Park Theatre on February 7, 1826.

Verdi, an idolator of Shakespeare, set Macbeth to music in 1847. The tragedy also became the libretto for Hippolyte-Andre-Jean-Baptiste Chélard's opera; in 1910 Ernest Block completed his operatic version of Macbeth. Commissioned by King Frederick William IV of Prussia, Felix Mendelssohn expanded his 1827 Overture to a Midsummer Night's Dream into a musical score for the entire play. Mendelssohn's complete score for A Midsummer Night's Dream included the world famous "Wedding March" to whose tempo countless brides have braved the journey down the aisle. The entire score was first performed in Potsdam on October 14, 1843.

Shakespeare's As You Like It was the basis for Hector Berlioz's 1862 opera Béatrice et Bénédict. Charles-François Gounod's extremely popular Roméo et Juliette appeared in 1867, overshadowing Vincenzo Bellini's 1830 I Montecchi ed i Capuleti, diminishing Niccolo Antonio Zingarelli's less notable version, and remaining superior to Riccardo Zandonai's 1922 Giulietta e Romeo. Charles-Louis-Ambroise Thomas's opera Hamlet was produced in 1868. Giuseppe Verdi's last opera was Falstaff (1893), based on Shakespeare's

The Merry Wives of Windsor and portions of Henry IV. Charles-
Camille Saint-Säens' operatic version of Henri VIII failed.

Seventy-three-year-old Giuseppe Fortunino Francesco Verdi
(1813-1901) dubbed his two-year operatic translation of Shakespeare's
Othello "the chocolate project." Verdi's Otello, with a libretto by
Arrigo Boito (omitting the entire first act of Shakespeare's Othello),
successfully premiered on February 5, 1887, at Milan's La Scala
Opera House, with Francesco Tamagno in the title role, Romilda
Pantaleoni as Desdemona, and Victor Maurel as Iago. The premiere
was conducted by Franco Faccio and, in the orchestra pit, was a
nineteen-year-old cellist named Arturo Toscanini.

The American premiere of Verdi's Otello was less successful.
The opera opened at New York's Academy of Music on Friday, April
13, 1888. It was produced by Italo Campanini and starred Marconi
as the Moor, Eva Tetrazinni as Desdemona, and Antonio Galassi as
Iago. Verdi's Otello gained greater recognition and fame on March
24, 1890, at the Metropolitan Opera House, with Tamagno in his
original title role, Giuseppe del Puente as Iago, and Emma Albani
as Desdemona. Historian George C. D. Odell felt Tamagno's international reputation exceeded his talent but wrote,

> Tamagno had a voice of tremendous power and of extraor-
> dinary range which soared easily above the noisiest of op-
> eratic finales, and, in moments of lyric ecstasy or passion
> could ring out like a clarion; but it had the nasal quality
> known as white--He was of fine presence, a commanding
> figure, and he portrayed Otello to the life, in magnificence
> of appearance, and in passionate acting not unworthy of
> Salvini.

The Metropolitan presented Jean de Reszke in the title role
of Otello on January 11, 1892, with Emma Albani as Desdemona and
Eduardo Camera as Iago. Odell noted, "the beautiful mellow tones
of de Reszke threw the violent vocalism of Tamango quite into the
background." On November 24, 1902, the Metropolitan Opera
opened their season with Otello. The title role was sung by Albert
Alvarez to Emma Eames's Desdemona and Antonio Scotti's Iago.

On December 25, 1908, Arthur Hammerstein presented six performances of a superb production of Verdi's Otello at his four-year-
old Manhattan Opera House, with Giovanni Zenatello in the title role,
Mario Sammarco as Iago, and the great Nellie Melba as Desdemona.
Czech tenor Leo Slezak (father of Walter) was lauded in his debut
at the Metropolitan Opera House on November 17, 1909, for his brilliantly sung and acted performance as the Moor in Otello, conducted
by Arturo Toscanini, with Antonio Scotti as Iago and Frances Alda
as Desdemona. Six-foot seven-inch Slezak lifted his Desdemona high
above his head and slowly crossed the stage to drop her on the bed
and strangle her.

After Slezak's departure from the Metropolitan, Otello was
shelved until December 22, 1937, when aging Giovanni Martinelli
superbly sang the title role, with Lawrence Tibbett as Iago and
Elizabeth Rethberg (who had replaced Eide Norena who had replaced Gina Cigna) as Desdemona. Oscar Thompson (the New York
Times) wrote,

> As Otello, Giovanni Martinelli, now in his twenty-fifth sea-
> son at the Metropolitan, shared with Verdi the proof that
> success is not the peculiar prerogative of the young. His
> characterization of the Moor must be ranked among his best
> achievements--Subtler Iagos than that of Lawrence Tibbett
> undoubtedly have walked the same boards.

Without a rehearsal, and having sung the role only once before in
Mexico City, Chilean tenor Ramon Vinay hurriedly replaced Torsten
Ralf in the title role of Otello at the Metropolitan on December 9,
1946, with Leonard Warren as Iago and Stella Roman as Desdemona.
Placido Domingo has played the Metropolitan's Otello during the
eighties with shining brilliance. A compilation of the Metropolitan
Opera's leading artists in their productions of Otello is included in
Appendix "A."

Besides being adapted for opera, Shakespeare's plays provided librettos for several adaptations to America's and England's
musical comedy stages. Earlier, Charles Lecocq's Marjolaine had
appeared in 1877. Lecocq's opera bouffe was loosely based on Cym-
beline and starred Marie Aimée. Richard Rodgers' remarkably talented lyricist Lorenz Hart suggested Shakespeare's The Comedy of
Errors as the basis for a Broadway musical comedy. The Comedy
of Errors was adapted (with one line of the original text), produced,
and directed by George Abbott, who turned it into a successful
musical comedy called The Boys from Syracuse. Blessed with a
spirited score by Rodgers and Hart and choreographed by George
Balanchine, The Boys from Syracuse opened on Broadway at the
Alvin Theatre on November 23, 1938; it ran for 235 performances.
Abbott and Shakespeare's musical twins were Eddie Albert (Antipholus of Syracuse) and Ronald Graham (Antipholus of Ephesus), with
Jimmy Savo and Teddy Hart romping in tandem as the Dromios.

Shakespeare's A Midsummer Night's Dream was adapted by Gilbert Seldes and Erik Charrell as Swingin' the Dream; the play
opened at New York's Centre Theatre on Wednesday, November 29,
1939. Jimmy Van Heusen's music, with lyrics by Eddie de Lange,
was augmented by Mendelssohn's "Spring Song" and "Wedding
March" and interpolated with various popular standards such as
"St. Louis Blues," "Ain't Misbehavin'," "Melancholy Baby" and others.

Transplanted somewhat "south of Shakespeare" to 1890 New
Orleans, Louisiana, Swingin' the Dream featured a predominantly

black cast headed by Louis Armstrong as Bottom, Maxine Sullivan
as Titania, Juan Hernandez as Oberon, Butterfly McQueen as Puck,
Oscar Polk as Flute, Jackie "Moms" Mabley as Quince, Bill Bailey as
Cupid, and Dorothy Dandridge as Second Pixie. The players were
backed by Benny Goodman's Sextet (Goodman, Lionel Hampton,
Fletcher Henderson, Charles Christian, Arthur Bernstein and Nick
Fatool) installed in a stage box. Swingin' the Dream, alas, be-
came a thirteen-performance casualty.

Cole Porter's sparkling musical comedy Kiss Me, Kate, with
Bella and Sam Spewack's clever libretto that interchanged Shakespeare's The Taming of the Shrew with a modern backstage tale,
opened on Broadway at the Century Theatre on December 30, 1948,
and completed 1,077 performances. Arthur Laurents brilliantly
transposed Romeo and Juliet to Manhattan's steaming summer streets.
The ongoing teenage gang-wars occurring between Puerto Rican
"Sharks" and American-born "Jets" replaced feuds that occurred
between the Montagues and Capulets. Laurent's West Side Story
was conceived, superbly directed, and choreographed by Jerome
Robbins, with music and lyrics by Leonard Bernstein and Stephen
Sondheim. West Side Story became one of the theatre's greatest
musical hits, opening on September 26, 1957, at Broadway's Winter
Garden Theatre. The musical compiled 981 performances on Broadway and 1,040 performances in London.

Your Own Thing, a rock-musical, spoofed Twelfth Night; music and lyrics were by Hal Hester and Danny Apolinar in a delightful adaptation by Donald Driver. The musical opened on January
13, 1968, at off-Broadway's Orpheum Theatre; it ran 937 performances. Ten days before the opening of Your Own Thing, another
musical reworking of Twelfth Night appeared at New York's Sheridan
Square Playhouse on January 3, 1968. Adapted and directed by
John Lollos, Love and Let Love retained Shakespeare's characters
and paralleled his text. Music was composed by Stanley Jay Gelber;
lyrics were written by Don Christopher and John Lollos. The show
disappeared after fourteen performances.

America's foremost and most capable play-doctor, the inestimably talented playwright-director George Abbott, at the age of
eighty-nine resorted to the Bard of Avon for yet another version
of Twelfth Night and rechristened it Music Is. Mr. Abbott strove
to maintain Shakespeare's verse and complex text, but his expertise
in transferring The Comedy of Errors to The Boys from Syracuse
in 1938 was not repeated on December 20, 1976, when Music Is
opened on Broadway at the St. James Theatre only to fade away
after eight performances.

Retaining Shakespeare's title, Two Gentlemen of Verona arrived on Broadway at the St. James Theatre on December 1, 1971.
John Guare and Mel Shapiro's joyous and successful adaptation
(music by Galt MacDermot and lyrics by John Guare) delighted

audiences for 613 performances. Hamlet hit the rocks on February
17, 1975, at Broadway's Minskoff Theatre. The rock musical devised by Cliff Jones and directed by Gower Champion was called
Rockabye Hamlet. The adaptation was pronounced "flashy and vulgar" and mercifully became a ghost after seven performances.
Rockabye Hamlet was first aired by the Canadian Broadcasting Company via radio in 1973 and staged under the title of Kronborg:
1582 on Prince Edward Island and in other places in Canada.

Othello had been successful as an opera, and it was inevitable
that the tragedy would eventually become grist for the mill of the
commercial, modern musical-makers. Englishman Jack Good, an
alumnus of Balliol College of Oxford University, reconstructed
Shakespeare's Moor into a black evangelist who was plagued by
malicious racist Iago. Iago was grappling for the souls of Othello
and Desdemona in a manner reminiscent of Mephistopheles' pursuit
of Faust in Goethe's poem. The Othello-Faustian motif was set in
America's Southwest. Music was by Ray Pohlman and Emil Dean
Zoghby.

Roosevelt "Rosy" Greer, a six-foot five-inch former Los Angeles Ram tackle trying to quarterback the art of acting, had originally been named for the lead in Good's Othellian opus, Catch My Soul.
Black actor William Marshall who, for several years, had frequently
played the title role in Othello, and was praised for his performance
as God in a 1951 Broadway revival of Marc Connelly's 1930 Pulitzer
Prize play, The Green Pastures, appeared in the role of Othello at
the world premiere of the musical at Los Angeles' Ahmanson Theatre
on March 5, 1968. Rock star Jerry Lee Lewis made his legitimate
stage debut as the racist Iago, and Julienne Marie, who had been
James Earl Jones's Desdemona in 1964, repeated her performance as
the Moor's wife and victim in this rock 'n' roll hymn to homicide.

The two-act, two hour and twenty minute Centre Threatre
Group production of Catch My Soul was riddled with contemporary
jargon and Elizabethan verse. It received mixed notices from the
Los Angeles press. Due to the radical, racist theme of the rock
musical, plans to transfer the show to Broadway were abandoned
after the murder of Dr. Martin Luther King on April 4, 1968. The
British premiere of Catch My Soul was at Manchester, England on
October 17, 1970. The production opened at London's Round House
Theatre on December 21, 1970, extending its run at the Prince of
Wales Theatre the following year.

In his Christian Science Monitor London review headlined
"Rocking the Bard," Harold Hobson questioned the validity of Catch
My Soul: "Is it a thing worth having? The answer unequivocally
is yes. What it seems to me to accomplish is to set out the background of turmoil and savagery from which, when it came to the
push, Othello's ultimate barbarism sprang." Jack Good described his
script and concept for Catch My Soul as

a collage. We took the various texts of Shakespeare's
Othello and cut them into little bits. We threw about half
the bits away and stuck the rest together again, interlard-
ing lines here and there from other Shakespearean plays,
sonnets, The Rape of Lucrece, etc. and then we improvised
occasionally with modern coloquial speech and kept some of
the resulting lines.

Helen Dawson, reviewing the London production for Plays and
Players, wrote,

It's an inspired and lively evening, an intelligent and inventive reworking of Shakespeare's Othello by Jack Good,
who also plays an old, ham-style, pitch-blacked-up Moor--
Strangely, and to his credit, Good has managed to marry
the fragments of authentic Shakespeare with almost contemporary slang and Hollywood scripts of a couple of decades
ago. Catch My Soul, if it were tightened, could certainly
stand along side other successful Shakespearean musicals
like Kiss Me, Kate and West Side Story.

Good's overblown performance as Othello almost played second
to his intense black makeup, which created one of the blackest
Othellos (other than Laurence Olivier's) in history. Lance Le Gault
was a show-stealing, reptilian Iago, "a full scale villain, a Ku Klux
Klan man." Sharon Gurney was a believable Desdemona, but P. J.
Proby was sadly miscast as Cassio; P. O. Arnold brightened the
stage as a black Bianca. Roy Pohlman and Emil Dean Zoghby's nineteen songs for Catch My Soul were classified as "derivative and
largely unmemorable" and included such titles as "That Handkerchief," "Willow," "If Wives Do Fall," "Good Name," and "Comfort
Forsake Me."

In 1973, Metromedia Producers Corporation produced Jack
Good's screen version of Catch My Soul. Directed by British actor
Patrick McGoohan, the film featured Richie Havens as Othello, Lance
LeGault as a hippie Iago, Season Hubley as flower-child Desdemona,
Tony Joe White as Cassio, and Susan Tyrrell as Emilia. The film
received deadly damning critical coverage. London critic Tom Milne
dismissed it as "a sort of comic strip travesty of the play--less
watchable than the unspeakable Godspell. Catch My Soul starts
with the disadvantage of an opportunistic book which simply lifts
the love-and-jealousy theme out of Othello, rephrases it in religious
terms in a Jesus freak milieu, and leaves it at that." Vincent Can-
by reviewed the film for the New York Times on March 23, 1974,
as "pricelessly funny though seldom meaning to be--It's the hybrid
plot and dialogue that keep one in what is genteelly called stitches."
Only three of Ray Pohlman and Emil Dean Zoghby's songs from the
original stage production were used. Tony Joe White, who was the
film's Cassio--"a wino from Baton Rouge, Louisiana"--composed most
of the film's songs to Jack Good's lyrics; additional numbers were
written by Delaney Bramlet.

During the 1965-1966 theatrical season, the Dance Theatre of
José Limon performed a ballet (The Moor's Pavane) based on Othello.
José Limon was Othello; Lucas Having danced Iago; and Betty Jones
was Desdemona.

THE REEL OTHELLO

Transition from stage to screen of Othello started early in
motion picture history with Cinés' 1907 short film, directed by Mario
Caserini, with Ubaldo Del Colle of the Italian stage as the Moor.
An unusual filming of Othello was made in Germany by director
Oskar Messter in 1907-1908. He used a process called Biophon by
which a recording of "The Death of Othello" from Verdi's opera was
synchronized with the film and lip-synched by Franz Porten, as
Othello, with his young daughter, Henny Porten, as Desdemona
(Henny was later to become Germany's great film star.)

J. Stuart Blackton produced several of Shakespeare's plays
in 1908 at the Brooklyn studios of the Vitagraph Company of America. The one-reel films were all directed by William V. Ranous and
included: The Comedy of Errors (February); Macbeth (April);
Romeo and Juliet (May); Richard III (September); Antony and Cleopatra (October); Julius Caesar (November); The Merchant of Venice
(December). Othello had no release date. William V. Ranous directed and played the title role in Vitagraph's 1908 Othello, with
Julia Swayne Gordon as Desdemona and Hector Dion as Iago. Denmark's Nordisk Films released a ninety-five meter screen version
of Othello on November 14, 1908; this version featured Carl Astrup
as the Moor.

The Societa Anonima Pineschi (Latium Film) produced a short
film of the play in 1909; the film was directed by Giulio Enrico
Novelli, son of the stage's Othello, Ermente Novelli. Film d'Arte
Italiana filmed Othello in Venice in 1909. The movie was directed
by Gerolamo Lo Savio, with Ferruccio Garavaglia as Othello, Cesare
Dondini as Iago, and Vittoria Le Panto as Desdemona. At the age
of eighty-three, the great Tommaso Salvini wisely declined a proposal to record his world famous Othello on film in 1912.

The Societa Anonima Ambrosio's full-length, five-reel feature
film of Othello was produced in Venice by the Photo Drama Company
and released by George Kleine in America on July 6, 1914. The
Venetian feature cast Paolo Colaci as Othello, Léna Lenard as Desdemona, and Riccardo Tolentino as Iago. Comedies based on the
jealousy motif in Othello, but on little else, were also produced.
Thomas A. Edison released a one-reel comedy on June 9, 1913, called
Othello in Jonesville. The film was written and directed by Herbert

Prior, who also played the leading role of James Reginald White-
stone. Paul Beckers was seen in a German travesty Der Fliegentuten-
Othello in 1915, and Camillo De Riso appeared in a 1920 Italian parody.

Leonce Perret, who had appeared in a short Gaumont comedy,
which was known as Leonce Plays Othello (1914), wrote a script titled A Modern Othello,* in which Robert Hyde, during rehearsals
for a charity performance of Shakespeare's tragedy, dreams he is
Othello killing his wife Clarice playing Desdemona. The five-reel
Harry Rapf production for Pathé was directed by Perret and retitled
first, The Shadow of Night and then, The Lash of Jealousy. On
July 22, 1917, the film was finally released as The Mad Lover, starring Robert Warwick as Hyde/Othello and Elaine Hammerstein as
Clarice/Desdemona.

A former Bensonian, Alexander Matheson Lang was born in
Montreal, Canada on Thursday, May 15, 1879, and was successful
in the title role in Othello at Manchester, England in January, 1907.
Twelve years later, Lang and H. C. M. Haringe translated Pordes
Milo's Italian play Sirocco for the English stage. Sirocco generously
borrowed the denouement of Shakespeare's Othello, and Lang and
Haringe retitled the play Carnival, which opened at London's New
Theatre on February 11, 1920, for a successful engagement of 188
performances. Lang played Shakespearean actor Silvio Steno whose
jealousy is aroused by his actress-wife Simonetta's (Hilda Bayley)
off-stage affair during carnival time in Venice with Count Scipione
(Dennis Nielsen-Terry). Steno, releasing his pent-up jealous fury
on-stage during a performance of Othello, tries to strangle his wife,
who is playing Desdemona.

During the run of Carnival, Lang also appeared to critical acclaim in his well-mounted production of Shakespeare's Othello. He
acted in fifteen matinee performances, with Arthur Bourchier as a
wicked, scarlet-clad Iago. But Lang's ambitious plan of reschedul-
ing Othello to evening performances and Carnival to matinees never
materialized. Audiences preferred the modern play to Shakespeare's
tragedy. W. M. Darlington (the Daily Telegram) pinpointed the
audience's whimsical choice, "To them Carnival had reality and
Othello had not: it was as simple as that."

The Moor, as Lang interpreted him, had dark, shoulder-length
hair and makeup "black as dead of night." His acting was favorably
compared to Salvini's masterful portrayal of Othello. W. MacQueen-
Pope (a descendant of Thomas Pope of Richard Burbage's early seventeenth-century Shakespearean company) reasoned in The Footlights
Flickered that Lang's performance as the Moor was due to "That im-

---

*A 1914 American film of the same title, featuring Margarite Fischer
and Harry Pollard was related to Shakespeare's play only by the
jealousy theme.

immense strength of personality which Lang possessed and which
made his Othello better than Tearle's. It can be safely said that
Lang's was a great Othello."

    Godfrey Tearle, son of the prominent English actor Osmond
Tearle, was born in New York City on Sunday, October 12, 1884.
He made his Broadway debut at the Forty-fourth Street Theatre,
on December 24, 1919, as the jealous actor in Carnival. The play
was frigidly received by critics and public. Margot Kelly and A. E.
Anson were considered hopelessly inadequate as Steno's wife and
lover, respectively. On April 21, 1921, Tearle won laurels in the
title role of Othello. The play was J. B. Fagan's production at
London's Court Theatre. Tearle played opposite Basil Rathbone's
Iago and Madge Titheridge's Desdemona. On April 30, 1948, Tearle
was Stratford-upon-Avon's Othello, with Anthony Quayle as Iago
and Diana Wynyard as Desdemona. Tearle repeated his performance
as the Moor at Stratford on June 17, 1949, with John Slater as Iago
and Wynyard, again, as Desdemona.

    W. Macqueen-Pope described Godfrey Tearle, half-brother of
screen star Conway Tearle and a descendant of William Augustus
"Handsome" Conway, as having the right height and "handsome, his
figure magnificent; he had a wonderful smile, great charm and a
splendid voice, which he knew exactly how to use." Two years before his death on Monday, June 8, 1953, at the age of sixty-eight,
Godfrey Tearle was knighted.

    Carnival was filmed in Venice with Matheson Lang, Hilda Bay-
ley, and Ivor Norvello. The film was directed by Harley Knowles
and released in England in April, 1921. M. A. Malaney (Moving
Picture World) found the acting rather heavy "But it was done dif-
ferently and divides interest with the beautiful settings. The New
York Times considered the film "all too theatrical to be dramatic.
And too wordy to be cinematographic." Lang revived the play on
June 9, 1923, at London's New Theatre; it played sixty-five performances.

    Ten years after Carnival was filmed in Venice, Herbert Wilcox
reproduced and directed the play for the screen in England, with
Matheson Lang (then the highest paid actor in English films) re-
enacting his role of Steno/Othello, Dorothy Bouchier as Simonetta/
Desdemona, and Joseph Schildkraut as the amorous Count Andreas.
The second film version of Carnival was released in England in
November, 1931. London critic Ernest Marshall lamented Herbert
Wilcox's "passion for photography, and not for one moment do the
actors in Carnival seem to be real flesh and blood--While Matheson
Lang has not added to his reputation by this film, he has not low-
ered it as Mr. Schildkraut has done."

    The greatest of the many European actors imported by Holly-
wood in the mid-1920s was Emil Jannings, who was born Theodor

Emil Janenz on Saturday, July 26, 1884, at Rorschach, Switzerland.
Jannings was a stage actor trained in Max Reinhardt's Berlin theatre
company prior to entering motion pictures. He attained international
fame in F. W. (Friedrich Wilhelm) Murnau's superb expressionistic
classic German film Der Letzte Mann (The Last Laugh) and in E. A.
(Ewald-Andre) Dupont's 1925 German film Variete.

Dimitri Buchowetzki directed Emil Jannings in Der Mohr (or
Othello), which was produced in Germany in 1922. Jannings had
portrayed the Moor on the German stage. His screen performance
was applauded when the German film version of Othello premiered
before a select audience at New York's Century Theatre Roof in
January 1923. The New York Times reported, "Janning's performance as Othello is an impressive piece of work. He makes you feel
the genuine character of the Moor, his simplicity, his strength and
his weakness." C. S. Sewell (Moving Picture World) wrote, "Emil
Jannings in the title role gives a magnificent performance, bringing
out the pathos and tragedy of the dark-skinned Moor's romance
with the fair Desdemona." Ica Lenkeffy performed beautifully as
Desdemona and Werner Klaus (another Reinhardt alumnus) was char-
acterized as vital and vigorous as Iago, though given to occasional
bursts of overacting.

On May 16, 1929, Emil Jannings became the first actor to receive the Academy of Motion Pictures Arts and Sciences Best Actor
Award. He was awarded this honor for his brilliant performances in
Paramount Pictures' The Way of All Flesh (1927) and The Last Command (1928). The advent of sound and the talking screen ended
Janning's career in America. He returned to Germany, where he
appeared as Professor Immanuel Unrath in Josef von Sternberg's
memorable film Der Blaue Engel (The Blue Angel), which launched
Marlene Dietrich to international stardom. On Monday, January 2,
1950, Jannings died at the age of sixty-five at Lake Wolfgang,
Stroblhof, Austria.

Based a story by Walter Reisch that utilized Shakespeare's
Othello as the basis of another love-hate triangle, Alexander Korda's
1936 film production called Men Are Not Gods was directed by Walter
Reisch. The film derived from a scenario by C. B. Stern, Iris
Wright, and William Hornbeck. In this reworking of the tale, actor
Edmund Davey (Sebastian Shaw) attempts to kill his pregnant actress-wife Barbara (Gertrude Lawrence) on-stage during a performance of Othello. Aware of his homicidal intentions, Davey's
astute mistress, Ann Williams (Miriam Hopkins), prevents Davey
from committing murder. Frank S. Nugent (the New York Times)
found Reisch's story traveling "an uncertain road with erratic steps
--Quite a muddle, really."

The interplay of Othello with off-stage characters was more
brilliantly realized in France in Jacques Prevert's innovative drama
which involved two historically famous French actors reflecting

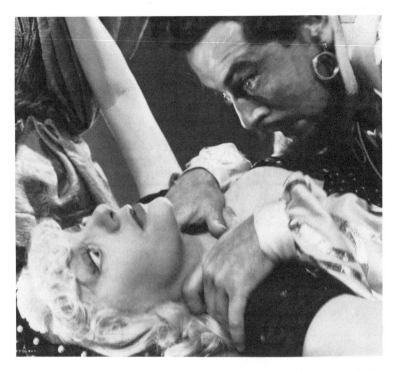

Gertrude Lawrence and Sebastian Shaw in Men Are Not Gods, 1936 (courtesy of The Free Library of Philadelphia Print and Pictures Dept.).

Shakespeare's Moor. Jean-Gaspard-Baptiste Deburau (France's most famous pantomimist, established in his interpretation of the "lovesick, languishing and yet potentially cruel" Pierrot Gilles in Le Boeuf enragé [1827]), became the world's prototype for poor Pierrot. Deburau and his contemporary at the Théâtre des Funambules, the celebrated French actor Frédérick Lemaître, became the protagonists of Jacques Prevert's original screenplay Les Enfants du Paradis (Children of Paradise); Prevert expertly captured the theatricality, style, and essence of the Romantic Period of the nineteenth-century French theatre.

Produced by Pathé Consortium Cinema, Les Enfants du Paradis was filmed in 1943 during the Nazi occupation of France in Nice. Prevert's brilliant script was directed by Marcel Carne; it premiered in Paris at the Palais de Chaillot, on March 9, 1945. The film lasted three hours and fifteen minutes and was a fictionalized competition of the two actors for the love of lovely actress Garance, who was

married to Count Edouard de Montray. Carefree Lemaître despairs
of playing the Moor, never having experienced jealousy until he
falls in love with Garance. Only through the character of Othello
can he release his submerged jealousy. Lovelorn Baptiste, however,
believes "One could make a nice pantomime out of Othello. A man
who kills for love, and dies of it!" Both actors expressed Prevert's
hypothesis, "Why ask people their names when they hide their real
selves?" Lemaître hid behind the blackface of Othello, and Baptiste
masked himself behind the white makeup of Pierrot.

Marcel Carne described the film in L'Homme Libéré (October
3, 1944) as "a tribute to the theatre; nowadays it would be known
as the children of the gods, they are actors, the beloved heroes of
the public." Jacques Prevert explained "the gods" as "the cheapest
seats in the theatre, the worst, the furthest away from the stage,
for the 'people'--that is why it was called Paradise, in those days"
and the actors became the Children of Paradise.

Les Enfants du Paradis was re-released in 1965 and verified
its established reputation as one of the world's classic films. The
performances of Pierre Brasseur as Lemaître/Othello, Jean-Louis
Barrault as Deburau/Pierrot and Arletty as Garance, with Marcelle
Monthil as Desdemona and Jean Lanier as Iago, maintained their
lustre even after twenty years.

In October, 1965, Raymond Durgnat (Films and Filming) cited
Les Enfants du Paradis as "one of the most profoundly Surrealistic
films ever made.... For this film the passing of the years has
proved a fountain of youth" which is "complex and rich in para-
doxes as only the work of genius can be (and the genius is Prevert's)." Viewed by Bosley Crowther (the New York Times) in
February 1947, Les Enfants du Paradis was seen as overlong but
also as a "frequently captivating film which has moments of great
beauty in it and some performances of exquisite note." Eric Rhodes
in A History of Cinema from Its Origins to 1970 perceptively wrote,
"on this occasion Carne brought such excitement to Prevert's ideas
that he really was able to incarnate a poet's dream. Seldom has
the feeling of life backstage, or of miraculous stage performance,
been so fully realized."

For their eclectic screenplay, A Double Life, produced by
Michael Kanin for Universal Pictures and directed by George Cukor
in 1947, Ruth Gordon and Garson Kanin used the same general
theme as found in The Mad Lover, Carnival, and Men Are Not Gods;
there were overtones of Dr. Jekyll and Mr. Hyde. The Gordon-
Kanin collaboration had actor Anthony John (Ronald Colman) strangling his mistress, waitress Pat Krol (Shelley Winters), and becoming
insanely, but unwarrantedly, jealous of his ex-wife actress Brita
(Signe Hasso) and their theatrical agent Bill (Edmund O'Brien).
During a performance of Othello, mentally deranged Anthony John
attempts to strangle Brita (Desdemona).

Time magazine found Colman's performance, "a pleasure in itself, but the real delight is to watch his delight in his job.   Colman
is not a great actor, but he gives an arresting demonstration of
what a good actor can do with great material when he cares enough
to do it."   Director George Cukor later said, "I question whether
he had the danger and madness for a great Othello, on the stage or
in real life.   Some can be scary, some can't, and Colman was a most
gifted actor who didn't have a sense of the demonic.   He played
Othello the way he saw it, within his vision, his strengths and his
limitations.

Walter Hampden, who had portrayed the Moor on Broadway in
1925, coached Colman for the film's Othello sequence, which was
filmed in New York's famous, late Empire Theatre.   After a long
and distinguished screen career, Ronald Colman won the Golden
Globe Award and the Academy Award as Best Actor of the Year for
his portrayal of Anthony John/Othello in A Double Life (March 20,
1948).

Correctly finding the climax of A Double Life predictable,
Bosley Crowther (the New York Times) reported, "But otherwise
Miss Gordon and Mr. Kanin, in collaboration with William Shakespeare, have whipped up a modern drama which thoroughly employs
the screen to demonstrate the strange excitement and deathless
romance of the theatre" while handing Ronald Colman "the role of
his lengthy career."

John Slater was the Moor in England's filming of Othello released in November 1946, with Lucanne Shaw as Desdemona and
Sebastian Cabot as Iago.   England also produced a series of scenes
from Shakespeare's plays in 1953.   They were performed by the
Young Vic Players, known as The World's A Stage series; the series
included Othello.

Orson Welles, with his usual frenzy of financial turmoil--and
his excessively prolonged and exhaustive creative chaos--freely
adapted, produced, directed and played the title role in Othello.
The Wellesian version became a four-year marathon project.   It was
interrupted by necessary financial excursions, which required Orson's appearance in the films The Black Rose and The Third Man
--there was also a London radio series based on his Third Man
character, Harry Lime.   The Othello odyssey progressed in falter-
ing pace from Mogador (with its fifteenth-century Portuguese fortress) to Marrakesh, Safi, Mazagram, Venice, Torcella, Tuscania,
Viterbo, Perugia, Rome, Paris, and London.

Initially, in 1948, several scenes were filmed in Venice, with
Welles's current romantic interest, Italian actress Lea Padovani,
playing Desdemona.   French actress Cecile Aubry succeeded Padovani for two swift and unproductive days; then American actress
Betsy Blair was signed for the role of the Moor's wife.   French-

Canadian actress Suzanne Cloutier eventually became the final Desdemona, although Padovani and Blair are glimpsed in fleeting shots
in the film, as are Joseph Cotten as a nameless senator and Joan
Fontaine as a page boy.

Irish actor Micheál MacLiammóir, a former associate from
Welles's youth and early theatrical training with the Dublin Gate
Theatre, was signed to portray Iago. MacLiammóir and Hilton Ed-
wards (who, bombastically, would play the role of Brabantio in
Welles's Othello) founded the Dublin Gate Theatre in 1928, where
Edwards played Iago to MacLiammóir's Othello. Under their man-
agement, sixteen-year-old Orson Welles appeared in seven plays
from October 1931 to February 1932 (Jew Suss; The Dead Ride
East; The Archduke; Mogu of the Desert; Death Takes a Holiday;
Youth's the Season; and, on February 2, 1932, Hamlet [as the
Ghost]). From January 27, 1949, to March 7, 1950, MacLiammóir
had maintained a diary, taking from it an entertaining and revealing account of the travels and travail of Welles's Othello (described
as a "chic but highly neurotic lumber camp"), which was published
by Methuen & Co., Ltd. in 1952. Using Iago's advice to Roderigo
in act 1, scene 3, MacLiammóir titled his book Put Money in Thy
Purse.

A crescendo critical chorus greeted the release of Welles's
Othello in 1952. Eric Bentley deprecated Welles's performance as
the Moor as follows: "he never acts, he is photographed." The
New Yorker magazine calculated that the film contained "half a hundred cinematic tricks," whereas Joseph McBride described the film
as "nevermore floridly expressionistic--self absorbed and rhetorically
diffuse--decadent indeed" but "this does not preclude the film from
many moments of spellbinding purity and grace." An English critic
wrote, "Visually, the film has the characteristic Wellesian excitement, and the equally characteristic lapses into the pursuit of showy
effects for their own sake. Infuriatingly perverse, Othello again
displays the strength and the limitations of its creator's aggressive,
undisciplined talent." MacLiammóir gave a confused portrayal of
Iago, offering little contest to Othello, and was "almost impossible
to understand." Additionally, fifty-three-year-old Micheál Mac-
Liammóir (born in Cork, Ireland on Wednesday, October 25, 1899)
was hardly credible as twenty-eight-year-old Iago.

During his 1953 lecture at the Edinburgh Film Festival, Welles
screened the first reel of his Othello. The reel opened with the
funeral cortège of Othello and Desdemona and the capture of Iago,
who is flung into a small cage and hoisted to the top of Mogador's
fortress. The Mogador Film Production of Othello was shown as a
Moroccan entry at Cannes on May 10, 1952. The Cannes Film Festival awarded Welles its highest award, The Grand Prix; his beleaguered Othello tied for first place with an Italian film, Two
Pennyworth of Hope.

On September 13, 1955, Bosley Crowther reviewed the film
for the New York Times, "Shakespeare himself set down before it,
might have a tough time recognizing his play." Crowther described
Welles's Moor as "hollow and heartless as a shell" then dismissed
the motion picture as having "just a little Shakespeare and a lot of
Welles." Time magazine noted "The film has all over it the stamp
of Orson Welles's brummagem genius." Robert Downing (Films in
Review) succinctly summarized the much traveled Othello as "full
of contradictions as its producer-adaptor-director-star ... the film
is stamped with Orson's amazing insight and gross negligence."

Jack C. Jorgens (Shakespeare on Film) wrote, "Welles's Othello
is one of the few Shakespeare films in which the images on the
screen generate enough beauty, variety, and graphic power to
stand comparison with Shakespeare's poetic images." But weighing
the mangled text and garbled soundtrack Jorgens added, "In short,
Welles's Othello is an authentic flawed masterpiece." Andrew Baz-
in's June, 1952 review of Othello in Cahiers du Cinema (the review
was translated by Charles W. Eckert) praised Welles's adaptation of
Shakespeare's tragedy as being

> profoundly faithful to Shakespeare's poetry. I can think of
> no other director in the world who could cut so much out of
> the original text and replace it with visual spectacle without
> inviting ridicule.... However, I cannot wholeheartedly
> praise Welles's editing, for it seems extremely fragmented,
> shattered like a mirror relentlessly struck with a hammer.
> Carried to such a degree, this stylistic idiosyncrasy be-
> comes a tiresome device.

Russia's reverence for Shakespeare's tragedies, especially
Othello, became increasingly evident three years after Welles's photographed Moorish architecture and "artistic improvements" to the
text. Sergei Yutkevitch, maintaining his credo of "The ideas of
the artist and author must become one if the translation is to suc-
ceed," brilliantly adapted and directed Othello. The Mosfilm-
produced Othello was filmed in the Crimea in Sovcolor and won
Yutkevitch the 1956 Cannes Festival Award for best direction.

Yutkevitch spent six weeks in rehearsal prior to filming. In
his article, "My Way with Shakespeare," for Films and Filming in
October 1957, he noted, "The actors had to enter and grow into
their roles. This task was eased considerably for them by the
method of taking scenes in sequence. We were able to film Shakespeare's acts in the order he wrote them (not always possible when
making films)." Later, Yutkevitch stated in a 1960 interview, "To
begin with mine is an adaptation of Shakespeare's play while Welles's
is a series of variations on a theme of Shakespeare." Referring to
Welles's opening sequence of the funeral of Othello and Desdemona,
Yutkevitch added, "I start from life. Welles from death."

Sergei Yutkevitch completed his exceptionally fine screen version of Othello in 1955, with Sergei Bondarchuk in the title role
after Paul Robeson had been unable to accept Mosfilm's invitation
to portray the Moor. Following the film's first showing in England
with the original Russian soundtrack and music by Khachaturian,
Yutkevitch's Othello was released in England in 1957 with a print
by Technicolor. It was dubbed into English by a group of talented
English actors directed by William de Lane Lea. The dubbed English voices were Howard Marion Crawford (Othello), Arnold Diamond
(Iago), and Kathleen Byron (Desdemona).

Three years later the Russian Othello opened in New York.
A. H. Weiler (the New York Times) ably described the Soviet film
as "beyond a doubt, a most beautiful, literally colorful and motion-
filled version of the tragedy that dwarfs any Othello constricted by
the confines of stage and proscenium arch." The English dubbing,
however, was poorly synchronized to Russian lips, and this flaw
weakened the impact of the original Russian version. Sergei Bondarchuk portrayed a powerful, exciting Othello and Andrei Popov
was an intensely disquieting Iago in contrast with Irina Skobtseva's
finely defined Desdemona.

In 1961, Bob Roberts and Michael Relph produced--and Basil
Dearden directed--a modern version of Othello called All Night Long.
During the English film, the displaced Shakespearean characters
were caught up in the miasma of the jazz world. Patrick McGoohan
(who later directed Jack Good's 1973 screen version of his rock
musical concept of Othello, called Catch My Soul) became Johnny
Cousin, a jazz-drumming Iago. Cousin convinces black jazzman
Aurelius Rex (Othello), played by Paul Harris, that his faithful
white wife singer, Delia Lane (Desdemona), acted by Marti Stevens,
is having an affair with Rex's white agent, Cass Michaels (Michael
Cassio), played by Keith Michell. Cousin's villainous friendship is
exposed only after Rex tries to strangle his wife. Betsy Blair, one
of Orson Welles's several aborted Desdemonas, was cast as Emily
(Emilia), Cousin's wife. All Night Long was properly and summarily
dismissed as follows: "To combine an all-star jazz jamboree and a
modern idiom version of Othello in one film is to make sure that no
one satisfied--both unconvincing and wearying."

In 1960, Russia's Gruziya-Film produced a markedly African-
inspired dance drama which, without a word of spoken text, closely
followed Shakespeare's play. Adapted by Uri Golovani and director
Vakhtang Chabukiani, the dance version of Othello, called Venet-
sianskiy maur, was released in the Soviet Union in September 1961.
The ninety-four minute Ballet of Othello with music by Alexei Macha-
variani was filmed in Sovcolor. Chabukiani was the Moor, Vera
Tsignadze was Desdemona, and Zurab Kikaleyshvili was Iago. They
appeared with members of the Paliashvili Opera Theatre and Georgia
State Ballet of Tbilisi for whom Chabukiani had originated the dance
role of Othello in 1957. The photographed ballet was viewed as

Laurence Olivier and Maggie Smith in the filmed National Theatre production of <u>Othello</u>, 1964 (courtesy of The Free Library of Philadelphia Print and Pictures Dept.).

reflecting "a DeMille surge and spectacle, and the progression of the film as a whole flows with the same vitality as the spatial rhythms which are an integral part of it." Howard Thompson, reviewing the film for the <u>New York Times</u> on May 7, 1964, called it "Shakespeare with electricity"; it "bulges with sound, fury, color and high-geared theatrically--sparked by Vakhtang Chabukiani as the hero, a lavish array of supporting performers, sets and costumes and a surging tidal wave of music--sinuous, barbed, bombastic and tender in turn."

The panegyrical publicity given to Laurence Olivier's

revolutionary and controversial interpretation of the Moor in the
National Theatre's production of Othello (London's Old Vic Theatre,
April 23, 1964) convinced producers Anthony Havelock-Allan and
John Brabourne of British Home Entertainment that it was important
to "preserve and enhance this Othello and more or less present it
as one might have seen it at the National Theatre and to recreate
completely the atmosphere, effect and immediacy of the theatre performance, using the basis of film technique."

During three weeks in July 1964 at England's Shepperton
Studios, the National Theatre's production of Othello was filmed in
Panavision and Technicolor under the direction of Stuart Burge.
The two-hour, fifty-minute film was the filmed play. Olivier's
Moor loomed larger than life but the motion picture never attained
emancipation from the proscenium. Frank Finlay's Iago, which had
been overshadowed on the stage, surfaced on film in a performance
praised as "fluid and brash." Maggie Smith's Desdemona was categorized as "vibrant" and "sensitive." But Olivier's Moor was once
again contested. Critical observations and assessments produced
no oblations.

In Shakespeare and the Film, Roger Manvell capsulized the
variables in the theatrical presentation and filming:

> Othello is a supremely difficult if not impossible part to
> render successfully except from the distance of the stage
> for which it was specifically written. Nevertheless, one is
> more than grateful to have this record of a performance
> which must rank as one of the great bravura achievements
> of the century in the British theatre.

Bosley Crowther's objurgatory review in the New York Times
appraised Olivier's Othello as "one of the boldest you'll ever see."
Crowther was as appalled at Olivier's blackface, as was Sir Laurence's good friend and staunch supporter actress Dame Sybil Thorndyke who, after seeing his performance at London's Old Vic Theatre
was aghast and exclaimed "Oh, that Negro!" Crowther compared
Olivier's makeup to "Rastus or an end man in an American minstrel
show. You almost wait for him to whip a banjo out from his flowing
white garments or start banging a tambourine."

In June, 1966, David Wilson (the British Film Institute) described Olivier's photographed stage performance as

> too calculated, too worked on. This is an all-African Othel-
> lo, from his looks--to his mannerisms, which at times border
> on parody and assumed the characteristics of (dare one say
> it?) nothing more complex than the chocolate-coloured coon.
> It is indeed a towering performance, but it is essentially a
> stage performance and matches ill with the more restrained
> subtleties of Frank Finlay's Iago.

The film industry had frequently borrowed Shakespeare's Othellian jealousy motif while also using Othello as background or focal point. Italy's Giaguaro Film produced Il peccato di Anna (Anna's Sin) in 1953, in which an American black actor (Ben E. Johnson), while in Rome rehearsing Othello, seeks revenge for a framed prison term. Johnson falls in love with his Desdemona, Anna Curti, played by actress Anna Vita.

A virtually unseen jazz version of Othello, conceived by Liz White and filmed on Martha's Vineyard with black actor Moses Gunn as the Moor, was first screened at Howard University during April 1980. Max H. Boulois wrote, produced, and directed a corruption of Shakespeare's tragedy in 1982. Busy Boulois also played the title role in his Othello, which was filmed in Spain under the aegis of Ambdiffusion and Eurocine Productions. The Boulois reworking of Othello demoted the Moor to the leader of a commando brigade operating in Central America. Tony Curtis was a Bronx Iago, and Joanna Pettet was Desdemona; both were involved in one of the daily revolutions of a tropic republic (an Allconfusion and Porcine Production).

Othello on the reel continues a challenge far greater than under the proscenium arch, despite the efforts of Lang, Welles, Bondarchuk, Chabukiani or "Oh, that Negro!" devised by Sir Laurence Olivier.

PART II:

EXODUS

PRELUDE TO A CABIN

The parade of whites masquerading as blacks from Titus Andronicus' Aaron to Othello, Oroonoko, Zanga in The Revenge, Gambia of Surinam in Thomas Morton's play The Slave (played by William Charles Macready on November 12, 1816) swept across the world's--especially America's--stages. In the colonies (according to Sterling Brown), Lewis Hallam's characterization of Mungo in The Padlock (1769), "fathered a long line of comic Negroes in the drama."

Andrew Barton's 1767 "comic opera" The Disappointment; or The Force of Credulity introduced the tune "Yankee Doodle," but Barton's character Racoon was not a Negro; he was a Frenchman murdering the King's English. Impersonations of blacks occurred in Colonel Robert Mumford's presumably unproduced 1770 play The Candidates, which introduced a Negro character called Ralpho. Black characters appeared in John Leacock's play The Fall of British Tyranny; or American Liberty Triumphant, published by Styner & Cist of Philadelphia in 1776. J. Robinson's The Yorker's Stratagem; or Banana's Wedding (May 10, 1792) had whites as West Indian natives; so did Prince Hoore's 1793 The Prize; or 2, 5, 38.

Sambo was recorded by historian Arthur Hobson Quinn as the first, full comic, native American Negro role written for the American stage. The part was played by William Bates on May 22, 1795, at Philadelphia's Chestnut Street Theatre, in John Murdock's comedy The Triumphs of Love; or, Happy Reconciliation. In 1798, Philadelphia barber Murdock's second play, called The Politicians, had four black characters--Pompey, Cato, Caesar, and Sambo. Obi; or Three-Fingered Jack by John Fawcett (music by Samuel Arnold) appeared in 1800 in England, with Ira Aldridge. MacLaren Meadows' play Negro Slaves was seen in Edinburgh, Scotland in 1799.

James Cobb's Paul and Virginia (music by William Reeve and Joseph Mazzinghi) was produced on May 7, 1802. The performance featured dusky Dominique (played by Joseph Jefferson) and a black slave Alambra. Negro songs were interpolated into 1802's A New Way to Win Hearts; Andrew Jackson Allen sang Negro songs in 1815's The Battle of Lake Champlain. A. B. Lindsley's 1807 play, Love and Friendship, or Yankee Notions, listed, in the cast, black Harry and Phillis. Black Caesar appeared in Beach's Jonathan

Postfree; or, The Honest Yankee in 1807, and blacked-up faces
were seen in George Colman's 1808 play, The Africans; or, War,
Love and Duty (music by Michael Kelly).

Various adaptations of Daniel Defoe's adventure novel Robinson Crusoe had their black Fridays. John Durang played a Harlequin Friday to Charles Biddle's Crusoe at Philadelphia's Southwark
Theatre on May 20, 1789, and William Bates was Friday to Charles
Whitlock's Robinson at Philadelphia's New Theatre on May 23, 1794.
Joseph Jefferson was a pantomime Friday in a production on May 11,
1801. A Mr. Bancker--on September 11, 1817--played Friday opposite Edmund Simpson's Crusoe in New York's Park Theatre production of Defoe's story, called The Bold Buccaneers; or The Discovery of Robinson Crusoe.

James Fenimore Cooper's novel The Spy; or a Tale of the
Neutral Ground was adapted to the stage by Charles Powell Clinch
and produced at New York's Park Theatre on March 1, 1822, with
Mr. Bancker as black Caesar. Sol Smith's The Tailor in Distress;
or A Yankee Trick was produced at Cincinnati, Ohio's Globe Theatre
on July 17, 1823, with young Edwin Forrest as the Negro, Cuff.
Samuel Woodworth, the lyricist of "The Old Oaken Bucket," wrote
a play called The Forrest Rose; or American Farmers, which was
staged at New York's Chatham Theatre on October 6, 1825; in the
play, Rose was the Negro slave of Deacon Forrest.

It was in Solon Robinson's 1828 play, The Rifle, in Louisville,
Kentucky, that Thomas D. Rice introduced a song and dance specialty "Jump Jim Crow," which would become tremendously popular
and herald the advent of the first original American form of entertainment called Minstrels. On November 28, 1828, William Dunlap's
A Trip to Niagara; or Travellers in America was performed at New
York's Bowery Theatre; it presented Job Jerryman as "a gentleman
of colour" aspiring to Shakespeare.

Joseph S. Jones's play The Green Mountain Boy was produced
in Philadelphia on March 19, 1833. It starred comedian George Hill,
with a black servant in the cast (Bill Brown). Three years later,
George Handel Hill collaborated with Bayle Bernard to write Old
Times in Virginia; or The Yankee Pedlar, in which comedy and
nostalgia were accompanied by plantation Negroes singing American
folk songs at London's Drury Lane Theatre (November 1, 1836).
George Lionel Steven's The Patriot (1834) had a dancing black servant Sambo doing Rice's "Jump Jim Crow." Cornelius A. Logan's
The Vermont Wool Dealer; or, The Yankee Traveller produced in
Cincinnati, Ohio, on June 4, 1838, utilized Bob, a Negro waiter, and
Betty, a mulatto. Heath's Whigs and Democrats (1839) included a
darkened Cato.

The most amusing comedy relief character was created in Zeke,
a pretentious elaborately uniformed black servant of nouveau riche

Tiffany's of New York, in Anna Cora Ogden Mowatt's (Mrs. William
Foushee Richie) satirical play Fashion. Zeke pompously accepts
Mrs. Tiffany's elevation of his given name of Ezekiel to the more
elegant A-dolphe. Zeke was played by George Skerrett in the
opening of Fashion at New York's Park Theatre on March 26, 1845.
Edgar Allan Poe, then a drama critic, reluctantly recanted his
original deprecating review of Fashion and wrote in The Broadway
Journal, "We can call to mind no drama, just now, in which the de-
sign can be properly stated as the satirizing of fashion as fashion."

Anna Cora Mowatt's comedy was successfully revived at New
York's Provincetown Playhouse on February 3, 1924, for 235 performances; George Brown was Zeke. The Provincetown Players'
"entirely new version" was arranged as a spoof of the original play
by Brian Hooker and Deems Taylor. It was augmented by period
songs such as "My Life is Like a Scentless Rose." The "entirely
new version" was directed by Robert Edmond Jones and James Light,
with Clare Eames as Mrs. Tiffany.

The perennial Negro mammy was first introduced in Mrs. Hexe-
kiah Linthicum Bateman's (actress Sidney Frances Cowell) play Self
as Aunt Chloe. The role was played by Mrs. Dunn at Barton's
Chambers Street Theatre in New York on October 27, 1856. The
same year the minstrel-vaudeville-type Negro appeared as the black
porter, Cuff, in John Brougham's play Life in New York. Mrs.
J. C. Swayze's drama (based on John Brown's Harper Ferry Raid)
called Ossawattomie Brown was produced at New York's Bowery
Theatre on December 16, 1859, and cast several blacked-up whites
as Brown's comrades-in-arms. James McCabe's play The Guerillas
produced in Richmond, Virginia on December 22, 1862, related the
unwillingness of a freed slave, Jerry, to leave the South and go
north.

All of the above was but prelude to the greatest and most enduring character who ever masqueraded in black and who began life
on the stage on New York's National Theatre on August 23, 1852,
and became synonymous with all blackface roles. In more recent,
liberalized times, the play that housed the character has become
anathema and his persona and name is now used in a derogatory
sense, and means subservience. But the longest-running blackface
characterization in the world was infinitely more popular during its
era than Shakespeare's Othello; it was Harriet Beecher Stowe's
creation--the gentle and tragic Uncle Tom.

UNCLE TOM'S CABIN

On November 25, 1862, Massachusetts Senator Henry Wilson took Harriet Beecher Stowe to the White House in Washington, D.C., to meet President Abraham Lincoln. The Great Emancipator Lincoln greeted the petite, ardent abolitionist and deeply religious writer with "So you're the little woman who wrote the book that made this great War?" Mrs. Stowe's inflammatory novel was possibly a great contributing factor to America's Civil War, but Mrs. Stowe did not create the War Between the States anymore than Adolf Hitler's Mein Kampf initiated World War II.

Dr. Gamaliel Bailey first advertised Harriet Beecher Stowe's novel in his Washington, D.C. antislavery periodical, the National Era (May 8, 1851) as Uncle Tom's Cabin; or, The Man That Was a Thing. When the first chapter appeared in the Era in serial form on June 5 the title became Uncle Tom's Cabin, or Life Among the Lowly. The serialized novel ran through fifty installments, which ended on April 1, 1852. John Punchard Jewett of Boston published a two-volume edition of Uncle Tom's Cabin, or Life Among the Lowly on March 20, 1852 (Paper covers $1; Cloth $1.50; Cloth with full gilt $2). Sales of the book reached ten thousand copies weekly by June, 1852 and within the year sold three hundred thousand copies. The phenomenal success of the melodramatic tale was later translated into twenty-three languages. Only the Holy Bible exceeded the popularity and sales of Uncle Tom's Cabin.

In the preface to her novel, Mrs. Stowe wrote,

> The scenes of this story, as its title indicates, lie among a race hitherto ignored by the associations of polite and refined society; an exotic race, whose ancestors born beneath a tropic sun, brought with them, and perpetuated to their descendents, a character so essentially unlike the hard and dominant Anglo-Saxon race, as for many years to have won from it only misunderstanding and contempt. But another and better day is dawning; every influence of literature, of poetry and of art, in our times, is becoming more and more in unison with the great master chord of Christianity, "good will to man."

Harriet Elizabeth Beecher Stowe, born on Friday, June 14,

1811, at Litchfield, Connecticut, was one of thirteen children of the Reverend Lyman Beecher. Harriet married the Reverend Calvin Ellis Stowe, an ardent abolitionist and professor at the Lane Theological Seminary at Cincinnati, Ohio, where her father was president and she and her sister Catherine were teachers. After living eighteen years in Cincinnati, Reverend Stowe accepted a professorship at Bowdoin College in Brunswick, Maine, and there Harriet began writing Uncle Tom's Cabin, or Life Among the Lowly.

The composition of the character of Uncle Tom came from several sources. Harriet's reading included Theodore Weld's 1839 abolitionist pamphlet, American Slavery As It Is, and Lewis Clark's 1845 Narrative of the Life of Frederick Douglass, An American Slave. She had also read Frances Trollope's antislavery novel, The Life and Adventures of Jonathan Jefferson Whitlaw, published fifteen years earlier. At the time of writing her famous novel, Harriet had not met a former slave named Henson but had read his autobiography, The Life of Josiah Henson, Formerly a Slave, Now an inhabitant of Canada, as Narrated by Himself, which was published in 1849. The Reverend Henson was a former escaped slave who became a minister and an activist in the Underground Railroad to Canada helping other escaped slaves to freedom.

Mrs. Stowe acknowledged her debt to Henson in a revised edition of his autobiography, Truth Stranger Than Fiction: Father Henson's Story of His Own Life, as "an exemplification of the truth of the character of Uncle Tom" (dated Andover, Massachusetts, April 5, 1858). Henson's story was further expanded in 1879 as An Autobiography of the Reverend Josiah Henson (Mrs. Harriet Beecher Stowe's "Uncle Tom") from 1789 to 1879 with a Preface by Mrs. Harriet Beecher Stowe. Introductory Notes by Wendell Phillips and John G. Whittier and an Appendix on the Exodus by Bishop Gilbert Haven. The illuminating history of Uncle Tom's Cabin is elaborately detailed in E. Bruce Kirkham's book The Building of Uncle Tom's Cabin, published by the University of Tennessee Press in 1977.

A year after the publication of her famous novel Mrs. Stowe wrote The Key to Uncle Tom's Cabin, in which she identified the sources and prototypes for various characters in the book and acknowledged reading Henson's autobiography (though she had not actually met him prior to the writing of her novel). In a letter to the Brooklyn Magazine editor in 1885, Harriet wrote, "I would say that none of the characters in Uncle Tom's Cabin are portraits—I knew several colored men who showed the piety, honesty and faithfulness of Uncle Tom—but none of them had a history like that I created for him."

Reverend Henson became so internationally identified with the character of Uncle Tom that, at the age of eighty-eight in the year 1877, when he was received at Windsor Castle, Queen Victoria affectionately called him "Uncle Tom." The genial, white-headed,

bearded and noble old man became a resident of Dresden, Canada
and a well-known lecturer. He related his years of bondage as a
slave when a brutal Maryland overseer Bryce Litton "broke my arms
and marred me for life" and spoke of his eventual escape to Canada.
At the age of ninety-two Reverend Henson still toured, giving lectures based on his fascinating life and reflected glory as the original, if controversial, Uncle Tom.

The enormous popularity of Uncle Tom's Cabin produced an
immediate request from Asa Hutchinson for dramatization rights.
Deeply religious Mrs. Stowe, who had filed on May 12, 1851, for
copyright but not for dramatic rights to her novel, wrote to Hutchinson,

> It is thought, with the present state of theatrical perform-
> ances in this country, that any attempt on the part of
> Christians to identify themselves with them will be produc-
> tive of danger to the individual character, and to the gen-
> eral cause--I fear it is wholly impracticable, and as a friend
> to you should hope that you would not run the risk of so
> dangerous an experiment.

Mrs. Stowe's reluctance to agree to the dramatization of Uncle
Tom's Cabin was "wholly impracticable" and a dangerous risk in
several experimentations. The proliferation of stage adaptations began soon after the publication of the novel. Harriet's son Charles
E. Stowe later estimated that various adaptations of the novel had
been performed over three hundred thousand times; but neither
Harriet Beecher Stowe (who died on Wednesday, July 1, 1896) nor
her estate ever received one bleak penny from the many dramatiza-
tions and performances.

Before the forty installments of Uncle Tom's Cabin had completed their course on April 1, 1852, in the Era, a Baltimore professor named Hewitt used the theme of the novel--but altered the
story--to express the Southern concept of happy slavery. The
Hewitt play, titled The Southern Uncle Tom (or Uncle Tom's Cabin
as IT IS), opened at the Baltimore Museum and Gallery of Fine Arts
on January 5, 1852. It was produced by John E. Owens, who also
portrayed noble Uncle Tom devoted to his kind and thoughtful master. Two years later, Dr. William T. Leonard's proslavery satire,
Uncle Tom in Louisiana, appeared at New Orleans' New Amphitheatre
on March 6, 1854, for twenty-three performances.

Charles Western Taylor's adaptation of Harriet Beecher Stowe's
novel was the first to appear on the New York stage. The one-
hour version by Taylor opened at New York's National Theatre on
Monday, August 23, 1852, with the playwright as Uncle Tom as part
of a bill featuring quick-change artist Herr Cline making three costume changes while walking a tight rope and T. D. "Jump Jim Crow"
Rice in an Othello travesty. Rice, as Othello, angrily responded to

black Desdemona's repeated agonizing request for her handkerchief, "Blow yah nose on yah sleeve, nigger, an' git on wid de show!" Taylor renamed several of the characters in the book. He completely omitted Topsy, Eva, and St. Clair, while blithely giving the melodrama a happy ending. The New York Sunday Dispatch found Taylor's remarkable reconstruction "dull--the piece is perfectly harmless, in fact, there is nothing in it whatever."

James Gordon Bennett's antiabolitionist New York Herald took a different view: "The success of Uncle Tom's Cabin has naturally suggested its success upon the stage; but the fact has been overlooked that any such representation must be an insult to the South.... The play, as performed at the National, is a crude and aggravated affair." The crusading Herald proceeded to uphold the institution of Southern slavery as protected by the United States Constitution striking a strong stance of antiabolition by advising a play based on Uncle Tom's Cabin should be dropped

> once and forever. It is a sad blunder; for when our stage
> shall become the deliberate agent in the cause of abolition-
> ism, with the sanction of the public and their approbation,
> the peace and harmony of this Union will soon be ended.
> The thing is in bad taste--is not according to good faith to
> the constitution--as calculated, if persisted in, to become
> a firebrand of most dangerous character to the peace of the
> whole country.

Handsome George Cunnabell Howard, born at Halifax, Nova Scotia in 1820, became manager of the Troy, New York, Museum Theatre in 1851. Seeking new material to produce, Howard asked resident actor-playwright George L. Aiken to adapt Uncle Tom's Cabin. In one week Aiken, born in Boston on Sunday, December 19, 1830, produced a stage version (retaining the character and essence of the novel) that George C. Howard reshaped into a playable script. Aiken's dramatization Uncle Tom's Cabin, or Life Among the Lowly opened on Monday, September 27, 1852, at Peale's Troy Museum. The immediate success of Aiken's four-act version inspired a two-act sequel, The Death of Uncle Tom, or The Religion of the Lowly (October 26, 1852) which introduced more major characters from the novel.

Aiken combined his two plays into one six-act, eight-tableaux, thirty-scene play on November 15, 1852. George C. Howard who had radically altered Aiken's plays into more cohesive and playable scripts also composed the words and music for Uncle Tom's Cabin. Songs included: "Oh, I'se So Wicked!"; "Eva to Her Papa"; "St Clair to Eva; or Tell Me, Where My Eva's Gone" (based on an old English folk song "Can I E'er Forget the Valley?"); "Little Eva in Heaven"; and "Uncle Tom's Religion." They augmented the play's musical theme, "Old Folks at Home," which was written by Stephen Foster and sung by Uncle Tom in act 5. The music was published in New York by Horace Waters in December 1853.

After 79 performances--not the extensively documented 100
performances--the Troy engagement of Uncle Tom's Cabin ended on
Wednesday, December 1, 1852.

The Uncle Tom's Cabin company was predominantly a family
affair. Matriarch of the clan was widow Emily Wyatt Fox (Aunt
Ophelia), who organized her four children into a theatre troupe
known as "The Little Foxes." Daughter Carolina E. Fox made her
legitimate stage debut at the age of four, with Charles Kemble in
The Stranger. While playing the part of Sally Lawton opposite
George C. Howard (the Cabin's St. Clair) in The Drunkard, Caroline married Howard. In Aiken's play, Caroline doubled in the roles
of Topsy and Aunt Chloe. Two more of Emily's children continued
in show business. George Washington Lafayette Fox (who had
played the part of Rideout Ruggles in The Fugitive Slave on March
19, 1850, prior to the publication of Mrs. Stowe's novel) and
Charles Kemble Fox played the roles of Gumption Cute and Phineas
Fletcher.

George L. Fox became America's highest paid actor as the
librettist and star of 1868's pantomime, Humpty Dumpty, in which
he played the title role for a phenominal run of 483 performances
until, as noted by Gerald Bordman in his masterful, comprehensive
chronicle American Musical Theatre, "His insanity caused him to be
forcibly removed from the stage." George Washington Lafayette Fox
died on Wednesday, October 24, 1877 at the age of fifty-two.
Joseph Jefferson, a cousin to the Fox family, carved out a career
as the stage's Rip Van Winkle and played Gumption Cute on September 26, 1853, at Philadelphia's Chestnut Street Theatre.

Joseph Jefferson's granddaughter, Mrs. Greene C. Germon,
played both Eliza and Cassy. Her husband, Greene C. Germon,
who died in March 1854 during the company's management in Chicago, was the original Uncle Tom. Cousin George L. Aiken wrote
the play and doubled in the roles of George Harris and George
Shelby--his brother Frank W. Aiken was the original Marks, the
lawyer. The greatest family asset--billed as "The Child of Nature"
--was five-year-old Cordelia Howard.

Cordelia Howard, born at Providence, Rhode Island on Tuesday, February 1, 1848, made her stage debut at the age of three
as Little Dick in Oliver Twist, with her mother Caroline in the title
role and Fanny Wallack as Nancy Sikes. "The Child of Nature's"
performance as Little Eva in Uncle Tom's Cabin was one of the large
contributing factors to the success of Aiken's stage version of the
novel. It is even more remarkable that such a young child could
retain the lines and intricacy of performance in the several plays
that alternated with Uncle Tom's Cabin.

Sterling Brown wrote about the beautiful, petite actress, "The
impersonation of Eva by Cordelia was one of the most charming and

affecting specimens of the art dramatique I ever beheld." Little
Cordelia continued playing Little Eva, while originating the title role
in Charles Western Taylor's play Little Katy, the Hot Corn Girl,
which premiered at the National Theatre at the December 5, 1853,
matinee. During the week Cordelia played Little Katy at four matinees and Little Eva in Uncle Tom's Cabin six nights and two matinees or, as George Odell noted, "The tender child Cordelia Howard
was thus performing twice a day for weeks. By the laws of the
health-books such a course should have carried her to a very early
grave." Cordelia, however, outlived the entire original Uncle Tom's
Cabin cast.

ORIGINAL CAST OF UNCLE TOM'S CABIN

Produced by Alexander H. Purdy at his National Theatre,
Chatham Square, New York on July 18, 1853. Dramatized
from the novel by Harriet Beecher stowe by George L. Aiken;
Directed by George C. Howard; Company manager, George
W. L. Fox

> Greene C. Germon (succeeded by James W. Lingard) (Un-
> cle Tom); Cordelia Howard (Little Eva); Mrs. G. C. How-
> ard (Topsy); George C. Howard (succeeded by S. M.
> Siple and J. B. Howe) (St. Clair); S. M. Siple (suc-
> ceeded by J. J. Prior) (George Harris); Charles K. Fox
> (succeeded by H. F. Stone) (Gumption Cute); George
> W. L. Fox (Phineas Fletcher); N. B. Clarke (Simon Le-
> gree); Mrs. W. G. Jones (succeeded by Mrs. J. J. Prior)
> (Eliza); Henry F. Stone (succeeded by M. Blake) (George
> Shelby); Mrs. Bradshaw (succeeded by Mrs. Emily Fox
> and Mrs. Myers) (Aunt Ophelia); J. Herbert (Marks, the
> lawyer); George Lingard (Tom Loker); Edward Lamb
> (Haley); Charles Toulmin (Wilson, the Quaker); William
> Henderson (Alf Mann); William H. Thompson (succeeded
> by Daymon Lyons) (Skeggs); Mrs. Nathaniel H. Bannister
> (Cassy); Herr John Cline (Waiter); Mr. Rose (Old Shel-
> by); Mr. Mack (Sambo); Mr. McDonnell (Jumbo); Mr.
> Mitchell (Adolph); Miss Barber (Emmeline); Mrs. J. W.
> Lingard (Aunt Chloe); Fanny Landers (Marie St. Clair);
> Master Murray (Harry, the child); James W. Lingard (suc-
> ceeded by George W. L. Fox) (Deacon Perry); Mr. Smith
> (Doctor); Mrs. Rose (Mrs. Shelby)

Six-year-old Cordelia appeared at the National Theatre's matinee on February 6, 1854, as Brother William in Lost and Won; or
The Gambler and originated the role of Marie Little in the American
premiere of The Child of Prayer; or Thirst for Gold at the April 17,

1854, matinee. The play later became popular as The Sea of Ice
and brought fame to Laura Keene. The Sea of Ice; or, The Prayers
of the Wrecked and the Gold Seekers of Mexico by D'Ennery and
Dugue was first produced at the Théâtre Ambigu-Comique in Paris
on October 20, 1853. These plays were alternated with parts in
The Lamplighter; or The Blind Girl and the Orphan on June 22,
1854, in which Cordelia played Little Gerty in the dramatization of
Maria S. Cummin's popular story and in Charles Western Taylor's
dramatization of Mrs. Ann S. Stephens's novel Fashion and Famine;
or the Strawberry Girl on September 11, 1854. Cordelia was seen
on September 17, 1855, at the Brooklyn Museum in The Youthful
King and at the National Theatre on April 7, 1856, in Ida May; or
the Kidnapped Child. She was cast as Mary Fuller in George L.
Aiken's adaptation of Mrs. Ann S. Stephens's novel The Old Home-
stead on November 3, 1856; on November 7, 1856, she played in
Old and Young.

On September 22, 1856, Cordelia created a minor sensation
when she appeared in blackface as Tom Tit in Charles Western Taylor's dramatization of Harriet Beecher Stowe's novel Dred, a Tale
of the Great Dismal Swamp. The book had been published by Phillips, Sampson and Company that year and serialized in the Saturday
Evening Post. A week after the opening of Dred, Taylor revised
his play; the new version played on September 29. Charles W.
Taylor portrayed Old Tiff, the "Gardener, coachman, cook, housekeeper and man of all work of the Peytons"; J. Reed was the runaway slave Dred. J. H. Allen was Harry, the white Gordon's quadroon slave brother, and Fanny Herring was Harry's black slave wife,
Lizette. The New York Tribune admired Cordelia's impersonation
of the "careless, good-for-nothing Tom Tit--devil-may-care rascal"
but looked "not for excellent miniature acting, but for a beautiful
child deformed by burnt cork and horse-hair wig" and found she
was "truly admirable." Taylor's stage version of Dred completed
forty performances at New York's National Theatre.

John R. Adams in his biography, Harriet Beecher Stowe,
wrote, "Although Mrs. Stowe nowhere in her published writings
admitted acquaintance with earlier anti-slavery novels, the situations
and characters of both Uncle Tom's Cabin and Dred are partly traditional." Adams cited Richard Hildreth's 1836 novel The Slave; or
Memories of Archy Moor as one source. Following the frequent
liberal, if not literal, adaptations of Uncle Tom's Cabin, various un-
authorized versions of Mrs. Stowe's novel Dred quickly surfaced.
John E. Brougham produced his adaptation of Dred at the Bowery
Theatre on September 29, 1856, with W. R. Denham as Tom Tit,
T. D. "Jump Jim Crow" Rice as the black slave, Old Tiff, and
Conrad Clarke as the outlawed slave Dred.

P. T. Barnum, at his New York American Museum, produced
Henry J. Conway's version of Dred on October 16, 1856. The event
featured his star attraction, the mighty midget "General Tom Thumb"

(Charles Sherwood Stratton) as Tom Tit, with James W. Lingard as
Old Tiff, and Mr. Havelock as Dred. Conway had made alterations
in his stage adaptation of Uncle Tom's Cabin. He also made changes
in his play, Dred, drastically altering Mrs. Stowe's story and increasing the importance of the character of Tom Tit while, at the
same time, completely eliminating others. The New York Tribune
reported that in the part of the little blackface slave "the little
General (Tom Thumb) made a decided hit." Barnum augmented
Dred by having the "Magnolia Grove Troubadours" sing ballads
such as "Pretty Carolina Rose." But the outlandish costumes designed for the blackface characters made Dred resemble the mounting of a dramatic minstrel show. Barnum's Dred closed on November 22, 1856.

     The Aiken-Howard "Tom" troupe left Troy for Albany, New
York, where Alfred B. Smith and France's Madame de Margueritte's
crackpot interpretation of Uncle Tom's Cabin offered no competition
other than amazement. On July 18, 1853, Aiken's Uncle Tom's
Cabin opened at Alexander H. Purdy's National Theatre on Chatham
Square in New York City. James W. Lingard succeeded Greene C.
Germon as Uncle Tom, and, on May 30, 1854, Charles Western Taylor replaced Lingard in Aiken's play. In America and England,
George C. Howard, his wife Caroline, and their remarkably talented
daughter Cordelia, created careers in their original roles. So great
were the profits from the huge success of Uncle Tom's Cabin that
manager Purdy turned his decrepit playhouse into "The Temple of
Moral Drama," proudly displaying in the lobby his commissioned
Alanson Fisher portrait of Harriet Beecher Stowe as well as a portrait of himself holding the Holy Bible in one hand and a copy of
Uncle Tom's Cabin in the other.

     Uncle Tom's Cabin played to enthusiastic capacity audiences
despite frenetic editorial damnation of the play by the New York
press. The New York Clipper called the play Abolitionism in New
Garb, the substance of which is worth recording.

          The Uncle Tom excitement is being renewed again in a new
     garb, and one of our public theatres is used as an aboli-
     tion hall in which to depict the alleged tyranny of the slave
     owners of the South over their slaves. Is this right! Is
     it proper that a fresh agitation of a question which at one
     time threatened the dissolution of the Union should be suf-
     fered to be revived in our midst by a theatrical manager,
     for the purpose of putting money in his pocket, and that,
     too, at the expense, perhaps, of bloodshed and riot! Is
     it right that these things should be--that the Southern peo-
     ple who are now thronging into our city should be insulted
     merely to gratify the whim of a man who would make capital
     out of dissensions and disorders. Business men from the
     South are daily arriving in the great City of New York,
     to make their fall purchases. On opening some of our daily

papers, what is their surprise to behold under the editorial
head, insulting language regarding the citizens and a con-
stitutional institution of the South. Many of them leave in
disgust and procure their supplies elsewhere, and thus, this
slavery revival robs the enterprise of our merchants, and
gives to strangers a false impression of the character of
our people.

In speaking of the theatre where the abolition play is
produced, the Tribune, while exulting over the effect produced is not wise very flattering in its description of the
audience. It says, "It was composed largely of the stuff
which demagogues, acting under oligarchs, have used for
the purpose of burning down halls, destroying printing
presses, assaulting public speakers, intimidating, striking,
killing." What do the auditors at the National Theatre
think of that! Very pleasant, isn't it! And yet you continue to visit this place. You approve by your presence
of those abolition principles, which are antagonistic to the
constitution of the United States, and which are sowing the
seeds of disorder, of contention, and of hatred, which may
ultimately shake to its centre, the glorious fabric of our
confederation. Look to it in time, friends of the Union.
Beware of Abolition Halls in disguise. Wake up!

The Clipper's paranoia was not shared by the entire press.
Although the Spirit of the Times reported, "We do not approve of
the spirit of this piece, with all its crudities and absurdities, but
what little there is to act is well performed.... It is creditably
put on the stage, and the little morality which here and there
peeps out unexpectedly, tells well with the audience." Later the
Spirit of the Times added, "If a constant succession of crowded
houses for now nearly nine weeks be any evidence of the popularity of a piece, or of the good reputation of the house, then is the
National on very sure ground. Eva, by Little Cordelia Howard, is
performed extremely well--and the plaudits of the audience attest
how highly they appreciate her performance."

As the success of Uncle Tom's Cabin continued, both newspapers recanted their original diatribes. The New York Clipper
reluctantly acknowledged the continuing success of Aiken's play
(after the National Theatre began advertising in the Clipper).
Various New York clergymen upheld and hailed the dramatization
of Uncle Tom's Cabin as "the opening of a new era in the history
of drama in New York City" and encouraged their congregations to
visit the National Theatre. The Spirit of the Times later decided
that "the various characters are admirably enacted, and hosts of
people have 'with moist eyes and refined feelings' admitted the
fact. Whatever may be the prejudice, political or otherwise, for
or against the 'colored bredren' of this country, the feelings provoked by the representation of Uncle Tom's Cabin do us credit.
The performance of this drama has made converts to the abolition

doctrine many persons, we have no doubt, who have never examined the subject, and know nothing of its merits." The newspaper extolled the excellence of Caroline Howard's performance as Topsy, saying that she, in combination with Cordelia's Eva, "has made the character and the performer subjects of interest."

Uncle Tom's Cabin was refurbished for its 186th performance on January 9, 1854. The play had new scenery and was repopulated with Aiken's constant introduction of new characters. The new production was presented in seven acts, twelve tableaux and thirty-four scenes. The play ran for 325 performances to May 13, 1854, and became the first production to be played without a curtain-raiser, afterpiece, or a divertissement. Uncle Tom's Cabin established a record for the play that would continue to be performed for nearly a century and rightfully earn its reputation as "The World's Greatest Hit." The complete history of Uncle Tom's Cabin is painstakingly recorded in Harry Birdoff's 1947 book, The World's Greatest Hit. George L. Aiken's dramatization of the novel remained the best adaptation and also the one that was most frequently performed. Among other plays dramatized by Aiken are The Gun-Maker of Moscow; Orion, the Gold Beater; and The Mystic Bride. He also wrote Helos, the Helot; or, The Revolt of Messene; Karmel the Scout; and The Ups and Downs of New York Life; or City Revelations.

During Uncle Tom's Cabin's run at the National Theatre, the New York Clipper observed, "Religious services are still held in this place every evening. Our Southern friends don't like the doctrines of the church and consequently don't hold pews there. Cullud pussons and white folks mingle together on the lower floor." The Clipper's National Theatre advertisement listed "Parquette for colored people--25 cents. Pit seats (for whites) 12-1/2 cents and Exclusive Private Boxes for five-dollars."

The resounding success of Aiken's Uncle Tom's Cabin produced other adaptations that "growed" as ambiguously and faster than Topsy. Clifton W. Tayleure's Southern sympathizing version appeared in Detroit, Michigan on October 2, 1852, with Lancing K. Dougherty as Uncle Tom. To offset the distortions of Tayleure's pro-Southern production, George L. Aiken produced, directed, and played the part of George Harris in his own adaptation in Detroit (October 2, 1854), with L. D. Ross as Uncle Tom and Mary Mowry as Eva.

Mrs. Anna Marble, the widow of actor Danforth (Dan) Marble, sister-in-law of John B. Rice and sister of actor William Warren (who originated the character of Penetrate Partyside, a character not in the novel but included in H. J. Conway's Boston Museum dramatization) had her tattered version of Uncle Tom's Cabin (which dispensed with both Eva and Topsy among other editorial excesses) produced by John B. Rice at his Chicago theatre on December 13, 1852

for a run of three weeks. Edwin Booth's future father-in-law was
James Hubert McVicker. McVicker's 1858 production of Uncle Tom's
Cabin featured his nine-year-old daughter Mary McVicker (later to
become the second wife of Edwin Booth) in her stage debut as Little
Eva, with A. D. Bradley as Uncle Tom, W. H. Leighton as Legree,
Mrs. Leighton as Topsy, comedian John D. Dillon as Deacon Perry,
and Mrs. Anna Marble as Aunt Ophelia. Mrs. Conway produced
Uncle Tom's Cabin on April 26, 1865. The play featured Thomas
McKeon (Uncle Tom) and actor Frank Drew--possibly the first male
performer to play Topsy.

Henry J. Conway's pro-Southern adaptation of the story first
appeared at the Boston Museum on November 15, 1852, with Frank
Whitman as Uncle Tom and Helen Western as Eva. Vigorously pro-
moted by P. T. Barnum with his usual ballyhoo and hyperbole,
Conway's creation of the Cabin opened at Barnum's New York American Museum on November 7, 1853, with J. L. Munroe as Uncle
Tom. The Conway concept was assailed by members of the press.
They actually encouraged the public to attend the National Theatre
to see Aiken's more authentic dramatization, which "did not pander
to the fears of the timid, nor gratify a perverted taste."

S. E. Harris produced his usurped version of the Aiken-
Howard play at his Philadelphia National Theatre on Thursday eve-
ning, September 8, 1853, in defiance of Purdy's claim to the ex-
clusive dramatization rights published in the New York Herald.
Producer-manager-director-appropriator Harris played Uncle Tom in
his Uncle Tom's Cabin through six acts, nine tableaux and thirty
scenes, with Clara Reed as Eva and Rose Merrifield as Topsy. The
Aiken-Howard Uncle Tom's Cabin opened in opposition to Harris on
September 26 at the Chestnut Street Theatre, with John Gilbert as
Uncle Tom, Laura Parker as Eva, Lizzie Weston as Topsy, George
Mason as Simon Legree, Joseph Jefferson (who also designed the
scenery) as Gumption Cute, Mrs. Jefferson as Marie, and Mrs. Gilbert as Aunt Ophelia.

Henry Edmund Stevens' stage version of Uncle Tom's Cabin
was produced by J. P. Waldron at New York's Bowery Theatre on
January 16, 1854, with Thomas D. Rice as Uncle Tom, Caroline
Whitlock as Eva, and Gertrude Dawes as Topsy. The Spirit of the
Times proclaimed Rice's interpretation of Uncle Tom the best seen
to date on the New York stage. On Sunday, February 5, 1854,
during a friendly wrestling match with actor William Hamilton (who
played Aunt Chloe in the Bowery production), Stevens was hurled
against a curbstone and broke his neck. Actor-playwright Henry
E. Stevens died on Thursday, February 9, 1854, while, at the
Bowery Theatre, performances of his adaptation of Mrs. Stowe's
novel continued until March 16.

Harriet Beecher Stowe had never been in a theatre in her
life, according to Francis H. Underwood, the managing editor of the

Atlantic Monthly, a magazine to which Mrs. Stowe began contributing, in 1857. Reluctantly, Mrs. Stowe allowed Underwood to persuade her to see the characters she'd invented come to life on the
stage of Boston's National Theatre. Underwood procured a box;
Mrs. Stowe, carefully secluded by the curtains of the box, watched
the performance without speaking, but, Underwood wrote, "I never
saw such delight upon a human face as she displayed when she
first comprehended the full power of Mrs. Howard's Topsy--her
expression was eloquent, smiles and tears succeeding each other
through the whole." Underwood added, "Mrs. Howard was beyond
comparison the best representative of the dark race I ever saw.
She was a genius whose method no one could describe. In every
look, gesture, and tone there was an intuitive revelation of the
strange, capricious and fascinating creature which Mrs. Stowe had
conceived."

Throughout the 1880's nearly a hundred, or more, touring
Tom Shows took to the road. They opened in every city, town,
and hamlet in America. Tom companies increased in number and
proliferated in proportion to demand; to be sure, they stretched the
imagination of the entrepreneurs and competitive showmen. The
cabins housing Uncle Toms eventually took on the aura of a circus
inhabited by an astonishing zoo of animals. Double Toms, double
Evas, double Topsys, believed to have been inaugurated by C. H.
Smith's Double Mammouth Uncle Tom's Cabin Company in Boston
in 1881 (admission 10, 20 and 30 cents), soon became an added in-
ducment to the public. Brass bands, Negro choirs, dancers, and
Jubilee singers accompanied many of the Tom Shows. Parades
through towns en route proclaimed constantly "bigger," "better,"
"mammouth," "original," "spectacular" Uncle Tom's Cabins. The
foundation of the old Cabin was beginning to quake. For nearly
eighty years Uncle Tom's Cabin was not so much a play as it was
an institution. Only a few days could pass without the Cabin being
performed in various languages in many places in the world. The
play's longevity spanned over three-quarters of a century to remain
"The World's Greatest Hit" and "the greatest propaganda play of all
time."

Uncle Tom's Cabin became a lifetime career for many performers. The nomadic Tom Shows and their "Tommers" were derisively
classified by elegant, although probably unemployed, "legitimate"
New York actors as "Jays--Tomming the Tanks." A listing of
"Tommers" would become a directory of show business. Some of
the Tom Show performers are included in an appendix, "Whites in
Blackface--Stage and Screen," which is but a sampling over the
years of performers spotlighted in burnt cork.

London went Cabin-crazy in 1852 with five theatres simultane-
ously offering productions of Uncle Tom's Cabin and all playing to
capacity business. Londoners dubbed the multiple versions of the
novel "Tomitudes." The Great National Standard Theatre presentation

opened on September 13, 1852, with Uncle Tom's Cabin; or The
Slave's Life in America. The Standard Theatre's production was an
English translation of a French interpretation of the novel in which
Uncle Tom does not die, Eva is miraculously restored to life, and
Topsy is engaged in a heavy romance with a "fancy darky" named
Julius, as they sing, dance and indulge in low comedy routines.

On September 20, 1852, the Olympic Theatre presented Uncle
Tom's Cabin; or Negro Life in America. Beginning September 27,
1852, the Royal Victoria Theatre's production of Uncle Tom's Cabin
completed 100 performances and was followed by a "new drama,"
The Slave Hunt; or The Fate of the St. Clairs and the Happy Days
of Uncle Tom, including Cassy's Story and the Death of Little Eva.
William Brough's burlesque of the novel Uncle Tom's Crib; or Negro
Life In London opened on October 25, 1852. It was produced by
Major Dumolton and featured The African Troupe (American whites
in blackface). C. M. Tideswell's adaptation of Uncle Tom's Cabin
was seen at the Royal Park Theatre on November 8, 1852.

Tom Taylor, later to gain fame as the author of the famous
comedy Our American Cousin, collaborated with Mark Lemon on an
English version of Mrs. Stowe's novel called Slave Life, which was
produced in London in November 1852. On November 29, 1852, at
the Adelphi Theatre, Madame Celeste directed the editors of Punch
magazine's illuminating dramatization, in which Simon Legree stabbed
Uncle Tom to death with a Bowie knife. Edward Fitzball's Christmas
pantomime Uncle Tom's Cabin; or, The Horrors of Slavery opened on
December 25, 1852, at London's Drury Lane Theatre in competition
with Frederick Neale's pantomime version Uncle Tom's Cabin and
Lucy Neal; or Harlequin Liberty and Slavery; at Ashley's Royal
Amphitheatre, Eliza and Uncle Tom escaped to freedom on horseback!

The city of London presented John Wilkin's adaptation of the
novel in January, 1853, with Mrs. Barnett as Topsy; her donkey
called Tom Tit, was named for the little black character in Dred.
The following month, Eliza and the Fugitive Slaves; or Uncle Tom's
Cabin appeared. Scotland had seen J. B. Johnston's version in
Edinburgh on September 24, 1852, and in October the Cabin was
erected in Dublin, Ireland, T. B. Lacey's dramatization was produced on February 1, 1853, in Manchester, England, and on February 15 Edmund Glover's adaptation of the novel appeared in Glasgow.
In conjunction with appearances by his star performer, General Tom
Thumb, P. T. Barnum sponsored Aiken's original Uncle Tom's Cabin
in London. George C. Howard, his wife Caroline, and their daughter Cordelia charmed and conquered London in 1857. The novel was
constantly being dramatized throughout the years. George Fawcett
Rowe's adaptation was produced in Manchester on August 19, 1878,
and paced by a later version by C. Hermann. W. Harris's adaptation was produced at Peckham's Theatre Royal on September 24,
1880, with John Buchenough as Uncle Tom. Still another version
by Sims and Raleigh, called simply Uncle Tom, opened at London's

Vaudeville Theatre on April 3, 1893. Marshall Moore's three-episode
version was at London's Court Theatre on April 4, 1914.

Fascination with Uncle Tom encouraged other "authentic" black
entertainments. J. S. Sweasey presented The Slave Troupe at London's Royal Music Hall in February 1870, featuring Beaumont Read
and J. E. Johnson in a cast of twenty-three "coloured brethren."
America's first billboard poster appeared in Cincinnati in 1878 showing Eliza crossing the ice-choked Ohio River. The first lithographic
posters produced in England were for Uncle Tom's Cabin (Currier
Company, 1880). Currier's nine-sheet in four colors depicted Eliza
crossing the ice pursued by bloodhounds. Advertisements ballyhooed
"a host of genuine freed slaves from the Southern States of America,
who will make their first appearance in Europe in their original
Plantation Festival scenes." The "host of genuine freed slaves"
were all recruited from the Plantation of Manhattan.

In Berlin, Germany's Köenigstadisches Theatre presented the
first German adaptation of Uncle Tom's Cabin called Negersleben in
Nord-Amerika (December 1852). The adaptation was written by
Dankwardt and Kahleis; it was soon competing with Ernest Nonne's
two-act version titled, Barbier und Neger; oder Onkel Tom In
Deutschland. Therese von Magerle's Onkel Tom's Hutte; oder
Negersleben in Den Sklavenstaaten von Nordamerika at the Verstad-
isches Theatre featured songs by F. L. Shubert: "Topsy, I Came
from Alabama"; "Elisa, When I lib'd in Tennessee"; and, "Chloe,
Now Niggers Listen to Me," all of which gained great popularity in
the Fatherland.

On October 20, 1853, German-Americans at the Deutsches
Theatre (New York's St. Charles Theatre) enjoyed Onkel Tom's
Hutte in Olfers's adaptation. Other German translations by Buch-
Pfeiffer and Therese von Magerle followed in 1856 and Herman
Muhr's dramatic play, Zuavenstreiche in Amerika, used some of the
characters from Uncle Tom's Cabin. Later, in 1901, Adolph Philipps's
musical comedy Der Kartoffelköenig had Uncle Tom's Cabin as a play-
within-the-play.

Holland's Cabin was called Der Negerhut, and Italy saw the
play as La Capanna dello Zio Tommaso; Luigi Ferrari Trecate developed it into an opera a hundred years later. Spain enthused over
Don Ramon de Valladares and Saavedra's La Cabana de Tom; ó, La
Esclavitud de los Negros in 1864; Russians sympathized with Khizhina
dyadi Toma.

Dumanoir and D'Ennery's French adaptaiton, La Case de l'Oncle
Tom, was staged in eight acts and fifty-five scenes at Paris's Théâtre
del Ambigu-Comique on January 18, 1853, for twenty-five performances. Parisians were offered another interpretation on January 23,
1853, at the Théâtre de la Gaieté. This version, by L. DeWailly and
Edmond Texier, was called L'Oncle Tom and ran for thirty-three

performances; it was later translated for the English stage by L.
Rae (September 30, 1878) as Uncle Tom. Arthur de Beauplan's
two-act Elisa; ou un Chapitre de l'Oncle Tom appeared at the
Théâtre au Gymnase on February 21, 1853.

    The enthusiasm of French audiences for the imaginative and
inventive translations of Mrs. Stowe's novel to the stage generated
additional antislavery plays, which continued playing in France until the end of the American Civil War. The productions of Jar's
1854 Zamire, ou la belle esclave, Louvier's 1856 operetta Sang Mêlé,
Lardereau's operetta Le Bon Nègre, Bouchardy's 1859 Micaël l'esclave, and Cauwet's 1864 Le Négrophile found eager audiences.
The French also enjoyed parodies on the story such as Casine de
l'Oncle Tom by Dormeuil and Paul Michel's Le Cave de l'Oncle Tom.

    Likewise, American Southern audiences laughed at parodies
and burlesques of Uncle Tom's Cabin, such as the Irish satire
Uncle Pat's Cabin (1853). Sam S. Sanford's Happy Uncle Tom; or
Real Life in Old Virginia in January 1854 and Dr. William T. Leon-
ard's spoof of Uncle Tom's Cabin in Louisiana, produced at Dan
Rice's New Amphitheatre in New Orleans for twenty-three performances beginning March 6, 1854, were followed by Joseph M. Field's
Uncle Tom's Cabin; or Life in the South AS IT IS in St. Louis on
April 24, 1854. George W. Jamieson, who originated the role of
Old Pete in Dion Boucicault's 1859 drama, The Octoroon, wrote a
play The Old Plantation; or, The Real Uncle Tom in which he played
an aging Tom in a New Orleans production and at New York's Bowery Theatre on March 1, 1860. The fascinating Lotta (Crabtree)
toured as Topsy in Uncle Tom's Cabin in 1876, with W. H. Bailey
as Uncle Tom and Nellie Pennoyer as Little Eva. Clay M. Greene's
"new" version of Uncle Tom's Cabin appeared on April 20, 1891,
with Milt G. Barlow as Tom and Carrie Dillon as Topsy.

    The first major revival of Uncle Tom's Cabin on Broadway was
William A. Brady's elaborately mounted production at the Academy
of Music on March 4, 1901. Wilton Lackaye played Uncle Tom, Maud
Raymond was Topsy, and Georgie Florence Olp was Eva. Edward
Harrigan's former leading lady Mrs. Annie Yeamans played Aunt
Ophelia and, according to the New York Times, "the best acting of
the evening was done by Theodore Roberts as Simon Legree--A picturesque background was furnished by a well-drilled crowd of negro
singers and dancers and the appearance of horses, carriages, pony
carts, donkeys and dogs added much to the realism of the performance."

    William A. Brady, who had been a "Tommer" as Lawyer Marks
in California during the eighties, toured his production of Uncle
Tom's Cabin for several years. In the spring of 1904 Theodore
Roberts (later as Moses to part the Red Sea for Cecil B. DeMille's
1923 motion-picture epic The Ten Commandments) was still cracking
the whip as Simon Legree. John E. Kellard (whose Hamlet would

exceed the performances of Edwin Booth and John Barrymore in
1912) was Uncle Tom. Edith Taliaferro was Eva, Maud Raymond
continued as Topsy, as did Mrs. Annie Yeamans as Aunt Ophelia.
Comedian Jefferson De Angelis joined the cast as Marks, the lawyer.

In 1904, Mike Thomashevsky produced Uncle Tom's Cabin at
Philadelphia's Columbia Yiddish Theatre. Petite six-year-old Molly
Picon played Topsy, and her sister Helen was Little Eva. Molly's
Topsy was played in Yiddish with a strange southern accent. She
sang "Sho Fly Don't Bother Me, I Belong to Company B," which
she augmented with a jig and somersaults. Boris Thomashevsky
was Uncle Tom and his wife, Bessie, was Topsy in another Yiddish
version of Uncle Tom's Cabin that played at New York's Bowery's
People's Theatre on March 16, 1906. The Thomashevsky version
of Uncle Tom was later satirized in a vaudeville sketch by Timothy
Gray. The sketch, Uncle Thomashevsky's Cabin, was acted at
Hammerstein's Victoria Theatre on February 8, 1915, with Bernard
Granville as Simon Levy, Jack Curtis as Uncle Thomashevsky, and
Lillian Shaw as Little Evavitch.

J. H. J. Ronner produced James W. Harkins' and Edwin Barbour's adaptation of Uncle Tom's Cabin at Broadway's Majestic Theatre on March 20, 1907. The play featured John Sutherland as Uncle
Tom, Gretchen Hartman as Little Eva, Viola La Bretta as Topsy,
Herbert Bostwick as Legree, and Lucille La Verne as Cassy and
Aunt Chloe. The Harkins-Barbour version had originally been produced in Boston on April 30, 1894, with Edwin Barbour as Tom,
Viola Fitzpatrick as Evan, Marion Elmore as Topsy, and Frank Losee
as Simon Legree. In 1918, Frank Losee would become Uncle Tom
in Paramount Pictures' screen version of the classic.

Elizabeth Corbett's article "Uncle Tom Is Dead" published in the
January 1931 Theatre Guild Magazine stated,

> This year, for the first time in more than three quarters of
> a century, there was no company playing Uncle Tom's Cabin
> in all America. This play, which boasts the longest continu-
> ous run in theatrical history, incorporated in itself a whole
> era of American drama and acting. This year the longest
> run in American history came to an end. It was, indeed,
> a run half as long as American history itself. "Uncle
> Tomming" was a profession in itself. Uncle Tom's Cabin
> was not only our most successful American play, it was an
> American institution. Its day is done. If the play is re-
> vived, it will be as a curiosity; and no one can revive the
> profession of "Uncle Tomming." Alas, we must pay a price
> for our sophistication.

Uncle Tom's Cabin did return to Broadway two years later--
and thirty-two years after Broadway's last production in 1901. The
Players' Club's twelfth annual revival of a famous play at the Alvin

Theatre on May 29, 1933, was George L. Aiken's adaptation of the
novel, with the text revised by A. E. Thomas. The Players' production gave twenty-four performances and successfully toured
the major East Coast cities to great acclaim. The cast and credits
are worth recording not only because the play was the last Uncle
Tom's Cabin to be seen on Broadway as straight drama and as
originally written by George L. Aiken but because the play featured
a remarkably talented troupe of players (whose names are listed
below).

UNCLE TOM'S CABIN. Opened May 29, 1933, Alvin Theatre,
New York--24 performances. Produced by The Players' Club
as their twelfth annual revival; A dramatization of Harriet
Beecher Stowe's novel by George L. Aiken, revised by A. E.
Thomas; Director, Earle Boothe (succeeded by John Hayden);
Settings and costumes, Donald Oenslager; Musical program
prepared by Edward T. Emery; Musical director, Harry Gilbert; Music compiled and arranged by Henry H. Hamilton;
Ten Litchfield County Hounds in charge of John LeDor; Stage
managers, Walter F. Scott, S. Ascher Smith; Orchestra conductor, Henry Klein

  Otis Skinner (Uncle Tom); Lois Shore [succeeded by Betty
  Lancaster] (Little Eva); Fay Bainter [succeeded by Queen-
  ie Smith] (Topsy); Thomas Chalmers [succeeded by Bran-
  don Evans] (Simon Legree); Elizabeth Risdon (Eliza);
  Pedro De Cordoba [succeeded by Frank Wilcox] (George
  Harris); Cecilia Loftus [succeeded by Gertrude Fowler]
  (Aunt Chloe); Kate Mayhew (Aunt Hagar); Gene Lockhart
  [succeeded by Earle Mitchell] (Gumption Cute); Ernest
  Glendinning [succeeded by Charles Laito] (St. Clare);
  Minnie Dupree [succeeded by Mary Horne Morrison] (Aunt
  Ophelia); Mary Nash [succeeded by Joanna Roos] (Cas-
  sie); George Gaul [succeeded by J. D. Seymour] (George
  Shelby, Jr.); Malcolm Duncan [succeeded by Robert Hud-
  son] (Shelby); Sylvia Field [succeeded by Maureen Mc-
  Manus and Regina Wallace] (Marie); Edward McNamara [suc-
  ceeded by Walter F. Scott] (Phineas Fletcher); Roy Le
  May (Harry); Lyster Chambers (Haley); John Daly Mur-
  phy [succeeded by Harry Tyler] (Marks); John C. King
  (Tom Loker); George Christie [succeeded by Doan Borup]
  (Mr. Wilson); Harold W. Gould [succeeded by George
  Christie] (Auctioneer Skeggs); Burford Hampden [suc-
  ceeded by Julian Johnson] (Caesar); Margaret Mullen
  [succeeded by Joanna Roos] (Emeline); Wright Kramer
  [succeeded by Earle Mitchell and Robert Hudson] (Major
  Mann); Frank Wilcox [succeeded by W. B. Taylor] (George
  Fisk); Ben Lackland [succeeded by Jonathan Hale] (Sambo); Harry Gresham [succeeded by Thomas Reddy]

(Quimbo); John Knight [succeeded by Guy Wright and
Bruce Elmore] (Adolph); Eleanor Goodrich [succeeded by
Betty Hanna] (Nurse); John Kramer [succeeded by Wesley
Givens] (Clerk); W. B. Taylor (Waiter); Oswald Hering
[succeeded by Francis H. Day and George Nichols] (First
Bidder); Edwin T. Emery [succeeded by Thomas Beck]
(Second Bidder); Earle Mitchell (Overseer); James Stan-
ley, Paul Parks, T. H. Montgomery, Joseph Cummings
Chase, Raymond Thayer, J. Scanlon, F. Mathieu, H.
Panter [Alternates: Harry Gilbert, Frederick Jagel, Sam-
uel Merwin, John Barnes Wells] (Singers); Florence Shot,
Kathleen Lockhart, Essie Emery, Katherine Doyle, Amy
Groesbeck, Janice O'Connell, Elizabeth Dewing, Nancy
Levering, Mrs. Edward D. Dunn, Grenville Vernon, Owen
Culbertson, George Riddell, William Fisher, Scudder Mid-
dleton [Alternates: Alice McKenzie, Oswald Hering, Rich-
ard Hoffman, Oswald Marshall, Russel Crouse, Harold
Staton, Edward Delaney Dunn] (Southern Ladies, Plant-
ers, Slaves, Etc.); Patricia O'Connell (Soprano Soloist)

Succeeding players appeared mainly in the road tour which
was sponsored by Lawrence Rivers, Inc.

Richard Lockridge (the _Evening Sun_) reported,

Otis Skinner was an Uncle Tom of quiet dignity and Fay
Bainter's inspired Topsy can hardly have been bettered in
all of the years of Tom shows--Doubtless it is no discovery
that the old play, for all its heavy moralism--has broad
bands of grand drama in it. Elizabeth Risdon's Eliza has
an appeal that nothing can shake--Several of the big scenes
will get you, if you don't watch out--The slave market
scene, for example, is stirring drama--It is not only authentic Americana; it is in its own right a pretty grand
evening.

Ironically the distinguished seventy-five-year-old Otis Skinner, born at Cambridge, Massachusetts on Monday, June 28, 1858,
began portraying Uncle Tom. Skinner came full cycle. He made
his last appearance on the New York stage as Uncle Tom in the
Players' 1933 production of Uncle Tom's Cabin. Otis Skinner, who
died on Sunday, January 4, 1942, had begun his impressive career
at the age of nineteen at Philadelphia's Museum Theatre in 1877,
playing Uncle Tom for twelve performances, with Little Fanchon
Campbell as Little Eva and Kate Large as Topsy. During the Broadway engagement of the Players' Uncle Tom's Cabin, Mr. Skinner,
drawing on his extensive knowledge of the theatre and its lore,
wrote a long, reflective, and authoritative article Uncle Tom and
Eva Take Another Bow for The New York Times Magazine on May 29,

Otis Skinner in <u>Uncle Tom's Cabin</u>, 1933 (courtesy of The Free Library of Philadelphia Theatre Collection).

1933. Percy Hammond (New York Herald-Tribune) described Skinner's characterization of Uncle Tom as "a deep, sincere and dramatic picture of the heroic and humble negro in the most prejudiced
and potent of the mission plays."

The Boston Herald on October 8, 1933, extolled the accomplishments and purpose of The Players' Club and their splendid revival of Mrs. Stowe's aging story with a brief résumé of former
famous "Tommers." Attending Boston's opening night performance
of The Players' Uncle Tom's Cabin on Monday, October 9, 1933,
was eighty-five-year-old Mrs. Edmund J. MacDonald.

Mrs. MacDonald shunned personal publicity but did enthuse
to the press about The Players' production and performance, "I
think this production is about as faithful to the original as has ever
been put on. But I think the play seems rather archaic. This
girl (Betty Lancaster) makes a darling Eva. She looks the part.
I like the way she plays it." But Mrs. MacDonald bristled on the
subject of Bloodhounds. "The original production," she said,
"didn't have them. In fact, the script doesn't call for them. They
were put in a long time after the original production when the play
was given in degraded forms such as two Evas, two Topsys and
Legrees and horses and mules."

There could have been no greater authority on the authenticity of 1933's Uncle Tom's Cabin than Cordelia Howard. She was the
original Little Eva who, at the age of twelve, retired from the stage
and, at the age of twenty, married Boston publisher Edmund J.
MacDonald, who died on May 9, 1887, shortly after the death of her
father George C. Howard. Mrs. Cordelia Howard MacDonald still
had the vestige of the four-year-old child who had originated the
role of Little Eva. At the age of eighty-five, Cordelia had small,
lively eyes above plump, rounded cheeks, and the tiny pursed
mouth was plainly visible. The former Cordelia Howard laughingly,
but correctly, referred to herself as "The Shirley Temple of my
Day."

Mrs. MacDonald in a letter to her brother Walter was enthusiastic and observant.

> Well, they did give me an ovation Monday eve. So many
> years since I have received the plaudits of an audience!
> And do you know I rather liked it! Mr. Skinner made a
> speech and said the original Little Eva was present and
> pointed to my box. The applause broke forth and I had
> to bow to the audience. Well, it was my swan song, that
> is the end. I saw Mr. Skinner afterwards. He was very
> complimentary about my looks, the old flirt! But as he is
> a widower and I am a widow it was all right....

The play follows our dramatization pretty closely. The

auction scene was excellent.... It is a good thing to show
the young people the conditions of those days. Mr. Skinner, of course was a fine Uncle Tom.... Eva was charm-
ing--her voice childish and her movements natural and
she is very pretty. Between ourselves, Topsy (Queenie
Smith) was awful! The first thing she did was to pick her
nose! Disgusting! Not the innocent, childlike Topsy of
our mother. Mr. St. Clair was rather old (Charles Laito),
I thought, and not very good-looking--not the handsome,
cultured gentleman that our father made it. But on the
whole the old play was well given and seemed to please the
audience. They played Father's song "I'se So Wicked."
I told the children it was their grandfather's composition.

The Players presented [me with] four dozen red roses. I
placed some on our father and mother's grave in Mt. Auburn. I thought it was appropriate....

Again, with love,
                                                    Delie

Cordelia Howard MacDonald died at the age of ninety-four at
her home in Belmont, Massachusetts (Sunday, August 10, 1941).
She is buried in Cambridge's Mt. Auburn Cemetery, not far from
her father George C. Howard, her mother Caroline Fox Howard,
and the founder of The Players' Club, Edwin Booth.

Cordelia's brother Walter Scott Howard of Buzzard's Bay,
Massachusetts, in a letter to the New York Times on October 25,
1936, confirmed his sister's denouncement of the bloodhound in-
vasion. "There were no dogs in the original production, and there
should never have been any dogs introduced at this period of the
play." Howard referred to his original George L. Aiken Uncle Tom's
Cabin manuscript. In it Aiken had Eliza escaping through a tavern
window--that is, until George C. Howard altered Aiken's script and
had Eliza make an exciting escape across the ice of the frozen Ohio
River. Noting that bloodhounds were not in Mrs. Stowe's book,
Howard explained that his father "had the greatest respect for the
creator of this famous novel" and "believed that a dramatization
should follow the work of the person who wrote it."

Uncle Tom's Cabin was produced at Martha's Vineyard,
Mass. during the summer of 1933, with Phidelah Rice as Uncle Tom
in Charles Emerson Cook's adaptation of Mrs. Stowe's novel. Cali-
fornia's Pasadena Playhouse produced George L. Aiken's Uncle
Tom's Cabin on July 4, 1933, with Ralph Freud as Uncle Tom,
Anita Deniston as Eva, Ruth Covell Leivson as Topsy, and Emmett
Vogan as Legree. Uncle Tom's Cabin was given another production
in December 1933 at London's Gate Theatre. Adapted and directed
by Peter Godfrey, the 1933 Cabin featured W. E. C. Jenkins as
Uncle Tom, Carol Rees as Topsy, Merle Tottenham as Eva, Gabriel
Toyne as Legree, and Walter Fitzgerald as St. Clair.

The demise and burial of Uncle Tom and dismantling of his
Cabin eventually occurred in America and in most countries in the
world (except in Russia where Mrs. Stowe's novel has remained
evergreen and popular). Moscow's Central Theatre of Transport
produced Uncle Tom's Cabin in April 1949, but any resemblance between Mrs. Stowe's novel and the Soviet bastardization was as remote as Marxism is remote from Christianity. Alexandra Burstein's
so-called adaptation included a prologue in which a black girl is
injured during a political rally; while a kindly white couple await
a doctor to attend to the girl, they tell her the story of Uncle
Tom's Cabin.

Burstein wildly mixed up the Cabin's characters with those
of Mrs. Stowe's Dred, discarding such characters as Topsy and
Eva. Middle-aged Tom and his wife, Chloe, are owned by the Gor-
dons (from Dred); George Harris is a brilliant inventor who is
bilked by a capitalist but escapes further persecution dressed to
the teeth as a Mexican caballero. Harris' wife, Eliza, escapes with
their thirteen-year-old daughter, May-"Blue Jay," and finds refuge
with kindhearted Senator Baird and his loving wife. Eliza and her
daughter are captured with Uncle Tom and put up for sale on the
auction block against a backdrop of a massive United States seals
emblazoned with "E Pluribus Unum" and a gigantic figure of Justice
--blind as usual. An American priest, heavy with cross and beads,
makes a bid for Eliza's attractive daughter. Seemingly abandoned
from a dismembered road company of The Three Musketeers and costumed as a rather effete D'Artagnan in burgundy velvet and a plumed
yellow velvet hat (which would have been the envy of the Court of
Louis XIII), a Red River planter named Simon Legree has Uncle
Tom hanged. Evil capitalist Legree storms to the footlights to de-
clare his intention of continuing to rule the world, where there will
always be slaves--either black, yellow, or white.

For the juicy epilogue Burstein returned to the poor Negro
girl of the prologue who still has not received medical attention from
an American doctor and is possibly in severe shock from the story
she has just heard. But not to worry! Niet! Her mother dismisses
her daughter's injuries and tells her to remember the face of Legree
as the face of the enemy, an enemy more deadly than her injuries.
Curtain.

"Uncle Tom" and "Tommer" eventually became synonymous
with subservience and as a derisive denouncement of one kowtowing
to whites or displaying obsequiousness to other nationalities.
"Simon Legree" entered the language as descriptive of a slave-
driving employer. It was, therefore, surprising that the Workshop
of the Players' Art revived Uncle Tom's Cabin 122 years after its
first production at their off-off Broadway Bowery Theatre on February 26, 1975.

Black actor Robert Stocking played a dignified, acceptable

Uncle Tom in the large cast of thirty. The adaptation by Lionel H.
Mitchell, directed by Hugh Gittens, with choreography by Quincy
Edwards and incidental music and spirituals arranged by David
Hollister and Lionel Mitchell, closely resembled George L. Aiken's
original play. Mel Gussow (the New York Times) found "the play
itself could use judicious cutting, less exposition and more interpretation, so that we can see with greater clarity the black point
of view today towards Uncle Tom's Cabin."

        Howard Sackler's Pulitzer Prize play The Great White Hope,
which opened at the Alvin Theatre on October 3, 1968, for 546
performances, was based on the flamboyant career of heavyweight
boxing champion Jack Johnson. The play included a second act
scene set in a Budapest cabaret where black Johnson (Jefferson
in the play)--reduced in glory and circumstances--and his white
common-law wife perform Uncle Tom and Little Eva in a travesty
of Uncle Tom's Cabin. The Trinity Square Repertory Company of
Providence, Rhode Island, in November 1978, produced the world
premiere of Adrian Hall and Richard Cumming's treatment of Mrs.
Stowe's story, called Uncle Tom's Cabin: A History.

        For all its historical significance and established reputation as
an American classic novel and play, Uncle Tom's Cabin, seen against
today's cultural background, would confirm Cordelia Howard Mac-
Donald's observation of some fifty years ago, "I think the play
seems rather archaic."

The motion-picture medium was a natural showcase for putting the classics and not-so-classics before the public especially when no royalties were demanded. Uncle Tom's Cabin appeared early on in Sigmund Lubin's May 1, 1903, short film and served as background the same year in Lubin's comedy The Troubles of a Stranded Actor, in which a Shakespearean hac-tor enacted the part of Little Eva. On July 30, 1903, Thomas A. Edison released a one-reel version of Uncle Tom's Cabin, directed by Edwin Stratton Porter. The Edison entry crowded fourteen settings (and a closing tableaux showing Abraham Lincoln promising to free the slaves) into fifteen minutes; in 1907 Lubin again attempted to film the Stowe story.

Vitagraph released three one-reel pictures on July 26, 29, and 30 (1909) of Uncle Tom's Cabin. The pictures, based on Eugene Mullin's screenplay, with E. R. Phillips as Uncle Tom, was directed by J. Stuart Blackton. Thanhauser's July 30, 1910, "complete on one reel" release had Frank Crane as Uncle Tom and Marie Eline as Eva. Mutual-Reliance's two-reel film of Forrest Halsey's scenario The Open Road, advertised as "Ben Tippet's Massive Production of Uncle Tom's Cabin--The Play Within the Play," was directed by Oscar Apfel and released on January 22, 1913, with Irving Cummings doubling as Uncle Tom and Eliza--and George Siegmann as Simon Legree. Del Henderson's short Biograph comedy An Uncle Tom's Cabin Troupe on April 10, 1913, featured a touring "Tom Show."

The first screen version of Uncle Tom's Cabin that approached the complete story was Universal-Imp's three-reel $15,000 August 25, 1913, release directed by Harry Pollard. Pollard also played Uncle Tom, with Gertrude Short as Eva, Margarita Fischer as Topsy, Robert Leonard as Simon Legree and Edna Maison as Eliza. On December 17, 1913, the Kalem Company released their two-reel motion picture of Uncle Tom's Cabin; the film was written and directed by Kenean Beuel, who also played Marks, the lawyer. Henry Hallam was Kalem's Uncle Tom, Doris Hollister was Eva, Miriam Cooper was Topsy, James Vincent was St. Clair, Anna Q. Nilsson was Eliza, and Hal Clements was Simon Legree.

World Pictures' August 10, 1914, five-reel feature film of Uncle Tom's Cabin was the first to cast a black actor in the role of

Uncle Tom. Seventy-two-year-old Sam Lucas, who would die less than two years later on Sunday, January 16, 1916, supposedly from illness developed during the filming of Uncle Tom's Cabin (he had been directed to leap into a frozen river to rescue Little Eva), was one of the foremost black actors and entertainers of his era. Known as "The Grand Old Man of the Negro Theatre," Sam Lucas, born at Washington, Virginia on Saturday, August 7, 1841, was the son of former slaves owned by Samuel Lucas whose name Sam was given. Lucas entered show business in the mid-nineteenth century and, in C. B. Smith's "Double" Uncle Tom's Cabin company, was documented as the first black actor to play Uncle Tom on the stage. Marie Eline was Eva, Boots Wall was Topsy, Irving Cummings was George Harris, Teresa Michelana was Eliza, Roy Applegate was Simon Legree, Walter Hitchcock and Hattie Delaro were the Shelbys, and Garfield Thompson was St. Clair. Universal's L-Ko comedy The Death of Simon Le Gree on January 24, 1915, had Pathe Lehrman as the villainous Simon. Kalem's August 23, 1915, four-reel feature, The Barnstormers, was another comedy based on a "Tom Show," with True Boardman and Ollie Kirby as the leading "Tommers."

J. Searle Dawley directed Adolph Zukor's Paramount Pictures' July 15, 1918, feature Uncle Tom's Cabin. Filmed primarily in Louisiana, Marguerite Clark was seen as both Eva and Topsy, with Frank Losee, a seasoned stage "Tommer," as Uncle Tom. Fred Niblo directed Thomas H. Ince's production When Do We Eat?-- another comedy satirizing a small town production of Uncle Tom's Cabin, with Enid Bennett as Little Eva. The picture was released by Paramount Pictures on August 13, 1918. Mack Sennett's Paramount comedy Uncle Tom Without the Cabin (August 31, 1919) featured cross-eyed Ben Turpin as an unlikely Uncle Tom, and Marie Prevost as Eliza; Charles Lynn cracked the whip as Simon Legree.

It was in 1927 that Carl Laemmle's Universal Pictures Studio released their extravagantly advertised reputed $2 million motion-picture version of Uncle Tom's Cabin. Laemmle spared no expense in constructing sixty-five different sets. He carefully and meticulously re-created Harriet Beecher Stowe's description of the St. Clair home, Legree's plantation, and the Shelby plantation, with its detailed rows of humble and squalid cabins along the slave quarter. Harry Pollard, who had directed Universal's three-reel 1913 Cabin, was once again in charge of the mid-twenties filming, and black actor Charles S. Gilpin was signed to play Uncle Tom.

Charles Sidney Gilpin was born on Wednesday, November 20, 1878 at Richmond, Virginia. He had been a leading player in various black theatre companies for nearly two decades when he first appeared on Broadway as the black clergyman, William Curtis, in John Drinkwater's drama Abraham Lincoln (Cort Theatre, December 15, 1919). Gilpin was the original Brutus Jones in Eugene O'Neill's drama The Emperor Jones in 1920-1921. But his seriously inflated ego, born of sudden fame and progressively serious drinking, led

to his replacement by Paul Robeson in the revival of The Emperor
Jones on Broadway and in London (1925). Charles Gilpin made
one film prior to being signed for the part of Uncle Tom. He
played the leading role of Joe Morgan in an all-black motion-picture
version of Timothy Shay Arthur's 1854 potboiler Ten Nights in a
Barroom (for the Colored Players Film Corporation of Philadelphia
released on December 27, 1926).

   Early in the spring of 1926, filming began on Universal's epic
production of the Cabin. The location was Plattsburg, New York,
where Eliza (played by Pollard's wife Margarita Fischer) was chased
across the ice-choked Saranac River by a team of thoroughbred,
registered English Ledburn bloodhounds. Gilpin's arrogant behavior
and heavy drinking (which followed him like a stumbling shadow)
and his arrogantly preconceived idea of how to interpret Uncle
Tom, militated against Universal's and Pollard's concept, and Gilpin
was summarily released from his contract. Three years later, on
Tuesday, May 6, 1930, at his farm at Eldredge Park, New Jersey,
Gilpin died at the age of fifty-one. He was replaced in Uncle Tom's
Cabin by black actor James B. Lowe.

   James B. Lowe had appeared in two movie Westerns (The De-
mon Rider and Blue Blazes) before replacing Charles Gilpin as Uncle
Tom. With the usual flamboyant Hollywood hyperbole, Universal
Studios press release on Lowe read:

> James B. Lowe has made history. A history that reflects
> only credit to the Negro race, not only because he has
> given the "Uncle Tom" character a new slant, but because
> of his exemplary conduct with the Universal Company.
> They look upon Lowe at the Universal Studios as a living
> black god. Of the director, critics, artists and actors who
> have seen James Lowe work at the studio there are none
> who will not say he is the most suited of all men for the
> part of "Tom." Those who are religious say that a heavenly
> power brought him to Universal and all predict a most mar-
> velous future and worldwide reputation for James B. Lowe.

Despite this preamble to deification, James B. Lowe never made
another film after Uncle Tom's Cabin; he died at the age of eighty-
three in 1963. Universal did export Lowe to London for personal
appearances at the opening of Uncle Tom's Cabin after it became
apparent their super-colossus Cabin was in danger of collapse.

   In the autumn of 1926 Pollard relocated his company in Natchez, Mississippi. He recorded some beautiful film footage including
frames of an old-fashioned river steamboat. On January 22, 1927,
the Moving Picture World reported, "The boat used by the Uncle
Tom company was the Kate Adams, the only remaining side-wheeler
on the river and one of the most famous of its day. This craft was
burned to the water's edge last week shortly after the Universal
company returned to California."

James B. Lowe as Uncle Tom and Virginia Grey as Little Eva in
Uncle Tom's Cabin, Universal Pictures, 1927 (courtesy of The Free
Library of Philadelphia Print and Pictures Dept.).

    Uncle Tom's Cabin opened a twice-daily, reserved-seat, road-
show schedule at two dollars, tops, on November 4, 1927 at New
York's Central Theatre on which Universal had taken a year's lease.
The two hour and twenty-one minute film was viewed by Mordaunt
Hall (the New York Times) as "an unremitting effort to make this
picture tearful, which is possibly to be expected--James B. Lowe
gives an excellent performance as Uncle Tom. He puts a good deal
of soul into the part, and it is a pity that Mr. Pollard should have
taken such unbounded delight in picturing the last moments of the
old slave."

    The long, over-drawn screening of Uncle Tom's Cabin was
played with one intermission. But Universal's proclamation of their
accurate and faithful adaptation of Mrs. Stowe's novel dissolved when
the studio extended her story to include Lincoln's freeing of the

slaves and General Sherman's march through Georgia; these changes
increased the film's poor reception in the South. Universal reissued
their 1927 <u>Uncle Tom's Cabin</u> several times with a synchronized
sound track and, in 1958, added a ponderously intoned prologue
spoken by Raymond Massey, who had spent several years freeing
the slaves on Broadway in the title role of Robert E. Sherwood's
Pulitzer Prize 1938 drama, <u>Abe Lincoln in Illinois</u>.

The cast and credits for Universal's 1927 <u>Uncle Tom's Cabin</u>
are listed below.

UNCLE TOM'S CABIN. Produced by Universal Pictures. Released November 4, 1927.

Carl Laemmle, producer; Director, Harry Pollard; Screenplay,
based on the novel by Harriet Beecher Stowe, by Harvey
Thew, A. P. Younger and Harry Pollard; Camera, Charles
Stumar, Jacob Krull; Titles, Walter Anthony; Musical score
(Movietone) by Hugo Riesenfeld; Technical adviser, Colonel
George L. Bryam; Production supervisors, Edward J. Mon-
tagne, Julius Bernheim; Film Editors, Gilmore Walker, Daniel
Mendell, Byron Robinson.

James B. Lowe (Uncle Tom); Virginia Grey (Eva St. Clare);
Mona Ray (Topsy); George Siegmann (Simon Legree); Mar-
garita Fischer (Eliza); Arthur Edmund Carew (George Har-
ris); John Roche (St. Clare); Gertrude Astor (Mrs. St.
Clare); Eulalie Jensen (Cassie); Adolph Milar (Haley);
Jack Mower (Mr. Shelby); Vivian Oakland (Mrs. Shelby);
Aileen Manning (Miss Ophelia); Lucien Littlefield (Lawyer
Marks); Gertrude Howard (Aunt Chloe, Tom's Wife); Nel-
son McDowell (Phineas Fletcher); Grace Carlisle (Mrs.
Fletcher); J. Gordon Russell (Tom Loker); J. Seymour
"Skipper" Zeliff (Edward Harris); Lassie Lou Ahern (Little
Harris); C. E. Anderson (Johnson); Dick Sutherland
(Sambo); Tom Amardares (Quimbo); Bill Dyer (Auction-
eer); Francis Ford (Lieutenant); Rolfe Sedan (Adolph);
Louise Beavers (Cook); Martha Franklin (Landlady); Marie
Foster (Mammy in St. Clare House); Madame Madilane Sul-
tu-Wan (Negress); Geoffrey Grace (The Doctor); Mattie
Peters, Spencer Bell, Curtis McHenry (Slaves); Alice
Nicholas (Dan's Wife); Hartwell Rice, Clark Moore (Coach-
men); Jim Anderson (Driver); Catherine Carrett, Anna
Johnson, Mary Washington (Housemaids); George West
(Servant)

While Universal was struggling to re-create <u>Uncle Tom's Cabin</u>

The Duncan Sisters in Topsy and Eva, 1924 (courtesy of The Free
Library of Philadelphia Theatre Collection).

on celluloid, in another part of the Hollywood wonderland--south of
Universal City--vaudevillians and musical-comedy performers Vivian
and Rosetta Duncan (United Artists studio) were busy putting their
1924 musical comedy, Topsy and Eva, before the cameras. Los
Angeles-born vaudevillians Rosetta and Vivian Duncan made their
New York debut, May 1917, at the Fifth Avenue Theatre. Their
popular sister act had no competitors, and later they headlined the
bill at the Palace. Prior to their greatest musical-comedy success,
Topsy and Eva, the sisters also appeared on Broadway with Fred
Stone in the 1920s musical comedy Tip-Top.

Topsy and Eva was a comedic adaptation of Uncle Tom's Cabin
by Catherine Chisholm Cushing, with music and lyrics by the Duncan Sisters. The adaptation included the sisters' sweetly sentimental
duet "Remembr'wring" as well as Topsy's outrageous song "I Never
Had a Mammy," encored by Rosetta with "When It's Sweet Onion Time
in Bermuda." Topsy and Eva opened at San Francisco's Alcazar
Theatre on July 9, 1923, and became a runaway hit. After over a
year's run in Chicago, where Ashton Stevens (Chicago Herald Examiner) commented that "Rosetta Duncan is funnier than Charlie
Chaplin," Topsy and Eva opened at Broadway's Sam H. Harris Theatre on December 23, 1924, with Rosetta as a very black, hilariously
impudent and belligerent Topsy, Vivian as golden-curled Eva, and
Basil Rysdael as Uncle Tom. Frank K. Wallace played Simon Legree,
and Myrtle Ferguson was a perfect foil for Topsy as Aunt Ophelia.
George Shelby became the show's romantic lead and was played by
several actors: Carl Gantvoort (San Francisco); Rex Cherryman
(Chicago); Robert Halliday (succeeding Cherryman on Broadway).
Morris Brown and Vernon Rickard played him during the road tour,
where Uncle Tom was acted by Edmund Fitzpatrick and later by
Virgil Johanson.

TOPSY AND EVA. (Opened December 23, 1924, Sam H. Harris Theatre, New York--159 performances.)

Produced by Tom Wilkes; A musical comedy based on Uncle
Tom's Cabin by Catherine Chisholm Cushing; Director, Oscar
Eagle; Music and Lyrics by the Duncan Sisters; Settings,
Dickson Morgan; Musical numbers staged by Jack Holland;
Costumes, Madam Keeler; Company manager, John R. Willad-
sen; Musical director, Jerome Stewartson; Stage director,
Wilbur Cushman; Stage manager, Ross Himes

Vivian Duncan (Eva St. Clare); Rosetta Duncan (Topsy);
Basil Ruysdael (Uncle Tom); Frank K. Wallace (Simon Legree); Harriet Hoctor (Henrique); Rex Cherryman (succeeded by Robert Halliday) (George Shelby); Wilbur Cushman (Augustine St. Clare); Florence Martin (Eliza); Ross
Himes (Rastus); Helen Case (Mrs. Shelby); Davis Goodman

(Gee Gee); Nydia D'Arnell (Mariette); Ashley Cooper (Erasmus Marks); Aimee Torriani (Chloe); Glory Minehart (Harry); Renee Lowrie (Helen); Lea Swan (Ann); Edith Maybaun (Jane); Antoinette Boots (Bessie); Myrtle Ferguson (Ophelia St. Clare); Philip Ryder, Harry Furney, Roy Collins, Floyd Carder (Plantation Quartette); Ernay Goodleigh, Alice Averill, Dixie Harkins, Renee Lowrie, Lea Swan, Antoinette Boots, Shirley Beauford, Jessie Pollard, Edith Maybaun, Natasia Verova, Lorraine Ray, Patricia Pattisson, Hazel Cushman (Old-Fashioned Girls); London Palace Theatre Dancers (especially contracted for the Duncan Sisters in Topsy and Eva, direct from the Palace Theatre, London, England:--Billie Bart, Hettie Ward, Toresa McSpirit, Rosie Swettenham, Violet Little, Rosa Thompson, Ethel Swettenham, Minnie Shaw, Elsie Thompson, Kitty Dolan (Pickaninnies)

Songs: Give Me Your and Give Me Your Hand; Um-Um-Da; Moon Am Shinin'; Rememb'wring; The Land of Long Ago; Do-Re-Mi; In the Autumn; Uncle Tom's Cabin Blues; Bird Dance; Cotton Time; Mariette; Kiss Me; I Never Had a Mammy; Wedding Procession

TOPSY AND EVA.   Released June 16, 1927.

Produced by Feature Productions, United Artists release; Director, Del Lord (D. W. Griffith refilmed and directed most of Topsy and Eva. Much of Del Lord's footage was scrapped. Lois Weber was the film's first director); Adaptation of Catherine Chisholm Cushing's musical comedy; Camera, John W. Boyle; Titles, Dudley Early; Continuity, Scott Darling; Production consultant, Myron Selznick

Vivian Duncan (Eva); Rosetta Duncan (Topsy); Gibson Gowland (Simon Legree); Noble Johnson (Uncle Tom); Nils Asther (George Shelby); Henry Victor (St. Clare); Myrtle Ferguson (Aunt Ophelia); Marjorie Daw (Marietta)

Critical opinion was divided on Topsy and Eva, reviews were acknowledged by Time magazine as a "savage disagreement." The New York Times noted "In brief, a reasonably discouraging play" while Percy Hammond (New York Herald-Tribune) declared it was "Something akin to a triumph." Burns Mantle (Daily News) tagged the show as "a freak of the season." Time magazine added, "The Duncan Sisters make the difference--to hear the Duncan Sisters harmonize is just as important as to subscribe to the Theatre Guild. The little Duncan [Rosetta] is in blackface, playing Topsy. Most people find her funny."

The Duncan Sisters played Topsy and Eva across the nation
for three years and, after their screen version of the musical comedy, took their show to London. London was neither impressed nor
delighted with Topsy and Eva until Rosetta's hospitalization brought
England's adored music hall star Gracie Fields into the musical as
Topsy's replacement; then Topsy and Eva became a London hit.
The Duncan Sisters made a cameo appearance in Paramount's 1927
film, Two Flaming Youths. On February 18, 1929, they were back
on Broadway in Ziegfeld's Midnight Frolic. Their talking-screen
debut was in Metro-Goldwyn-Mayer's 1929 musical, It's A Great Life,
which had originally been known as Cotton and Silk and later was
known as Imperfect Ladies.

Producer Martin Jones engaged the Duncan Sisters to headline
Leonard Sillman's New Faces of 1936 when business at Broadway's
Vanderbilt Theatre declined. Rosetta and Vivian reenacted their
aging Topsy and Eva routines on Broadway and on tour in New
Faces, a title not reflecting their image. Leonard Sillman, in
shock of discovering that the Duncan Sisters* were starring in his
revue, later recalled they performed a song "Who'll Buy My Doughnuts" and "While the girls sang this fetching ditty they pelted the
audience with doughnuts. It was absolutely obscene."

Lois Weber was assigned as director for the filming of 1927's
Topsy and Eva, but she resigned in protest because of the en-
croaching racist aspect of the material (although Weber had adapted
the play herself and written the scenario). Del Lord replaced Weber
and managed to mangle the project. United Artists president Joseph
Schenck asked D. W. Griffith to resurrect Lord's directorial disaster. Griffith shot many additional scenes and rearranged and recut
the entire picture, virtually remaking the film. The screen version
of Topsy and Eva did not echo the success of the stage production
(although the Broadway engagement completed only 159 performances); nor did the personal appearance of the Duncan Sisters in
conjunction with the showing of the motion picture increase attend-
ance. Rosetta and Vivian Duncan reprised their stage roles with
black actor Noble Johnson as Uncle Tom, Gibson Gowland as Simon
Legree, and Nils Asther (who married Vivian Duncan) as the romantic George Shelby.

Although D. W. Griffith salvaged Topsy and Eva, he could
not redeem a blackface comedy of his own. On May 23, 1923,
D. W. Griffith announced his next project would be a screen version of Arthur Caesar's story Mammy's Boy (starring Al Jolson),
to be filmed at Griffith's Marmaroneck, New York studio. Jolson
closed his Broadway show, Bombo, on Saturday, June 9, 1923, and
preliminary shooting on Griffith's film (then known as Black and
White) began. The famed director told the press he was delighted

---

*The Duncan Sisters were satirized in 1926's Grand Street Follies
by Lois Shore as Topsy (Rosetta) and Dorothy Sands as Eva (Vivian).

with Jolson's screen work and persona. But "The World's Greatest Entertainer," after seeing a few reels of Black and White, with a cast including Harlan Knight, Mrs. Stuart Robson, Frank Puglia, Erville Alderson, Annie Eggleston and James Phillips, appraised his screen debut as "the worst bit of junk I've ever seen." Jolson suddenly sailed for Europe with J. J. Shubert on the S.S. Majestic on June 23. He wired Griffith from the ship, "Ordered by physicians to take ocean voyage immediately owing to my nervous condition."

Griffith and his company sued Jolson for breach of contract. They had had a "gentleman's agreement" (no signed contract) by which Jolson was to receive $25,000 in advance--and the same amount upon the completion of the picture. Anthony Paul Kelly, who had written the scenario for Black and White, testified that Jolson was terrified he would not be successful on the silent screen. Jolson's attorney admitted that the great Jolson was badly afflicted with stage fright and felt he could not act well enough for the uncompromising camera. The breach of contract suit was not settled until mid-September, 1926; at that time, Griffith, Inc. was awarded a settlement of $2,627.28.

Added to Griffith's problems with Jolson was the death of his white, blackface character actor Porter Strong who, on Monday, June 11, 1923, was found dead of a heart attack at the age of forty-four in his New York apartment. Black and White resumed filming in August 1923 with Educational Comedies star Lloyd Hamilton playing Jolson's blackface part of Claude Sappington, a white amateur detective, disguised in blackface, who infiltrates the Black Cat Cafe (which was reserved for "culled folk 'sclusively") to capture a gang of blackface bootleggers and save innocent Uncle Eph from hanging (Eph had been falsely accused of a murder committed by Bill Jackson). The completed five-reel comedy, directed by John W. Noble (not D. W. Griffith), was released by W. W. Hodkinson Corporation on March 16, 1924, as His Darker Self. The whites in blackface were Lucille La Verne (Aunt Lucy); Irma Harrison (Darktown's Cleopatra); Tom Wilson (Bill Jackson); Tom O'Malley (Uncle Eph), and Edna May Sperl (Jackson's sweetheart).

Uncle Tom's Cabin served as background for several motion pictures and several specialty numbers were based on the Cabin's characters. Among them was Thomas Beer's Saturday Evening Post story, "Little Eva Ascends" produced by Metro Pictures in 1922. Blanche St. George's (Unice Vin Moor) tank-town touring Tom Show features her sons: Roy was Little Eva (Gareth Hughes); John was Uncle Tom (Benjamin Haggerty). Ham actor Richard Bansfield was Aunt Chloe (W. H. Brown). Madge Bellamy played a stranded Tom-Show actress in Truart Film Corporation's 1925 film, The Reckless Sex. In Tiffany's 1927 picture, Lightning, Jobyna Ralston and Margaret Livingston performed Eva and Topsy with Pat Harmon as Simon Legree (as part of Zane Gray's story Hosses).

The misadventures of a troupe of hammy Tom-Show actors and
their one ragged bloodhound stranded in Hiawatha, Kansas was called
Fly By Night. It was written by Kenyon Nicholson and John Golden.
Based on Nicholson's one-act play, The Marriage of Little Eva, it
opened at Atlantic City's Apollo Theatre on April 2, 1928, and closed
on May 12 after a four-week stand at Chicago's Cort Theatre.
Thomas Mitchell was the troupe's Simon Legree. He was in love with
an aging but unretiring Little Eva, played by Gladys Hurlbut. Produced by John Golden and Edgar Selwyn, the comedy arrived on
Broadway at the Little Theatre on August 28, 1928: it had been
recast and retitled Eva the Fifth. Claiborne Foster was aging actress Hattie Hartley. Hattie permits her little sister, Oriole Hartley (Lois Shore), to play her part of Little Eva. Jealous of Oriole's
instant success in Uncle Tom's Cabin, Hattie plies her gullible sister
with delicious chocolates. When Oriole, the fifth Eva of the acting
Hartley family, cannot continue in the death scene she wishes were
real, Hattie naturally retrieves her wig of golden curls and resumes
her part as Little Eva. Buford Armitage replaced Thomas Mitchell
as Hattie's lover, Mal Thorne, and the Cabin's Simon Legree.
Metro-Goldwyn-Mayer filmed Eva the Fifth in 1929 as The Girl in the
Show. The project was directed and adapted by Edgar Selwyn, with
Bessie Love as the reluctant-to-retire Little Eva, Nanci Price as the
chocolate overdosed Oriole, and Raymond Hackett as Mal and Legree.

Shirley Temple played Little Eva opposite Jack Clifford's Uncle
Tom and Betty Jean Hainey's Topsy in 20th Century-Fox' Dimples
(1936); Frank Morgan was Shirley's broken-down actor grandfather,
who was evading police disguised as blackface Uncle Tom. Twentieth Century-Fox's second-string moppet Jane Withers as Little Eva
sang "Uncle Tom's Cabin Is a Cabaret Now" in Can This Be Dixie?
(1936). Judy Garland was Topsy in MGM's Everybody Sing (1938),
caroling Uncle Tom's more modern routines with Eliza crossing the
ice in a limousine while Simon Legree shook his tambourine. For
the Lincoln Birthday holiday sequence in Paramount Pictures' 1942
Irving Berlin's Holiday Inn, Bing Crosby blacked-up as Uncle Tom,
with Marjorie Reynolds as Topsy, performing Berlin's song "Abraham." Crosby and Sonny Tufts blackfaced the "Accentuate the
Positive" number in Paramount Pictures' Here Come the Waves
(1944), and Betty Grable and June Haver went blackface as double
Topsys for a specialty number in 20th Century-Fox's 1945 The
Dolly Sisters.

Hollywood's frequently creative, though often infelicitous, fascination with blackface had started in the dawn of motion pictures.
But after Uncle Tom's Cabin was reduced primarily to sequences in
Hollywood musicals or, when the film capital was not occupied with
various clonings of Uncle Tom, actors in blackface or minstrels
(either as background, characterization, or pivotal points) were
used in many films. Warner Bros. produced a 1927 feature comedy,
Ham and Eggs at the Front, which headlined Tom Wilson as Ham and
Heinie Conklin as Eggs, with Myrna Loy as Fifi, a Negro waitress

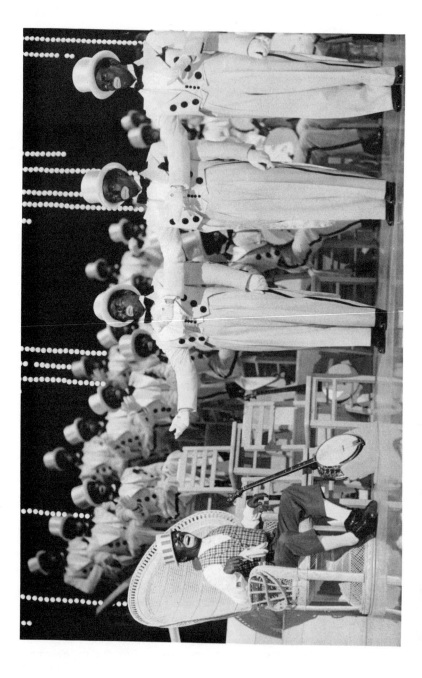

spying for the Germans. Wesley Barry and Wade Boteler resorted
to burnt cork as U.S. Army spies in Anchor Films' Top Sergeant
Mulligan (1928); the same blackface ploy was used by Marion Davies
in MGM's Operator 13 (1934).

Paramount Pictures released Sono-Art's production of The
Rainbow Man in 1929. The film starred Eddie Dowling as minstrel
man Rainbow Ryan. Fox Film Corporation's extravaganza Happy
Days (filmed in large screen Grandeur process) had an all-star cast
coming to the aid of Colonel Billy Batcher to help him save his
floundering Memphis Mammouth Minstrels. Happy Days was described
by Photoplay as the "latest in the big parade of photoplay revues.
It wears a minstrel suit and carries a huge red banner." The protagonist in Pathé's The Grand Parade (1930) was an alcoholic minstrel
man in a story closely paralleling George Manker Watter's and Arthur
Hopkins' successful Broadway play Burlesque (1928), which had been
pristinely filmed by Paramount Pictures as The Dance of Life (1929).
Warner Bros. picture Mammy (1930), with songs by Irving Berlin,
starred Al Jolson as end man Mr. Bones, with Mitchell Lewis as Tambo and Lowell Sherman as the minstrel show's interlocutor. Supposedly, Mammy was based on an unproduced "Musical Comedy of
Minstrel Days in Two Acts" by Irving Berlin and James Gleason
(Mr. Bones).

There were many burnt-cork characterizations, among them
was George M. Cohan in his first talking picture as medicine show
performer Doc Peter Varney in Paramount's The Phantom President
(1932). For the first time in his career, Fred Astaire appeared in
blackface in Jerome Kern and Dorothy Fields's tribute to the great
Bill Robinson, singing and dancing "Bojangles of Harlem" in RKO's
Swing Time (1936). Martha Raye torched "Public Melody Number
One" in Vincente Minnelli's staged sequence for Paramount Pictures
Artists and Models (1937). In 1939, even Edgar Bergen's alter-ego
Charlie McCarthy went blackface (Universal Pictures, You Can't
Cheat an Honest Man).

Metro-Goldwyn-Mayer's Babes in Arms (1939) included a minstrel show finale led by blacked-up Judy Garland and Mickey Rooney
singing "My Daddy Was a Minstrel Man." The sequence also included such old favorites as: "Oh, Susanna"; "Ida, Sweet as Apple
Cider"; "De Camptown Races"; "On Moonlight Bay"; "I'm Just Wild
About Harry" (Eubie Blake's song hit from Broadway's 1921 Shuffle
Along). Busby Berkeley, whose most tasteless and tactless directed
film sequence was Al Jolson's blackface "Going to Heaven on a Mule"
number in Warner Bros. Wonder Bar (1934), directed a musical segment arranged by Roger Edens for MGM's 1941 sequel to Babes in
Arms, called Babes on Broadway, in which Garland and Rooney

[Opposite:] Mickey Rooney (left) as Sambo in the minstrel show
finale of Babes on Broadway, M-G-M, 1941 (courtesy of the Doug
McClelland Collection).

again applied burnt cork, Rooney strummed a banjo to "Swanee
River." He was backed by a blackface chorus with banjos and
tambourines, and Garland belted out Harold Rome's infectious song
"Franklin D. Roosevelt Jones" from George S. Kaufman and Moss
Hart's satirical Broadway revue Sing Out the News (1938), which
presented the United States Congress as a minstrel show.

Paramount Pictures' Technicolor Dixie (1943) was a highly fictionalized biography of Dan Emmett, which had no pretense of authenticity. Composer and minstrel man Dan Emmett was played by
Bing Crosby; Dixie also featured Eddie Foy, Jr. and Billy De Wolfe
as Tambo and Bones, with Lynne Overman as Billy Whitlock. The
blackface semicircle of the minstrel show included John "Skins"
Miller, Donald Kerr, Fred Santley, Warren Jackson, Jimmy Ray,
Hal Rand, Charles Mayon, Allen Ray, Jerry James, and Jimmy
Clemons. Dixie remains probably the best produced and most
definitive screening of a minstrel show in its era. Interpolated
with new songs by Jimmy Van Heusen and Johnny Burke were several of Dan Emmett's memorable songs, including "Old Dan Tucker."
Most of the blackface sequences have been deleted and cut from
these films for today's television audiences.

Melodie Film CCC Filmkunst Avala Film-S.I.P.R.O., Debora
Film, Aldo von Pinelli, producer, filmed Uncle Tom's Cabin (1964).
Released in West Germany as Onkel Tom's Hutte (April 1965), the
film was directed by Geza Radvanyi and featured John Kitzmiller
as Uncle Tom; Herbert Lom as Simon Legree; Gertraud Mittermayr
as Little Eva; Rhet Kirby as Topsy; Catana Cayetano as Eliza; and
Olive Moorefield as Cassy. Eartha Kitt was cast as a singer. The
film was released in the United States in January 1969. Mrs.
Stowe's story was considerably altered to include President Lincoln's
freeing of the slaves who revolt, find shelter in a monastery, and
escape by flooding the cotton fields.

Philip Langner produced an updated Uncle Tom's Cabin (1969)
for the Theatre Guild Films-Slaves Company and the Walter Reade
Organization. Retitled Slaves, the adaptation of the final chapters
of Harriet Beecher Stowe's novel was made by director Herbert J.
Biberman, Alida Sherman, and John O. Killens. Stephen Boyd
played Nathan MacKay (Simon Legree), with Dionne Warwick as
Cassy and Aldine King as Emmeline. Uncle Tom became Luke. He
was played by Ossie Davis, who is flogged to death by MacKay as
the slaves torch the cotton sheds and escape with the help of Arthur
Stillwell (Sheppard Strudwick).

The passing of Uncle Tom was observed by Peter Noble in
1948 (The Negro in Film, London):

> The Uncle Tom who possessed the qualities of brotherly love
> and humility was, in his time, an argument against slavery,
> but Negroes have in recent years discovered militancy, and

the meek Beecher Stowe character now offends the sensibilities of most coloured thinkers, writers and workers. In
the eyes of the Negroes, Uncle Tom has long been a figure
of contempt, and his name associated with a kind of sub-
missive, servile, passive Negro, the "good nigger" who would
not fight against oppression.

With the advent of sound, Hollywood rediscovered Negro talent. Blacks began to appear on the screen in parts previously
played by whites in blackface. The first all-black film produced by
a major Hollywood studio was Metro-Goldwyn-Mayer's Hallelujah; the
motion picture was written and beautifully directed by King Vidor,
mainly on location in Memphis, Tennessee. Hallelujah featured black
actors Daniel Haynes--an understudy in Ziegfeld's Show Boat--and
Nina Mae McKinney, who had been on Broadway in Lew Leslie's
Blackbirds of 1928. For three years, Vidor, the renowned director
of The Big Parade (1925) and La Boheme (1926) planned (and fought
to make) his all-black (and first "all-talking") feature film. Hallelujah was released on August 20, 1929, and played twice-daily in
New York at the Embassy and Lafayette Theatres. Called "a magnificent film and a remarkable achievement," Hallelujah was selected
one of the ten best pictures of 1929. It was one of the finest films
made by King Vidor (although it failed to recover its cost of almost
$600,000); today the film might appear to be patronizing.

While Vidor was getting Hallelujah ready for release, Fox Film
Corporation released their shorter all-black feature film Hearts in
Dixie (May 10, 1929). Hearts in Dixie was originally scheduled as a
two-reeler short subject, with Charles Gilpin (whose continuing arrogance, unreasonable demands and drinking resulted in the studio
replacing him with George Reed). Advertised as "the first authentic
screen record of the Old South ever produced," Hearts in Dixie featured a fine black actor Clarence Muse, who had replaced Tony
Lucas, brother of the late, talented Sam Lucas. Muse was supported
by Gertrude Howard and Stepin Fetchit.

Lincoln Theodore Monroe Andrew Perry, better known as
Stepin Fetchit, enacted what became the stereotype of the shuffling, slow-moving, servile servant for over a decade in many Hollywood films. Fetchit was later unjustly accused of debasing his race
while, in reality, he was merely making a living. Fetchit later
lashed back at his accusers, "People don't understand any more
what I was doing then, least of all the young generation of Negroes.
Maybe because they don't really know what it was like then. Hollywood
was more segregated than Georgia." Fetchit died in November 1985.

The casting of whites in blackface was common practice in the
early years of the motion-picture industry. This practice grew out
of the dearth of Negro actors in California and from precedents established in the theatrical world, which dictated that only white
actors could impersonate blacks or take black parts. Beyond those

whites masquerading in black mentioned in the text, a small sampling
of some of the players who faced the cameras in burnt cork disguised as slaves, servants, mammys, mulattos, or black "natives"
is included in Appendix "B."

ETUDES ON UNCLE TOM

The popularity of Uncle Tom's Cabin inevitably inspired composers and lyricists to inject music into the Cabin. Caryl Floria's
(William James Robjohn) opera with a libretto by H. Wayne Ellis
was produced at Philadelphia's Chestnut Street Theatre on May 22,
1882, and was found to "laden the theatre with gloom." Paolo
Giorza's score for the ballet I Bianchi ed i negri, retitled La
Capanna dello Zio Tom, was heard when the ballet was performed
at Milan's La Scala Opera House on November 10, 1853. Uncle
Tom's Cabin was set to music in London's 1894 operetta by Ivan
Caryll, with a libretto and lyrics by George R. Sims.

A Newark, New Jersey cafe owner, Rosewell G. Tompson,
wrote a satire on Uncle Tom's Cabin (1901) for which a sixteen-
year-old Newark High School student wrote his first score for a
"book" musical. The student's name was Jerome David Kern.
Uncle Tom's Cabin was directed by Tompson's partner, former
actor Robert Neil. It opened on Kern's seventeenth birthday
(January 27, 1902) at Newark's Kreuger Auditorium. The leading
roles were acted by members of the community. Playwright Tompson was Little Eva, Gustave Troxler was Svengali Legree, Nicholas
J. Tynan was Topsy Wheatcake, and Daniel Blakeman was Aunt
Ophelia Sophedelia Obeleia Prim. Two different men were reported
for the amateur actor playing Uncle Tom. The composer of Show
Boat and numerous other musical successes--who later became world
famous--composed some eight songs for Uncle Tom's Cabin. Unfortunately, Jerome Kern's first score for a "book" show has vanished.

Uncle Tom characterizations or Uncle Tom songs emerged in
other shows, such as When Johnny Comes Marching Home which
opened on Broadway at the New York Theatre (December 16, 1902).
Julian Edwards composed the music for Stanislaus Stange's melo-
dramatic libretto played against the background of the Civil War.
The second act opened with Uncle Tom (Will H. Bray) singing "My
Honeysuckle Girl." The musical was revived on May 7, 1917, by
F. C. Whitney and staged by Fred Bishop at the New Amsterdam
Theatre, with Wilbur Cox as the old slave Uncle Tom. The Planta-
tion Darkies were played by: Lillian Franko (Chloe); Ethel Young
(Mandy); Ida Lodge (Eliza); Florence Lee (Harriet); Carrie Sager
(Rebecca); Jennie Faas (Matilda); Lilian Chambers (Susannah);
Ethel Phillips (Lindy); Harry Leclair (Ephraim); Ed Douglass (Chan);

Jack Roberts (Marmaduke); Albert Wyatt (Rastus); Kris Dahl (Jefferson Clay); David Adler (Washington Clay); Ben Tillson (Nick Bomby); and Marshall Stone (Abraham).

Operettas, musical comedies, varieties, and minstrels had early on featured whites masquerading as blacks. A blackface production of Gilbert and Sullivan's The Mikado (appropriately renamed The Black Mikado; or the Town of Kan-Ka-Kee) presented Chauncey Olcott, Ed Marble, Billy Rice, and George Edwards in burnt cork, and on January 25, 1886, Thatcher, Primrose, and West presented their minstrel version of The Black Mikado at Niblo's Garden.

The first musical comedy produced, written, and performed entirely by blacks was Bob Cole and Billy Johnson's A Trip to Coontown, which opened on September 27, 1897, in South Amboy, New Jersey and braved Manhattan exposure on April 4, 1898, at the Third Avenue Theatre. Clorindy; or the Origin of the Cakewalk (produced by George W. Lederer) opened July 5, 1898, at the Casino Roof Garden Theatre and headlined talented black performer Ernest Hogan (Reuben Crowders of Bowling Green, Kentucky who was a former "Tommer" and composer of a popular song "All Coons Look Alike to Me"); Hogan had advertised himself as "The Unbleached American." Clorindy had a book and lyrics by Paul Laurence Dunbar and music by Will Marion Cook.

The cakewalk was a favorite minstrel feature "peregrinating for the pastry" and was highlighted earlier in 1877 by Harrigan and Hart in "Walking for dat Cake, an Exquisite Picture of Negro Life and Customs" at their Theatre Comique. The cakewalk gained greater popularity in 1892 when the first Annual Cakewalk Jubilee ran for three nights at Madison Square Garden, featuring M. Sissieretta Jones (Matilda S. Joyner) known as "The Black Patti." The infectious, strutting, high-kicking, back-tilting cakewalk was polished to perfection by black dancers Charlie Johnson and Dora Dean in Sam T. Jack's 1893 revue The Creole Show. The finale of John W. Isham's 1895 black show, The Octoroons, was a cakewalk.

The cakewalk originated on Southern plantations, described by Robert C. Toll (Blacking Up) as follows: "when Negroes dressed in their masters' and mistresses' discarded finery and competed for a prize, usually a cake. This was, then, simply another feature of plantation life. Since the audience decided the winner by shouting out the number of its favorite couple, the black people threw themselves into a frenzied series of contortions--almost like puppets on strings." Bert Williams and George Walker were expert "cakewalkers." Their musicals--A Senegambian Carnival (1899--later known as A Lucky Coon); The Policy Players; Sons of Ham (1900); In Dahomey (1903); Abyssinia (1906); and Bandanna Land (1908)--became popular all-black entertainments.

Bert (Egbert Austin) Williams, born in Antigua, British West

Indies on Thursday, November 12, 1874, became the first celebrated
black comedian in American theatrical history. He was described
in Theatre magazine as "a vastly funnier man than any white comedian now on the American stage." After the death of his partner
George Walker who died at the age of thirty-eight on Friday, January 6, 1911, at the Central Islip, Long Island, New York Sanitorium
of paresis during the terminal stage of syphilis (this illness would
also bring early deaths to John McCullough, Maurice Barrymore,
Tony Hart, George L. Fox, Thomas B. Campbell, and many others
in the profesison), Bert Williams became the brightest comedian of
Ziegfeld's Follies.

Fanny Brice and Bert Williams each made their Follies debut
in 1910. Williams appeared as prizefighter Jack Johnson's double
in a sketch "A Street in Reno" and the following year sang his
famous song, "Nobody" (1905), which was forever to be identified
with him. Bert was Othello to Don Barclay's Desdemona in a travesty on Othello (Ziegfeld's Follies of 1916). Because of his light,
bright skin, Williams was forced to use burnt cork throughout his
career to conform to public acceptance of a black comedian. His
last stage appearance was on February 21, 1922 at Detroit's Shubert-
Garrick Theatre, where he collapsed during the first act of Under
the Bamboo Tree. Bert Williams died at his Manhattan home, 2309
Seventh Avenue, on Saturday, March 4, 1922; he was forty-eight.

The expert black comedians Flournoy Miller and Aubry Lyles
had smash hits with Shuffle Along (504 performances in 1921); they
used costumes from Eddie Leonard's 1919 show Roly Boly Eyes.
Shuffle Along featured "Uncle Tom and Old Black Joe," sung
as a duet by Charles Davis and Bob Williams and introduced Eubie
Blake and Noble Sissle's perennial favorite song, "I'm Just Wild
About Harry." Miller and Lyles continued their Broadway success
with 213 performances of Runnin' Wild (1923). The cakewalk had
been replaced by the more energetic, frenetic Charleston, but black
performers in musicals and dramatic plays had established themselves
as potentially popular and gifted entertainers on Broadway.

Minstrels had had their day. Burnt-cork performers were
gradually disappearing from the American entertainment world, except for the persistence of Jolson, Cantor, Leonard, Moran and Mack,
and those few vaudevillians whose trademark was blackface. Eventually Amos and Andy revived and popularized blackface comedy on
radio, but the art of minstrelsy and the reconstructions of Uncle
Tom's Cabin had all but passed. The emergence and acceptance of
exceptional black talent was challenged if not threatened in 1927
when a musical drama featuring whites in blackface made its inevitable appearance on Broadway. The drama was called Golden Dawn.

The opening of the 1927-1928 theatrical season on Broadway
saw the inauguration of three new theatres built specifically for
musical comedies. Abraham Lincoln Erlanger opened his new

Erlanger Theatre (September 26, 1927) with George M. Cohan's
musical comedy The Merry Malones. Two Philadelphia-born men of
the theatre, Alex A. Aarons and Vinton Freedley, produced George
and Ira Gershwin's musical comedy Funny Face. It was the first
attraction in their new theatre (named by a combination of their
first names), the Alvin (now the Neil Simon Theatre). Arthur
Hammerstein unveiled his memorial to his famous father Oscar Hammerstein, I on Wednesday, November 30, 1927. The new Hammerstein Theatre at 1697 Broadway between Fifty-third and Fifty-fourth
Streets was designed by architect Herbert J. Krapp, who had designed many of Broadway's more notable theatres.

     The distinguished and flamboyant Oscar Hammerstein, I, who
blacked-up to appear on the New York stage for a one-night-stand,
was as easily recognized in Manhattan as the Statue of Liberty was
to millions of emigrants, of which he was one. Perpetually, a large
black cigar could be seen above his grey Mephisphelean goatee,
an outsized top hat extended his five-foot-five-frame. He wore a
Prince Albert coat.) Oscar I was born on Saturday, May 8, 1847,
in Stettin (or Berlin), Germany. He became one of the most notable
and colorful impresarios of the American theatre, exceeding Florenz
Ziegfeld in extravagant productions and fiscal irresponsibility.

     The first show young Oscar saw in New York was Bryant's
Minstrels at Mechanic's Hall. In 1874, he rented Bryant's former
Fourteenth Street Tammany Hall Theatre and renamed it the Ger-
mania Theatre, where several of his own plays and music were presented in German until 1877, when Tony Pastor acquired the house
as a variety theatre. Ten years earlier, Oscar had seen the Booth
brothers (Edwin, John Wilkes, and Junius Brutus, Jr.) in their
special performance of Julius Caesar given to raise funds for a
statue of Shakespeare in Central Park; but Oscar's abiding love
was opera.

     Oscar I had a remarkable disinterest in money, despite making
and losing millions. He built and lost several theatres, the first
being the Harlem Opera House between Seventh and Eighth Avenues
and 125th and 126th Streets, which opened on September 30, 1889.
Among others, he lost the Olympia Theatre where he produced,
wrote, and composed an adulteration of Goethe's Faust called Marguerite (February 10, 1896)--creating no threat to Faust's composer
Charles-François Gounod. Hammerstein's consuming passion was
Opera. This passion resulted in his building his 3,100-seat Manhattan Opera House on Thirty-fourth Street and Eighth Avenue.
The Manhattan Opera House, the construction and decor having been
supervised by his son Arthur, opened December 3, 1906, with Vincenzo Bellini's opera I Puritani di Scozia, with Alessandro Bonci and
Mario Ancona; the conductor was Cleofante Campanini. Hammerstein successfully challenged and vigorously competed with the
more elegant and social-conscious Metropolitan Opera by signing such
famous artists as Nellie Melba, Luisa Tetrazzini, Mary Garden,

Ernestine Schumann-Heink, Emma Trentini, Emma Calvé, Mario Sammarco, and John McCormack. His production of Verdi's Otello (December 25, 1908, with Giovanni Zenatello) was a triumph.

Hammerstein's dedication to opera was evidenced in Philadelphia where he built his magnificent, acoustically perfect 4,100-seat Philadelphia Opera House, again leaving the intricate details of construction and decor to Arthur. The poorly-located Philadelphia Opera House opened on November 17, 1908, with Bizet's Carmen, featuring Maria Labia and conducted by Campanini. Through financier Otto Kahn, Oscar's rival, The Metropolitan Opera Association forced the dedicated impresario out of Opera in New York and, under their name, took title to his elegant, failed Philadelphia white elephant Opera House.

Oscar I was the pioneer of the theatrical district in and around Times Square when his Victoria Theatre opened on March 2, 1899, with a variety show and then became a legitimate theatre. Hammerstein built the Republic Theatre. It adjoined the Victoria and opened September 7, 1900, with James Herne starring in his own play Sag Harbor. The cast including Lionel Barrymore, Chrystal Herne, and William Hodge. Widely advertised as "The One, the Only, the Original Oscar Hammerstein" in his "Debut Extraordinary," the colorful impresario appeared on-stage for one night at the Victoria Theatre in March, 1905. He blacked-up as an end man in Lew Dockstader's Minstrels and performed a monologue in his everlasting German accent, singing one song to a wild fifteen-minute ovation.

Hammerstein commissioned Victor Herbert to write an operetta for his failing Manhattan Opera Company and its current star Emma Trentini. In 1910, he successfully produced Herbert's Naughty Marietta and, in 1912, produced Rudolf Friml's operetta The Firefly. Also in 1912, the ebullient Oscar--flushed with his financial gain from The Metropolitan Opera deal--lost nearly a million dollars competing with London's Covent Garden. Lavishly advertising himself as "Oscar Hammerstein, Builder of Opera Houses," he opened his London Opera House on Monday, November 13, 1911, with Jean Nouguès' opera Quo Vadis? (staged by his New York director Jacques Coini), but in less than a year the London Opera House was memory.

The enigmatic, unaffectionate genius known as Oscar Hammerstein, I died at the age of seventy-two on Friday, August 1, 1919. John McCormack sang two songs at Oscar I's funeral in Temple Emanuel on the morning of August 4th. One of McCormack's songs, "The Lost Chord," unintentionally reflected Oscar's lifelong, dedicated pursuit of opera. Four years later, Hammerstein's Theatre, with its domed, vaulted lobby exhibiting a bronze statue of Oscar Hammerstein, I, was renamed the Manhattan; in 1934 it became the Billy Rose Music Hall. The Columbia Broadcasting System purchased

the property in 1936; since 1967, Arthur Hammerstein's memorial to
his father has been the Ed Sullivan Theatre.

Golden Dawn was virtually a Hammerstein family enterprise.
Arthur Hammerstein, who died at the age of eighty-three (Wednes-
day, October 12, 1955, in Palm Beach, Florida), produced the show.
Arthur's brother William, who passed away at the age of forty
(Wednesday, June 10, 1914), had two sons--Oscar Greeley Clen-
denning Hammerstein, II, who co-authored the book and lyrics with
Otto Harbach, and Reginald Kent Hammerstein, who directed the
musical drama. The music was composed by two men: Vienna-born
Emmerich Kalman, whose best work is represented by his lovely
score for Countess Maritza (1926) and Herbert Stothart who later
became musical director for Metro-Goldwyn-Mayer in Hollywood.
Ziegfeld's genius designer Joseph Urban created the opulent settings for Golden Dawn.

The musical drama was accompanied by Viennese music, which
incongruously wafted through an African jungle as whites cavorted
in blackface. White and blonde Dawn (Louise Hunter) has been
raised as an African Princess by black Mooda (Marguerite Sylva),
matriarch of an East African tribe under German rule in 1917.
Mooda's ruthless overseer Shep Keyes (Robert Chisholm) is jealous
of Dawn's love for an imprisoned British officer Steve Allen (Paul
Gregory) and vindictively dedicates Dawn as the bride of their
tribal pagan god. Two years later, the tribe is plagued by a
drought and loss of crops. Shep, again repelled by Dawn, incites
the natives to rebel against Dawn; she has rejected their god
Mulunghu and embraced Christianity. Dawn seeks refuge at the
gate of a convent where Mooda confesses the white girl is really
the daughter of a dead white trader. Shep furiously attacks Dawn
and Mooda kills him with a crucifix. As the rains suddenly come
to relieve the drought and reduce the rebellion of her tribe, Dawn
is reunited with her English lover, Steve.

Percy Hammond (New York Herald-Tribune) called Golden Dawn,
"a stately opera, swimming in luscious tunes, depicting unusual
dramatic circumstances, and sung and acted by a superb troupe of
artists and performers." Burns Mantle (Daily News) dismissed the
show as "a pretentious operetta" and Robert Coleman (Daily Mirror)
said that "Joseph Urban's sets are breathtaking." Brooks Atkinson
(the New York Times), noting the more than three hours playing
time, wrote, "If the drama seems artificial and rather more prolonged than necessary, the score and singers make ample amends."
Gilbert Gabriel (New York Sun) extolled Golden Dawn as "a most
lavish 'music drama,' tirelessly romantic, scenic and songful."
Walter Winchell tersely described the operetta as "The Golden Yawn."

The New Yorker magazine admired the show's excellent score
(by Kalman and Stothart) and endorsed Golden Dawn as a "good
operetta" well sung by Metropolitan Opera's Louise Hunter and the

entire cast. The New Yorker headed their review "Art Attack";
their subject was the new theatre, which was not calculated to have
brought joy to Arthur Hammerstein or to architect Krapp, "It's
ugliness is so overpowering as to assault the senses" with "stained
glass windows which are illuminated at appropriate moments. Hammerstein's is, above all, a home for the Operetta Reverent."

Playing the small part of Australian soldier Anzac with one
line of dialogue was a young Englishman who had been a former
Coney Island stilt-walker. His name was Archie Leach. Eventually,
Leach gained international fame as Cary Grant. Hugh Fordin (in
his biography of Oscar Hammerstein, II, Getting to Know Him, published by Random House in 1977), wrote about Golden Dawn, "The
most memorable features of the presentation were the first topless
girl to be seen on a Broadway stage and the American debut of
Cary Grant."

Golden Dawn completed 184 performances on Broadway and in
1930 it became a motion picture. Directed by Ray Enright in Technicolor for Warner Bros., Golden Dawn was released on June 14, 1930,
with Vivienne Segal as Dawn, Alice Gentle as black Mooda, basso
Noah Beery as the blackface villain, Shep, and Walter Woolf as Dawn's
lover, Steve. The Warner Bros. African revels in three-quarter time
were described as "pretty dull."

Three years after the impressive Players' Club revival of Uncle Tom's Cabin and twelve years after Topsy and Eva opened on Broadway, another musical adaptation appeared. It was "a musical drama interpolated with choral numbers" and was called Sweet River. Produced, adapted, and directed by one of the theatre's master talents, George Abbott, Sweet River, following its opening on October 28, 1936 at Broadway's 51st Street Theatre, flowed quickly by after five performances. Black actor Walter Price was Sweet River's Uncle Tom, with seven-year-old Philadelphian Betty Philson as Little Eva, Harlem actress Inge Hardison as Topsy, Matt Briggs as Simon Legree, and white actress Margaret Mullen as Eliza. Excellent choral work was performed by an all-black chorus. The musical score had been arranged and directed by Juanita Hall who later became the celebrated Bloody Mary of South Pacific.

Burns Mantle (Daily News) reported,

> George Abbott has laid loving hands on the manuscript of Uncle Tom's Cabin and brought a new entertainment out of it. Not a very exciting entertainment but one that provides a pleasantly sentimental evening in the theatre. It is a reverent attempt to do justice to the old play and as such is entirely disarming.

George Abbott admitted in a program note that his adaptation (in which Little Eva does not die) rearranged Mrs. Stowe's story, eliminated various characters and "makes no pretense of being an honest adaptation--true to the original neither in the letter nor the spirit."

John Mason Brown (New York Post) commented that "In spite of all of Mr. Abbott's rewriting and omissions, it remains in its major outlines the same old play that every one knows." Richard Watts (Herald-Tribune) saw Sweet River as "probably the best looking and least exciting Uncle Tom's Cabin that has yet been devised" and John Anderson (Evening Journal) viewed it as "This Uncle Tom's Cabin is a lavish, handsome production with elaborate scenery by Mr. Oenslager and singing by a Negro choir. I fear, however, that like its own Little Eva, it is not long for this world." Stark Young (the New Republic) added, "Curiously the very integrity

with which Mr. Abbott has tried to keep out raw stage hokum,
forcing and highlights, has mainly served to cut down the play's
impact and weaken its unity. The original novel, take it or leave
it, did hang together."

Further dramatic or musical constructions of Uncle Tom's Cabin
were left to another day and another decade except for sporadic
interpolations on the musical stage. Two months after Sweet River
quickly ebbed on Christmas night, 1936, the Shuberts presented
Vincente Minnelli's revue The Show Is On at Broadway's Winter
Garden Theatre; the revue starred Beatrice Lillie and Bert Lahr.
The first act finale (called "Parade Night" by Norman Zeno and Will
Irwin) was a miniature version of Uncle Tom's Cabin, with Fred Nay
as Uncle Tom; Evelyn Thawl as Little Eva; Pearl Harris as Topsy;
Gracie Barrie as Eliza; Willem Van Loon as Aunt Chloe; Andre
Charise as Legree--Mitzi Mayfair and Paul Haakon danced a "Cake-
walk."

John C. Wilson produced Bloomer Girl at the Shubert Theatre
on October 5, 1944. The book was by Sig Herzig and Fred Saidy;
the show was based on a play by Lilith and Dan James, with music
and lyrics by Harold Arlen and E. Y. Harburg. One of the musical's
highlights was the opening of the second act "Sunday in Cicero
Falls," which combined Sunday strolling with a Tom Show parade.
As the play-within-the-play, Uncle Tom's Cabin opened in 1861 at
Cicero Falls, New York's Opera House with admission fifty cents--
Ladies in bloomers were admitted Free. Runaway slave Pompey
was Uncle Tom. (He was played by Dooley Wilson who is remem-
bered tenderly for his performance as Sam, the piano player at
Rick's Cafe Americain singing the memorable song "As Time Goes
By" in the Warner Bros. classic 1943 film Casablanca.) Joan Mc-
Cracken, as Topsy, sang "I Never Was Born" ("jes growed like
cabbage and corn") in the Uncle Tom segment and stopped the
show. "Liza Crossing the Ice" was executed by dancer Emy St.
Just. She was pursued by Joseph Florestana as Simon Legree.

Richard Rodgers' and Oscar Hammerstein, II's enchanting
musical The King and I, starring the late, great Gertrude Lawrence
with Yul Brynner, opened on Broadway at the St. James Theatre
(March 29, 1951). The King and I contains many memorable moments. One of its most delightful is Jerome Robbins' ingenuous
and charming ballet "The Small House of Uncle Thomas," "by Harriet
Beecher Stow-a"). In act 2, the Royal dancers of the Siamese
Court interpret the story of Uncle Tom's Cabin that is narrated by
Tuptim (Doretta Morrow). Dusty Worrall was Uncle Thomas and
black-masked Topsy was danced by Ina Kurland, with Shellie Farrell
as Little Eva and Yuriko as Eliza. Simon Legree became King Simon
of Legree of The Kingdom of Kentucky and was danced by Gemze
DeLappe.

MINSTRELSY OVERTURE

The blacking-up of whites eventually led to the formation of American Minstrels which started during the early days of colonization. Lewis Hallam blacked-up as Mungo in the comic opera The Padlock (New York's John Street Theatre, May 29, 1769). On December 30, 1799, a Mr. Graupner appeared at Boston's Federal Street Theatre, darkened with burnt cork to sing "The Gay Negro Boy" in Oroonoko. William Bates was black Sambo singing and dancing in John Murdock's 1795 play The Triumphs of Love; or Happy Reconciliation. "Pot-Pie" Herbert, who later appeared at New York's Park Theatre, hawked his wares by blackening his face and publicly singing a song based on the popular air "Boyn Water," called "Siege of Plattsburgh," which Andrew Jackson Allen (later to become Edwin Forrest's dresser), sang between the acts of The Battle of Lake Champlain (Albany, New York Theatre, 1815). The song later became known as "Back Side of Albany"; it was also performed by Sam Tatnall.

Between jail sentences for his irascible behavior and scurrilous, libelous writings, George Washington Dixon's blackface buffo singing of "Zip Coon" in a voice of nominal tonal quality at Philadelphia's Arch Street Theatre on June 19, 1834. His appearance created a minor sensation as did his performance at New York's Park Theatre when he rendered John Clement's song "Coal Black Rose." The Boston Courier's critique of Dixon's singing was this: "He is the most miserable apology for a vocalist that ever bored the public ear." In 1836, the great Phineas Taylor Barnum blacked-up in Camden, South Carolina with Aaron Turner's Circus, to sing, "Zip Coon" and other "Ethiopian" songs.

Thomas Allston Brown, in his New York Clipper series "Early History of Negro Minstrelsy," wrote,

> Ethiopian minstrelsy, with its accompaniments of wit and
> drollery, became one of the standard amusements because
> of the strong appeal it made to the masses who were touched
> by its simple melodies and its effusions of genuine wit....
> Many people wonder why minstrel music has so broad a hold
> upon the public taste, and why the cork opera, with its
> threadbare smartness and everlasting repetitions, so stub-
> bornly defies the ordinary revolutions of the public taste--

But the explanation is furnished on the one side by the
talent and ever springing "animal" wit of such men as Billy
Birch and Charley Backus--it is the unseen shrine at which,
through these touching minstrel tunes, the millions of our
race on both sides of the Atlantic who love music solely for
its melody bow down and worship.

William Dean Howells wrote, "Our one original contribution
and addition to histrionic art was negro minstrelsy, which, primiti-
tive, simple, elemental, was out of our own soil, and had the characteristics that distinguish autochthonic conceptions."

Historian George Clinton Densmore Odell acknowledged the
Birth of Negro Minstrelsy as "inaugurating an art that was to endure for as many decades the artless disposition of our countrymen
could permit." Minstrels were unique, entertaining escapist fare
for the average citizen. They provided the healthiest antidote for
everyday traumas: laughter. Fred Stone, in his 1945 autobiography, Rolling Stones, wrote, "In those days the best way to become
a comedian was from black to white, that is, by way of blackface
minstrelsy. It was the best school the beginner could find. Francis Wilson, Nat Goodwin, Eddie Foy, Chauncey Olcott had all started
that way, and more of the great comedians than there would be space
to name."

Fred Stone's assessment of the number of comedians to start in
minstrelsy is quite correct, and beyond those mentioned previously
in this text there were blackface beginners such as Joseph Cawthorn, who blacked up for Haverly's Minstrels in 1873. Cawthorn's
stage and screen career spanned an incredible seventy years. It
was Cawthorn who invented the mythical "whiffenpoof" animal that
later was adopted by Yale University as the name of their choral
group and immortalized in "The Whiffenpoof Song." Raymond Hitchcock substituted in blackface for George "Honey Boy" Evans in
Cohan and Harris Minstrels.

William George Evans, born on Thursday, March 18, 1870, at
Pontytlin, Wales, and who later wrote the perennial favorite "In the
Good Old Summertime" with Ben Shields, achieved fame and personal
identity by singing his song "I'll Be True to My Honey Boy." Evans
made his last stage appearance at Birmingham, Alabama, in February
1915 with his act The Seven Honey Boys. He died at Baltimore's
Union Protestant Infirmary at the age of forty-five (Friday, March
5, 1915).

Jack Norworth, né John Knauff, who died at the age of eighty
(Tuesday, September 1, 1959, in Laguna Beach, California), was a
one-time Ziegfeld Follies star; he'd entered vaudeville in blackface
as "The Jailhouse Coon." Norworth wrote the lyric for "Take Me
Out to the Ball Game." With his more-famous wife Nora Bayes, he
composed the nostalgic "Shine on Harvest Moon." Dutch-dialect

comedians Weber (Joseph Morris) and Fields (Lewis Maurice Shan-
field) did a burnt-cork act in the 1880s.

Prior to the organization of the highly touted vaudeville act
The Avon Comedy Four, with John Coleman and Will Lester, Smith
(Joe Sultzer) and Dale (Charles Marks) did a blackface act (March
15, 1899) at New York's Bowery Atlantic Gardens. Smith and Dale
played their whiteface, two-man act (Dr. Kronkheit or Hungarian
Rhapsody) for six decades; their career was later the basis for
Neil Simon's play The Sunshine Boys.

William H. Crane was "Tambo" (minstrel left end man); he
shook the tambourine with Pell's Minstrels. John S. Clarke was
"Brudder Bones" (right end minstrel man) and played the bones.
William Henry Crane later teamed with comedian Stuart Robson in
the Broadway successes Our Boarding House (1877) and The Henri-
etta (1887). Henry Robson Stuart had made his blackface debut as
Stuart Robson in Hewitt's bowdlerized version of Uncle Tom's Cabin
(Baltimore in 1852). Crane's greatest success came in 1900; it was
then he originated the title role in David Harum, a play by R. and
M. W. Hitchcock. John Sleeper Clarke first performed in blackface
with his future brother-in-law, Edwin Booth.

Francis Wilson, born in Philadelphia on Tuesday, February 7,
1854, was the first president of Actors' Equity. His term extended
from 1913 until his retirement in 1921. Wilson teamed with James
Macklin in a blackface comedy act with Sanford's Minstrels in his
home town of Philadelphia. Sam S. Sanford built the first exclusively minstrel theatre there in August 1853 at Twelfth and Chestnut
Streets. Wilson attained stardom in the musical comedy version of
Robert Macaire, called Erminie (1886); he played the role of Cad-
eaux nearly thirteen hundred times. Wilson later wrote in his 1924
autobiography, Life of Francis Wilson by Himself, "To be a minstrel
and sing and dance in blackface was my original ambition."

Luke Schoolcraft, considered by James McIntyre of McIntyre
and Heath "The greatest of all impersonators of the real Southern
Negro on the American stage," persuaded Tom Lewis (Maguire) to
form his own single act; this was after he'd partnered for years
with James Pell--and also Sam Ryan--as a blackface team that appeared with several of the top minstrel companies. Lewis has been
credited with coining the phrase "Twenty-Three" (to which later
was added "Skiddoo"). The man was a master at spouting scram-
bled oratory, this talent perpetuated by the twentieth century's
"Professor" Irwin Corey. Tom Lewis amplified "stump speaking,"
which had been perfected by such a performer as Addison "Ad"
Ryman. Tom later abandoned blackface. He appeared in the Ziegfeld Follies and many other Broadway shows and had a career in
motion pictures. Lewis later recalled, "My happiest, carefree days
in the ever-shifting show world were in the wandering vagabondage
of oldtime minstrelsy--But minstrelsy has slipped into decadence.

There are no more real impersonators of true Negro character; no successor to Schoolcraft, Billy Emerson, George Primrose, Willis Sweatnam and their kind."

A talented performer with an excellent tenor voice and an overwhelming compulsion for gambling, Ireland-born William "Billy" Emerson (Redmond) died in poverty at the age of fifty-six at Diman's Hotel in Boston on Saturday, February 22, 1902, while appearing with William H. West's Minstrels. Emerson made his debut in blackface as a youngster with Joe Sweeney's Minstrels and with Sanderson's Minstrels before his New York debut at Tony Pastor's Theatre in 1866. Billy Emerson, according to one appraiser, was "the personification of grace, gifted with a voice an opera singer might have envied" who "stood absolutely alone in his chosen profession; never before his advent had his equal been seen, nor will we ever again."

Born in London, Ontario, Canada, in 1852, George Primrose (George H. Delaney) began his career as a blackface performer at the age of fiteen with MacFarland's Minstrels in Detroit. Primrose became a partner in several famous minstrel companies, notably Barlow (Milt), Wilson (George), Primrose and West (William). Primrose and West were joined for nine years by George Thatcher; on October 27, 1894, they produced The Mick-Ah-Do, the travesty that later became extended as The Black Mikado. Primrose later joined forces with Lew Dockstader. George is said to have been the first to introduce highly colored evening clothes as a minstrel costume. Primrose returned to vaudeville as a blackface single act in 1918 at Proctor's Fifth Avenue Theatre. He died at the age of seventy-two on Wednesday, July 23, 1919. He had been a blackface performer for fifty-six years.

George Thatcher made his stage debut at the New Idea Concert Hall in his native Baltimore. He gained fame with Simmons, Slocum and Sweatnam's Minstrels in Philadelphia. Thatcher spent three years with the prestigious San Francisco Minstrels (produced in the Bay City by Thomas Maguire in the mid-nineteenth century). This group became the longest running permanent New York minstrel company (1865 to 1883). In 1883, it was acquired by John H. Haverly's Mastadon Minstrels. The San Francisco Minstrels featured minstrelsy's premier end men, Charley Backus (Tambo) and Billy Birch (Bones). Their travesties of current plays (e.g., Uncle Tom's Lament) and expert performers became famous. On December 20, 1880, they produced a spoof of Tommaso Salvini's Othello. It starred Signor Charles Salvini Backus in the title role with Signor Billy Maccorini Birch as Desdemona. After Thatcher's partnerships with Barlow, Wilson, and West--and later with Lew Dockstader--his minstrel days diminished. George became a talented legitimate stage actor (albeit in blackface) playing Sassafras Livingston in The County Chairman, old slave Croup in Cameo Kirby, and faithful slave Uncle Billy in The Littlest Rebel.

The progression from blackface minstrel to legitimate actor was a common path; one of its earliest travelers was Dan Bryant of the famous Bryant Minstrels.

Daniel Webster O'Brien was born on Thursday, May 9, 1853, at Troy, New York. In 1844, he made his blackface debut with his brother Jerry at New York's Vauxhall Gardens. Following his apprenticeship and after experiencing increasing fame with several minstrel companies, Dan, with his brothers Jerald (Jerry) and Cornelius (Neil), formed Bryant's Minstrels, which opened on February 23, 1857, at Mechanics Hall in New York. In 1859, after Dan's requesting a walk-around finale song, Dan Emmett wrote "Dixie." Handsome, versatile Dan Bryant made his legitimate stage debut on July 2, 1863, at New York's Winter Garden Theatre, where he performed in the title role of William R. Floyd's play Handy Andy.

Bryant's excellent acting and warm personality were described by William Sykes as follows: "His handsome face, fine figure and his graceful dancing eminently fitted him for Irish comedy." These qualities carried him through leading roles such as: Tim O'Brien in The Irish Emigrant at Wallack's Theatre on July 26, 1864, Myles-na-Coppaleen in Boucicault's The Colleen Brawn, and the lead in Born to Good Luck in 1865. During this year, Bryant was also successful on the legitimate stage in England and Ireland. He returned to minstrelsy with his company then reappeared at Wallack's Theatre on July 30, 1866 to play four roles in Thomas B. McDonough's and Fred G. Maeder's play Shamus O'Brien, the Bould Boy of Glengall (Shamus, Owney Dugan, Denny Doyle and Highen O'Leary).

Dan returned to his minstrel company (May 18, 1868 to July 24, 1869) in their Fourteenth Street Bryant's Opera House. There they continued presenting outrageous travesties on plays and operas like Il Trovatore (called Ill-True-Bad-Doer), with their "wench" performer Eugene as Leo Norah, Nelse Seymour as As-You-Chain-Her, and Dan as Man-Wreak-Oh. The popular minstrel specialty dance "Essence" was performed no better by anyone than by Dan Bryant. The dance was described by T. Allston Brown as follows: "He made an immense hit in his "Essence of Old Virginny"--a characteristic dance which has since been attempted by many men in the business, but up to the day of his demise Dan never met with a successful rival."

Beginning June 10, 1867, Dan was back at Wallack's Theatre playing The Irish Emigrant, Handy Andy and Shamus O'Brien in repertory. From July 3 to July 27, he starred as Barry O'Leary in The Bells of Shandon. Dion Boucicault's 1865 play Arrah-na-Pogue; or the Wicklow Wedding was revived at Niblo's Garden on August 2, 1869. It starred Dan as Shaun the Post and Rose Eytinge as Arrah Meelish. Dan opened his new Opera House on November 23, 1870, in New York on Twenty-third Street and Sixth Avenue; he made his last appearance in his theatre on April 3, 1875.

Dan Bryant fell into a deep depression following the sudden death of his close friend and professional compatriot, minstrel great Nelse Seymour (Thomas Nelson N. Sanderson), who died at the age of thirty-nine on Tuesday, February 2, 1875. Dan developed a terminal case of pneumonia on April 3, 1875, and died at his Manhattan home, 20 East Sixtieth Street, on Saturday, April 10, 1875, at the age of forty-two. On April 29, 1875, eleven Broadway theatres held a benefit for his family. Virtually every notable performer on Broadway participated, including: Harrigan and Hart, Mrs. John Drew, Stuart Robson, John Wild, Mlle. Aimée, Francis Wilson, Charley Backus, and many others.

Willis Palmer Sweatnam first dipped into burnt cork as a young boy at Cincinnati's Western Museum. Then he joined Frank Clark's Lilliputian AEolians as "Master Willie, the Castanettist" at the age of seven and graduated to play in minstrels aboard the show boats, Huron and Dixie. Sweatnam's success soared at Philadelphia's Arch Street Opera House where he was end man for Simmons (Lew) and Slocum's (E. N.) Minstrels in 1875. He later took over Simmons and Slocum's Minstrels with John L. Carncross. Sweatnam's vast popularity preceded him to New York. There, he had his Broadway debut and was advertised on June 24, 1878, as "the funniest Ethiopian comedian living, Philadelphia's favorite, Billy Sweatnam." George Odell wrote of Sweatnam's Manhattan debut, "Well, if Willis Sweatnam was not the funniest, he certainly came close to being it, especially in his later years."

Sweatnam's later years did not include minstrels. But his legitimate stage performances with Dan Daly and David Warfield in The City Directory (1891); A Society Fad (1893), and About Town (1894) established him as a leading comedian on the Broadway stage. It was his performance as black politician Sassafras Livingston in George Ade's successful comedy The County Chairman at Wallack's Theatre (New York, November 24, 1903) that assured him a place among the comedic greats of the era. Willis reenacted his Sassafras Livingston role in Paramount Pictures' 1914 screen version of the play. Seeing Rupert Hughes's comedy Excuse Me (Broadway's Gaiety Theatre, February 13, 1911) dismissed any doubts about Sweatnam's talent; in the play, Sweatnam played the pivotal role of a black Pullman porter on a train. The production ran 160 performances; for several years Sweatnam starred in the comedy on the road.

Sweatnam reminisced about his career in 1911,

> It takes more than a coat of burnt cork to make a minstrel comedian; he must have a natural aptitude for comedy, regardless of the color. Modern minstrelsy no longer gives the schooling that it used to give. Formerly, the company played all sorts of burlesques and sketches, varying them from week to week. Now, instead of changing the bill, companies change their scene of activity.

Willis P. Sweatnam died at the age of seventy-six (Tuesday, November 25, 1930) at New York's Lambs Club.

The 1911 Friar's Frolic opened at Broadway's New Amsterdam Theatre. The highlight of that year's Frolic was a minstrel show, with Jerry Cohan as interlocutor; his son George M. Cohan and another actor, David Montgomery, were the end men, Tambo and Bones. In the minstrel circle in blackface were George Beban, Tom Lewis, William Rock, Richard Carle, Raymond Hitchcock, Fred Niblo, Vaughn Comfort, and Robert Dailey, with Irving Berlin singing his song "Ephraim." William Collier spread burnt cork to appear in George M. Cohan's sketch The Pullman Porter's Ball, with female impersonator Julian Eltinge as a seductive black femme. Collier and George M. were a blackface duo singing "Two Dandy Darkies" in Cohan's musical Hello, Broadway (December 25, 1914) at Broadway's Astor Theatre.

Jeremiah John Keohane, born in Boston, Massachusetts on Monday, January 31, 1848 became better known as Jerry Cohan, father of George M. and spent approximately seven years in blackface with several minstrel groups. In July, 1869, Jerry Cohan was with The Associated Artists of Kelly and Leon's Minstrels in Baltimore, performing a blackface sketch The Lively Bootblack. Cohan made his last minstrel appearance performing Irish songs and dances and such specialties as Paddy Miles, the Irish Boy and The Dublin Dancing Master with Sharpley's Minstrels in the spring of 1874 at Elgin, Illinois. In June of that year, Jerry Cohan married Helen Frances Costigan. Together with their children Josephine (born in 1876) and George Michael (born on July 3, not July 4, in 1878), they became the famous Four Cohans.

Chauncey (Chancellor John) Olcott, born in Buffalo, New York on Saturday, July 21, 1860, began his career as a blackface balladist at the age of twenty and joined Haverly, Primrose and West's Minstrels as a featured singer. Olcott later became the leading tenor in Gilbert and Sullivan operas with the Duff Light Opera Company; in 1886, he appeared in blackface as Nanki-Poo in an all blackface production of The Mikado. Retitled The Black Mikado, or the Town of Kan-Ka-Kee, the transformed Gilbert and Sullivan comic opera featured Ed Marble as the Mick-ah-do, Billy Rice as Ko-Ko, Bert Shepard as Yum-Yum, and George Edwards as Katisha (a Back Number).

Chauncey abandoned blackface on March 16, 1886, to play the lead opposite Lillian Russell in Pepita, or the Girl with the Glass Eyes at New York's Union Square Theatre. Olcott became America's favorite Irish tenor and introduced many songs ever beloved by the public, especially in the Emerald Isle. Although most of Olcott's plays were fastidiously fustian, the music from them became famous and everlasting favorites. On January 9, 1899, Olcott introduced his own composition ("My Wild Irish Rose") in a dreary piece called

A Romance of Athlone at New York's Fourteenth Street Theatre.
With Ernest R. Ball he wrote several memorable songs, including
"Mother Machree" (which he sang in 1911's Barry of Ballymore)
and composer Ball's title song of 1912's Macushla. On January 13,
1913, at New York's Grand Opera House, Olcott introduced Ball's
"When Irish Eyes Are Smiling" in The Isle o' Dreams and again sang
"Mother Machree." From 1906 to 1920, Olcott recorded several of
his famous songs for Columbia Records, including those mentioned
plus "Where the River Shannon Flows," "In the Garden of My
Heart," and "Too-Ra-Loo-Ra-Loo-Ra, an Irish Lullaby." Chauncey
Olcott died at the age of seventy-two (Friday, March 18, 1932) at
his home in Monte Carlo.

Philadelphia-born (1844) minstrel man Hougline "Hughey"
Dougherty graduated from a Civil War drummer boy to his blackface
debut at the age of fourteen with Sandford's Minstrels in Philadelphia. Dougherty perfected the art of minstrelsy's "stump speaking,"
which later was extensively improvised and perpetuated by Ad Ryman, Tom Lewis, and others. Dougherty starred in Edward Marble's
burnt-cork comedy and variety play Tuxedo at New York's New
Park Theatre on October 3, 1891. In the minstrel show sequence,
he was an end man opposite George Thatcher and supported by Tom
Lewis, and James and William Powers, in the blackface semicircle.
Dougherty died at the age of seventy-five on Tuesday, August 20,
1918.

Edwin Fitzgerald, born in New York's Greenwich Village on
Sunday, March 9, 1856, became the famous Eddie Foy. After being
supernumerary in several Shakespearean plays (starring Edwin Booth
in Chicago), Eddie and his partner, Ben Collins, became Tambo and
Bones with Sam Begley's Minstrels and played tank towns in the
Midwest. Foy joined Billy Emerson's Minstrels on the West Coast for
several seasons. Then he trekked east with partner Jim Thompson
to join Charlie Dockstader, George Alfred Clapp (Lew Dockstader)
and ballad singer Chauncey Olcott for twelve weeks with Carncross's
Minstrels at Philadelphia's Eleventh Street Opera House.

Foy left the blackface world to star in many Broadway shows.
He appeared in The Crystal Slipper (1888); Bluebeard, Jr. (1889-
1890); Off the Earth (1894); Hotel Topsy Turvy (1898); An Arabian
Girl and Forty Thieves (originally called Ali Baba in 1899); The
Strollers (1901); The Wild Rose (1902); Piff! Paff! Pouf! (1904);
The Orchid (1907); Mr. Hamlet of Broadway (using his personal
observation of Edwin Booth's Prince of Denmark in 1908); Up and
Down Broadway (1910); and, in 1912, Over the River. After being
widowed twice, Eddie married his third wife, ballerina Madeline
Morando, in 1896; they produced seven children--Bryan, Charlie,
Mary, Madeline, Richard, Eddie, Jr., and Irving. Eddie Foy and
the Seven Little Foys debuted on August 12, 1910 for the Lambs
Club and soon became one of vaudeville's most famous family acts.
Eddie Foy continued performing until his death at the age of

seventy-two at the Baltimore Hotel in Kansas City where he was appearing at the Orpheum Theatre in Tom Barry's sketch The Fallen
Star.

Years after minstrels were consigned to theatrical nostalgia,
Broadway saw a return of the blackface art in a full-blown, short-
lived revival of minstrelsy in Kilpatrick's Old-Time Minstrels (Royale
Theatre, April 19, 1930). Produced by Thomas Kilpatrick, staged
by Walter F. Scott and J. A. Shipp from material selected and
edited by Henry Myers, the old-fashioned minstrels opened with the
traditional semicircle centered with the interlocutor, flanked by end
men Tambo and Bones, and followed by an olio and afterpiece as had
been presented in the past. Kilpatrick's resurrection of minstrelsy
by an all-black company overlaid with burnt cork and outlandish
white circles enlarging their mouths was "not the most exhilarating
entertainment," according to Brooks Atkinson (the New York Times).
"When this minstrelsy, composed exclusively of Negroes, gets round
to the 'olio' which is vaudeville, the fun is labored and spasmodic,
and you realize that good talent is essential to any show--Even for
sentiment's sake you like the fooling to be talented." Kilpatrick's
Old-Time Minstrels closed after a one-week run.

Samuel L. "Roxy" Rothafel produced the inaugural program of
the Radio City Music Hall. The program was directed by Leon
Leonidoff, with settings and costumes by Robert Edmond Jones.
Erno Rapee conducted the Music Hall Symphony Orchestra (with
Charles Previn, Joseph Littau and Macklin Marrow). Ballets were
by Florence Rogge, with Russell Markert's superb precision dancers
(then, they were called the Radio City Music Hall "Roxyettes").
The originally scheduled two and one-half hour show of nineteen
separate acts began on Tuesday, December 27, 1932, about 9:00
P.M. before a standing-room-only audience of sixty-two hundred
when a red satin-clad squad of trumpeters sounded a fanfare her-
alding a parade of the theatre's smartly dressed ushers down the
aisles and onto the stage; thus began Roxy's lavishly produced
entertainment, which became an interminable embarrassment of
riches, ending in the early hours of Wednesday, December 28, 1932.
The weary audience had considerably dwindled by the time act 19
(the finale called "Minstrelsy") began.

The minstrelsy finale featured "the entire company" with the
exception of those who assembled for the final curtain: Martha
Graham and her dance group; Coe Glade, Arnoldo Lindi, and Titta
Ruffo who had appeared in six scenes from Bizet's Carmen; acro-
batic teams, The Wallendas and The Kikutas; Martha Wilchinski and
Robert T. Haines, who performed the "Dedication" with soloist
Caroline Andrews; fraulein Vera Schwartz of Berlin's Staats-Oper
making her American debut singing "Libeswalzer" from Johann
Strauss's Wiener Blut; London Music Hall dancers Kirkwhite and
Addison; Ballet dancers Harald Kreutzberg and Margaret Sande;
soloist Jennie Lang; premiere danseuse Patricia Bowman; Otto

Fassell, Josie and Jules Walton and Jimmy McHugh and Dorothy
Fields (in her stage debut), who had appeared in the first act finale "Night Club Revels."

  Jimmy McHugh and Dorothy Fields wrote two songs, "Happy
Times" and "Journey's End," for the "Minstrelsy" finale, which was
introduced by DeWolf Hopper. The "Minstrelsy" finale also included
Glenn and Jenkins, and John Pierce (later known as Jan Pierce of
the Metropolitan Opera). They were joined by performers featured
in other acts, Ray Bolger, Taylor Holmes, "Doc" Rockwell, The
Sisters of the Skillet (Ralph Dumke and Ed East), the Berry Brothers, Joan Abbott, the Tuskegee Choir (under the direction of William L. Dawson); the Radio City Roxyettes, Corps de Ballet and
Chorus; and, last but not least, in their first appearance of the
evening, the old-time great comedy team of Weber and Fields, who
undoubtedly--by that hour--had aged perceptively awaiting their turn.

  Honoring the hundredth anniversary of the founding of minstrelsy by The Virginia Minstrels, the Radio City Music Hall, on
September 9, 1943, produced a huge thirty-eight-minute minstrel
show. The event was advertised as follows:

> It's tambourine time at the Music Hall as the Rockettes,
> Corps de Ballet and Glee Club bring back merry minstrel
> days in a joyous, nostalgic cavalcade of laughter and mel-
> ody--produced by Russell Markert with brilliant settings
> by Nat Karson. Molasses 'n' January (Pick and Pat) as
> rib-tickling end men--Borrah Minevitch's melody-making
> Harmonica Rascals--Frank Brooks, Jack Spoons, Frank
> Condos and others all join in this mammouth parade of
> minstrelsy.

  The extravaganza included a minstrel parade and Regis Joyce
as interlocutor. Time magazine reported, "Manhattan's Radio City
Music Hall last week honored a great anniversary in show business.
One hundred years ago The Virginia Minstrels, at the Bowery Amphitheatre, introduced Manhattan to a new art form, conceived in blackface and dedicated to the proposition that the white man could equal
Negro comedy, song and dance."

  Beautiful Dreamer, a musical play by William Engvick, based
on the life and music of Stephen Foster (played by James Morris)
was produced at New York's Madison Avenue Theatre on December
27, 1960. Ted Lawrie played minstrel man E. P. Christy and Don
Liberto and Stephen Lloyd were the end men, Tambo and Bones.
London's popular BBC television show The Black and White Minstrels
(1957) was transferred to the stage at London's Victoria Palace Theatre (May 25, 1962). The revue produced by Robert Luff was
devised and directed by George Inns and featured the George Mitchell Minstrels, plus other performers. The two-hour minstrel show
accumulated an astonishing 4,344 performances!

Eric Johns headlined his 1973 <u>Theatre</u> review <u>The Magnetism of Minstrels</u>. He reported,

> <u>The Black and White Minstrels</u> are an outstanding theatrical phenomenon of our time. They are now in their fourteenth year and during that time their stage shows have been seen by 25,000,000 people in this country and overseas--The audience hears snatches of some hundred songs during the two-hour show, songs which they love because they evoke precious memories for them. Melody is the most potent magnet of the Minstrels.

The bell has tolled for minstrelsy in America. Robert C. Toll, in his 1976 history <u>On with the Show</u>, perceptively wrote,

> The minstrel show was the first uniquely American show business form. As the most popular entertainment form in the nation for a half-century, it had great impact on vaudeville, burlesque and its other show business successors. But the minstrel show also created and perpetuated negative stereotypes of Negroes that endured in American popular thought long after the minstrel show had disappeared.

Whites in blackface today are considered anathema in the liberated culture of the fading days of the twentieth century. Most ethnic characterizations have become passé--but in the beginning there was Thomas D. "Daddy" Rice who lit the torch of minstrelsy. Rice and a few of his followers are screened in the succeeding text, while the endless parade of thousands in blackface have passed, never to be seen again.

Although preceded by Lewis Hallam, William Bates, Charles
Mathews, and many others masquerading in blackface, T. D. "Jump
Jim Crow" Rice has been documented as the father of American minstrelsy. If Rice was not minstrelsy's sire, he certainly was the man
who popularized and inspired the creation of minstrel shows, which
became the first, original, American musical theatre.

Legend has it that while playing a blackface role in Solon
Robinson's play The Rifle with Samuel Drake's Company in Louisville, Kentucky, in 1828, Rice became fascinated with and studied
the erratic twitching, loose-jointed jig performed by a crippled and
deformed black stableman named Jim Crow. The old slave's right
shoulder was held high and his stiff and crooked left leg did not
prevent his shuffling feet from maintaining rhythm and from keeping
time to his singing of an old tune with his own lyric:

"First on de heel tap, den on de toe
Ebery time I weel about I jump Jim Crow
Weel about and turn about and do jis so
An' ebery time I weel about I jump Jim Crow."

Rice added additional lyrics, perfectly copied Crow's dance and
singing, and introduced his "Jump Jim Crow" in his role in The
Rifle. The Louisville audience "went mad with delight, recalling
him on the first night at least twenty times" (according to Edmon S.
Connor of the New York Times).

The foggy folklore and apocrypha regarding the origins of
"Jim Crow" vary with the interpreter and with the time of retelling.
Jim Crow has been authoritatively and geographically "discovered"
in Louisville, Pittsburgh, Cincinnati, New Orleans, and obscure
outposts of the Great Southwest. Progenitors of "Jim Crow" surfaced all over the land with blackface singers, known as "Ethiopian
Delineators," proclaiming parenthood. Purdy Brown's Theatre and
Circus blackface clown George Nichols, who popularized the Negro
song "Clare de Kitchen," claimed he had performed "Jim Crow"
years before Rice; Blackface comedian James Roberts made that
claim too when he had appeared at New York's Chatham Gardens in
1824 singing Micah Hawkins's song, "Massa George Washington and
General La Fayette." Burnt-cork performer George Washington Dixon,

known as the writer of "Turkey in the Straw" (originally called
"Old Zip Coon"), maintained that he introduced the song and dance
before Rice, Roberts, and Nichols. Rice's employer Noah M. Ludlow in his 1880 memoir, Dramatic Life as I Found It, produced in-
contestable evidence that established Louisville as the city of origin
of Jim Crow. For all the authoritative geographical assumptions
and avowed declarations of fatherhood, it was T. D. Rice who made
"Jump Jim Crow" internationally famous, and it was he who became
forever identified with its origin.

Thomas Dartmouth Rice was born on Tuesday, May 20, 1808
(or 1806, or 1807), in New York City. He made his stage debut as
a supernumerary at the Park Theatre and later played a comedy
lead in Bombastes Furioso. Rice also played the leading role in
The Mogul Tale at the Lafayette Theatre in 1828. He then joined
Noah M. Ludlow's and Sol Smith's touring company. After his phenomenal success performing "Jim Crow," Rice played Wormwood in
The Lottery Ticket in Cincinnati with Ludlow and Smith's troupe;
then he headed north where he soon became famous and forever
identified with "Jump Jim Crow."

During the summer of 1832, Rice appeared at Philadlephia's
Walnut Street Theatre, where on July 28 he played in Whirligig Hall
and increased his growing fame by singing and dancing "Jump Jim
Crow." News of the burgeoning success of his blackface routines
soon reached the Island of Manhattan. Daily bulletins announcing
his imminent appearance began in the late autumn of 1832 in the
New York press. On Monday, November 12, 1832, during the intermission between two dramas (The Hunchback and Catherine of
Cleves), Rice introduced "Jump Jim Crow" to New York at the American Theatre in the Bowery. At the next performance, Rice sang
and danced "Jump Jim Crow" between the theatre's two plays The
Fire Raiser and The French Spy. On November 15th, he mitigated
the tragedy of Othello (in which Junius Brutus Booth played the
Moor, Thomas S. Hamblin played Iago, and Naomi Vincent portrayed
Desdemona) with his enthusiastically received blackface routine.
Rice's benefit on November 17 was a tour de force in which he impersonated six characters in A Day After the Fair.

One hundred years later, Frederick R. Sanborn wrote an article Jump Jim Crow--The Opening of an Era for the New York Times
Magazine (November 13, 1932), recalling Rice's tremendously acclaimed introduction of "Jim Crow" to New York.

> One hundred years ago last night the Bowery Theatre roared
> with such applause as greets few actors in any generation.
> The orchestra pit and the four circling balconies rocked
> and cheered, forgot the tragedy that had opened the pro-
> gram, forgot that another play was to come, forgot even
> to munch peanuts and throw their shells about in the ac-
> cepted manner of those times. A song sung in the

intermission by a tall, thin blackface comedian had set the
patrons wild with delight. Six times they brought back the
singer to repeat the song before they would let him go.
The song was "Jump Jim Crow," the singer, Thomas Dartmouth Rice."

Sanborn's supposition that "Rice is conceded to have been the greatest popularizer of Negro minstrels" is open to conjecture, but the
following statement by him is not: "He was not the first blackface
comedian, but no earlier actor in his field attained to a tithe of his
popularity. To Rice goes the credit of bringing in the reign of
Negro minstrels."

Significantly, Rice's "Jim Crow" became rooted in the English
language as firmly as Uncle Sam, Miss Liberty, Santa Claus, and
John Bull. With the passing of years, the connotation of "Jim Crow"
was applied to laws, segregation of public transportation, rest rooms,
and elsewhere; in these applications, the term meant discrimination
against blacks. Webster defines "Jim Crow" as a "stereotype Negro
in a nineteenth-century song and dance act; (1) Negro--usually
taken to be offensive; (2) discrimination especially against the
Negro by legal enforcement of traditional sanctions."

T. D. Rice came on stage carrying a sack and sang, "Ladies
and Gentlemen, I'd have for you to know that I've got a little darkey
here that jumps Jim Crow." Rice upended the sack and out tumbled
a small boy made-up in blackface and costumed to resemble Rice.
The small boy did an excellent imitation of Rice singing and dancing
"Jump Jim Crow." The lad's name was Joseph Jefferson; Jefferson
later wrote about his blackface stage debut--he also wrote about
Rice.

Joseph Jefferson, in his Autobiography published by The Century Company in 1889, recalled this about Rice,

In London he acted in two theatres nightly. Of course this
fantastic figure had a great influence upon me, and I danced
Jim Crow from the garret to the cellar--He put me in a bag,
which almost smothered me, and carried me upon the stage
on his shoulders--and turning the bag upside down he emp-
tied me out head first before the eyes of the astonished
audience. Rice was considerably over six-feet high, I was
but four years old [born in Philadelphia on Friday, February 20, 1829], and as we stood there, dressed exactly alike
the audience roared with laughter.

Following their alternate singing of several stanzas of "Jump Jim
Crow" and their encoring their dance, the audience tossed twenty-
four dollars in coins on the stage, which Rice gave to a wide-eyed
Joseph Jefferson.

England rejoiced in Rice's performing, and "Jump Jim Crow" took London by storm. It was especially beloved by the Cockney population and equally admired by London's elite. Rice played two theatres in London in 1836. At the Adelphi Theatre, he appeared in Leman Rede's sketch (which was especially written for him and called Twelve Hours in New York) with Mrs. Stirling and John Reeves in the cast; then he danced and sang "Jump Jim Crow" the same night at London's Pavilion Theatre. Rice's provincial tours of England outgrossed all other touring companies. "Jump Jim Crow," published by E. Riley of Chatham Street, New York City, included forty-four stanzas of the song; in England special lyrics were written geared to English audiences.

Inevitably, imitators of Rice emerged--those known as "Ethiopian Delineators." But they never overshadowed his popularity and talent. Many of his imitators, however, attained fame as Negro impersonators, singers, and dancers. The shuffling, limp-jointed dance of "Jump Jim Crow"--and the later "Essence of Old Virginia" dance routine featuring leaps and jumps--eventually became refined into what is known as "The Old Soft Shoe," which was performed to perfection by Eddie Leonard and other minstrel men.

Rice appeared as Guffee at the Bowery American Theatre (January 9, 1833) in his "Ethiopian Opera," Long Island Juba; or, Love by the Bushel, with T. H. Hadaway as Sambo, Mr. Sowerby as Gumbo, and Mr. Hanson as Rosa. Billed as "Mr. Rice, the Celebrated Jim Crow," he enlivened Jonas B. Phillips's play Life in New York; or, The Major's Come in his character of Jim Crow, which was especially written into the script for his performance at the American Theatre (May 21, 1834), with W. F. Gates as Major Jack Downing. Rice presented his farce Where's My Head? (May 23), in which he played Squash.

Bone Squash Diavolo; or Il Nigeretta (obviously playfully synonymous with Daniel F. Auber's 1830 comic opera Fra Diavolo and Verdi's Rigoletto) featured a very popular song--"Sich a-Gittin' Upstairs" (music and lyrics by Joe Blackburn, who left the Roman Catholic priesthood to become a clown)--that was described by George Odell as "running like a flame down a part of the nineteenth century." Bone Squash Diavolo with an afterpiece The Masquerade (Rice was Caesar Cudjo) was the American Theatre's bill for November 8, 1834. Bone Squash was structured on the Faustian motif. Bone Squash sells his soul to the Yankee Devil Sam Switchell for the love of Junietta Ducklegs. Junius Brutus Booth supported Rice in Bone Squash Diavolo; he was Sam Switchell at Baltimore in 1840. Francis Courtney Wemyss, in his Theatrical Biography of Eminent Actors and Authors, wrote, "His Bone Squash was an amusing affair, the music truly delightful and ably executed. The Virginny Mummy, although vulgar even to grossness, met a good reception." Rice's Oh, Hush! was generously borrowed from the song "Coal Black Rose" (both in characterization and melody); it was one of his most successful sketches.

T. D. Rice's sketches <u>Corn Meal</u> (1836) and <u>Black and White</u>
on September 16, 1837, with Charles Western Taylor as Colonel
Clover and Rice as Sambo, were followed by his sketch <u>Black Cupid</u>
on September 20. During 1838 Rice appeared on September 14 as
the cook Mephistopheles Faust in his <u>Midshipman Easy</u> at the Franklin Theatre, and on September 17 in <u>The Peacock and the Crow</u> and
<u>Jumbo Jim</u>. Rice wrote and appeared in the following: <u>Jim Crow</u>
<u>in Foreign Service</u>; <u>The Virginny Mummy</u> (also known as <u>The Sar-</u>
<u>cophagus</u>)--his character was Ginger Blue; <u>Uncle Pap</u> (as Bamboo
Sappotash); <u>Black Hercules</u> as Tom Cringle (1839 and 1840). In the
following years Rice introduced <u>Janggaroo</u>; <u>The Hypocrite</u> (as Black
Mawworm); <u>Wheugh! Here's A Go!</u> and <u>Ten Miles from London</u> (as
Pompey). George Odell properly described Rice's work: "These
Rice sketches were certainly precursors of the sketches ultimately
incorporated in the bills of Negro Minstrels in the future."

T. D. "Daddy" Rice was well-cast as Uncle Tom in Henry E.
Steven's stage version of <u>Uncle Tom's Cabin</u> on January 10, 1854,
at New York's Bowery Theatre (in which he was succeeded by one
founder of <u>The Virginia Minstrels</u>, Frank Brower) and as the black
slave Old Tiff in John Brougham's stage adaptation of <u>Dred</u> at the
same theatre on September 29, 1856. Ironically, Rice was a member
of <u>Henry Wood's Minstrels</u> at New York's Marble Palace in August
1859, participating in--and watching--his "Jump Jim Crow" specialty
matured into modern minstrelsy. During his last years, paralysis
and loss of speech plagued Rice. His last appearance on the New
York stage was on July 28, 1860, at the Canterbury Concert Hall
where he completed six performances. Rice died at the age of fifty-
two in New York City (Wednesday, September 19, 1860). "Daddy"
Rice did receive "credit in bringing in the reign of the Negro Minstrels" and lived to become a member of them.

Four blackface performers joined forces to create what would
eventually become America's minstrel show or, as Gerald Bordman
wrote in his superb, definitive <u>American Musical Theatre</u>, "What
did evolve was the first genuinely American Musical Theatre, the
first great indigenous entertainment." The four men were Dan Emmett, Billy Whitlock, Frank Brower, and Dick Pelham.

THE VIRGINIA MINSTRELS

DAN EMMETT

Daniel Decatur Emmett, born on Sunday, October 29, 1815, in Mt. Vernon, Ohio, was one of the founders of American minstrelsy. Emmett was a blackface banjoist in 1840 with the Cincinnati Circus Company orchestra. On November 2, 1841, he made his debut in Charleston, South Carolina as a blackface performer and appeared with Frank Brower who introduced "bone-playing." He had an 1841 engagement with Raymond and Waring's Circus in a building that later would become Philadelphia's Grand Central Variety Theatre. In 1842, he made a tour as a musician in Edward Kendell's Brass Band. Afterward, Emmett teamed with Frank Brower at New York's Chatham Square Franklin Theatre on November 14, 1842, appearing on a bill with Richard W. Pelham and Tom Backus, "The Negro Paganini." Emmett and Brower's act, "Negro Holiday Sports in Carolina and Virginia" was performed at New York's Bowery Republic Theatre on January 1, 1843. Emmett and Brower were "at liberty." Toward the end of January, another unemployed performer, Billy Whitlock, requested that they join him and another "at liberty" blackface performer to rehearse their songs. The rehearsal unwittingly established what would become the first totally American theatrical enterprise: The Minstrel Show.

The four men rehearsed in Emmett's room in Mrs. Brooke's New York boarding house at 37 Catherine Street. Rejecting previous classifications of blackface performers of "Ethiopian Delineators" for "Minstrels," they based their name on the name of the recent successful American tour of The Tyrolese Minstrel Family and called themselves The Virginia Minstrels. The group members tested their new act on January 31, 1843, at New York's Chatham Theatre. Using Emmett's song "Old Dan Tucker" (composed in 1831), Frank Brower played "the bones"; Billy Whitlock strummed the banjo; Dick Pelham rattled the tambourine; and Dan Emmett played the violin--all for the official debut of The Virginia Minstrels on February 6, 1843, at the Bowery Amphitheatre. The Virginia Minstrels were advertised as a "Negro Concert" and as an exhibition of the "Oddities, peculiarities, eccentricities, and comicalities of that Sable Genus of Humanity." The four minstrels included two brief sketches in their act--"Dan Tucker on Horseback" and "The Serenade."

The New York <u>Herald</u> reported,

> First night of the novel, grotesque, original and surpris-
> ingly melodious Ethiopian band, entitled the <u>Virginia Min-</u>
> <u>strels</u>, being an exclusively musical entertainment combining
> the banjo, violin, bone castanets, and tambourine, and en-
> tirely exempt from the vulgarities and other objectionable
> features which have hitherto characterized negro extrava-
> vaganzas.

The quartet added additional material to their act, including Whitlock's "Negro Lecture on Locomotives" and Frank Brower's "A Definition of the Bankrupt Laws." Dick Pelham contributed "A Brief
Battering of the Blues," and the band enlarged its "Dan Tucker on
Horseback" sketch.

The Virginia Minstrels' success continued through six weeks
in Boston. On April 23, 1843, the troupe sailed for England, giving their first performance at Liverpool's Concert Hall on May 25,
1843. Using Emmett's songs (including "Dandy Jim"), <u>The Virginia</u>
<u>Minstrels</u> completed six successful weeks at London's Adelphi The-
atre (the engagement began June 19, 1843). Dick Pelham left the
group and was replaced by Joe Sweeney, an expert American banjoist. After touring Ireland and Scotland, Billy Whitlock returned to
America. Frank Brower and Sweeney joined <u>Cooke's Circus</u> for a
tour of Scotland, and Emmett and Pelham performed for eight weeks
at London's Astley's Theatre. Within a year the renowned <u>Virginia</u>
<u>Minstrels</u> had disbanded. But they had inaugurated more than a
half-century of native-born American entertainment: <u>Minstrels</u>.

Emmett's minstrel sketch <u>Hard Times</u> was first performed at
White's Opera House in New York on October 12, 1855, with Dan as
a black reluctant worker and Charlie White as Old Dan Tucker.
Dan joined <u>Bryant's Minstrels</u> in 1857. At Bryant's request, he
wrote a song for a "walk-around" plantation finale, which was introduced at New York's Mechanics Hall on April 4, 1859, and called "I
Wish I Was in Dixie's Land." The song, which later became better
known as "Dixie," was undoubtedly the most famous song ever composed for minstrels. (Firth, Pond & Company first published the
song in New York, with a piano arrangement by W. L. Hobbs.)

"Dixie" was played at the inauguration of former Mississippi
Senator Jefferson Davis as President of the Confederate States of
America (Montgomery, Alabama, February 18, 1861) and became the
national anthem of the Confederacy. On Palm Sunday, April 9,
1865, General Robert E. Lee surrendered the Confederate Army of
Northern Virginia to Union General Ulysses S. Grant at the MacLean
House at Appomattox, Virginia, and, in Washington, D.C., an enormous, jubilant crowd gathered in front of the White House in antici-
pation of a "Victory" speech from President Abraham Lincoln. But
after a few conciliatory remarks and congratulatory comments

regarding the end of the war, The Great Emancipator said to the throng, "I propose closing this interview by the band performing a particular tune--I have always thought 'Dixie' one of the best tunes I have ever heard."

Brander Matthews wrote,

> The song was introduced by Mrs. John Wood into a bur-lesque she was playing in New Orleans just before the out-break of the Civil War. The sentiment and the tune took the fancy of the ardent Louisianians and they carried it with them into the Confederate Army, where it soon estab-lished itself as the war song of the South.

Emmett formed his own minstrel company in 1864 and three years later retired to his home in Mt. Vernon, Ohio. He emerged from retirement in 1881 to join Leavitt's Gigantean Minstrels. On August 21, 1895, Al G. Field gave white-haired, eighty-year-old "Uncle Dan" (the impoverished composer of "Dixie") a farewell tour, which lasted until April 11, 1896.

Called "The Dean of American Minstrelsy," Alfred Griffith Hatfield was born at Leesburg, Virginia on Tuesday, November 4, 1848. He died at the age of seventy-two on Wednesday, April 3, 1921. In 1881, Hatfield had his name legally changed to Al G. Field by the Franklin County, Ohio Probate Court. Field recalled in his autobiography, Watch Yourself Go By, published in 1912, "Uncle Dan was not in his best voice after he marked his fourscore years, but every time he appeared before the footlights to sing 'Dixie' the audience went wild--It recalled to the widows, wives and daughters the occasions on which 'Dixie' had been sung while the men were valorously fighting the cause that was dear to all of them."

Dan Emmett, one of the four originators of the American min-strel show, was the composer of many songs such as "Old Dan Tuck-er," "De Blue Tail Fly," "Early in the Morning," "Walk Along, John," and others. But he was best remembered for "I Wish I Was in Dixie's Land," known as "Dixie." Emmett died at the age of eighty-eight (Tuesday, June 28, 1904) at his home in Mt. Vernon, Ohio.

BILLY WHITLOCK

William H. Whitlock, the self-proclaimed originator of the pio-neer band of blackface minstrels called The Virginia Minstrels was born in New York City in 1813. While employed by the New York Herald as a typesetter, Whitlock made his stage debut at New York's Patriot House in Chatham Square; he played Cuff in T. D. Rice's popular blackface sketch <u>Oh, Hush!</u>, in which his brother-in-law, Dan Gardner, was the blackface wench dancer. Whitlock resigned his typesetting job at the <u>Herald</u> in 1837. On March 5, 1838, without having previous experience, he made his debut as a blackface singer with <u>Whipple's Circus</u> near Savannah, Georgia.

During the Whipple tour, Whitlock met Joe Sweeney, master of the banjo, in Lynchburg, Virginia. Sweeney taught Whitlock to play a popular banjo song "Sittin' On the Rail," and Whitlock became proficient on the instrument. Minstrelsy's favorite instrument was the banjo. The banjo closely resembled the ancient Egyptian lyre and consisted of four strings pegged to the shaft-head and running across a stretched oblong hoop of calfskin. James Buckley improved the banjo by adding an iron ring around the hoop of the previously nailed calfskin. Joe Sweeney further altered the instrument by adding a short catgut string thus making the instrument a five-string banjo. Later, Whitlock learned to make banjos and taught the fine banjoist Tom Briggs how to play the instrument.

Whitlock gave his first New York City performance on July 6, 1838, and, at Richmond Hill Theatre, he was billed as "Billy Whitlock, the Celebrated Ethiopian Singer and <u>Original</u> Banjoist." There he sang "The Raccoon Hunt" and played the banjo for the <u>first</u> time in public. P. T. Barnum engaged Whitlock to play the banjo for John Diamond's jig dancing. The hedonistic, unmanageable Diamond was fired by Barnum (he would later die at the age of thirty-four on October 29, 1857, at Philadelphia's Blockley Alms House). Whitlock continued his banjo accompaniment for the second John Diamond (Frank Lynch) in 1840.

Whitlock asked Dan Emmett to "practice the fiddle and banjo with me" in late January 1843. He invited Frank Brower to join in with "the bones" and asked Richard Ward "Dick" Pelham to beat the tambourine. The result of this practice session was <u>The Virginia Minstrels</u>. Whitlock enthusiastically suggested, "Let's go in together as a band of minstrels," and he later wrote in his <u>Autobiography</u>, "The origination of the Minstrels I claim as my own idea, and it cannot be blotted out!" While touring with dancer Diamond at the Walnut Street Theatre in Philadelphia, Whitlock had first tested the combination of banjo and violin by persuading Dick Myers to fiddle as he strummed. The February 6, 1843, debut of <u>The Virginia Minstrels</u> at the Bowery Amphitheatre was the original American Minstrel Show. After their enormous success in England, the company disbanded; Whitlock was the first of the four original blackface minstrels to return to America.

Billy Whitlock returned to P. T. Barnum's minstrel band and, in 1844, toured extensively with Barnum's exhibition <u>The Funeral of Napoleon</u>. Ten years later Whitlock was cast as Julius in the Bowery Theatre January 16, 1854, production of <u>Uncle Tom's Cabin</u>, starring T. D. Rice as Uncle Tom and Whitlock's daughter Caroline as

Little Eva. Billy toured across the country in <u>Katy, the Hot Corn</u>
<u>Girl</u>, with his daughter Caroline. His last appearance was in black-
face with Duke Morgan, in <u>Dan Rice's Circus</u>.

Hoping to end the controversy of the authorship of two famous
minstrel songs, Whitlock, in his <u>Autobiography</u>, insisted he was the
composer of "Lucy Long" and "Mary Blane" (lyrics by Thomas G.
Booth). Whitlock retired to Jersey City, New Jersey, where he was
employed for four years in the U.S. Customs office. From 1862,
Billy Whitlock was paralyzed. He remained an invalid until his death
on Friday, March 29, 1878, at Long Branch, New Jersey.

FRANK BROWER

Francis Marion Brower, born on Sunday, November 30, 1823,
in Baltimore, Maryland, was among the most talented of the minstrel
men. He made his blackface debut at the age of fifteen performing
a song and dance routine at Dick Myer's Third and Chestnut Streets
Museum in Philadelphia in 1838; the following year he toured with
the <u>Cincinnati Circus Company</u>. Brower sang and danced to "Jim
Along Josey" and "Zip Coon" on April 23, 1841, with <u>Charles J.</u>
<u>Rogers' Cincinnati Circus</u>. In Lynchburg, Virginia, on July 4,
1841, Brower introduced rhythmic "bone-playing" to the tune of
"Old Tar River," with Dan Emmett accompanying him on the banjo.
The same year he performed with Emmett in <u>Raymond and Waring's</u>
<u>Circus</u> in Philadelphia and appeared in New York City as a "single"
blackface act.

Frank teamed with Dan Emmett in November 1842 in New York
at the Franklin Theatre and the Bowery Amphitheatre. Advertised
as "Dan Emmett, 'the great Southern Banjo Melodist' and Frank
Brower, 'the perfect representation of the Southern Negro characters'," the team opened their act "Negro Holiday Sports in Carolina and Virginia" on January 1, 1843, at the Bowery Theatre.

Monday, February 6, 1843, marked the birth of the American
Minstrel Show at New York's Bowery Amphitheatre, when Brower,
playing the bones, joined Dan Emmett, Billy Whitlock, and Dick Pelham in the historical debut of <u>The Virginia Minstrels</u>. But each of
the four founders of the world's first minstrel show considered himself a "single-act"; after winning acclaim in London, <u>The Virginia</u>
<u>Minstrels</u> disbanded. Brower and banjoist Joe Sweeney toured Scot-
land with <u>Cooke's Circus</u>. On April 22, 1844, they rejoined Dan
Emmett and Billy Whitlock as <u>The Virginia Minstrels</u> for four successful weeks at Dublin's Theatre Royal. The group made an acclaimed tour of Ireland and Scotland and gave their final performance in Glasgow.

Brower returned to England in 1851 as a blackface clown with

Risley and McCollum's Circus. His singing and dancing received
high praise, as did his acting as Gumbo Cuff in T. D. Rice's
sketch, Oh, Hush!, or The Virginny Cupids. Brower's performance
in the title role of Wood's Minstrels' parody of Uncle Tom's Cabin,
called Happy Uncle Tom in 1854, was lauded by The New York
Clipper--"as perfect a piece of acting as has ever been witnessed
upon any stage." Frank's "perfect acting" as Happy Uncle Tom
went from comedy to tragedy when he succeeded T. D. Rice as
Uncle Tom in Henry E. Stevens's adaptation of Uncle Tom's Cabin
at the Bowery Theatre in the spring of 1854.

For the next decade, Brower continued to play Happy Uncle
Tom. In the play, "he had the happy faculty of completely merg-
ing his personal identity in the character which he assumed." On
July 7, 1862, he was in the original company of Henry Wood's newly opened Theatre Comique in New York. Frank was a comically
threatening Othello to Nelse Seymour's terrified Desdemona at Wood's
Theatre on March 23, 1863, in a ribald parody of Shakespeare's
Othello. Thomas Nelson N. Sanderson (known as Nelse Seymour)
was one of minstrels' finest performers. Born in Baltimore, Maryland, on Friday, June 5, 1835, Nelse Seymour gave his last performance on January 27, 1875, as the lead in Bryant Minstrels' production of Kaliko; or, Harlequin, King of the Sandwich Islands; he died
a week later in New York City (Tuesday, February 2, 1875).

The original "Brudder Bones" Brower retired in 1867 and
opened a saloon in Philadelphia. His last appearance as a minstrel
was on October 28, 1867, at Philadelphia's Seventh Street Opera
House, with Tunison's Minstrels. Brower's last appearance on the
stage was at the Walnut Street Theatre (Philadelphia, from November
25, 1867, to December 20, 1867), where he performed an "Ethiopian
scene" in the concert segment of John Brougham's play Lottery of
Life, A Story of New York.

Frank Brower died at the age of fifty at his home, 1422 Master
Street, in Philadelphia (Thursday, June 4, 1874).

DICK PELHAM

Blackface song and dance man, Richard Ward Pelham, was born
in New York City on Monday, February 13, 1815. Pelham made his
stage debut in 1835 at the Bowery Theatre, with T. D. Rice in Oh,
Hush!; or The Virginny Cupids. He later toured with Turner's
Circus performing his burnt-cork routines. On his twenty-fifth
birthday, February 13, 1840, Pelham entered a match-dance contest
at the Chatham Theatre against P. T. Barnum's former protégé
John Diamond. The famous Negro dancer Master Juba frequently
defeated Diamond in such matches, but Dick Pelham lost five hundred dollars. Dick toured with his brother Gilbert W. Pelham in

Negro Peculiarities, Dances and Extravaganzies, which included a
comedy sketch and the song "Massa is a Stingy Man."

Gilbert later became known as Gil Pell of the Boston Serenaders and gained fame as a "bone" player. The Boston Serenaders,
organized in 1843, included George Harrington, Gilbert Pelham,
Moody Stanwood, Frank Germon, and Tony Winnemore. President
John Tyler invited the group to entertain at the White House in
1844, and, in 1846, The Boston Serenaders were a tremendous success at London's St. James Theatre. The blackface troupe gave a
Royal Command performance at Arundel Castle for Queen Victoria,
the Royal Family, and the Duke of Wellington. Gil Pell (as Brudder
Bones) explained why he was like the Duke of Wellington--"cos I
beat the bony part!"

Dick Pelham performed sixteen songs and danced as a Negro
clown on January 16, 1842, at the Bowery Amphitheatre. He was
invited to join Billy Whitlock, Dan Emmett, and Frank Brower in a
new blackface act. The newly formed Virginia Minstrels first performed for Pelham's benefit on January 31, 1843, and made their historical debut on February 6, 1843 at the Bowery Amphitheatre, with
Pelham shaking the tambourine. The Virginia Minstrels left for England and greater acclaim.

The London press advertised the appearance of the newly
formed group at the Adelphi Theatre:

> NEW AND NOVEL ENTERTAINMENT!! Grand Ethiopian
>   concerts by
> the four highly celebrated
> VIRGINIA MINSTRELS FROM AMERICA
> who will appear in London on
> MONDAY, JUNE 19, 1843.
> TO THE CITIZENS AND LONDON AND WESTMINSTER:

The Virginia Minstrels would, with great respect, say that, in
their delineations of the sports and pastimes of the Southern
slave race of America, they offer an exhibition that is both
new and original, which they illustrate through the medium of
songs, refrains, lectures and dances, accompanying themselves
on instruments of a peculiar nature, which, in their hands,
discourse most exquisite music. Their melodies have all been
produced at great toil and expense, from among the sable in-
habitants of the Southern States in America, the subject of
each ascribing the manner in which the slaves celebrate their
holidays, which commence at the gathering-in of the sugar and
cotton crops; and they flatter themselves that, from the great
success--in their own country, to introduce not only a chaste
and pleasing school of negroism, but also a true copy of Ethiopian life, that they cannot fail to please all who will honor
them with their patronage, their exhibition being void of any
objectionable feature, either in word, look, or motion, which
could offend the most fastidious.

After The Virginia Minstrels received acclaim in England, Pelham partnered with Dan Emmett for an eight-week engagement at London's Astley's Theatre; then he left his American compatriots to remain in England.

During 1849, Dick Pelham managed Pell's Serenaders. The company included his brother Gil Pell, Tom Briggs, and the great Negro dancer, Juba (William Henry Lane), who would die two years later in England. Dick Pelham's last engagement in England was with Samuel Hague's Liverpool Minstrels. Pelham composed several Negro-inspired songs and wrote a column for Liverpool's monthly Ethiopian Anecdotes.

Richard Ward "Dick" Pelham died of cancer in Liverpool, England, on Wednesday, October 8, 1856.

BLACKFACE BIOGRAPHIES

AMOS AND ANDY

McIntyre and Heath's The Georgia Minstrels had been heard on radio, but the famous blackface team declined an invitation to transfer their talents to the airwaves on a recurring basis in the early 1920s. A blackface vaudeville act known as Sam 'n' Henry, featuring Gosden and Correll performing comedy routines that were augmented by some forty songs, was heard over Chicago radio station WGN on January 12, 1926. The popularity and novelty of the broadcasts prompted Victor Records to release several Sam 'n' Henry blackface routines in 1926: Sam 'n' Henry Buying Insurance; Rollin' the Bones; At the Fortune Teller and At the Colored Lodge. Despite the team's noticeable lack of musical talent, several vocal duets were recorded.

Freeman Fisher Gosden, born on Friday, May 5, 1899 at Richmond, Virginia, and Charles James Correll, born on Sunday, February 2, 1890, at Peoria, Illinois, had made their radio debut in New Orleans in 1920 and first met in Durham, North Carolina in 1919. For several years they staged musical shows and circuses for the Shriners, American Legion, and other brotherhoods across the country. Settling in Chicago in 1923, Gosden and Correll appeared in a 1925 vaudeville-revue Red Hot before relocating their Sam 'n' Henry blackface routines to radio in 1926.

Two years later, Sam 'n' Henry signed with Chicago radio station WMAQ, and, on March 28, 1928, Gosden and Correll introduced two new blackface characters called Amos and Andy. The Amos and Andy Show soon became the most popular radio show of The Great Depression. Sponsored by Pepsodent toothpaste on the Columbia Broadcasting System, on August 19, 1929 until the end of 1937, and by Campbell Soup Company from January, 1938 until February, 1943, the adventures of Amos and Andy kept America laughing during its grimmest decade.

America came virtually to a standstill six nights a week (reduced to five nights weekly in 1931) at 7:00 P.M. as fans listened to the fifteen-minute broadcast, opening with the playing of the show's musical theme "The Perfect Song." The theme, with lyrics by Clarence Lucas and music by Joseph Carl Briel, was derived from Briel's principal theme in his score for D. W. Griffith's motion picture The Birth of a Nation, originally adapted from Gaetano Braga's "La Serenata," or "Angel's Serenade."

During the show's first decade, Gosden and Correll wrote their own material. Later, writers contributed to the script: Octavus Roy Cohen; Robert J. Ross; Harvey Helm; Bill Moser; Paul Franklin; Bob Fischer; Arthur Slander; Bob Connolly, and others. The often hilarious adventures of Amos Jones (Freeman F. Gosden)--an honest, hard-working taxicab driver and family man--and Andrew Halt Brown (Charles J. Correll)--Jones's lazy, gullible, ne'er-do-well, woman-chasing partner--gained millions of fans.

Amos Jones and Andrew H. Brown, owners of one rustic, top-less, windshield-less automobile known as Harlem's "Fresh-Air Taxi-cab of America, Incorpulated," were members of "The Mystic Knights of the Sea" Lodge, which was headed by an unscrupulous con-artist, George "Kingfish" Stevens, who was assisted by a slower-than-molasses janitor, Lightnin'. Gosden and Correll supplied a wide

Amos Jones [Freeman F. Gosden; right] and Andrew Halt Brown [Charles J. Correll] (courtesy of The Doug McClelland Collection)

variety of voices, with Gosden creating many of them (including
Lightnin' and The Kingfish, an appellation later applied to Louisiana's controversial Senator Huey P. Long).

Miller and Lyles were a black comedy team that had become
Broadway stars in their 1921 musical comedy Shuffle Along. They
brought a lawsuit against CBS claiming that the Amos and Andy
characters were based on their Jim Town characters, originated in
Shuffle Along. Miller and Lyles contended that Amos was based
on Miller's character Steve Jenkins and that Andy was modeled after
Lyles's loudmouth Chief of Police, Sam Peck. The case was settled
out of court.

Amos and Andy became one of vaudeville's highest paid "In
Person" acts, broadcasting their nightly radio show from theatre
dressing rooms. They inspired a widely syndicated Chicago Daily
News comic strip and, in 1928, made two recordings for Victor
Records--"Is Everybody in Your Family as Dumb as You Is?" and
"The Presidential Election." President Herbert Hoover invited the
team to entertain at the White House, and one of the few things
George Bernard Shaw claimed never to forget about his trip to
America in the spring of 1933 was Amos and Andy. On the screen,
Amos and Andy starred in RKO Pictures' 1930 film Check and Dou-
ble Check, featuring Duke Ellington and his Orchestra and Russell
Powell in blackface as The Kingfish. Paramount Pictures' Big
Broadcast of 1936 featured Amos and Andy with several other top-
rated radio stars.

Beginning October 8, 1943, their broadcast was increased to
a half-hour weekly show sponsored by Rinso Soap. But in 1948,
Amos and Andy left CBS for NBC and $2.5 million. From 1949 until
1954 their sponsor was Rexall Drugs. Defending the blackface comedy against growing criticism, Gosden told Newsweek magazine in
1948, "What we have tried to do over the years is mirror the trials
and tribulations of Negroes of whom we are very fond." Although
Gosden and Correll created most of the voices (approximately 166
different characters) other characters on the show were added later
and played by Elinor Harriot (Amos's wife, Ruby); Henriette Widmer
(Madame Queen); Eddie Green (Lawyer Stonewall); Lou Lubin (Shorty
the Barber); Ernestine Wade (Kingfish's wife, Sapphire); Amanda
Randolph (Sapphire's mother); and Terry Howard (Ardabella).

Amos and Andy became the first all-black show on television
on June 28, 1951 (but without Freeman Gosden and Charles Correll).
The cast included Alvin Childress (Amos); Spencer Williams, Jr.
(Andrew Halt Brown); Tim Moore (George "Kingfish" Stevens);
Horace Stewart (Lightnin'); Ernestine Wade (Kingfish's wife, Sap-
phire); Jane Adams (Amos's wife, Ruby); Lillian Randolph (Madame
Queen); Amanda Randolph (Sapphire's mother); and Patty Marie
Ellis (Amos and Ruby's daughter, Ardabella), plus others. The
television version of Amos and Andy was vigorously opposed by the

National Association for the Advancement of Colored People. The association asserted that the show was demeaning to blacks and that it was hindering the progress of the emerging black civil rights movement. Television's Amos and Andy ended on June 11, 1953, and was withdrawn from syndication in 1966.

Freeman Gosden was stunned by the critical reaction to the television version of Amos and Andy. He later commented, "Both Charlie and I have deep respect for black men. We felt our show helped characterize Negroes as interesting and dignified human beings." Gosden and Correll retired as millionaires on November 25, 1960, after the demise of their Amos and Andy Music Hall program on CBS radio.

Charles J. Correll suffered a fatal heart attack at the age of eighty-two, while visiting Chicago (Tuesday, September 26, 1972). Freeman F. Gosden died ten years later at the age of eighty-three (Los Angeles, Friday, December 10, 1982).

JAMES BARTON

Born on Saturday, November 1, 1890, in Gloucester, New Jersey, James Barton had the unusual distinction of being the only white performer to recreate a role written specifically for a black performer (Bert Williams). The great Ziegfeld Follies black comedian Bert Williams starred in Al H. Woods's musical comedy The Pink Slip, which opened at Atlantic City's Wood's Theatre on August 21, 1921. The Shuberts took over the production of The Pink Slip and reopened it on the road as Under the Bamboo Tree. Bert Williams collapsed in Detroit during the first act of Under the Bamboo Tree and died in his New York City home on Saturday, March 4, 1922. The Shuberts reopened the show under the title of In The Moonlight, at Atlantic City's Apollo Theatre, on April 23, 1923. The production starred James Barton in Williams' part of black porter Ananias Washington. When the musical comedy reached Broadway at the Astor Theatre on May 17, 1923, it was called Dew Drop Inn.

Barton told the press, "When Mr. Shubert suggested that I play the part of Ananias in Dew Drop Inn, I hesitated, because I had practically forgotten even how to put on burnt cork. I would like to make it emphatic that I do not attempt in any way to imitate Bert Williams, one of the greatest artists who ever appeared in blackface on the stage."

At the age of four, James Barton first appeared in blackface as Topsy in a touring company production of Uncle Tom's Cabin (he had made his stage debut at the age of two when his parents carried him on-stage in a touring production of The Silver King). His mother, Clara Barton, had appeared in what is considered the first

American musical comedy, <u>The Black Crook</u>. His father, James
Barton, was once the interlocutor for <u>Primrose and West Minstrels</u>
and his grandfather, former actor James M. Barton, reputedly organized the world's first women's softball baseball team and was
manager of Baltimore's Front Street Theatre.

        James Barton was a protean performer accurately described
by Joe Laurie, Jr. as "An all-around artist--who was a burly comic,
a skater, a storyteller, a dancer, a singer, a dramatic actor, and
a pic, radio and TV star." Barton spent years touring with several
repertorial companies and appeared in burlesque in <u>Twentieth Century Maids</u> and <u>The Garter Girl</u>. He made his Broadway stage debut at the Winter Garden Theatre on October 23, 1919, in <u>The
Passing Show of 1919</u>. In 1921 Barton alternated between <u>The Last
Waltz</u> at the Century Theatre and <u>The Mimic World</u> at the Century
Theatre Roof Theatre; he gained additional recognition at the former
theatre on March 7, 1922, for his performance as the Valet in <u>The
Rose of Stamboul</u>. He was featured in <u>The Passing Show of 1924</u>
and was the principal performer in Florenz Ziegfeld's <u>The Palm
Beach Girl</u>, which became <u>Ziegfeld's American Revue</u> and later op-
ened as <u>No Foolin'!</u> on June 24, 1926, at Broadway's Globe Theatre.

        Headlining vaudeville at the Palace Theatre performing his
well-known drunk act in a sketch called <u>Moonshine</u>, Barton alternated between the two-a-day and the Broadway stage in 1930's
<u>Artists and Models</u> and <u>Sweet and Low</u>. When Henry Hull left the
cast of Jack Kirkland's dramatization of Erskine Caldwell's novel
<u>Tobacco Road</u>, James Barton succeeded him as Jeeter Lester, play-
ing the part for five years (1,899 performances). Dirty, ragged
Jeeter Lester was later portrayed by James Bell, Eddie Garr, and
Will Geer, but it was James Barton's Uncle John who finally established the record for performances. John Barton played the part
of Jeeter in <u>Tobacco Road</u> 2,016 times. In a quick Broadway casualty, <u>Bright Lights of 1944</u>, James Barton spoofed Jeeter Lester in the
revue. Billy Lynn replaced Barton on the road in the musical comedy <u>The Girl From Nantucket</u> (1945).

        <u>The Iceman Cometh</u>, the last play of Eugene O'Neill's produced
in his lifetime, was a four-hour dramatic marathon. It opened at the
Martin Beck Theatre at four-thirty on Thursday afternoon, October
9, 1946, allowing for a dinner intermission. In the long, demanding
part of the protagonist, Theodore Hickman, the former blackface
comedian, dancer, singer, and musical comedy star James Barton,
gave a superlative performance. Before the end of the Broadway
run of <u>The Iceman Cometh</u>, Barton's voice failed and he was succeeded by E. G. Marshall.

        Producer Cheryl Crawford starred James Barton in Alan Jay
Lerner's and Frederick Loewe's frolicking 1951 musical <u>Paint Your
Wagon</u>, which opened on Broadway at the Shubert Theatre on Novem-
ber 12, 1951, for 289 performances. Barton's last appearance on

Broadway was at the Cort Theatre on March 13, 1957, in a short-lived play The Sin of Pat Muldoon. Barton's film career was sporadic and unimpressive. His last screen appearance was in the cameo role of Grizzle in John Huston's 1960 film The Misfits.

James Barton died at the age of seventy-one in Mineola, New York (Monday, February 19, 1962).

EDDIE CANTOR

Eddie Cantor's last Broadway show was Banjo Eyes. The show was a musical version of George Abbott's and John Cecil Holm's comedy hit Three Men on a Horse, which had been adapted by Joe Quillan and Izzy Elinson, with a musical score by Vernon Duke and lyrics by John Latouche and Harold Adamson; the show opened on December 25, 1941, at the Hollywood Theatre. In most of Cantor's shows or films, he managed--often without rhyme or reason--to emerge in blackface. Cantor closed Banjo Eyes in blackface, singing a medley of his famous old song hits. His expertise in burnt cork developed early in his career and was finely polished by his association with the inestimably talented black comedian Bert Williams, a mulatto who had been forced to black-up so that he would be acceptable as a "Negro" comedian.

Cantor later wrote that Bert Williams was

> The best Negro comedian to trod the boards. The best teacher I ever had. Working alongside him in the Ziegfeld Follies I studied his extraordinary powers as a pantomimist, his incomparable way with an audience--manipulating their emotions as if they were puppets on strings. A moment of silence as they watched his gestures, his shuffle, his expressive face and hands--then--thunderous applause! From Bert Williams I learned what little panotmime I possess. To my mind he was one of the greatest pantomimists in the world and he proved it. For any man who could stand on the stage for five minutes at a time in blackface and tell stories like the famous poker game, using only his hands, established his supremacy.

Born over a Russian tearoom on Eldridge Street on Manhattan's Lower East Side on Sunday, January 31, 1892, Isidor Iskowitch--as Eddie Cantor--made his professional vaudeville debut at the age of fifteen at Clinton Music Hall. From Frank B. Carr's burlesque unit, Indian Maidens, Eddie migrated to Carey Walsh's Coney Island saloon as a singing waiter. At the saloon, he was accompanied by an ebullient ragtime pianist named Jimmy Durante. Contingent on changing his act, a sixteen-week booking was offered Cantor by ex-furriers Adolph Zukor and Marcus Loew and two former drug store clerks,

Eddie Cantor (courtesy
of the Free Library of
Philadelphia Theatre Collection)

Joseph and Nicholas Schenck, on
their newly formed People's Vaudeville Company circuit. Cantor
retained the same act but quickly
switched to burnt cork.

S. N. Behrman in his De-
cember 10, 1932, New Yorker
magazine profile on Cantor wrote,

> At his wits' end for new
> material, he got the
> bright idea of doing the
> same act in blackface.
> That was the genesis of
> the familiar figure, the
> scholarly darky with
> great eyes staring from
> behind horn-rimmed spec-
> tacles, and the oblong of
> white skin around the
> lips to exaggerate their
> thickness. From this
> time, too, dated the char-
> acteristic epileptic style,
> the frenetic hand-clapping,
> the revivalist ecstasy in
> rendering a song.

Cantor's blackface persona was
the sophisticated, effete burnt-
cork character closely resembling
Florian Slappey, Octavus Roy
Cohen's Saturday Evening Posts's
colored dude and the principal
character in Cohen's 1920 comedy, Come Seven. Cantor defended his perpetual burnt-cork
routine as "It is much harder to
work in blackface with only one's
eyes and mouth to denote expression than in whiteface where every
feature can register."

Cantor spent two years as
the stooge for the vaudeville team
of Bedini and Arthur. In 1912,
he was featured in Gus Edwards'
hugely successful vaudeville act

Kid Kabaret. Eddie married Ida Tobias on June 9, 1914, in Brooklyn and sailed for England on their honeymoon where he joined
Charlot's revue Not Likely at London's Alhambra Theatre. Returning to the states, Eddie partnered for two years with Al Lee in a
vaudeville act Master and Man. On the West Coast he played blackface chauffeur Sam Beverley Moon in Oliver Morosco's production of
Canary Cottage (1916). Eddie and Ida Cantor eventually produced
five daughters: Marjorie, Natalie, Edna, Marilyn, and Janet. Will
Rogers finally sent Cantor a telegram, "If you want a boy--send for
Western Union!"

Florenz Ziegfeld engaged Cantor for his Midnight Frolics on
the New Amsterdam Theatre Roof where his suggestive singing of
"Oh, How She Could Yacki, Yicki, Wicki, Wacki, Woo!" graduated
him to the Ziegfeld Follies of 1917, which opened on June 12, 1917,
with Will Rogers, Fanny Brice, W. C. Fields, and Bert Williams.
Cantor appeared in a skit as blackface Abner Jones, the effeminate, college-educated son of illiterate blackface Red-Cap Porter
Murgatoyd Jones (Bert Williams). Eddie was equally successful in
Ziegfeld Follies of 1918 and in what was possibly the greatest revue
in Ziegfeld's career, The Ziegfeld Follies of 1919.

The finale of the first act of Ziegfeld Follies of 1919 was "The
Follies Minstrels," which featured Eddie Cantor as "Tambo," Bert
Williams (in his last Follies) as "Bones," George Lemaire as interlocutor, and Ray Dooley as "Mandy." Marilyn Miller (appearing in
her last Follies) was minstrel man George Primrose. The score by
Irving Berlin featured his song "Mandy," originally written for Camp
Upton's 1918 soldier show, Yip Yip Yaphank, that was sung by Gus
Van and Joe Schenck. Cantor scored a personal hit with Berlin's
suggestive, popular song "You'd Be Surprised" and the 1919 Follies
also introduced Irving Berlin's "A Pretty Girl Is Like a Melody,"
which became the theme song of all Follies.

Thunderous applause greeted Eddie Cantor throughout forty-
five years in show business. His enormous energy and frenetic
movement created the illusion that he was an expert song-and-dance
man just as his superb sense of timing made him excel in comedy:
talents combined to keep Cantor rollicking through such Broadway
successes as The Ziegfeld Follies (1917, 1918, 1919, and 1927);
Make It Snappy (1922); Kid Boots (1923); and Whoopee (1928).
For many years Cantor was one of radio's top stars. His screen
career covered four decades. And, from 1917 to 1942, his phonograph records sold millions of copies.

Cantor's screen career began with an early experimental talk-
ing picture for Thomas A. Edison called Widow at the Races, with
George Jessel and Truly Shattuck. His first feature film was Para-
mount Pictures' 1926 silent-screen version of Kid Boots, with Clara
Bow and Billie Dove. On August 16, 1927, Eddie returned to
Broadway's New Amsterdam Theatre for his last Ziegfeld Follies.

Following Paramount Pictures' 1927 feature comedy, <u>Special Delivery</u> (directed by William Goodrich--a pseudonym for the fallen comedy idol Roscoe "Fatty" Arbuckle), Cantor had his biggest Broadway success in Florenz Ziegfeld's <u>Whoopee</u>.

Adapted by William Anthony McGuire from Owen Davis's 1923 comedy hit, <u>The Nervous Wreck</u>, with music by Walter Donaldson and lyrics by Gus Kahn, <u>Whoopee</u> opened at the New Amsterdam Theatre on December 4, 1928, for 379 performances. During the run of <u>Whoopee</u>, Cantor made two short subjects at Paramount's Astoria, Long Island studio, <u>Midnight Frolics</u> and <u>That Party in Person</u>, and reenacted his hilarious tailor-shop sketch from Broadway's <u>The Midnight Rounders</u> and <u>Make It Snappy</u> in Paramount's 1929 picture <u>Glorifying the American Girl</u>.

Florenz Ziegfeld and Samuel Goldwyn produced a Technicolor screen version of <u>Whoopee</u> in 1930. Samuel Goldwyn signed Eddie to a lucrative contract, and, in 1931, he was seen on the screen with Charlotte Greenwood in Goldwyn's <u>Palmy Days</u>. Eddie joined his former Gus Edwards cohort, George Jessel, in a fantastically successful vaudeville engagement on October 31, 1931, at Broadway's Palace Theatre. With two box offices open to satisfy the demand for tickets, the Cantor-Jessel show, in which the team of George Burns and Gracie Allen also appeared, extended the original two-week engagement to New Year's Eve.

Cantor left Broadway to appear in Goldwyn's films <u>The Kid from Spain</u> (1932); <u>Roman Scandals</u> (1933); <u>Kid Millions</u> (in which he reprised "Mandy" in blackface in 1934); and <u>Strike Me Pink</u> (1936). His final eight motion pictures were made for several other studios, but they never attained the success of his Goldwyn-era films. Eddie Cantor was president of the Screen Actors Guild and the Jewish Theatrical Guild. Indefatigably, he combined these responsibilities with charity work that included initiating The March of Dimes held annually on President Franklin Delano Roosevelt's birthday. He made his last screen appearance in an epilogue to the Warner Bros. 1953 film <u>The Eddie Cantor Story</u>. The movie failed to attain the acclaim and success of Columbia Pictures' <u>The Jolson Story</u>. Cantor's last appearance on Broadway was at Carnegie Hall in <u>An Evening with Eddie Cantor</u> (1952).

Ida and Eddie Cantor reaffirmed their marriage vows on their 39th wedding anniversary over national television on Sunday, June 7, 1953; Eddie's famous protégée Dinah Shore was matron of honor. In 1964, President Lyndon B. Johnson awarded Cantor a Presidential Citation for his long service to the United States and to humanity. On Saturday, October 10, 1964, Eddie Cantor died at his home in Beverly Hills, California, at the age of seventy-two.

The State of Israel Bond Committee sponsored a gala sixtieth birthday party in the grand ballroom of New York's Hotel Commodore

(January 31, 1952) to show their appreciation of Cantor's strenuous and lucrative efforts in selling bonds for Israel. Cantor's address, I'm Glad I Spent These Sixty Years, was later published. Among the hundreds of telegrams received that evening was one from Cantor's former employer Samuel Goldwyn. The telegram read,

> It is fitting that we join in paying you the richly deserved tribute which your dedication to the cause of humanity has earned for you. What you have done on behalf of American service men, the unstinting devotion you have given to charities and worthy causes of every nature and your complete consecration to the causes of Israel and its people have been an inspiration and a shining beacon to all of us.
>
> Your heart is as great as the world itself, and your spirit knows no boundaries of color, race or creed. I am proud to call you friend and to join with your friends from all over the world in hailing you.

E. P. CHRISTY

Edwin Pearce Christy, born in Philadelphia in 1815, founded the most famous and best known of all the many minstrel organizations. As a young man Christy was a blackface singer with Purdy and Welch's New Orleans Circus. He studied the impromptu routines of Negro performers in New Orleans Congo Square. Relocating to Buffalo, New York in 1835, he later formed a blackface variety act with Dick Sliter, John Daniels, and Negro jig dancer John Perkins in Rochester. The same year, Christy married widow Harriet Harrington. Their sons E. Byron Christy (1838-1866) and William A. Christy (1839-1862) became minstrel men. Christy's stepson George Harrington adopted his stepfather's surname to become the brightest of minstrelsy's stars. It was in Buffalo in 1843 that Christy organized his first minstrel band, The Virginia Minstrels, which soon became Christy's Minstrels with Christy himself as balladier. George Christy rhythmized the bones. Lansing Durand beat the tambourine; Thomas Vaughn, Enom Dickerson, and Zeke Backus completed the company.

Christy's Minstrels made their New York City debut on April 27, 1846, at Palmo's Opera House on Chambers Street. After playing at several New York theatres, the group settled at Mechanics Hall, 472 Broadway, on March 22, 1847, giving performances every night there (and infrequently elsewhere) until July 13, 1854. Historian George Odell noted, "Possibly no civic institution met with warmer response from happy, simple-minded citizens than at the performances of Christy's Minstrels domiciled at Mechanics Hall." The company included E. P. Christy singing ballads; George Christy playing the bones, singing and dancing and playing a variety of parts including remarkable wench-impersonations; R. H. Hooley playing the violin; and Earl H. Pierce playing banjo and tambourine. M. Zorer was the falsetto prima donna of the troupe.

The songs of Stephen C. Foster did much to popularize
Christy's Minstrels. Conversely, much of the fame attained by
Foster's songs was via Christy to whom the composer gave permission to sing his songs from manuscript, prior to publication.
Christy paid Foster ten dollars for his famous song "Old Folks at
Home" (popularly known as "Way Down upon the Swanee River"),
and the song was published as written by E. P. Christy. Foster
finally became aware of the fame his songs had attained through
Christy's Minstrels and other minstrel companies. In May 1852, he
wrote to Christy, "I have concluded to reinstate my name on my
songs and to pursue the Ethiopian business without fear or shame
and lend all my energies to making the business live, at the same
time that I will wish to establish my name as the best Ethiopian
songwriter."

Stephen Collins Foster, who unlike George M. Cohan, was
born on July 4 in the year of 1826 in the village of Lawrenceville,
near Pittsburgh, Pennsylvania, wrote "Old Uncle Ned" at the age
of nineteen in 1845; the song was published in 1848. Aside from
introducing "Old Folks at Home," Christy introduced several of
Foster's songs, including "Massa's in the Cold, Cold Ground" and
"Ellen Bayne." The title page of one published collection of Foster's
songs read "Foster's Ethiopian Melodies as sung by the Christy
Minstrels--Written and Composed by S. C. Foster."

George Christy quit his stepfather's show in October 1853,
and Odell correctly observed, "But Christy could not for long survive the departure of George Christy, the heart of the machine."
The admission to New York's principal minstrel show was twenty-five
cents--children "half-price," and their program advised, "Gentlemen
are requested not to beat time with their feet as it is annoying to
the audience and confuses the performers." Christy also imaginatively, if not altogether factually, ballyhooed his minstrels following
the departure of George Christy as

> The first to harmonize negro melodies, and originators of
> the present popular type of Ethiopian entertainments, au-
> thors of all the most popular negro melodies that have been
> introduced in concerts of this character, and whose success
> in this city, for a continued succession of seven years past
> is without precedent in the annals of public amusement in
> New York. The present company (with additional members)
> comprise the same, and every person now living, who con-
> stituted the band at its organization in 1843 (with the ex-
> ception of George N. Harrington, late bone castanet per-
> former of this establishment). The company, comprising a
> versatile and talented "corps" of experienced performers,
> under the personal supervision of Edwin P. Christy, sole
> proprietor and manager, the only individual at this time, or
> previous, of the name of Christy engaged as a performer in
> representations of Ethiopian minstrelsy.

E. P. Christy retired on Saturday, July 14, 1854, and, after 2,792 performances, his famous Minstrels closed. Ironically, on August 18, 1854, George Christy returned to Mechanics Hall, which he and Henry Wood leased for their Christy and Wood's Minstrels. Depressed and beset with personal problems, Edwin P. Christy leaped from the second floor window of his home at 78 East 18th Street in New York City, on Friday, May 9, 1862. He died on Wednesday, May 21, 1862, at age forty-seven. T. Allston Brown's epithet for E. P. Christy was "Mr. Christy was a man of violent temper and not a pleasant man to deal with. He was entirely self-willed and had too little regard for the feeling of others."

Christy's Minstrels was hugely successful in England, but the English Christy's was purely generic; E. P. Christy had no interest in it whatsoever. Christy's Minstrels opened at London's Polygraphic Hall in January 1858, featuring George W. "Pony" Moore and J. W. Raymer. "Pony" Moore, born in New York City on Tuesday, February 22, 1820, became England's favorite minstrel until his death in London on Friday, October 1, 1909. William Makepeace Thackeray found England's Christy's Minstrels inspiring and wrote,

> I heard a humorous balladist, a minstrel with wool on his head, and an ultra Ethiopian complexion, who performed a negro ballad that I confess moistened these spectacles in the most unexpected manner--a vagabond with a corked face and a banjo sings a little song, strikes a wild note, which sets the heart thrilling with happy pity--Humor! Humor is the mistress of tears.

William Frawley impersonated Edwin P. Christy in Mascot's 1935 film Harmony Lane in which Douglass Montgomery portrayed Stephen Foster. Don Ameche was Foster in 20th Century-Fox's 1939 picture Swanee River, with Al Jolson as Christy.

GEORGE CHRISTY

One of the most noted minstrel performers was born George N. Harrington on Saturday, November 3, 1827, at Palmyra, New York. His mother, Harriet Harrington, became the first wife of Edwin P. Christy, and they became the parents of E. Byron Christy (1838-1866) and William A. Christy (1839-1862). Harrington adopted his stepfather's surname and became George Christy, making his stage debut at Buffalo's Eagle Street Theatre as a jig dancer with E. P. Christy's variety company. George was a featured performer and played the "bones" when E. P. Christy formed a minstrel group called The Virginia Minstrels (1842) that soon became known as Christy's Minstrels.

Christy's Minstrels' New York debut was on April 27, 1846, at

Palmo's Opera House. Established at Broadway's Mechanics Hall on
March 22, 1847, Christy's Minstrels became the most famous company
in minstrelsy. Its success was heightened by the exceptional talent
and popularity of George Christy as well as by the songs of Stephen
C. Foster. Historian George Odell observed, "negro minstrelsy had
become almost synonymous with Christy's. But, of course, the heart
of that famous organization was George Christy." George gained
great popularity as Christy's star performer and became one of the
first minstrel blackface "wenches." His graceful, dusky female impersonations were highly praised and, in 1849, to refute Barney
Williams' claim as having introduced "Lucy Long" in drag in the early 1840's, George publicly announced he was the original "Lucy
Long" and "Mary Blane" (two songs and impersonations he had
made famous). George also popularized minstrel parodies of current
plays, as well as frequently hilarious lampoons of current events.

George left E. P. Christy on October 23, 1853, and formed
Christy and Wood's Minstrels with Henry Wood on October 31.
Christy and Wood produced what is considered the first minstrel
parody of Uncle Tom's Cabin ("Life Among the Happy"). The paro-
dy was based on Mrs. Stowe's book's subtitle--Life Among the Lowly.
At their "famous hall of minstrelsy" (444 Broadway), Christy and
Wood also produced an "operetta" (April 1854) based on Uncle Tom's
Cabin. The "operetta" was called "Happy Uncle Tom." George
Christy played Topsy and restaged a blackface parody of Shake-
speare's play Macbeth (previously produced by Wood on April 26,
1852).

George Christy and Wood's Minstrels opened at Wood's Marble
Hall of Minstrelsy, 561 Broadway on October 31, 1857. George Holland, a former Wallack's Theatre legitimate stage actor, joined the
company on December 21, alternating blackface "wench" roles with
George Christy. Holland returned to the legitimate stage the next
year and Christy left his partnership with Henry Wood to form his
own minstrel company, which opened in San Francisco at Maguire's
Opera House on June 7, 1858. Christy returned to New York but
under a court-approved injunction filed by Wood could not perform
until November 1, 1859, when he headlined the bill at Niblo's Garden
with great success until July 28, 1860.

George Odell observed, "Wood never recovered from the loss
of George Christy" and "Wood's without George Christy slowly went
to pieces as a metropolitan attraction." But when Henry Wood retired on December 25, 1865, his minstrels had run fifteen years in
New York City. According to Odell, George Christy's departure
from Christy's Minstrels left "a darkness never quite lighted up
again in Mechanics Hall" and "the heart of that famous organization
was George Christy." Within nine months after George's defection,
Christy's Minstrels folded forever.

George Christy's Minstrels, featuring the remarkable sixteen-year-old female impersonator Francis Leon as the show's "wench," opened in Charleston, South Carolina on December 20, 1860, the night of South Carolina's "Independence Day" (the state had passed their Ordinance of Secession from the United States and Major Robert Anderson was busy trying to evacuate Fort Moultrie). Since minstrelsy was basically anti-Negro, and most of its participants were uninvolved and unimpressed with the abolitionist movement, Charleston's audience was hastily assured that Christy's Minstrels did not sympathize with the Northern cause. Nevertheless, after one performance, Christy and his blackface performers scurried back to the North.

After an engagement in Havana, Cuba, Christy appeared as part of a variety show (February 10, 1864). With G. W. H. Griffin, the man opposite whom he had parodied Desdemona to Griffin's Othello in a travesty of Shakespeare's tragedy, Christy leased a building on West Twenty-fourth Street and Fifth Avenue, which he converted to the Fifth Avenue Opera House, opening there (November 30, 1865) as Jim in Handy Andy. Christy and Griffin abandoned the Fifth Avenue Opera House on July 4, 1866, after a less than successful season.

Christy's drawing power at the box office was noticeably diminishing. He joined Kelly and Leon's Minstrels when they opened their new minstrel hall (October 1, 1866) where they were featuring a travesty on the great Italian actress Adelaide Ristori's recent Broadway success in Medea, called My-Deah Restore Her. In the late summer of 1867, Christy and Griffin unsuccessfully attempted to restore their own minstrel company. Christy's one-time partner R. M. Hooley engaged the fading star for five weeks, beginning December 2, 1867, when, in Brooklyn, he portrayed Pete in a burlesque of Augustin Daly and Joseph Howard's play Norwood, with Hooley's Minstrels.

In January 1868, Christy rejoined Kelly and Leon's Minstrels where he made his last Broadway appearance in their hugely successful burlesque of Offenbach's operetta La Grande Duchesse de Gerolstein called The Grande Dutch S. (February 1868). On April 20, 1868, George returned to Hooley's Minstrels in Brooklyn and played Kurtiss in The Ku Klux Klan closing May 2nd. Christy was engaged to open May 11, 1868, in Boston with the Morris Brothers' Minstrels, but during rehearsals he was taken ill and returned to New York.

George Christy died in New York City at the age of forty (Tuesday, May 12, 1868). T. Allston Brown later wrote, "He was one of the funniest of the funny in everything he did." George Odell Recorded, "George Christy, ... for nearly a quarter-century, had been the acknowledged leader of the profession of minstrelsy."

LEW DOCKSTADER

Hal Reid's "Emotional and Stirring Melodrama of War Times," entitled <u>Dan</u>, was filmed by the All Star Feature Company and released on July 4, 1914. Dan was described as "a gray-haired darkey slave--at once servant and friend--of great service in the family that owns and loves him, and in the end he gives his life to free his young master--he is shot at sunrise by Union Soldiers." <u>Dan</u> starred "The Most Famous Black Face Character delineator and fun maker in the World"--Lew Dockstader.

"The most famous Blackface Character delineator and fun maker in the World" was born George Alfred Clapp at Hartford, Connecticut on Thursday, August 7, 1856. Clapp made his blackface stage debut in 1873 with the <u>Earl, Emmett and Wilde Minstrels</u>. He appeared as Lew Clapp with <u>Harry Bloodgood's Comic Alliance</u> and toured the West Coast with <u>Whitmore and Clark's Minstrels</u>. Three years later, Lew Clapp teamed with Charles Dockstader in an act known as "The Dockstader Brothers" and, wisely, changed his surname to Dockstader. On October 31, 1881, Lew appeared at New York's Fourteenth Street Theatre with <u>Haverly's Minstrels</u>. Three years later, he formed his own minstrel company. George H. Primrose became Dockstader's partner, and their Minstrels opened at New York's Grand Opera House on October 27, 1894.

Before the turn of the century, Dockstader was shuttling between minstrel shows and vaudeville. The <u>New York Dramatic Mirror</u> in February 1903, wrote about the genial minstrel, "The American public dearly loves the man that can make it laugh, and if there is a comedian on the stage today who can do this in greater measure than Lew Dockstader he has yet to be discovered." Dockstader and his minstrels headlined Hammerstein's Victoria Theatre on January 4, 1904, and Lew's songs "Peter, You're in Luck this Morning," "Oh, Mr. Austin," and "He Used to Breakfeast with us Every Morning," became popular. Dockstader recorded several of his famous songs for Columbia Records: "Everybody Works But Father" (1905); "Uncle Quit Work Too" (1906); and "Fiddle-Dee-Dee" (1912). Lyrically reflecting the extensive employment of women and children, <u>Everybody Works But Father</u> became a short film in 1905. It was based on Dockstader's famous song and released in two versions--one white, one black.

Dockstader returned to Broadway on January 15, 1906, presenting the first half of his show in the traditional minstrel format and combining variety and political satire in the closing half. He also sang "Nobody," a song introduced by, and forever identified with, the great Bert Williams in 1905. Al Jolson joined <u>Dockstader's Minstrels</u> on the West Coast. Recognizing Jolson's superlative talent, Dockstader featured him in the prime next-to-closing spot (usually reserved for Lew) at New York's Fifth Avenue Theatre (February 1909). Jolson later wrote about Dockstader, "With this king of burnt cork, I learned all that there was to know about the black face game." Jolson, Elizabeth Murray, and Dockstader made guest appearances at the Broadway Theatre on May 25, 1912, to bolster the opening of a one-week musical comedy casualty, Mama's Baby Boy.

Despite the declining interest in minstrels, Lew Dockstader kept the fading art of minstrelsy alive, headlining vaudeville in hilarious impersonations of well-known public figures such as Colonel Theodore Roosevelt of the Rough Riders and, pre-dating Will Rogers, keeping his audiences au courant with the latest gossip and national and local political shenanigans. Dockstader later abandoned blackface as he had once done earlier in his career by playing the role of Sir Joseph Porter in a Boston production of Gilbert and Sullivan's H.M.S. Pinafore. He last appeared on Broadway on April 15, 1922, at Jolson's Fifty-ninth Street Theatre, with De Wolf Hopper's "Funmakers" in a revue called Some Party that featured such aging comedians as Jefferson De Angelis, William Courtleigh, De Wolf Hopper, and Jed Prouty. Some Party creaked with more than the advanced age of its cast and closed after seventeen performances.

Dockstader fell while returning from a vaudeville performance at New Brunswick, New Jersey's Star Theatre in January 1923. A bone tumor developed in his left leg, and his health slowly deteriorated. His last stage appearance was with Julian Eltinge in a vaudeville bill.

The famous blackface minstrel Lew Dockstader died at the age of sixty-eight on Sunday, October 26, 1924, on Riverside Drive in New York, at the home of his daughter, Mrs. Warren Palmer.

JAY C. FLIPPEN

Tagged "the second Bert Williams," Jay C. Flippen was born on Tuesday, March 6, 1900, in Little Rock, Arkansas. At the age of sixteen he made his stage debut in Al. G. Fields' Minstrels; four years later he replaced Bert Williams during the road tour of George Le Maire's Broadway Brevities of 1920.

Broadway recognition came for Jay C. Flippen as the blackface janitor Johnson in June Days, a musical version of Alice Duer Miller and Robert Milton's play, The Charm School, which opened at the Astor Theatre on August 6, 1925, for eighty-eight performances. Flippen returned to Broadway in blackface as Genesis in the short-lived musical version of Booth Tarkington's novel and play Seventeen called Hello Lola at the Eltinge Theatre (January 12, 1926). He was featured in The Great Temptations with Jack Benny, Hazel Dawn, and Miller and Lyles on May 18, 1926, at the Winter Garden Theatre. Alternating between black and white face, he starred with (Mary

Louise) "Texas" Guinan and Lillian Roth at the Shubert Theatre on
July 5, 1927, in Padlocks of 1927.

Flippen carried his blackface act to vaudeville's mecca on
Broadway--the Palace, and toured the country on the Keith-Albee
vaudeville circuit. He explained his preference for blacking-up as
follows:

> Burnt cork and woolly wig have a psychological effect upon
> me which is essential to whatever success I make for myself
> on the stage. I should feel undressed and embarrassed out
> in the spotlight without them. I wouldn't be able to work.
> They are my equipment just as surely as the football is the
> football players'. They are as important to my act as the
> lion to the lion tamers. I believe with the ostrich that if
> my head is hidden the rest of me is too. It gives me a feel-
> ing of security and confidence. Without it I should be self-
> conscious, miserable, certainly never in the theatrical busi-
> ness.

Despite his preference for blackface, Flippen returned to
Broadway without it in The Second Little Show, which opened September 2, 1930, at the Royale Theatre. When Olsen and Johnson
left the Broadway company of Hellzapoppin, Jay C. Flippen and
Happy Felton replaced them in 1939. He made a three-month tour
as master of ceremonies in a vaudeville bill masquerading as a revue
called Merry Go Rounders. The revue closed in Washington, D.C.
After a twelve-performance run in another vaudeville Broadway
production, headlining Chico Marx, called Take a Bow (Broadhurst
Theatre, June 13, 1944), Flippen relocated on the West Coast where
he appeared in over fifty films.

During the filming of Cat Ballou in 1963, Flippen developed an
infection in his right leg that resulted in gangrene. His last screen
appearance in The Seven Minutes (20th Century-Fox, 1971) was
played from a wheelchair. Surviving the amputation of his leg, he
sporadically continued his motion-picture career (which was augmented by television appearances). Jay C. Flippen died in Los
Angeles at the age of seventy (Wednesday, February 3, 1971).

FOX AND WARD

Joseph E. Fox correctly called his professional association with
William H. Ward "The oldest theatrical partnership in the world."
Sixty years as a blackface team established Fox and Ward as the
longest-running team in the history of vaudeville.

Fox (born at Ogdensburg, New York on Friday, May 7, 1852)
and his partner Ward (born at Canandaigua, New York on Wednesday,

September 17, 1851) first met at the Adams House in Chicago in 1866 where they both were bellboys. Fox made his stage debut dancing an Irish jig in Dan Bryant's production of Shamus O'Brien at Chicago's McVicker Theatre. Fox and Ward first performed as a team in January 1867 at Wood's Theatre in Cincinnati, Ohio, where they appeared with the Worrell Sisters' Company.

In 1870, they joined Duprez and Benedict's Minstrels which, according to Ward, was the first minstrel company to cross the continent on the Union and Central Pacific Railroad. The team performed at San Francisco's old California Theatre. Nine years later, they joined Barlow, Wilson, Primrose and West's Minstrels, and, in 1882, Fox and Ward formed their own minstrel company. Their dance routines ("Silver Statue Clog" and "The Marble Pedestal Clog") gained as much prominence as their nationally known song, "Shoo Fly, Don't Bother Me."

Celebrating their Golden Anniversary as a team, they were signed by E. F. Albee for a national tour on the Keith-Orpheum circuit in 1918 at $350 per week. Fox and Ward retired from vaudeville in 1927 and established residence in Philadelphia. Their last public appearance was at Philadelphia's Earle Theatre in 1927, together with the second oldest blackface team in show business, McIntyre and Heath (whose partnership began six years after Fox and Ward's) during a benefit for the N.V.A. (National Vaudeville Actors Association) Fund. The four men were considered pioneers and thought of as the best of the blackface comedy teams.

Fox, commenting on his and Ward's Golden Jubilee as a team, recalled,

> I guess we must have used nearly five hundred pounds of burnt cork in our time. Our property man used to make it up for the whole company in big pailfuls but nowadays we buy it in prepared tins just like grease paint or makeup powder. We figure on staying in vaudeville until the end. The street parades of the minstrel companies are too strenuous. There was a time when we right there at 11:45 every morning. Ward with his horn and I with my snare drum, but those days are gone for us.

Fox and Ward remained inseparable companions on stage and off (unlike their longevity runners-up McIntyre and Heath). William H. Ward died at the age of eighty-three at Philadelphia's General Hospital (Wednesday, May 23, 1934). Joseph E. Fox died at the age of eighty-four in Philadelphia (Monday, January 25, 1937).

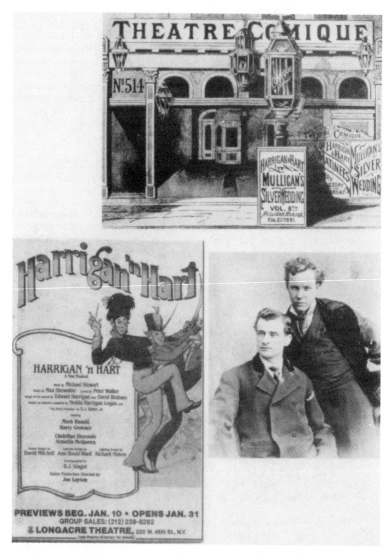

Harrigan and Hart (courtesy of The Free Library of Philadelphia
Theatre Collection).

HARRIGAN AND HART

The American theatre produced several extremely talented and popular teams, which included Weber and Fields, Montgomery and Stone, McIntrye and Heath, and Gallagher and Shean. But none of the many show-business partnerships flourished with such soaring talent and acclaim as did the team of Harrigan and Hart in the autumn years of the nineteenth century.

William Dean Howells called Edward Harrigan "The Dickens of America." He said that Harrigan's comedies "are much decenter than the comedies of William Shakespeare" and, in his time,

> he was perhaps the most important playwright in the United States, and certainly the most American American playwright. Consciously or unconsciously he is part of the great tendency toward the faithful representation of life which is now animating fiction. Mr. Harrigan is himself a player of the utmost naturalness, delicate, restrained, infallibly sympathetic; and we have seen no one on his stage who did not seem to have been trained to his part through entire sympathy and intelligence.

In his autobiography, Nat C. Goodwin enthused about his friend Tony Hart, "To refer to him as talented was an insult. Genius was the only word that could be applied. He sang like a nightingale, danced like a fairy, and acted like a master comedian-- His magnetism was compelling, his personality charming."

Edward Green Harrigan was born on Saturday, October 26, 1844*, at 31 Scammel Street, Corlears Hook, New York City. At the age of sixteen, he made his stage debut at the Bowery Theatre between acts of Pierce's Original Campbell's Minstrels when he recited a self-composed monologue. Harrigan made his San Francisco debut at the Olympic Theatre in 1867, performing in blackface and whiteface, playing the banjo, singing songs, and acting in his own sketches (Irish Comicalities, Jessie at the Bar and The Finnegans). He later played the Belle Union Theatre, the West's foremost Variety Hall, until late 1870 where he shared billing with Lotta Crabtree, Maggie Moore, Joseph Murphy and, possibly the best end men in the field of minstrelsy, the famous Tambo (Charley Backus) and Bones (Billy Birch) of the renowned San Francisco Minstrels.

Harrigan toured the western states with a partner, Alexander O'Brien, an alcoholic later confined to an asylum. Then he teamed with Sam Rickey (Richard T. Higgins). The pair was known as "The Noted California Comedians" and performed in Harrigan's sketch The Little Frauds, in which Harrigan was a German baker and Rickey was his "Fraulein." They first appeared in the sketch on Broadway

*Harrigan's obituary records his birthdate as October 26, 1843.

at the Globe Theatre on November 21, 1870 and, in their second
week, performed Harrigan's sketch The Mulcahy Twins. Harrigan
dissolved his partnership with heavy-drinking Rickey and joined
Manning's Minstrels. During the summer of 1871 in Chicago, Harrigan met an angelic-face, petite, "beautiful" blue-eyed sixteen-
year-old escapee from a reform school named Anthony J. Cannon.

Anthony J. Cannon, born in Worcester, Massachusetts on
Wednesday, July 25, 1855, escaped from a reform school, joined a
circus and migrated to Billy Arlington's Minstrels. By 1870 Cannon
was billed as "Master Antonio, the Boy Soprano" and, as "a cute
little girl," was the hit of Madame Rentz's Female Minstrels, owned
by Tony Pastor's former partner M. B. Leavitt--there was no Madame
Rentz. Cannon's poignant singing of "Put Me in My Little Bed"
stopped the show. Harrigan enlisted young Cannon as his new
partner and changed the youngster's name to Tony Hart.

Their debut was at Chicago's Winter Garden Theatre as "The
Nonpareils, Harrigan and Hart" in Ned's sketch The Big and Little
of It. This performance was followed by a two-month engagement
at Boston's Howard Athenaeum starting August 14, 1871. On October 9, 1871, they opened for a week at Brooklyn's Academy of Music. The new team first appeared on Broadway at the Globe Theatre
(with Adah Richmond's Burlesque and Vaudeville Company, October
21, 1871) in Harrigan's sketch The Mulcahy Twins. They repeated
their routines (including Harrigan's blackface sketch You 'Spute Me?)
at Tony Pastor's Theatre on September 16, 1872. Tony Pastor's
Opera House featured The Slave's Dream on October 19, 1872, with
Harrigan as faithful, contented slave Uncle Zeke, Hart as Joe "a
musical darky," and Billy Carter as "a discontented nigger."

Harrigan and Hart's rise to fame began at the Theatre Comique
at 514 Broadway. The building was originally a synagogue and had
become a carriage stable before it was rebuilt and converted into a
400-seat theatre by Henry Wood, who called his theatre Wood's Minstrel Hall and opened it on July 3, 1862. William Horace Lingard renamed the house the Theatre Comique in 1867, and Josh Hart became
manager of the theatre on October 16, 1871. Harrigan and Hart
opened at the Theatre Comique on December 2, 1872, in Harrigan's
sketches The Day He Went West and The Big and Little of It.

Uncle Tom's Cabin was given a robust comedic outing at the
Theatre Comique on October 27, 1873, with Harrigan as Uncle Tom,
Hart as Topsy, and Jennie Yeamans as Eva. Several Harrigan
sketches followed in 1874: Who Owns the Line? (March 2); A
Terrible Example and The Italian Padrone (March 9); Was She Led
or Did She Go Astray? (April 6); Cushla Machree (April 20) and
Who's Got de Flo?; or Scenes from the South Carolina Legislature
(May 4). Later in the year, The Skidmores; Going Home Again,
and Patrick's Day Parade were presented on December 21; Fee-Gee
was performed on December 23, 1874.

Harrigan's most famous sketch, The Mulligan Guard, first
performed on July 15, 1873, at Chicago's Academy of Music and at
the Theatre Comique on September 8, 1873, was the progenitor of
several of his most acclaimed and popular plays. The Mulligan
Guard continued their escapades in The Mulligan Guards' Ball,
which opened on January 13, 1879, for 100 performances and closed
on May 24, 1879. The Mulligan Guards' Chowder ran 105 performances from August 11, 1879, to November 5, 1879; The Mulligan
Guards' Christmas ran from November 17, 1879, to February 14,
1880; The Mulligan Guards' Surprise opened on February 16, 1880,
and closed on May 15, 1880; The Mulligan Guards' Picnic began on
September 23, 1878, and was revived on August 9, 1880, through
November 20, 1880. It was followed by The Mulligan Guards' Nomi-
nee (November 22, 1880, to February 21, 1881). The popular The
Mulligans' Silver Wedding opened on February 21, 1881, and was
the last production to be seen at the Theatre Comique, which closed
on April 30, 1881. The marching of The Mulligan Guard was described by Rudyard Kipling in his 1901 novel, Kim.

Harrigan later wrote about The Mulligan Guard,

> It is a fancy title and a burlesque upon local target excur-
> sions that take place in New York and vicinity. In the dif-
> ferent wards of New York the young men form military or-
> ganizations, which they name after some prominent ward
> politician. These companies arrange a target excursion,
> engage a band, and after marching to the residences of the
> leading politicians, and paying their compliments, and re-
> ceiving wreaths of flowers, etc., they march to the depot or
> steamer landing for the picnic ground, where the target fir-
> ing takes place. The target is carried in the rear of the
> company by a negro, hired for the occasion. These excur-
> sions sometimes finish with a terrible riot, in which people
> were killed or wounded. After the target shooting, the
> companies return to the city, march through the principal
> streets, decked with prizes and flowers (many being drunk
> and disorderly), with a calcium light, fireworks, and so on.

New York City in 1853 had a plethora of "Guards": The Pickwick
Guard; Atlantic Light Guards; The Hudson Guard; Fulton Light
Guards; Lindsey Blues; Dry Dock Light Guards; Moore's House
Smith's Guards; Gage Guard and many other Guard and Target
Companies. Over twenty years their number increased. Harrigan's
"Guard" was trained by Major John Edmund Burke of the Duryea
Zouaves.

Montrose J. Moses (Theatre Arts Monthly) in March 1926
wrote,

> The American drama offers no more graphic record of con-
> temporary life than the mass of manuscripts left by Edward

Harrigan--They throb with the spirit of New York of their
day; they catch with a photographic distinctness those pal-
pitant strains of unusual life in a large city, which very
few dramatists besides Harrigan have had sufficient interest
to study and embody in plays.

During his lifetime Ned Harrigan wrote over eighty vaudeville
sketches. London's St. James Hall Variety Theatre, on November
7, 1877, presented Harrigan's sketch Walking for dat Cake featuring
David Braham's title song. One of Harrigan's earliest and best
plays was Old Lavender (produced at the Theatre Comique on
September 3, 1877). The play was based on his vaudeville sketch
Old Lavender Water or Round the Docks. Harrigan gave a fine performance as the gentle, genial drunkard Lavender, which became
one of his favorite roles.

The fame of Harrigan and Hart increased yearly, and, on
August 7, 1876, they became the proprietors of the Theatre Comique.
The team and their theatre were described by the New York World
as a "bright little spot that shines like an oasis of light amid the
surrounding gloom of lower Broadway." Historian George Odell
recorded the Theatre Comique with the Harrigan and Hart Company
as "probably the best variety theatre then in New York."

The Mulligan plays cast Harrigan as warm-hearted, garrulous,
ex-Civil War veteran and corner-grocer Dan Mulligan. Hart was
sassy, brassy Rebecca Allup, the Mulligans' black cook. Expert
comedienne Annie Griffiths Yeamans appeared as Dan's wife, Cordelia. Mrs. Annie Yeamans, born on the Isle of Man, first appeared
with Harrigan in 1872 in The Slave of the Harp. Her daughters,
Jennie, Lydia and Emily (all of whom had played Topsy in Uncle
Tom's Cabin), later joined the Harrigan company. John Wild was
urbane, black barber Captain Simpson Primrose and William Gray
(born Cornelius O'Donnell in Philadelphia) played Reverend Palestine
Putter, Chaplain of the Skidmore Guards. Gray and Wild had been
a successful blackface comedy team before joining Harrigan's well-
trained ensemble acting company.

Harrigan told Harper's Weekly (February 2, 1889) that he
depicted these lives because "their trials and troubles, hopes and
fears, joys and sorrows are more varied and more numerous."
Minstrelsy generously borrowed Harrigan's material but never captured the depth and human diversification or racial pride of the integrated immigrant elements that was Harrigan's genius. Although
Harrigan burlesqued New York's mania for "Marching Clubs," minstrels lampooned his Ginger Blues and Skidmore Guard black march-
ers.

Harrigan, in an interview with the New York Dramatic Mirror
in 1894, said,

The audiences recognize the authenticity and correctness of the types I endeavor to reproduce on the stage, and I suppose that the success of the Mulligan series and subsequent plays of local life was due in large measure to that fact. At the same time I wish to give no small measure of credit to the songs that Dave Braham composed for these plays, many of which have been whistled and sung all over the country.

Harrigan became Gilbert to David Braham's Sullivan. London-born Braham composed hundreds of songs for the comedies. He was a violinist and former conductor of orchestras at minstrelsy's Mechanics Hall; he was also orchestra leader at the opening of Wood's Theatre Comique on July 7, 1862. Braham's songs with Harrigan's lyrics became the popular song hits of the period. In November, 1876, Harrigan married the oldest of Braham's eight children, sixteen-year-old Annie Theresa. Annie Theresa Braham and Ned Harrigan produced ten children, seven of whom lived: Edward, Jr., Nolan, Philip, Anthony Hart, Adelaide, William, and Grace (who became Nedda and later wed Joshua Logan after the death of her first husband, actor Walter Connolly).

The Mulligans' Silver Wedding, in which Dan and Cordelia celebrated twenty-five years of married life "wid niver an angry word, only what passed between ourselves" gave the last performance at the soon-to-be-demolished Theatre Comique on April 30, 1881. Harrigan and Hart opened their New Theatre Comique at 728 Broadway --"a gem of mechanical art--acoustic properties perfect--17 exits-- Architects, Kimball and Wisedell--Builder, George T. Dallinger--new stock of scenery by Charles W. Witham--Dave Braham, musical director." The New Theatre Comique opened on August 29, 1881, with one of Harrigan's greatest hits, The Major. Harrigan was rhetorical con-man Major Gilfeather, and Hart--predating George Bernard Shaw's professor in Pygmalion--was Enry Iggins.

The New Theatre Comique produced Harrigan's plays Squatter Sovereignty* (January 9, 1882); Mordecai Lyons (October 26, 1882); McSorley's Inflation (November 27, 1882); The Muddy Day (April 2, 1882); Cordelia's Aspirations (November 5, 1883); Dan's Tribulations (April 7, 1884); and Investigation, in which Harrigan played a frantic Romeo to Annie Yeaman's Juliet (September 1, 1884). The New Theatre Comique burned down on Tuesday, December 23, 1884 and was mourned by Harrigan as "the worst night I ever spent. Tony Hart and I stood at a window and watched $70,000 worth of our property go."

Harrigan and Hart moved to the New Park Theatre where they

---

*M. W. Hanley produced Squatter Sovereignty for a road tour in September 1882, with Sam E. Ryan in Harrigan's role and J. H. Ryan playing Hart's Widow Nolan.

opened in Ned's latest play McAllister's Legacy on January 5, 1885.
The show ran until March 2, 1885, when they transferred to the
Fourteenth Street Theatre for three months. Harrigan's Park Theatre, Broadway and Thirty-fifth Street, opened on August 31, 1885,
and contained a good deal of the equipment and furnishings of the
dismantled Booth Theatre. The opening play at Harrigan's Park
Theatre was a rewritten version of Old Lavender, which had originally been produced on September 3, 1877, at the Theatre Comique,
with Harrigan in the title role and Hart as Dick, the Rat, a Negro
bootblack. After 100 performances of Old Lavender, Harrigan's new
play The Grip followed on November 30.

In London, on July 15, 1882, Tony Hart married twice-divorced
English-born actress Gertie Granville. Within three years her unreasonable demands and constant interference, in combination with
imposed assistance and advice from members of both families, had
caused the breakup of one of the most beloved and talented teams
in show business.

The last New York City appearance of Harrigan and Hart was
at the Fourteenth Street Theatre on Saturday, May 9, 1885. The
New York Dramatic Mirror on May 9, 1885, deplored the separation
of Harrigan and Hart in an article "Goodbye Mulligan," eulogizing
the end of the famous team as follows:

> the dissolution of the firm of Harrigan and Hart breaks up
> an institution that had been in existence for about a dec-
> ade. It was an institution peculiar to the Metropolis.
> American-Irish comedy, negro minstrelsy, and Dutch spe-
> ciality work were welded together, and from this, through
> the brainwork of Mr. Harrigan and his father-in-law Mr.
> Braham, was evolved the famous Theatre Comique, or
> Mulligan series--Since the fact of the dissolution was first
> made known, neither partner has given any satisfactory
> explanation to the public.

Threatened with a law suit to honor a previous contract, Harrigan and Hart made their final appearance as a team on-stage at
Brooklyn's Park Theatre in The Major and Investigation (June 1 to
June 15, 1885). Harrigan temporarily replaced Hart in his company
with Richard Quilter. Ned returned to Manhattan in a revival of
Old Lavender on August 31, 1855, with Dan Collyer, a member of
the cast of Martin W. Hanley's May 11, 1885, eleven-performance
production of Harrigan's unsuccessful play Are You Insured?, assigned to Tony Hart's former blackface, drag and comedic male roles.
The glowing fourteen-year reign of Harrigan and Hart was ended.

Tony and Gertie Hart headed the cast of a dreary play by
William Gill called Buttons, which opened in August 1855 in Burling-
ton, Vermont. They closed the fiasco on November 19, 1885, in St.
Paul, Minnesota. Ned Harrigan had opened in his play The Leather

Patch in February, and, on Saturday, February 20, 1886, Tony
Hart returned to Broadway at the Comedy Theatre as editor Isaac
Roast in William Gill's farce The Toy Pistol, a reworking of Gill's
prior year's comedy A Bottle of Ink. Hart's return was greeted
with wild enthusiasm by his devoted followers, but Gill's inane
comedy was not; in April it closed to tour.

Harrigan leased the Park Theatre and renamed the house
Harrigan's Park Theatre, advertising it as "the only theatre in
America producing original comedy and local drama, all written, directed and the principal characters impersonated by the author,
Mr. Edward Harrigan." Harrigan's Park Theatre opening, scheduled for August 31, 1885, was postponed until September 1, 1885,
when the curtain rose on an expanded version of Old Lavender,
accumulating 104 performances by its closing on November 28, 1885.
Harrigan's performance as alcoholic George "Old Lavender" Coggs-
well was critically considered as artistic as Joseph Jefferson's acclaimed portrayal of the title role in Rip Van Winkle. The New
York Times reported, "His impersonation is remarkable for elabor-
ation and delicacy as it is for humor--it is a wonderful piece of
acting."

During Harrigan's seasons at the Park Theatre, he produced
several new plays and revived nine of his past successes, among
them: The Grip (November 30, 1885); The Leather Patch (Febru-
ary 15, 1886); The O'Reagans (October 11, 1886); McNooney's Visit
(January 3, 1887); Pete (November 22, 1887); Waddy Googan
(September 3, 1888); The Lorgaire (originally produced on November
25, 1878 and on December 10, 1888); and 4-11-44 (a reworking of
McNooney's Visit March 21, 1889). After four seasons at the Park,
Harrigan took most of his resident company on tour to the West
Coast and in 1890 he built his own theatre.

Tony Hart, as moonshiner Upton O. Dodge, paired with Lillian
Russell as maid Virginia at the Standard Theatre on August 16,
1886, in The Maid and the Moonshiner. Charles Hale Hoyt's play,
with music by Edward Soloman, was directed by Julian Mitchell, but
the play could survive only sixteen performances. The popularity
of the two stars could not overcome devastatingly harsh reviews or
sustain the elaborately mounted musical comedy. Hart returned to
Broadway at the People's Theatre on December 13, 1886, in another
disaster called Donnybrook. Tony and Gertie Hart toured in Donnybrook until May, 1887 when Hart made his last appearance on the
stage of Boston's Howard Athenaeum, the place where he and Harrigan, on August 14, 1871, had realized their first success as a
team. Harrigan had successfully survived without Hart, but Tony
never regained the acclaim he had known as Ned's partner.

On Sunday, December 15, 1887, the New York Herald headlined Hart's decline as "That Telltale Lisp. Tony Hart's Trouble
Begins Like That of John McCullough. All the Symptoms of Paresis.

Why Ned Harrigan's Former Partner Has Been Forced To Leave the
Stage." A "Grand Testimonial Benefit" was held for Tony Hart on
March 22, 1888, at New York's Academy of Music. With the glaring
exception of Harrigan, most of Hart's contemporaries in the theatre
appeared. The highlight of the performance was an unintended
hilarious assassination scene from Shakespeare's Julius Caesar, featuring Broadway's leading comedians determinedly dedicated to playing tragedy. But Nat C. Goodwin, William H. Crane, Francis Wilson, Stuart Robson and others inadvertently turned tragedy to
comedy. The performance was virtually halted when Hart was recognized by a cheering audience; he had disguised himself in a toga
and was mingling amid a group of Roman senators.

Released from the Worcester Asylum in February, 1889, Hart
attended a performance of Pete. Harrigan played the title role
of his play as an ex-black slave and faithful servant; the play had
opened on November 22, 1888. Hart went backstage to congratulate
his former partner on his splendid performance as Pete. It was to
be their last meeting. Tony Hart died completely paralyzed from
paresis in the asylum at Worcester, Massachusetts at the age of
thirty-six (Wednesday, November 4, 1891); he was interred in Worcester's St. John Cemetery.

East of Sixth Avenue on Thirty-fifth Street, Harrigan built
his own theatre, which had been designed by architect Francis H.
Kimball. Harrigan's Theatre opened on December 29, 1890, for
a successful run of 202 performances of Harrigan's new play Reilly
and the Four-Hundred, which featured Braham and Harrigan's
popular song hit "Maggie Murphy's Home." Harrigan's next new
play, Last of the Hogans, opened on December 21, 1891, and his
play The Woollen Stocking premiered on October 9, 1893. His drama
Notoriety opened on December 10, 1894, and, on February 5, 1895,
Harrigan revived The Major.

Following the death from peritonitis of his eighteen-year-old son,
Edward, Jr., on February 17, 1895, Ned Harrigan retired from the
stage (February 23). Harrigan leased his theatre to Richard Mans-
field for an annual rental of $18,000. Mansfield renamed Harrigan's
Theatre the Garrick and opened it on April 23, 1895, when he
starred in George Bernard Shaw's comedy Arms and the Man.
Charles Frohman leased the theatre until 1915. The following year
it was sold at auction but purchased by Otto Kahn prior to its proposed demolition. The Theatre Guild established their first home
at the Garrick Theatre opening on April 19, 1915, with their production of Nobel Prize winner Jacinto Benavente's play The Bonds
of Interest. Harrigan's once beautiful theatre was demolished in
1932 after a devastating fire had once again destroyed a Harrigan
creation (the event was similar to the burning of the New Theatre
Comique in 1884).

Harrigan's play My Son, Dan closed on the road, and Harrigan returned to Broadway at the Bijou Theatre on August 13, 1896, in his new play, Marty Malone. On May 3 and September 20 in 1897, Harrigan appeared on the vaudeville stage at Proctor's Twenty-third Street Theatre in a short version of his play Last of the Hogans called Sergeant Hickey; he then spent two years touring on the Keith-Proctor vaudeville circuit in abbreviated versions of several of his plays. Former heavyweight boxing champion Bob Fitzsimmons was billed above Harrigan in a tab version of The Mulligan Guards' Ball. Harrigan topped the bill at Tony Pastor's Theatre on April 10, 1899, in his playlet Larry Logan. In December of that year at the Grand Opera House, he replaced Wilton Lackaye as Uncle Tom in Uncle Tom's Cabin.

The Mulligans was published in 1910. Harrigan's novel was dedicated to the memory of Tony Hart. Harrigan received glowing notices in a bad play when he returned to Broadway at the Bijou Theatre on January 12, 1903, for forty performances as an Irish labor leader in Clyde Fitch's play The Bird in a Cage, starring Arnold Daly. Liebler and Company produced Harrigan's new and last play, Under Cover, off-Broadway at the Murray Hill THeatre (September 14, 1903).

Convinced that his former popularity had been forgotten by a fickle public and that his prestige and career were passé, Harrigan regained appreciable renewed--if reflected--glory on February 3, 1908, when his great admirer George M. Cohan invited him to the opening of his new musical comedy Fifty Miles From Boston at the Garrick--Harrigan's former theatre! Cohan's new effort ran only four weeks, but the show's hit song by George M. (sung by James C. Marlowe) became a standard: "Harrigan" ("H-A-Double R- I-GAN spells Harrigan").

On October 6, 1908, at Wallack's Theatre, sixty-five-year-old Harrigan made his last Broadway appearance in his role as Corporal O'Carroll in George Egerton's unsuccessful play His Wife's Family. The play starred Arnold Daly, with Harrigan's son William in the cast as Curly Desmond. Ned Harrigan closed the year 1908 in December when he toured in the small role of Croup, a Negro servant in Booth Tarkington and Harry Leon Wilson's new play, Cameo Kirby, which starred Nat C. Goodwin. The play closed at the Lyric Theatre in Philadelphia before the end of the year, and it was withdrawn. Cameo Kirby finally opened on Broadway at Hackett's Theatre on December 20, 1909. It starred Dustin Farnum; former minstrel man George Thatcher was Croup.

Substituting for his son William, Harrigan was greeted by a ten-minute ovation in the Lambs Gambol on May 9, 1909, at the Metropolitan Opera House. A medley of his famous old songs was played, and his career came full cycle when he blacked-up for the minstrel show finale. But the great old trouper Edward Harrigan, whose days of theatrical glory had passed like his century, was

suddenly stricken before the finale and taken from the Opera House
in a wheelchair. He spent the last two years of his life as an invalid and, at the age of sixty-seven, still convinced the public had
forgotten him, died at his New York home, 249 West 102nd Street,
on Tuesday, June 6, 1911. A massive funeral service was held on
Friday, June 9, 1911, at the Church of the Ascension, 107th Street
and Broadway. The Reverend Michael J. Tighe celebrated a Requiem
Mass, and the multitalented, beloved Edward Green Harrigan was
entombed in Woodlawn Cemetery.

Harrigan and Hart reappeared on July 20, 1984, at the Chester, Connecticut 200-seat Norma Terris Theatre, operated by the
Goodspeed Opera House of nearby East Haddam, in a work-in-
progress production. Michael Stewart's play Harrigan 'n Hart was
based on E. J. Kahn, Jr.'s definitive biography of the famous team,
The Merry Partners, published by Random House in 1955; it was
also based on data provided by Harrigan's daughter Nedda Harrigan
Logan, who owns the stage rights to Kahn's biography of her father
and his talented partner. Staged by Edward Stone, Harrigan 'n
Hart had music by Max Showalter and lyrics by Peter Walker.

The musical score of Harrigan 'n Hart was augmented with
songs unearthed from Harrigan's nineteenth-century plays. The
original songs written by David Braham (with Harrigan's lyrics) included "The Mulligan Guard" (1873); "Clara Jenkins' Socialistic Tea"
from The Major (1881); "The Old Feather Bed" and "McNally's Row
of Flats" from McSorley's Inflation (1882); "Maggie Murphy's Home"
from Reilly and the Four-Hundred (1890); and "Savannah Sue" from
Marty Malone (1896), plus others.

Christopher Wells portrayed Edward Harrigan, and versatile
Mark Hamill, the Luke Skywalker of the Star Wars films, made his
musical debut in a remarkably telling performance as Tony Hart.
Mark Hamill sang Hart's "Put Me in My Little Bed" from Madame
Rentz's 1870 Female Minstrels but performed no blackface numbers
in which Hart excelled. Tony Hart was one of the best female impersonators in the business. He was laughable, convincing, and
memorable as black Mrs. Welcome Allup in the Mulligan series where
he belligerently warns "I'se a member ob de Baptist Church--don't
push me!" Hart was equally effective in whiteface as the Widow
Nolan in Squatter Sovereignty, Mollie Gouldrich in McAllister's Legacy, and Norah Donovan in The Donovans. In 1881, Augustin Daly
wrote this about Hart's impersonations: "I know of no leading woman who could even touch the hem of his petticoat in the part."
Tony was equally believable in male roles: the Confederate soldier
Dan in The Blue and the Gray; Matteo Verslani in The Italian Padrone; Dennis Mulligan (doubling as Rebecca Allup) in The Mulligan
Guards' chowder; Dennis in The Mulligans' Silver Wedding; and
Enry Iggins in The Major.

Nedda Harrigan Logan recently said of her father, "He was the father of musical comedy. He put three acts together, with music, and made it something other than vaudeville." The Harrigan shows were the precursors of later musical comedies. But the latter-day musical based on the life of Harrigan and Hart--which returned their names in lights to Broadway--quickly flickered and died.

Harrigan 'n Hart was produced by Elliot Martin, Arnold Bernhard, and the Shubert Organization. Joe Layton restaged Michael Stewart's play (which began previews on January 10, 1985) at the Longacre Theatre and opened there on January 31. Talented Harry Groener was featured as Ned Harrigan (Christopher Wells, who had originated the part of Harrigan in the Goodspeed Opera House 1984 production, understudied both Harry Groener and Mark Hamill) and Mark Hamill reenacted his past-summer's role of Tony Hart. Christine Ebersole was cast as the bitchy Mrs. Gertie Hart, and Armelia McQueen was Mrs. Annie Yeamans. The longed-for successful return of Harrigan and Hart to Broadway did not occur. Harrigan 'n Hart closed on Saturday, February 2, 1985, after four performances.

"This is a dull, if dutifully professional evening in which endless medleys of vintage vaudeville songs and sketches are periodically interrupted by newly composed numbers and scenes imparting the history of the title characters," reported Frank Rich (the New York Times), "The old comedy routines are frantic but mirthless--Harrigan 'n Hart is bustling with kinetic energy, however aimless, and the ferociously peppy chorus mug as if they were being paid by the wink."

Brendan Gill (the New Yorker) felt "the feverishly animated cast evoked not that place and time but the amateur ebullience of a contemporary class play at Scarsdale High" in their efforts to recreate New York City of one-hundred years ago and that Harrigan and Hart "themselves defy being reincarnated--In seeking to pay homage to the Harrigan originals they achieved only a courteous anonymity."

Probably no chapter in the history of American show business more aptly personifies the nineteenth-century advancement of Broadway musical comedy from the variety stage than does the chapter featuring the careers of Harrigan and Hart. George M. Cohan acknowledged his indebtedness to Ned Harrigan not only in his dedication of his 1907 song "Harrigan" but also in 1914 when he wrote, "Edward Harrigan was a fine artist, a great writer of human comedies, and one of the grandest men it has ever been my pleasure to meet. I live in hopes that some day my name may mean half as much to the coming generation of American playwrights as Harrigan's name has meant to me."

AL JOLSON

By proclamation of press and public, and more frequently himself, Al Jolson was "The World's Greatest Entertainer." According to Michael Freeland, in his 1972 biography Jolie: The Story of Al Jolson, his father, Moses Hesselson, changed the family name to Yoelson. Al was born Asa Yoelson in Srednicke, Russia, which is now the town of Seredzius in the Lithuanian Republic. Preferring a spring birthday, Al decided that the date of his birth was Wednesday, May 26, 1886. But, in an interview for Everybody's Magazine in 1921, playwright George S. Kaufman more accurately gave Jolson's age as thirty-eight, thus establishing the year of his birth as 1883. The month and day of Jolson's birth have not been definitely established, both because of the absence of birth records and because of Jolson's unreliable memory.

The Yoelson family migrated to Washington, D.C. where father Moses Yoelson was a Jewish cantor and young Asa impulsively started a theatrical career from the gallery of Washington's Bijou Theatre by joining minstrel Eddie Leonard in singing "I'll Leave My Happy Home for You." Jolson's stage debut was in Washington, D.C. for three performances as a supernumerary in a mob scene in Israel Zangwill's play The Children of the Ghetto. A brief stint with Walter L. Main's Circus was later followed by an engagement in 1901 with Al Reeve's Burlesque company at New York's Star Theatre, where he sang "When the Roses Bloom Again" with Aggie Behler.

Jolson appeared with his brother Hirschel with a burlesque unit "The Mayflowers" in an act called The Hebrew and the Cadet. Hirsch (changed to Harry), Joe Palmer and Asa (altered to Al) were appearing at Kenney's Theatre in Brooklyn in a vaudeville sketch A Little of Everything when blackface monologist James Francis Dooley suggested their sagging act would be more successful in blackface. An offer from the manager of Poli's vaudeville circuit of a five-week booking as a "blackface single"--plus a tour with the Sullivan-Considine circuit--convinced Jolson to switch to blackface, a switch he maintained throughout most of his brilliant career. Not until March 17, 1931, when he returned to Broadway in the less-than-memorable musical comedy The Wonder Bar, did he appear in whiteface; except for his role in a travesty of the play My Lady's Dress, a brief sketch in the 1914 musical comedy Dancing Around.

Success in vaudeville in California prompted Jolson to advertise himself as "The Blackface with the Grand Opera Voice." It was in Portland, Oregon, that Jolson luckily joined Dockstader's Minstrels. Experienced and talented minstrel man Lew Dockstader taught Al the intricate timing of comedy and how to control an audience. Dockstader was so impressed with Jolson's talent that he relinquished his own featured spot in the minstrels to the young blackface singer (New York's Fifth Avenue Theatre, February, 1909). After gaining invaluable experience and recognition with

Al Jolson (courtesy of The Doug McClelland Collection)

Dockstader's Minstrels, Jolson made his Broadway musical comedy
debut.

The Shuberts inaugurated their new Broadway theatre, the
Winter Garden, on March 20, 1911, with a glorified vaudeville presented as a musical comedy, called La Belle Paree (A Jumble of
Jollity) in which Jolson made his bid for fame toward the end
of the show when he played the minor role of blackface Erastus
Sparkler, singing "Paris is a Paradise for Coons." After appearing
in Vera Violetta (Winter Garden, November 20, 1911), the Shuberts
featured Jolson in another Winter Garden three-part pastiche, Whirl
of Society, in which Jolson created the blackface character of Gus
that would become his stage persona in the following Winter Garden
shows: The Honeymoon Express (February 6, 1913); Dancing
Around (October 10, 1914); Robinson Crusoe, Jr. (February 17,
1916); Sinbad (February 14, 1918) and Big Boy (January 7, 1925).
The Shuberts opened a new theatre (October 6, 1921), which was
named for their star--Jolson's Fifty-ninth Street Theatre--with the
production of the musical comedy Bombo starring Jolson as Gus--
and Bombo.

Joe Laurie, Jr. described Jolson as "the greatest of all American entertainers," and Alexander Woollcott once wrote, "There is
no other performer who holds such an absolute dictatorship over his
audience." This appraisal might explain Jolson's manic compulsion
to entertain and his insatiable craving for applause and adoration
from his audiences. Jolson's inexhaustible energy extended to many
successful phonograph records over four decades, lengthy road tours
in several of his Broadway hits despite his hatred of touring, and
the interpolation into his shows of many songs that have become
standards. "Rock-A-Bye Your Baby with a Dixie Melody" and "My
Mammy" were interpolated during the run of Sinbad, and George
Gershwin and Irving Caesar's classic song "Swanee" was introduced
during the road tour of that musical. Jolson added to Sigmund
Romberg's undistinguished score for Bombo, "April Showers," "Toot,
Toot, Tootsie!" and, while on tour, "California, Here I Come."

In 1916, Jolson made his screen debut in a short film for the
Vitagraph Company that was produced for the Traffic Police's
Benefit Fund. Although displeased with his appearance on the
screen, Jolson, in May 1923, made a "gentleman's agreement" with
D. W. Griffith to star in the pioneer director's motion picture
Mammy's Boy. Mammy's Boy (retitled Black Magic) after two weeks
of rehearsals began shooting at Griffith's Mamaroneck, New York
studio. After seeing the rushes of Griffith's comedy--then called
Black and White--Jolson, claiming nervous exhaustion, immediately
sailed for Europe on June 23, 1923. Griffith sued Jolson for over
a half-million dollars but in 1926 settled for less than three thousand. The Griffith silent picture was completed and released in
1924 as His Darker Self, starring Lloyd Hamilton. It was not successful.

To celebrate the fifteenth anniversary of the opening of the
Winter Garden Theatre, Jolson starred in the second edition of the
Shubert's revue Artists and Models for four weeks beginning March
20, 1926. At the Four Cohans Theatre in Chicago, Jolson replaced
Phil Baker in the Shubert revue A Night in Spain on March 11, 1928,
closing April 7, 1928. In 1932 he had unbelievably ambitious plans
to play the title role of the black cripple in an operetta based on
the play Porgy. The Theatre Guild had made the arcane proposal
that Jerome Kern and Oscar Hammerstein, II should write a musical
version of Du Bose Heyward's successful play Porgy, which would
star Al Jolson. This proposal met with opposition from the author.
Heyward wisely waited for George Gershwin's operatic version, which
became Porgy and Bess.

Jolson reappeared before the camera at the Manhattan Opera
House in September 1926 for a Warner Bros. Vitaphone short film.
Photographed against a plantation log-cabin setting and costumed
in overalls, Jolson in blackface sang "April Showers," "Rock-A-Bye
Your Baby with a Dixie Melody," and "When the Red, Red, Robin
Comes Bob, Bob, Bobbin' Along." Jolson's segment closed the hour-
long Vitaphone film which opened with the Mignon overture played
by the New York Philharmonic Orchestra and featured: baritone
Reginald Werrenrath; four songs by Elsie Janis; Willie and Eugene
Howard in a comedy sketch Between the Acts at the Opera; and,
registering none-too-well, George Jessel.

Warner Bros. signed Jessel to reprise his successful 1925
Broadway portrayal of Jackie Rabinowitz in a screen version of
Samson Raphaelson's play The Jazz Singer. Jessel's repeated, excessive, and intransigent demands for additional money angered the
Warners, and Al Jolson was signed for the film during his California
tour of Big Boy in 1927. Premiering October 6, 1927, The Jazz
Singer was basically a silent picture, with four Vitaphone talking
and singing sequences. The film, erroneously, was called "the first
talking picture." Jolson's first line in the film was his old audience
titilating ballyhoo, "You ain't heard nothin' yet, folks!" And he
sang seven songs: "Mammy"; "Toot, Toot, Tootsie"; "Blue Skies";
"Goodbye"; "Dirty Hands, Dirty Face"; "Mother, I Still Have You";
and "Kol Nidrei." Jolson became the "talkies" first major star.
During the same period, George Jessel made two quickly forgotten
films--Lucky Boy and Love, Live and Laugh (1929)--and retreated
to vaudeville.

Jolson's historical success in The Jazz Singer and the advent
of talking pictures changed the future of Hollywood and Broadway.
His screen success continued with The Singing Fool (1928); Say It
with Songs (1929); and Mammy and Big Boy (1930). Jolson returned to Broadway in 1931. The small Nora Bayes Theatre atop
the Forty-fourth Street Theatre was converted into a cabaret by the
Shuberts to showcase their German imported musical, The Wonder
Bar, in which Jolson was a whiteface Monsieur Al, proprietor of

Paris's cabaret The Wonder Bar. For the first time Jolson appeared
on Broadway without blackface in a straight role paced with songs.
The Wonder Bar was no wonder and closed shop in less than three
months.

The "Mammy" singer returned to Hollywood to film Hallelujah,
I'm a Bum in 1933. After appearing in the screen version of Wonder
Bar and co-starring with his third wife, Ruby Keeler, in 1935's
Go into Your Dance, Jolson's film career faded. Meanwhile he found
success on Radio in NBC's Presenting Al Jolson (1932); Kraft Music
Hall (1933); 1935's Shell Chateau. From 1936 to 1939, he starred in
the Lifebuoy Program, and, on June 13, 1936, he was with Ruby
Keeler on radio's Lux Theatre in the play Burlesque.

United Artists' announcement in 1936 that Jolson would return
to the screen in a film version of the Broadway musical Sons O'Gun
never materialized. He did make an uninteresting musical film for
Warner Bros. that year called The Singing Kid. Jolson reappeared
on the screen in 1939 playing supporting roles in Rose of Washington
Square and in Hollywood Calvacade. He also was famed minstrel man,
E. P. Christy, in Swanee River. Jolson's last screen appearance
was as himself in the Warner Bros. 1945 film Rhapsody in Blue.

For the first time Jolson shared top billing (with Martha Raye,
Jack Whiting and Bert Gordon) in his last Broadway show Hold On
to Your Hats (September 11, 1940 at the Shubert Theatre) in which
he played "The Lone Rider" in whiteface. After four months the
musical folded due to Jolson's dislike of New York winters; he reported "poor health." Jolson gave a sincere, straight performance
as Uncle Tom in E. A. Ellington's adaptation of Uncle Tom's Cabin
(August 10, 1941, on radio's Star-Spangled Theatre over NBC station WJZ), with Jackson Beck as Simon Legree and Edna May Gordon
reading the female parts; Loney Haskell excelled in creating the off-
stage howling of bloodhounds.

The Jolson magic and acclaim, however, resurfaced in 1946
with the smashing success of Columbia Pictures' biographical film,
The Jolson Story, and its less successful sequel, Jolson Sings Again.
Larry Parks expertly portrayed Jolson and mouthed the songs to
Al's still-powerful voice. Decca Records' album of the sound track
from The Jolson Story (as recorded by the great mammy singer)
sold millions of copies.

The American Veterans Committee gave Jolson a Testimonial
Dinner at New York's Hotel Astor on October 1, 1946, in appreciation of his extensive, exhausting entertaining of overseas troops
during World War II. After returning from a long USO tour of
Korea, Al Jolson died of a heart attack on Sunday, October 23,
1950, in San Francisco (it was in San Francisco that he had first
gained eminence as a blackface singer).

Larry Parks as Jolson in <u>The Jolson Story</u>, Columbia Pictures, 1946 (courtesy of The Doug McClelland Collection).

Despite opposition from various quarters--including an earlier request by Jolson that George Jessel should not eulogize him--on October 26, 1950, at Los Angeles Temple Israel, George Jessel delivered the eulogy for Al Jolson. The Columbia Broadcasting Company distributed more than fifteen thousand copies of the speech. Toward the end of the eulogy Jessel said, "But history must record the name Jolson, who in the twilight of his life sang his heart out in a foreign land to the wounded and the valiant ... I am proud to have basked in the sunlight of his greatness, to have been part of his time...."

Twenty-three years later Jessel's appraisal of Al Jolson would be published by Time magazine (July 30, 1973): "He was a no-good son-of-a-bitch, but he was the greatest entertainer I've ever seen."

EDDIE LEONARD

The most noted minstrel of his day was born Lemuel Gordon Toney (Wednesday, October 18, 1871) at Church Hill, Richmond, Virginia. Nicknamed "Dots," in 1883 young Toney made his stage debut at the age of twelve, performing a song-and-dance routine at Richmond's Putnam's Theatre Comique for three dollars a week while working days as a water boy at Belle Isle Tredegar Iron Works. After an unsuccessful tryout as a center-fielder for John McGraw's Baltimore Orioles baseball team, "Dots" performed for George Primrose, who hired the young boy for his minstrel company.

Toney changed his name to Eddie Leonard after joining Primrose and West Minstrels in 1890 at the Ford Grand Opera House in Baltimore, where he sang his song "Just Because She Made Them Goo-Goo Eyes"--with "artful innuendo." Eddie appeared in an 1893 touring production of The South Before the War in which a talented young Richmond-born black dancer named Bill Robinson made his stage debut. After headlining Haverly's Minstrels in 1902, Leonard was on Broadway at the Victoria Theatre in January 1904 for a month's engagement; he was featured with Lew Dockstader's Minstrels. Four months later Eddie Leonard made his legitimate Broadway stage debut.

George W. Lederer's integrated musical The Southerners ("A Musical Study in Black and White") opened at the New York Theatre on May 23, 1904, with a musical score by black composer Will Marion Cook. Leonard was featured in blackface as Uncle Daniel, and, for the first time, a real black chorus performed a cakewalk. Leonard appeared in Lifting the Lid at the Aerial Gardens (atop the New Amsterdam Theatre) on June 5, 1905, singing "Coonland" for 112 performances. Cohan and Harris Minstrels opened at the New York Theatre on August 3, 1908. The show featured the great minstrel George "Honey Boy" Evans, Eddie Leonard, George Thatcher and, dancing as a dusky Salome, female impersonator Julian Eltinge.

Leonard's deceptively easy soft-shoe, sand dance and his unique singing of his own songs established him as the country's leading minstrel man. Billed as "The Prince of Minstrels," he starred as Billy Emerson for 100 performances in John Cort's production of Roly-Boly Eyes (the title of one of Leonard's songs, derived from George Nichols mid-nineteenth century song "Roley Boley") at the Knickerbocker Theatre on September 25, 1919. Alexander Woollcott reviewed the show as "Eddie Leonard singing 'Ida' again, Eddie Leonard going back to his old favorite, 'Ro-Oly, Bo-oly Ah-ah-ah-ah-eyes', Eddie Leonard sang softly and easily his wonderful steps, Eddie Leonard and not much more." During the show's run Leonard sang his classic, national song hit "Ida, Sweet as Apple Cider," a song later to gain additional fame when performed by Eddie Cantor.

Eddie Leonard (courtesy of The Free Library of Philadelphia Print and Pictures Dept.).

Called "a whale of a hit," Leonard and His Banjo Boys' forty minute vaudeville act at Broadway's Palace Theatre on March 18, 1924, was further praised at the Hippodrome Theatre on October 15, 1924. Critic Burns Mantle (Daily News) wrote, "Mr. Leonard is a gentle minstrel with a curiously appealing note in his voice and a decidedly individual gift, both for singing and writing negro melodies. He needs no more to guarantee him the popularity he enjoys." Leonard continued headlining New York and national vaudeville stages until the end of 1929, at which time he went to Hollywood under contract to Universal Pictures.

Eddie Leonard starred in Universal's musical film with a vaudeville background, Melody Lane. The film, released on July 28, 1929, had overtones of Al Jolson's 1928 film, The Singing Fool. Eddie sang his "Roly-Boly Eyes" and other songs during the course of the soggy story, but Melody Lane received withering reviews and failed to establish "The Prince of Minstrels" as a screen star. Leonard returned to the death throes of vaudeville, making his last appearance at The Palace on April 23, 1932. He personally published his autobiography, What a Life; I'm Telling You (1935), which he dedicated to his wife and one-time vaudeville partner Mabel Russell --"To my dear wife Mabel Russell Leonard, who is responsible for my good health and good behavior." In the same year Eddie opened a short-lived bar and grille in the Bushwick section of Brooklyn.

The demise of vaudeville and the death of minstrelsy ended Eddie Leonard's long career, but in 1940 he returned to Hollywood to appear with other one-time vaudeville and Broadway stars--Blanche Ring, Trixie Friganza, Julian Eltinge, and Grace La Rue--in Bing Crosby's Universal Pictures' musical, If I Had My Way. Once again Leonard sang "Ida, Sweet as Apple Cider." Returning to New York, Leonard performed his old blackface routine for the last time from May 1940 until March 1941, at Billy Rose's Diamond Horseshoe cabaret. Staged by John Murray Anderson, with costumes and settings by Raoul Pene DuBois and choreographed by Gene Kelly, Rose's nostalgic revue Nights of Gladness showcased aging show-business veterans Julian Eltinge, Blanche Ring, Pat Rooney, Harland Dixon, Gilda Gray, Eddie Leonard, and others, with Noble Sissle's twelve-piece orchestra.

The widely acclaimed "greatest minstrel of his day," Eddie Leonard, was found dead of natural causes in a room at Broadway's Hotel Imperial on Tuesday, July 29, 1941.

Leonard truly "transformed burnt cork into a thing of beauty" and probably no other performer executed a better soft-shoe dance than Eddie. Leonard composed many songs, among them, "Ida, Sweet as Apple Cider"; "Roly Boly Eyes"; "Sweetness"; "Oh, Didn't It Rain?"; "Just Because She Made Them Goo-Goo Eyes"; "I Lost My Mandy"; "Don't You Never Tell a Lie"; "Sugar Baby"; "Mandy Jane"; "Molasses Candy"; "Beautiful"; "I'm On My Way"; "Pick on

Your Old Banjo"; "Big, Brown Booloo Eyes"; and "I Wish I was Some Little Girlie's Beau."

Eddie Leonard's singing of "Water Boy" was electrifying. Critic Mabel Brundage described him in this way: "Others have done Negro spirituals but Leonard stands in a class by himself--One lives with Leonard, in the Georgia prison camp where the poor rockbreaker calls for water--Great artistry, Eddie Leonard. What more can one say?"

McINTYRE AND HEATH

"The greatest of all the blackface acts" was Joe Laurie, Jr.'s description of McIntyre and Heath in his illuminating show-biz history, Vaudeville.

James McIntyre, born in Kenosha, Wisconsin on Saturday, August 8, 1857, and Thomas K. Heath, born in Philadelphia, Pennsylvania on Wednesday, August 11, 1852, became a blackface comedy team at Harris' Vaudeville Theatre (San Antonio, Texas, 1874). They formed McIntyre and Heath's Mammoth Southern Minstrels at Omaha, Nebraska in 1881 but returned to vaudeville to become headliners for fifty years. Over the years their vaudeville sketches included Skedaddle; Way Down South; The Arrival of Gilbert; Flying To Jail; Happy Days; Gentlemen of Leisure; Back to the Stable; Waiting at the Church; Chickens; The Man from Montana; Hello Alexander. Called "the greatest of all blackface acts," their classic sketch The Georgia Minstrels was first performed by them at Brooklyn's Gaiety Theatre in 1894. Another famous sketch The Ham Tree was used throughout their long career.

During the 1890s an understudy was employed for heavy-drinking McIntyre (whose imbibing occasionally interfered with his locating the theatre). The understudy frequently went on-stage for McIntyre, but because he played his parts behind the protective blackface, audiences were never aware of Heath's substituted partner. Nor were audiences aware that the highly compatible team of McIntyre and Heath spoke to one another only on-stage.

Klaw and Erlanger presented McIntyre and Heath in an extension of their sketch The Ham Tree--"A Musical Vaudeville"--at the New York Theatre on August 28, 1905, for ninety performances in which McIntyre was cast as Alexander Hambletonian, Heath as Henry ("Hennery") Clay Jones, former juggler, W. C. Fields as Sherlock Baffles, and Belle Gold as a blackface maid called Desdemona. McIntyre and Heath toured for several years in The Ham Tree and returned to Broadway on August 30, 1909, at the Circle Theatre as the stars (for 56 performances) of In Hayti. They opened on October 26, 1916 at the Winter Garden Theatre for 209 performances in

McIntyre and Heath (courtesy of The Free Library of Philadelphia
Theatre Collection).

the Shubert's revue The Show of Wonders, and, on October 7, 1919, they starred (for 56 performances) in Hello Alexander (a revised version of The Ham Tree) at the Forty-fourth Street Theatre. The team's last appearance on the Broadway legitimate stage was in Red Pepper (May 29, 1922, at the Shubert Theatre).

After fifty years of headlining in vaudeville and appearing in several Broadway shows, McIntyre and Heath announced their premature retirement on Saturday, October 4, 1924, after completing their celebrated thirty-three minute act, The Georgia Minstrels (reminiscent of their 1891 stint as end men with Lew Dockstader's Minstrels), at Broadway's Palace Theatre. Rhode Island's governor, William S. Flynn, presented the famous blackface team with a loving cup inscribed "1874--Golden Jubilee--1924--McIntyre and Heath" on October 16, 1924, at Providence's E. F. Albee Theatre. The cup was given to commemorate their remarkable fifty-year partnership. Only the blackface team of Fox and Ward exceeded McIntyre and Heath in show-business longevity.

Following their "retirement," McIntyre and Heath returned to vaudeville in 1926. In 1928, they starred as Alexander and Henry in a musical comedy Headin' South, which closed in Buffalo, New York after eight weeks on the road. The Shuberts coaxed the team out of retirement once again in 1934, and they appeared in a musical based on the life of Stephen Foster (America Sings). McIntyre appeared as minstrel man Dan Bryant, and Heath was seen as minstrel Billy Rice. America Sings, featuring Allan Jones as Foster and Jules Bledsoe as Old Black Joe, opened on October 9, 1934, in Boston and closed there on October 20, 1934.

Three years after their final stage appearance, James McIntyre died at the age of eighty-one on Wednesday, August 18, 1937, at Southampton, Long Island, New York; he was buried in Noyack, Long Island. Thomas K. Heath died one year to-the-day later, on Thursday, August 18, 1938, at his home in Setauket, Long Island. He was eighty-five at the time of his death and unaware that his lifetime partner in burnt cork had preceded him.

MONTGOMERY AND STONE

The twenty-two year partnership of David Montgomery and Fred Stone began on March 20, 1895. After joining Haverly's Great Mastadon Minstrels in Galveston, Texas, they made their debut at Chicago's Hall's Casino. Billed as "Montgomery and Stone, Eccentric Blackface Comedians," they played B. F. Keith's Theatre in Boston and were first seen in New York at Miner's Bowery Theatre. Later they were the closing act on a vaudeville bill headlining the famous blackface team of McIntyre and Heath, and, in the spring of 1899, they were billed at Proctor's Theatre in New York as "The Burnt

Cork Swells." In 1900, their burnt-cork act was highly successful
for a three-month engagement in London at the Palace Theatre.

Fred A. Stone was born on Tuesday, August 19, 1873, in Val-
mont, Colorado, but his given name, Val, was soon changed to
Frederick. Fred joined the Walter Kirby Circus at the age of ten
as a tightrope walker and acrobat and made his stage debut in
D. P. Sutton's road company of a "Double" Uncle Tom's Cabin, with
his brother Edward J. Stone as "Double Topsys." David Craig
Montgomery, born on Thursday, April 21, 1870, in St. Joseph,
Missouri, made his stage debut at Stockbine's Gardens (March 20,
1887).

Charles Frohman engaged Montgomery and Stone for their
Broadway legitimate theatre debut, as pirates, in the musical comedy
The Girl from Up There, which opened at the Herald Square Theatre
on January 7, 1901, for 96 performances. The former "Eccentric
Blackface Comedians" gained stardom on Broadway at the Majestic
Theatre on January 21, 1903, in a musical version of The Wizard of
Oz in which, for 293 performances, Stone was acclaimed as "The
Scarecrow" and Montgomery as "Nick Chopper, the Tin Woodman."
Their success continued in Victor Herbert's musical comedy The Red
Mill, which opened on September 24, 1906, at Broadway's Knicker-
bocker Theatre for 274 performances. The team's fame was extended
in the musicals The Old Town (Globe Theatre, October 28, 1912, for
232 performances) and in their last co-starring musical comedy, Chin
Chin, which opened on October 20, 1914, at the Globe Theatre for
295 performances.

It was during the national tour of Chin Chin that David Montgomery became ill in Kansas City. Montgomery gave his last complete performance in Chin Chin in his home town of St. Joseph,
Missouri. On March 12, 1917, Montgomery collapsed during the
Chicago engagement of the show. David C. Montgomery died at the
age of forty-seven at Chicago's Presbyterian Hospital (Friday, April
20, 1917).

Fred Stone, in his autobiography Rolling Stones (Whittlesley
House, 1945) wrote,

> I don't seem to associate Dave Montgomery with anything
> but laughter.... For twenty-two years we had been to-
> gether. We had built our careers together, so closely that
> they seemed like one career. We had in common a whole
> lifetime of shared experiences, and deep-rooted friendship
> and trust. We supplemented each other, as in the case with
> all enduring partnerships. He had a gayety and sparkle
> and love of life that aroused a response in his audience
> and friends....

Fred Stone, who married his leading lady, Allene Crater, and sired three talented daughters--Dorothy, Paula and Carol--died at the age of eighty-five on Friday, March 6, 1959, in Hollywood, California.

MORAN AND MACK

The New York Times (October 1926) editorialized, "Of all the comedians who extract laughs from the public without the aid of slapstick, hokum or 'props,' Moran and Mack are probably best known to New Yorkers." The two comedians, known as "The Two Black Crows," also became known throughout the country and were favorite entertainers in England, where they played fourteen consecutive weeks in London. Moran and Mack were hailed as "the top blackface act of their era."

George Searcy (Moran), born in Elwood, Kansas, in 1881, started his career playing Sambo in a touring company of Uncle Tom's Cabin and later entered vaudeville. Charles E. Sellers (Mack), born on Tuesday, November 22, 1887, in White Cloud, Kansas, was encouraged by Alexander Pantages to try vaudeville in California with his blackface routines. While playing at San Francisco's Market Street Theatre, Mack survived the great earthquake of April 18, 1906, and later joined Hi Henry's Minstrels in Chicago. After appearing in burlesque and teaming with Bert Swor in a vaudeville blackface act, he was then cast in the musical revue Maid in America, which opened at Broadway's Winter Garden Theatre on February 18, 1915. Mack, as Henry, teamed with John Swor, as Alexander--characters made famous by McIntyre and Heath--in blackface routines (Winter Garden Theatre, June 22, 1916) in The Passing Show of 1916.

Moran and Mack first met in Astoria, Oregon where Moran and his partner Garvin were appearing on the same vaudeville bill. After appearing individually in the musical comedy Over the Top (originally called Oh, Justine!) at the Forty-fourth Street Roof Theatre on November 28, 1917, the blackface team of Moran and Mack was formed. "The Two Black Crows" (Moran as Willie Crow and Mack as Amos Crow) became successful in vaudeville, and their acclaim continued in Ziegfeld Follies of 1920. They "stopped the show" in The Greenwich Village Follies of 1924 and 1926 and were applauded for their second-act routine in Ziegfeld's musical No Foolin' at the Globe Theatre on June 24, 1926.

Moran and Mack's Broadway success became national when Columbia Records released their tremendously successful "Two Black Crows" 1927 recording of "The Early Bird Catches the Worm." Columbia Records followed the best-selling record with the team's "All About Lions"; "Curiosities--On the Farm" and "No Matter How Hungry a Horse Is--He Cannot Eat a Bit" in 1927. "Two Black

Crows in Jail" and "Two Black Crows in Hades" followed in 1928, and "Foolishments" and "Esau Buck and the Buck Saw" came afterward in 1929.

Their last appearance on the Broadway stage was in Earl Carroll's Vanities of 1926, in which they performed their hilarious sketches Rock Pile and On the Locomotive. Moran, logically disturbed that Mack would not agree to a fifty-fifty split of their earnings, left the Vanities and was replaced first by Mack's old partner Bert Swor and, later, on the road, by James Barton. Charles Mack was the business manager, writer, and owner of the team, having copyrighted the material and legally registered the name as a trademark. Despite the team's high weekly earnings, Mack paid Moran a meagre salary of some $200 per week and a flat donation of $150 for each phonograph record.

"The Two Black Crows" reunited in 1927, returning to Broadway in vaudeville at the Palace (where they had first appeared in 1918) and making their motion-picture debut as one of several comedy teams in Paramount Pictures' 1927 feature comedy, Two Flaming Youths, starring W. C. Fields and Chester Conklin. Moran and Mack were heard for twenty weeks in 1928 on radio's The Majestic Hour (they had been heard over the airwaves on radio's first variety show The Eveready Hour). The following year the team made their talking-picture debut.

Why Bring That Up? (the title derived from one of their classic lines) was released on October 4, 1929. The film was directed by George Abbott and written by the Jewish writer of blackface comedy, Octavus Roy Cohen. Paramount Pictures advertised the feature comedy as "You've heard them on the radio. You've laughed your head off at their phonograph records. Now hear them real as life in one of the funniest, most thrilling, ALL-TALKING entertainments ever screened." Noting that Moran and Mack "are black only part of the time," Photoplay magazine judged that "The two idols of the phonograph records are at their best in burnt cork. Without the shellac it is evident that they aren't much on heavy emoting. When they get going about the early bird and the worm and other comedy skits they are superb."

Their successful venture with Why Bring That Up? did not deter Moran from suing Mack in 1929 to restrain Mack from using his name. But Mack's legal hold both over their material and over the team's name was upheld in court. Moran left the team once again and was replaced by Mack's old vaudeville partner, Bert Swor, who had been in the cast of Why Bring That Up? Swor became "Moran" in Paramount Pictures' 1930 second-rate feature Anybody's War, which was based on Mack's 1928 story, Two Black Crows in the A.E.F.

The original George Moran returned late in 1930 for an extensive

vaudeville tour, and, in 1932, Moran and Mack were back on Broadway headlining the Palace. They starred in their last motion picture that year, an unheralded and unpopular comedy called Hypno-
tized, which was produced by Mack Sennett.

Mack left California, driving with his wife (former dancer
Marion Robinson), their daughter Mary Jane, partner George Moran,
and comedy-master Mack Sennett, to film a series of "Two Black
Crows" comedy shorts for Sennett in New York. The car overturned,
causing only minor injuries to Mack's passengers but crushing Mack
beneath it. Charles Mack died in the Mesa, Arizona Hospital at the
age of forty-six, on Thursday, January 11, 1934.

George Moran continued in show business with various partners and last performed during World War II on an USO tour.
Moran died at the age of sixty-seven on Monday, August 1, 1949,
at Oakland, California.

BERT SWOR

"A very funny man was Bert Swor," wrote Joe Laurie, Jr.,
and Swor, indeed, was one of the most original blackface mono-
logists in show business.

Born in Paris, Tennessee in 1878, Bert Swor started his long
career with Dr. Joseph Bramlee's Medicine Show. He taught his
brothers--John, James, and Albert--the art of minstrelsy. Brother
Will Swor became a comic tramp in vaudeville. Bert was seen in
the part of the Scarecrow (made famous by Fred Stone on Broadway) in the road company of The Wizard of Oz. He appeared with
his younger brothers John and James, who later gained prominence
as minstrels and as vaudeville's blackface team The Swor Brothers.
For twenty years Bert was featured in Al G. Field's Minstrels. He
was the original partner of Charles Mack, who gained fame with
George Moran as "The Two Black Crows."

Bert's hilarious blackface monologues brightened vaudeville
stages for many years. During the 1925-1926 season he replaced
Frank Tinney in the fourth edition of Earl Carroll's Vanities and in
the fifth edition of the Vanities he replaced George Moran to become
(temporarily) Moran of Moran and Mack. Bert was in the cast of
Moran and Mack's 1929 motion picture Why Bring That Up?, and,
when Moran again defected in 1930, Bert once more became Moran
in Paramount Pictures' Anybody's War.

Swor's amusing vaudeville monologues--"A Colorful Sermon"
and "Ducks and Deducts"--were filmed in 1930 as Warner Bros.
Vitaphone shorts. Edgar Smith's 1928 musical Headin' South (starring McIntyre and Heath, with music by Jean Schwartz, lyrics by

Al Bryan, dances staged by LeRoy Prinz) never reached the Mason-Dixon line and folded on the road. Bert Swor played the part of Bruce Skinner and dueted a song "Shining Shoes" with Rudolph Williams; he was an end man with the starring team in the minstrel show finale of act 1.

Without wearing burnt cork, Bert returned to Broadway's Masque Theatre on April 23, 1931, in the part of Pink Jones in Du Bose Heyward's drama of miscegenation, Brass Ankle, which starred Alice Brady. He retired in 1933 to his home of thirty years in Dallas, Texas, where in 1941 he played a Negro butler in the Dallas Little Theatre production of Where the Dear Antelope Roam. Swor's last stage appearance was in a benefit minstrel show for servicemen in Tulsa, Oklahoma, which had been sponsored by the show business organization Hey Rube, Inc. On Tuesday, November 30, 1943, Bert Swor was found dead of a heart attack in his room at Tulsa's Bliss Hotel. Glenn Condon, president of Hey Rube, Inc., told the press, "Bert Swor died with only a few dollars but a thousand friends."

FRANK TINNEY

Frank Tinney probably had no peer among the innumerable blackface comedians. He was accurately described as "one of the funniest men in the annals of the stage." Joe Laurie, Jr. recalled, "Frank Tinney was the most natural comedian I ever saw ... one of our greatest blackface comics...." Contemporary comedian Joe Cook called Tinney "the greatest natural comic ever developed in America." Press agent Joe Flynn added another concept of Tinney as "Peck's Bad Boy of the Prohibition Twenties." Paul Sann, in his book The Lawless Decade, classified Tinney as "the great blackface comedian of the postwar years" and described Tinney's offstage life as "The Blackface Blues."

Born on Friday, March 29, 1878, in Philadelphia, Frank Aloysius Robert Tinney made his stage debut in blackface at the age of four at Philadelphia's Bijou Theatre. After appearing with Barlow and Dumont's Minstrels, Tinney became a vaudeville headliner. His blackface comedy routines were performed without the usual Negro dialect, and he was the first comedian to use orchestra leaders as straight men. Tinney extended his vaudeville success to the Broadway musical stage. Variety reported that his blackface specialty was "the one bit hit" in The Revue of Revues at the Winter Garden Theatre on September 27, 1911. Ziegfeld's A Winsome Widow opened at Broadway's Moulin Rouge on April 11, 1912, with the Dolly Sisters--Leon Errol, Mae West, and Frank Tinney--in blackface as "Noah, a waiter."

Variety's Sime Silverman lauded Tinney's return to vaudeville on January 6, 1913, at Hammerstein's Victoria Theatre with "If there

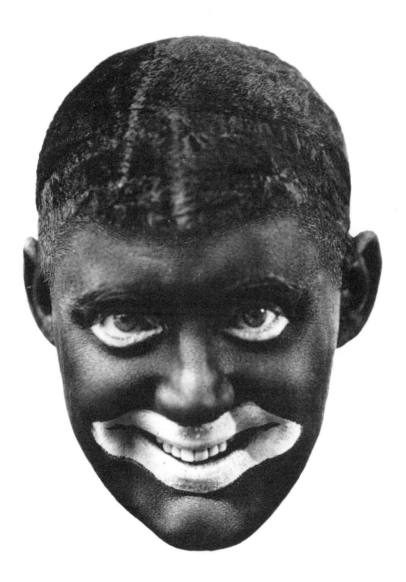

Frank Tinney (courtesy of The Free Library of Philadelphia Theatre
Collection and the Billy Rose Theatre Collection, The New York
Public Library at Lincoln Center, Astor, Lenox and Tilden Founda-
tions)

are natural comedians on earth Tinney is one of them." A British
critic hailed Tinney's London debut at the Palace Theatre on February 10, 1913 as "the most irresistible entertainer that America has
sent us." He was a hit on June 16, 1913 at the New Amsterdam
Theatre in Ziegfeld's Follies of 1913. On May 11, 1914, London
again enthusiastically welcomed Tinney at the Hippodrome Theatre
in the second edition of Max Pemberton and A. P. De Courville's
revue Hullo Tango. Acclaim continued for his blackface performing
as a Pullman Porter, a Carriage-Caller, and a Coat-Room Boy, on
December 8, 1914, in Irving Berlin's musical comedy Watch Your
Step, which headlined Vernon and Irene Castle at the New Amsterdam Theatre for 175 performances.

Tinney's comedy routines highlighted the Broadway musicals
The Century Girl (Century Theatre, November 6, 1916) and Doing
Our Bit (Winter Garden Theatre, October 18, 1917). Army Quarter-
master Captain Frank Tinney was featured with soldiers from the
Aberdeen Proving Ground in Atta Boy for twenty-four performances
at the Lexington Theatre on December 23, 1918. In the spring of
1919, civilian Tinney recaptured his past British success for sixteen
weeks at London's Stoll's Alhambra Theatre.

Despite Tinney's progressively heavy drinking, he starred in
Arthur Hammerstein's musical comedy Tickle Me at the Selwyn Theatre on August 17, 1920, opening the show in blackface but, for the
first time, completing his performance without burnt cork. Tinney
explained his emergence from black to white as follows:

> Naturally, when I went into vaudeville I did a blackface act,
> and the longer I did it the longer I had to do it. Vaude-
> ville audiences, in the first place, get used to having their
> favorites do familiar acts in a familiar way. So if I had
> changed my number from black to white face during my
> variety engagements I would have lost my following. All
> this time, however, I had been longing for a sustained
> comedy part and the chance to throw off my dusky face
> covering. Yet, though I did gain the comedy roles, it was
> not until Tickle Me that I really had the opportunity in New
> York to expose my real skin to the footlights.

Tinney continued his metamorphosis as the star of Arthur
Hammerstein's Daffy Dill (the original title, Tit for Tat, was--even
for the Roaring Twenties--considered too risqué) which opened at
the Apollo Theatre on August 22, 1922. Tinney told the press, "I
guess I am the only comedian who hasn't been longing to do Hamlet,
Beau Brummel or Dr. Jekyll and Mr. Hyde. My one ambition to is
be myself. I want to be Frank Tinney himself and not his blacked-
up shadow." In the chorus of Daffy Dill was a beautiful young
girl named Imogene Wilson whose headlined love affair with Tinney
would soon become a national scandal.

Returning to vaudeville, Tinney appeared at Broadway's
Palace on March 12, 1923, with his wife, Edna Davenport, dueting
a song "Driving Down the Avenue." Irving Berlin's Music Box
Revue opened on September 22, 1923. It featured Grace Moore,
John Steel, Florence Moore, Phil Baker, and Frank Tinney (who
received dismal reviews). Tinney made his motion-picture debut
with several other Broadway stars in a cameo role in a Warner Bros.
production Broadway After Dark. On August 25, 1924, he garnered
praise at London's Empire Theatre for his vaudeville routines. During a performance before King George V and Queen Mary, Tinney
complained to His Majesty. He said that for six weeks he had been
unable to take a bath because everytime he started to sit down in
the tub someone played "God Save the King." To quell a British
tax-collectors justifiable query about his excessive deduction for
makeup and burnt cork Tinney replied, "But I use champagne
corks!"

Imogene "Bubbles" Wilson, born in Louisville, Kentucky December 18, 1902, was called "the most beautiful blonde on Broadway,"
but her highly publicized love affair with Frank Tinney ended her
Broadway career, and Tinney's marriage and brilliant career were
soon destroyed. Imogene propelled their affair into scandalous national headlines when she had Tinney arrested for felonious assault
on May 27, 1924. A Grand Jury refused to indict Tinney, and
"Bubbles'" damage suit for $100,000 never reached court. Due to
the lurid newspaper coverage Florenz Ziegfeld, who had once described Imogene as "the most beautiful girl I ever glorified," dismissed her from his Follies. The once battered and bruised "Bubbles" left for London to join Tinney who was enjoying great success
on the vaudeville stage. Tinney's London accolades continued when
he opened on February 5, 1925, at London's Vaudeville Theatre in
the musical comedy Sometime.

Edna Davenport Tinney filed for divorce and custody of Frank
Tinney, Jr., naming Imogene as corespondent. The sadomasochistic
love affair between the blackface comedian and former Follies beauty
continued until Imogene signed a contract with U.F.A. and defected
to Germany to find fleeting fame on the screen as Imogene Robertson. In the late twenties, "Bubbles" went to Hollywood where she
made several films under the name of Mary Nolan.

Tinney's last appearance on Broadway was on December 28,
1925, when he opened in Earl Carroll's Vanities. The enthusiastic
audiences of the past were gone. His on-stage chatter about his
personal life, booze, and blondes was critically assaulted and cold-
ly received by the audience. Tinney collapsed in Detroit during
the road tour of Vanities and was replaced first by Frankie Heath
and later by Bert Swor. On May 16, 1927, he attempted a come-
back at Chicago's Club Bagdad but collapsed on the cabaret floor
after his fourth show. Tinney's physical decline was attributed to
paresis.

    Following long periods in and out of Veterans Hospitals, Frank
Tinney died at the age of sixty-two (Thursday, November 28, 1940)
at the U.S. Veterans Hospital in Northport, Long Island, New York.

Actors originally played female roles in Shakespeare's plays and female impersonators had been seen in the theatre for centuries before the advent of minstrelsy's creation of the blackface "wench" or "prima donna" role. Dan Gardner is presumed to have been, in 1855, the first minstrel "wench." Irish comedian Barney Williams (Bernard Flaherty), Sam S. Sanford, and George Christy created coquettish dusky damsels with the song "Lucy Long" and by doing outrageous sketches. Lew Dockstader was a memorable Camille, and Nelse Seymour and others were darkened Desdemonas. Charles Heywood, Charlie Backus, minstrel impressario Henry Wood, composer M. S. Pike, and many others donned drag in blackface for laughs.

Farceur George Holland was an uninhibited wench whose funeral became more famous than his career. The not-so-very-Reverend Lorenzo Sabine refused services for "actors" dead or alive but did recommend "a little church around the corner" to Holland's friend Joseph Jefferson where religion was less segregated and restrictive. Consequently, New York's Protestant-Episcopal Church of the Transfiguration at 1 East Twenty-ninth Street became famous as "The Little Church Around the Corner." It was there that the Reverend Dr. George H. Houghton conducted the funeral service for George Holland. Edwin Booth's massive funeral was held there in 1893, and, through the years, the church has gained prominence and popularity by holding weddings and funerals for people in the theatrical profession.

Tony Hart perfectly portrayed the opposite sex in Edward Harrigan's plays and sketches. Hart's flippant black cook, Mrs. Welcome (Rebecca) Allup, in The Mulligan Guard series, was hilariously accurate, and he was totally convincing in whiteface--both as the Widow Nolan in Squatter Sovereignty and as Norah Donovan in The Donovans. Hart was not the only wench in Harrigan's comedies. James Tierney was Caroline Melrose, and John Queen played Mrs. Honora Dublin in the Mulligan plays. After Hart's defection from Harrigan, Dan Collyer was assigned Hart's former drag roles in Harrigan's company. Collyer played Catherine O'Hollerhan in The Grip; Airy McCafferty in The Leather Patch; and Vi'let in Pete, with Richard Quilter as Ruth Callowfoot, Dan Burke as Auntie Charlotte, and John Decker as Susie Rivers. Pacing Collyer in the

Harrigan comedies were Joseph Sparks as Mary McQuirk and John
Decker as Clara Grizzle in 4-11-44. Sparks was Lizzie Calhoun in
Reilly and the Four Hundred, with Charles White as Mrs. Jackson
and John Decker as Bessie Bowlow.

James McIntyre, of the blackface team of McIntyre and Heath,
appeared in drag in their sketches "Waiting at the Church" and
"Chickens." Other blackface performers alternated in wench parts
or played Topsy in Uncle Tom's Cabin. Originally played for broad
burlesque, the "wench-prima donna" role was later refined to elegant characterization after blackface faded. William Henry Rice's
chic costumes created current fashion trends predating the later
haute couture of Francis Renault (Anthony Oriema) and the most
famous female impersonator of all, Julian Eltinge, who had pranced
in blackface with Cohan and Harris Minstrels (as had female impersonator Bothwell Browne). In contrast with the elegance of Eltinge
and Renault, was Karyl Norman (George Raduzzi), known as "The
Creole Fashion Plate." Bert Savoy created an overdressed, bitchy
trollop, and the Russell Brothers made a career portraying Irish
biddies and servant girls.

Julian Eltinge was born William Julian Dalton at Newtonville,
Massachusetts on Sunday, May 14, 1882. He had his biggest success on Broadway in Charles Klein and Jerome Kern's musical
comedy, Cousin Lucy; Eltinge played the dual role of Gerald Jackson and his "Cousin Lucy" in the production, which opened on August 29, 1915, at the George M. Cohan Theatre. The New York
Sun announced, "The annual visit of Julian Eltinge to Broadway is
almost on par with a society event in which the latest gowns are
assured of proper attention," and critics proclaimed "the handsomest woman on the stage today is a Man!--Julian Eltinge!"

England has enjoyed and supported female impersonators far
more than America has. W. S. Penley was Brandon Thomas's original Charley's Aunt, which opened at London's Royalty Theatre
on December 21, 1892, to become known as one of the longest-
running and most hilarious comedies ever written. Etienne Girardot
was America's cigar-smoking "Aunt from Brazil where the nuts come
from" when the play opened on October 2, 1893, at New York's
Standard Theatre.

Prior to the emergence of the vogue of whiteface female impersonation, minstrelsy had its own wench stars. So perfect was
the impersonation of minstrelsy's Eugene (Eugene d'Anseli) that
audiences at home and abroad were convinced he really was a woman. But none was more accomplished or talented in singing, dancing, or acting gracefully feminine than Leon, called by the New
York Clipper in 1870, "The best female actor known to the stage.
He does it with such dignity, modesty and refinement that it is truly
art."

Patrick Francis Leon Glassey was born in New York City on
Thursday, November 21, 1844. He studied ballet with Madame Gil-
etti, voice with Senor Errani, and made his stage debut at the age
of fourteen in 1858 at Wood's Marble Hall of Minstrelsy with Christy
and Wood's Minstrels. Leon formed his own troupe in 1864 with
Dublin-born (1835) Edwin Kelly, a widower with two daughters who
had trained as a surgeon at London's St. George's Hospital. After
migrating to America, Kelly became a blackface comedian, balladist,
and minstrel interlocutor with Ordway's AEolians (Boston, August
30, 1858).

Kelly and Leon converted Hope Chapel at 720 Broadway into
a first-floor saloon and a second-floor auditorium for their newly
formed minstrel company, which opened on October 1, 1866. Kelly
and Leon Minstrels successfully burlesqued Italian actress Adelaide
Ristori's recent Broadway triumph in Medea as My-Deah Restore Her
featuring "the wonderful Leon" with George Christy, Frank Moran,
Johnny Allen, and Edwin Kelly. An operatic burlesque of the opera
Lucrezia Borgia was performed on January 7, 1867, by "The Great
Leon" whose soprano voice reached a high "D." The 233rd performance of the landmark musical The Black Crook, which had opened
at Niblo's Garden on September 12, 1866, to pursue an incredible
history of 475 performances, coincided with the 115th performance
of Kelly's and Leon's Great Black Crook Burlesque advertised "With
The Only Leon, the greatest Prima Donna of the age, burlesque
actress, and danseuse, in his celebrated vocal waltzes, encored
nightly by the most fashionable audiences." Their second season
opened July 29, 1867, and a travesty on Verdi's opera Kill Trovatore was performed on August 26. Gounod's Faust was burlesqued
on November 4th as Le Petit Faust, with Kelly as Mephisto and Leon
as Marguerite. But the phenomenal success of Kelly and Leon soon
erupted in a major scandal.

Several minstrel managers were envious of Kelly and Leon's
quick success, and Samuel Sharpley (born Samuel Sharpe in Philadelphia on Monday, June 13, 1831) was particularly bitter at the
defection of three members of his Sharpley's Minstrels. End man
Ad Ryman and clog dancers (William Henry) Delehanty and (Thomas
Michael) Hengler had signed for a year with Kelly and Leon (opening July 29, 1867). Delehanty and Hengler had agreed to alternate
between the two troupes, but they elected to remain with Kelly and
Leon.

Kelly and Leon attended a matinee of Sharpley's Minstrels at
the Fifth Avenue Opera House on Wednesday, December 11, 1867.
After the performance, Sam Sharpley started a brawl with Edwin
Kelly on Twenty-fourth Street. Sharpley's brother Thomas Sharpe
fought Kelly while Sam chased the quickly disappearing Leon. Kelly
drew a revolver and fatally shot Thomas Sharpe in the head. Sam
Sharpley drew a revolver and wounded Kelly. Sharpley was taken
into custody, and Kelly was arrested and jailed.

Kelly and Leon's Minstrels reopened on December 17 without
Kelly and Leon. Rollin Howard, another popular female impersonator, replaced Leon. Nelse Seymour, Dave Reed, G. W. H. Griffin,
Sam Price, and others kept the company performing. On January
6, 1868, George Christy, once minstrels' brightest but fading star,
joined the troupe.

After the murder of thirty-one-year-old Thomas Sharpe, Leon
reluctantly shed his opposition to returning to the stage on February 3, 1868. "The Only Leon" returned in "one of the greatest of
all minstrel burlesques" (The Grande Dutch S.), which recorded the
longest consecutive run in the history of minstrelsy. Kelly and
Leon's Minstrels were lavishly produced, musically brilliant, and
one of Broadway's most popular entertainments.

Jacques Offenbach's La Grande Duchesse de Gérolstein, starring Lucille Tostee, originally opened at the Théâtre des Variétés
in Paris on April 12, 1867, and was first seen in New York on
September 24, 1867. Kelly and Leon's burlesque The Grande Dutch
S. was, according to Odell, "mounted and costumed with a lavish-
ness hitherto unknown in such things; much of Offenbach's melodious music was retained; and--to do him justice--Leon was remarkably
good as a female impersonator."

Kelly and Leon's long-running travesty The Grande Dutch S.
closed on June 6, 1868, and, on June 8, a burlesque of Offenbach's
La Belle Hélène (which had closed May 2) was produced. Called
La Bell L.N. with "costumes imported from Paris," Leon was Helen
and Edwin Kelly, released from prison and freed on a self-defense
murder charge, returned to the stage to play the part of Paris.

Offenbach's Barbe Bleue opened at Niblo's on July 13, 1868,
and Kelly and Leon's Minstrels, starring "The Only Leon, Founder
of a New School of Minstrelsy," opened their third season on August
31, 1868, with another Offenbach burlesque, Barber Blu. The New
York Herald called Leon's playing of Boulotte "his greatest hit,"
and the New York Tribune found the "astonishing burlesque a triumph." Leon's Eruydice in Orphée Aux Enfers followed on November
9 and Gin-nevieve De Graw closed the hall on January 15, 1869.
At that time, Kelly and Leon had given 625 performances at their
theatre.

Kelly and Leon opened in London on May 17, 1869, at St.
George's Hall with Montague Christy Minstrels and appeared in Saucy
Sal, Twice Married, and Barber Blu. Their success continued for
over one hundred performances and was "said to be the greatest
success ever achieved in London in minstrelsy." The London Times
reported,

> Among the most novel apparitions of the day may be men-
> tioned a singular artiste who has lately joined the Royal and

Original Christy Minstrels at George's Hall and who is styled
in the programme "The Only Leon." Leon takes you by a
start. The artlessness of the by-play is marvelous. We do
not venture on praise when everything is done so exceptional!

The London Telegraph enthused,

Mr. Edwin Kelly is a really accomplished vocalist, dancer,
comic actor and "mime."... Leon is still a more extraordinary
performer, whose peculiar and remarkable male soprano in-
duces him to assume the "crinoline" in which his apt impersonations are only rescued, by the assumption of burlesque,
from being too natural and lifelike ... these really clever
actors make one regret that any disguise, however popular,
should hinder them from taking rank on any stage where
genuine humor and comic talent of the highest order might
find a place.... Mr. Kelly and his remarkable associate
"The Leon"--"The Only Leon" as the announcements state--
and, certainly, a "Leon" who on any modern stage has, as
yet, never known a rival or counterpart--weave up an
amount of fun, frolic, droll acting and capital staging...."

Returning from England in August, Kelly and Leon toured the
States and reopened their Broadway hall on February 7, 1870, with
Le Petit Faust. On April 18, they romped through a travesty of
Augustin Daly's adaptation of Meilhac and Helévy's play Frou Frou
(called Frow Frow). Featuring Babes in the Woods, Kelly and Leon
opened at Haverley's Theatre in Brooklyn for four months beginning
January 1, 1871. On April 1, 1871, they announced that their minstrel careers were over and that henceforth they would appear only
in whiteface. The announcement was premature; their popularity
continued in Chicago and in Australia where they opened their own
Opera House.

Leon, without Kelly, joined Haverly's Minstrels in October
1881 at $300 per week. His wardrobe of some three hundred dresses
and haute couture designed gowns, pink-padded petticoats trimmed
with lace or elaborately embroidered sparkling white flounces with
an assortment of expensive silk stockings and size two slippers,
were offset by diamond earrings valued at $4,000. In 1881, The
Cleveland Press described Leon's stage appearance:

As to Leon's make-up as a representative of the softer sex,
it is in itself a work of art, for there is not, from the time
of his entrance until he quits the stage, the slightest sug-
gestiveness of a disguised member of the sterner sex. From
the tiny shoe, above which only a small instep is occasionally
allowed to peep forth; the modishly-cut skirt, the lines and
contour of the face and neck, slope of the shoulders, the
feminine expression of the face, the small ears, and finally

the hair bound tightly around the well-shaped head in a
modest Grecian knot--all combine to form one of the most
perfect illusions possible. Leon's performances can, without any reservation or qualifications, be placed under the
category of "truly wonderful."

Ten years later Leon joined the cast of A High Roller at
Doris's Eighth Avenue Museum. Leon personified the elegant, definitive female impersonator with incredible grace and singing abil-
ity. The era also produced the inestimably talented Tony Hart of
Harrigan and Hart, famous for his Irish biddies and, especially, for
his blackface character, Mrs. Welcome (Rebecca) Allup. Gerald
Bordman (The Oxford Companion to American Theatre) wrote,
"Probably the two most famous impersonators of the nineteenth century were Francis Leon who worked largely in the minstrel tradition
and who spoofed famous figures as well as characters from contemporary plays, and Neil Burgess who specialized in dear old spinsters
or widow ladies."

Neil Burgess, born in Boston on Monday, June 29, 1846, made
his New York debut in 1872 at Tony Pastor's Theatre where he was
billed as an "Ethiopian Comedian." He did one of his first female
impersonations at Harrigan and Hart's Theatre Comique in 1877, in
The Coming Woman. On March 15, 1880, at New York's Haverly's
Lyceum Theatre, Burgess appeared in the title role of David Ross
Locke's comedy The Widow Bedott. Burgess' characterizations were
called "wholesome and jolly," and, in 1882, he created Tryphena
"Betsy" Puffy in Vim; or A Visit to Puffy Farm. Charles Bernard's
play The County Fair (Proctor's Twenty-third Street Theatre,
March 5, 1889) provided Burgess with his best role, Aunt Abigail
"Abby" Prue. Burgess played Widow Bedott and Abby Prue through-
out his career. He died at the age of sixty-three on Saturday,
February 19, 1910.

The leitmotif of miscegenation became a popular theme in the theatre. The theme was expanded to include not only white and black mixed-blood dramas but dramas about Indians, Chinese, and other races considered to be non-white. (Also, whites were fascinated masquerading as blacks and dusky-hued natives.) Variations on the theme occurred in many plays, but among the best of the genre was Edwin Milton Royle's 1905 hit drama The Squaw Man, which related Jim Carston's (William Faversham) marriage to dusky Indian Nat-u-Ritch (Mabel Morrison), who commits suicide hoping to give her husband and son a better life. Richard Walton Tully's 1912 drama The Bird of Paradise had Laurette Taylor (as South Seas-hued Luana) leaping into a volcano to appease her pagan god and save her American husband (Lewis Stone). Interracial conflict threatened the love of Chinese Ming Toy (Fay Bainter) for a young American (Forrest Winant) and fascinated Broadway for 680 performances in Samuel Shipman and John B. Hymer's 1918 play, East Is West.

Tragedy in the Orient was represented in John Luther Long's 1897 Century magazine story "Madame Butterfly," adapted for the stage by David Belasco and John Luther Long, and produced and directed by Belasco at the Herald Square Theatre on March 5, 1900, for three weeks. Blanche Bates starred as Cho-Cho-San, with Frank Worthing as U.S. Navy Lt. B. F. Pinkerton. Giuseppe Giacosa and Luigi Illica supplied the libretto based on the American play for Giacomo Puccini's opera Madama Butterfly, which unsuccessfully premiered at Milan's La Scala Opera House on February 17, 1904. The first New York production of the opera at the Garden Theatre on November 12, 1906, featured Florence Easton. The Metropolitan Opera's acclaimed first performance of Madama Butterfly on February 11, 1907 (with Geraldine Farrar as Cho-Cho-San and Enrico Caruso as Pinkerton) assured Butterfly of continued fame.

The most successful of the color-conflict plays was Leon Gordon's "Vivid Play of the Primitive" (White Cargo), which was based on Ida Vera Simonton's novel Hell's Playground and produced by Earl Carroll at the Greenwich Village Theatre on November 5, 1923; later it was transferred to Broadway at Daly's Sixty-third Street Theatre. The play, directed by the author, completed 702 performances with Annette Margules (succeeded by Betty Pierce) as the dusky half-caste

Tondeleyo. Richard Stevenson (succeeded by Harris Gilmore) played her white lover, Langford. Playwright Gordon directed the even more successful London White Cargo, which was produced by Ida Molesworth and Templer-Powell at London's Playhouse Theatre on May 15, 1924. It featured Mary Clare as the tropic sexpot and Brian Aherne as her victim. London supported White Cargo for 821 performances. The play has been revived for so many years that "Me, Tondeleyo" has become as much of a silly cliche as "Me, Tarzan-- You, Jane" or "Twenty-three, Skidoo."

Gordon's potboiler told of Fred Ashley (reduced to "dry rot" by quinine and whiskey) being sent home to England from a West African Coast rubber plantation and replaced by young, enthusiastic, and adventurous Allen Langford. Aware that the requirements of the four-year assignment could reduce men to Ashley's state, Langford scoffs at cynical, old-timer Witzel's prediction that he too will eventually succumb to the emotional, mental, and moral damp rot of the place (the old-timer has cited the disreputable and once famous surgeon camp doctor as an example). Witsel's theory that "color's only a point of geography and morals a matter of longitude" is discredited by Lanford, who is revolted by Witzel's suggestion that he, too, will soon become like the rest of them, unshaven, unclean and in pursuit of "Mammy-palaver"--an affair with a willing black native. Handsome Langford eventually meets the beautiful, notorious half-caste Tondeleyo who succeeds in seducing him. Fighting to retain his respectability, Langford marries sexually promiscuous Tondeleyo. In another year, he has been reduced to the state of Fred Ashley and is sent home--another shipment to England of "white cargo." Langford's friends force Tondeleyo to drink a poisoned potion she had prepared for Langford.

White Cargo was filmed in England as a silent picture in 1929 by Neo-Art Productions. It was based on Leon Gordon's screenplay and featured Gypsy Rhouma as Tondeleyo and Maurice Evans as Langford. Metro-Goldwyn-Mayer's screen version of White Cargo (directed by Richard Thorpe from Leon Gordon's screenplay) starred, of all people, Hedy Lamarr as the very dusky, sexy "Me, Tondeleyo," with Richard Carlson as white Langford.

Edward Sheldon's miscegenation motif--deplored in The Nigger --raised its ugly head in Eugene O'Neill's controversial play All God's Chillun Got Wings. The play had been published by George Jean Nathan in the February 1924 issue of the American Mercury. Prior to the opening of the play a hue and cry was raised when it became known that white actress Mary Blair would kiss the hand of black Paul Robeson, who played her husband in the play. There were predictions of riots. Agonized cries from leading moralistic orators received strong support from inflammatory newspaper coverage (led mainly by William Randolph Hearst's American and the crusading Brooklyn Eagle).

Eugene O'Neill's perceptive declaration that "These prejudices will exist until we understand the Oneness of Mankind. Life is hard and bitter enough without, in addition, burdening ourselves with prejudice" was ignored. O'Neill's published statement that "Prejudice born of an entire ignorance of the subject is the last word in injustice and absurdity--of the sensation-mongers and notoriety hounds" had no effect.

There were threats of deadly reprisals from the Ku Klux Klan. The fray was quickly joined by opportunistic politicians, notably Mayor Hylan and District Attorney Jacob H. Benton of New York City. Manhattan's license commissioner served an injunction prohibiting the appearance of child actors in the opening scene of the play. James Light, director of the drama, appeared before the opening-night audience to announce that the first scene, in which O'Neill clarified children's unawareness of the color-line, could not be played. Light then read the expository scene and the play continued.

Augustus Thomas had written a magnolia-scented play called Alabama, which was produced on April 1, 1891, at New York's Madison Square Theatre. In the play, Reub Fax played a burnt-cork character, Decatur. The Brooklyn Eagle interviewed Thomas about the casting of O'Neill's play. Thomas rose to the occasion and apotheosized, "In the first place, I should never have written such a play, and in the second place, I should have been willing to do what is usually done in such cases, to permit a white man to play the part of the negro. The present arrangement, I think, has a tendency to break down social barriers which are better left untouched."

Despite all the puerile hue and cry, All God's Chillun Got Wings (produced by Kenneth Macgowan) opened at the Provincetown Playhouse on May 15, 1924, to play forty-three times without incident, and it reopened at the Greenwich Village Theatre on October 10 for a respectable run. But Chillun became a great disappointment to the rabble-rousers when it was almost unanimously reviewed as a dull play. "All God's Chillun Got Wings," wrote Heywood Broun (New York World),

> is a very tiresome play--Paul Robeson is a far finer actor than any white member of the cast. Before the play ends she (the wife) is stark raving mad. So instead of the problem of white and black, we have the problem of sane and insane--In the uneven career of Eugene O'Neill I think All God's Chillun will rank as one of the down strokes.

Percy Hammond (Herald-Tribune) found the play "mildly dull and audacious--A vehement exposition of a marriage between a stupid Negro and a stupid white woman. If it is possible for you to get an emotion out of that situation, here is your opportunity." Alexander

Woollcott (the New York Times) wrote, "Those who attended its first
performance in hope of seeing a few ructions, or possibly even a
bloody riot to put in their diaries, were doomed to disappointment
--those who attended in the hope of seeing a great play or even a
good one were also disappointed." But Robert Gilbert Welsh (Tele-
gram-Evening Mail) predicted the play "is likely to take a permanent
place in the American Theatre."

O'Neill's drama reduced Ella Downey (Mary Blair) to insanity
as she struggles with her inculcated racial prejudice and love for
her black husband Jim (Paul Robeson); Jim strives, and fails, to
become a lawyer but remains faithful and devoted to his demented
white wife, watching as her mind slowly reverts to the mental state
of a child. It was probably not so strange that O'Neill gave the
first names of his own parents, Ella and Jim, to his protagonists.

The New York World questioned the legality and permissive-
ness of the theatre in allowing a play to be produced that was
clearly "illegal and punishable as a crime in all Southern and border
States." Columnist Jay E. House (Philadelphia Public Ledger) wrote,
"It was inevitable, of course, that Mr. O'Neill finally would write a
play about marriage between the whites and blacks. He has already
written plays about nearly all the other revolting topics." Time
magazine considered the play "hardly living up to the provocative
possibilities of its background" while The Times' John Corbin, commenting on Robeson's performance, mused "one also thought of
Othello."

Years later Eugene O'Neill wrote,

> The preliminary furor over the suggestion that miscegena-
> tion would be treated in the theatre obscured the real in-
> tention of the play. In the eyes of those who had not seen
> it, or even read the manuscript, it became an incendiary
> drama threatening to stir up race riots. The actual produc-
> tion must have disappointed the howlers. Nothing happened.

O'Neill's play opened on March 13, 1933, at London's Embassy
Theatre with Paul Robeson in his original role and the brilliant actress Flora Robson as his wife. London's Sphere reviewed the opening:

> All God's Chillun Got Wings. Yes, and voices, too. And
> the ability to use them. Which is a lucky thing for Mr.
> Eugene O'Neill, who is one of God's children with a gift
> for pouring out great floods of words, which are by no
> means always winged words. In some of his plays he seems
> to take more words to arrive at, or to leave a simple situa-
> tion, than any other dramatist, and even his silence is elo-
> quent--It is irritating to find that he has no point to prove,
> and that the play does not take shape at all--Without Mr.

Paul Robeson as the black man and Miss Flora Robson as
the white woman, All God's Chillun would have been barely
tolerable. For, that those parts would have been better
acted, or acted half so well, I cannot believe--The Robeson-
Robson combination is indeed a formidable one, and it is a
pity that circumstances do not permit of it being brought
into play more frequently--Mr. Robeson singing off-stage in
that superbly rich voice of his, and saying his lines almost
as musically, proved again what a fine actor he is.

All God's Chillun Got Wings was revived at New York's Circle
in the Square Theatre on March 20, 1975. Directed by George C.
Scott, with Robert Christian as Jim and Trish Van Devere as Ella,
the play had fifty-three performances, but its turgid dramaturgy
had not improved over fifty-one years, and it was still considered
"a very poorly written play."

Like Ol' Man River, miscegenation jes' kept rollin' along in
Show Boat. Edna Ferber's fascinating novel Show Boat, with its
background patterned on James Adams' Floating Theatre, ran in
serial form from April to September in 1926 in the Women's Home
Companion magazine. The novel was published by Doubleday, Page
and Company in August 1926, and a year later Show Boat was
adapted for the stage and became one of the most famous musicals
produced on the American stage. Lavishly produced by Florenz
Ziegfeld and abundantly blessed with Jerome Kern's loveliest score,
Oscar Hammerstein, II's charming lyrics, and Joseph Urban's lush
settings, Show Boat opened at New York's Ziegfeld Theatre on December 27, 1927. Show Boat docked for 572 performances and became the most revived of all musicals in America and England; it
was produced three times as a motion picture.

The miscegenation subplot of Ferber's story involved beautiful
Julie La Verne, the star of Cap'n Andy's Cotton Blossom Show Boat
Floating Palace Theatre. Julie is married to the Show Boat's leading man Steve Baker. Born of a white father and a black mother,
Julie (Helen Morgan) is threatened with arrest on the levee at
Natchez when she is exposed as having Negro blood and is accused
of being illegally married to a white man--a criminal offense in the
state of Mississippi. Steve (Charles Ellis) cuts Julie's forefinger
and sucks her blood, thereby making him, legally, a Negro. Julie
and Steve leave the Show Boat--and the South--for Chicago.

The part of Show Boat's black Joe was specifically written for
Paul Robeson, but, due to contractural commitments, Robeson could
not join the cast. Robeson did sing the role in the London produc-
tion at the Drury Lane Theatre in 1928 and in Ziegfeld's 1932 Broad-
way revival of Show Boat. The fine baritone Jules Bledsoe played
Joe and sang "Ol' Man River" in the 1927 production. Among later
Broadway Joes were black baritones Kenneth Spencer (1946), William
C. Smith (1948), Lawrence Winters (1954), Arthur Fierson (1961),

William Warfield (1966), and Bruce Hubbard (1983). Joe's Mammy-type wife, Queenie, was delightfully portrayed by Aunt Jemima in 1927 (who actually was Tess Gardell in burnt cork).

Therese Gardella was born in Wilkes Barre, Pennsylvania in 1897. She was named Aunt Jemima by Lew Leslie after black min-strel man Billy Kersand's late-nineteenth century song "Old Aunt Jemima." Tess sparked George White's 1921 Scandals as a blackface singer and played a burnt-cork sketch with Lou Holtz. Gardella, the Italian dusky Mammy, became a vaudeville headliner as Aunt Jemima. She made Vitaphone shorts for Warner Bros. in 1927 and appeared in the musical prologue that had been added to Universal Pictures' basically silent screen version of Show Boat (1929). Black actress Gertrude Howard played Queenie in the 1929 film.

Tess Gardell appeared as herself in the 1934 film Stand Up and Cheer. Minus blackface, she returned to the legitimate stage in Eddie Dowling's 1940 musical comedy, The Little Dog Laughed, which closed during tryouts on the road. Rotund, jovial, and a fine singer, Tess Gardell as Aunt Jemima played vaudeville's Mecca --the Palace--on Broadway in 1949. She died at the age of fifty-two on Tuesday, January 3, 1950. In later revivals of Show Boat, Queenie was played by black actresses.

Some of the actresses who have played the unfortunate Julie were the following: Helen Morgan (1927, 1932 and 1940); Margaret Carlisle (1930 and 1938); Estelle Taylor (1933); Gladys Baxter (1934 and 1942); Natalie Hall (1938); Carol Bruce (1944, 1946 and 1948); Maxine Adams (1947); Marthe Errolle (1947); Terry Saunders (1950); Nancy Andrews (1951); Mariquita Moll (1952); Eleanor Lutton (1953); Helena Bliss (1954, 1956 and 1957); Rosalind Elias (1955 and 1963); Betty Colby (1956); Marion Marlowe (1958); Julie Wilson (1960); Anita Darian (1961); Jean Sanders (1964 and 1968); Constance Tow-ers (1966); Gale Sherwood (1967); Gloria Hodes (1974); Beth Fowler (1976); Kelly Garrett (1976); and Lonette McKee in 1983.

Julies on film were Alma Rubens (1929); Helen Morgan (1936); and Ava Gardner in 1951. Lena Horne was Julie in Metro-Goldwyn-Mayer's ersatz screen biography of Jerome Kern, called 'Till the Clouds Roll By (1946), in which a fifteen-minute miniature version of Show Boat opened the picture.

Ransom Rideout's drama Goin' Home opened on Broadway at the Hudson Theatre on August 23, 1928, for seventy-six performances. Produced by Brock Pemberton, who co-directed the play with Antoin-ette Perry, Goin' Home examined miscegenation in a French seaport village after World War I. New Orleans Negro Israel Du Bois (Rich-ard Hale) emerges a hero from the French Foreign Legion and mar-ries white Frenchwoman Lise. Israel and Lise (Barbara Bulgakov) become the owners of a café on the waterfront of a small French vil-lage. White American officer Major Edward Powell (Russell Hicks),

Helen Morgan as Julie in <u>Show Boat</u>, 1927 (courtesy of The Doug
McClelland Collection).

for whose family Israel once worked, finds his family's former servant. Powell ferments a race riot; he persuades Israel to abandon
his impossible marriage in a foreign land and return to the United
States.

Three years later, Brass Ankle, another drama on the taboo
subject, was seen on Broadway.

Miscegenation returned to Broadway in DuBose Heyward's play
Brass Ankle. Heyward's tragic story concerned Ruth Leamer (Alice
Brady), who was blighted with the inheritance of the brass ankle
of Negro ancestry from her grandfather John Chaldon (he had been
legally certified as a "white" soldier under the Civil War Conscrip-
tion Law but uncertified by nature). Ruth's white supremacist
husband, General Store owner Larry (Ben Smith), whose "social
position has no assurance but complexion" is a member of Riverton's
school board. Larry has been instrumental in having the Jackson's
children thrown out of the Southern town's white school after he
discovers that the Jacksons are contaminated with one-sixteenth
Negro blood. He takes this action even though, for years, the
family has been accepted as white. Larry's rationale for this para-
doxical behavior is "one drop of black blood makes a man a nigger!"

Ruth's baby is born black. Liberal, aristocratic Dr. Wain-
wright (Lester Lonergan) explains that John Chaldon's heritage
and the South's "brass ankles" is unacceptable to blacks and whites,
but this does not appease racist Larry, who screams in drunken
disbelief, "My Son--A Nigger!" Ruth is aware that she and her
black son will not be accepted by her Chaldon family relatives who
have been "passing fair" as whites for many years. To protect her
young, unsuspecting daughter June (Jeanne Dante) and frantically
desperate Larry, Ruth invites her female neighbors to their apartment above the General Store. Feigning drunkenness, she fabri-
cates a tale of an affair with Larry's deceased black handyman Davey
rather than confess the significance of her brass ankle. Drunken
and enraged, Larry kills Ruth and her black baby son with a shot-
gun Ruth has conveniently loaded and left at the bedroom door.

Edwin DuBose Heyward, who was born in Charleston, South
Carolina, on Monday, August 31, 1885, and who died at the age of
fifty-five, on Sunday, June 16, 1940, originally titled his drama
The Leamer Tragedy. Guthrie McClintic, who would produce Heyward's fine drama Mamba's Daughters (co-authored with his wife
Dorothy Kuhn Heyward) and star Ethel Waters in it eight years
later, optioned The Leamer Tragedy. The Theatre Guild planned
production of the play after McClintic dropped his option, but the
play (retitled Brass Ankle) was finally produced by James W. Elliott
Productions on April 23, 1931, at Broadway's Masque Theatre for
forty-four performances. Aging former minstrel star Bert Swor--not
wearing burnt cork--made his last Broadway stage appearance in
Brass Ankle as Larry's ignorant, bigoted friend Pink Jones.

Brass Ankle was DuBose Heyward's only solo playwrighting effort for Broadway. He wrote the famous drama Porgy with his wife Dorothy. The drama was produced by the Theatre Guild in 1927. Porgy had initially been called Porgo in Heyward's novel, after the name given by South Carolina Negroes to blackfish. Porgy was a name that had been used for an overweight, robust and roisterous character in several novels by William Gilmore Simms. In 1847, Simms had written a play Norman Maurice; or, The Man of the People for actor Edwin Forrest, but Forrest rejected the play. Heyward later collaborated with Ira Gershwin on the libretto for George Gershwin's brilliant folk opera, Porgy and Bess. (Cecil B. DeMille, in May 1927, optioned the screen rights to Porgy and announced plans to film the play, with an all-black cast starring Paul Robeson as Porgy and Florence Mills as Bess. The DeMille project never materialized.)

Richard Lockridge (the Evening Sun) wrote,

> Granted that its obvious colors are more of the theater than of life--even that Brass Ankle is sustained at times only by the failure of the characters to see fairly obvious solutions of their woes, something still remains beside the fine acting of Alice Brady and Ben Smith. There is an emotional intensity in the writing which bulges the tight little patterns-- One believes in Mr. Heyward's people, and in the bitter problem which confronts them, despite one's firm disbelief in the mechanics of the play.

Burns Mantle (Daily News) pinpointed the failure of Heyward's play, "Miscegenation is not a popular theme, either north or south."

Brooks Atkinson (the New York Times) felt Heyward's "hysterically inadequate" writing and "unequal telling" of the tragedy with its "volcanic end to a convulsive play" coupled with the miscasting of Alice Brady as Ruth, "never gets far enough from the theatre to get under the skin of life." Atkinson added that "in the writing of Porgy, in collaboration with his wife, Mr. Heyward had a more fluid style--But the play and performance barely expresses the depth of passion contained in the theme."

DuBose Heyward explained his play as follows:

> There are groups who inhabit that twilight zone between white and black, and in addition to the blood of the two races claim a strong strain of American Indian. In a certain section of South Carolina these people are described as Brass Ankles, the name deriving from the copper cast of their complexions. It is a type of individual predestined never to fit into the civilization which has produced it. The question of whether he can win out in our present civilization is one that challenges the imagination.

DuBose Heyward's Brass Ankle had been approached from a
black viewpoint in Ridgely Torrence's one-act tragedy Granny Maumee, produced by the Stage Society and Emily Hapgood on a bill
with Thomas Heywood's A Woman Killed With Kindness, at New York's
Lyceum Theatre at a special matinee (March 30, 1914). Dorothy
Donnelly was the original Madame X in Alexandre Bisson's long-
running tear-jerker translated for the English stage by John Raphael
in 1910. Donnelly became Sigmund Romberg's librettist and was
adept at translating other plays to the musical stage such as Blossom Time (1921), The Student Prince (1924), and My Maryland in
1927. Donnelly played the part of elderly black and blind Granny
Maumee; she was supported by June Mathis and Lola Clifton.

Torrence dramatized the fury and hatred of Granny Maumee
when her granddaughter returns to their wretched cabin with a
white baby boy sired by the grandson of a man who had killed
Granny's son by burning him at a stake. Granny conjures up a
voodoo curse against the white males, but her acquired Christianity
overcomes her native hatred, and she dies forgiving the white men
who have disgraced her black family.

Ridgely Torrence's Three Plays for a Negro Theatre included
Granny Maumee, Simon the Cyrenian, and The Rider of Dreams.
The three one-act plays were produced by Emily Hapgood for one
week at New York's Garden Theatre on April 4, 1917. They played
another week at the Garrick Theatre, beginning April 16, 1917.
The plays were directed by Robert Edmond Jones. A Negro choir
performed between the plays under the direction of J. Rosamond
Johnson. Marie Jackson-Stuart, Fannie Tarkington, and Blanche
Deas were the three women in Granny Maumee. The New York
Dramatic Mirror called Torrence's three plays "one of the big events
of the season and deserve every possible enocuragement."

Mae West's novel was first published by Macauley as Babe
Gordon; in later editions the title was changed to The Constant
Sinner. Mae wrote about her steamy novel, "It made literary critics
sit up and turn pale. It sold well. The book went through five
editions and was the biggest seller Macauley had had in five years."
J. J. Shubert persuaded Mae to adapt her novel to the stage, and
The Constant Sinner opened at Broadway's Royale Theatre on
September 14, 1931. Sultry, sexy Mae directed her play and
starred as amoral Babe Gordon, "the kind of woman every man
wants to meet--at least once." Babe had a ruinous love affair with
the black owner of a Harlem speakeasy for sixty-four performances,
despite equally ruinous reviews. George Givot in blackface played
amorous Money Johnson, the Harlem speakeasy king. The critics
pilloried The Constant Sinner. The least treacherous review was
the New York Herald Tribune's comment, "That she is an atrocious
playwright and appears in her own dramas is her only failing as an
actress."

Jerome H. Wallace's production of George Bryant's comedy
The Second Comin' opened at the Provincetown Playhouse on December 8, 1931, for one week. Bryant related the frantic effect
of white Reverend Wilbur's (Irving Hopkins) efforts to supply a
miracle for his doubting black congregation. The miracle occurs
on Christmas Day when the virginal black girl Glory (Enid Raphael)
gives birth to a pure white baby boy conceived through the not-so-
miraculous activities of the Reverend Wilbur.

Annie Nathan Meyer's drama Black Souls (produced by William
Stahl at the Provincetown Playhouse on March 30, 1932 for thirteen
performances) related the tragic affair of a white and a black. White
Senator Verne's daughter Luella (Guerita Donelley) seduces black
college professor of literature David Lewis (Juan Hernandez) into
resuming an affair which had begun in France in earlier years.
David and Luella are discovered during their rendezvous in a forest
cabin, and outraged whites lynch David. Senator Verne's (Alven
Dexter) interest in Negro Magnolia College quickly wanes as does
his sexual interest in the black college founder Andrew Moran's
(Morris McKenney) attractive mulatto wife Phyllis (Rose McClendon).
Richard Maibaum's drama (produced by Ira Marion and directed by
Robert Rossen at New York's Park Lane Theatre on April 12, 1931,
called The Tree, became the lynching post for black David (Thomas
Moseley) who had been falsely accused of strangling white Ruth
(Sylvia Lee) with whom he was in love. After David's lynching,
redneck Matt (Barton MacLane) confesses he has murdered Ruth.

James Mercer Langston Hughes, the celebrated black poet,
author, and playwright, was born in Joplin, Missouri on Saturday,
February 1, 1902; he died in New York City at the age of sixty-
five on Monday, May 22, 1967. To Jasper Deeter, Langston Hughes
contributed another case history of miscegenation, it was written in
1926. Deeter produced the play at his famous Hedgerow Theatre in
Moylan, Rose Valley, Pennsylvania. Hughes later converted his
play (called Mulatto) into a short story (Father and Son). Produced, directed, and "reconstructed" by Martin Jones, Mulatto
opened on Broadway at the Vanderbilt Theatre on October 24, 1935.
The program for the play included Hughes's 1925 poem "Cross,"
which had inspired Mulatto:

My old man's a white man,
And my old woman's black.
If ever I cursed my white old
man,
I take my curses back.
If ever I cursed my black old
mother
And wished she were in hell,
I'm sorry for that evil wish,
And now I wish her well.
My old man died in a fine big
house,

My ma died in a shack,
I wonder where I'm gonna die
Being neither white nor black.*

Colonel Thomas Norwood (Stuart Beebe) is the richest land-
owner in the county. He has sired several children by his black
housekeeper, Cora Lewis (Rose McClendon), on his rural Georgia
Plantation. Norwood sends their youngest son Robert (Hurst
Amyx) and their daughter Sally (Jeanne Greene) to be educated
in a Northern college. Robert becomes a football hero and gradu-
ates with honors. Returning home, Colonel Norwood puts young
Robert to work in the cotton fields where he is treated as a "field
nigger" by the bullying white overseer Talbot (John Boyd), who
has seduced Sally. Unlike his brother, William Lewis (Morris Mc-
Kenney), who has conformed to status as a servant in his father's
house, Robert rebels. When his father threatens him with a pistol
for using the front door and for his rebellious nature, Robert
strangles his father to death. While his mother Cora grieves over
the body of the Colonel, a drunken, inflamed white posse hunt
Robert with bloodhounds so they can lynch him. Robert escapes
and returns to the house; he commits suicide with his father's pistol as the posse enter the front door.

Mulatto was a great success on Broadway for 373 performances
and marked the final appearance on the New York stage of a fine
black actress--Rose McClendon--who gave a powerful, dignified performance as Cora Lewis. Brooks Atkinson (the New York Times)
wrote about Rose McClendon,

> As for Cora Lewis, she has the honor to be played by Rose
> McClendon, who is an artist with a sensitive personality and
> a bell-like voice. Plays are not very numerous for Miss
> McClendon, but it is always a privilege to see her adding
> fineness of perception to the parts she takes. In spite of
> its fatal weaknesses as a drama, Mulatto offers the combina-
> tion of Rose McClendon and a playwright who is flaming with
> sincerity--After a season dedicated chiefly to trash it is a
> sobering sensation to sit in the presence of a playwright
> who is trying his best to tell what he has on his mind.

But Atkinson also felt that Hughes's earnest effort was "muddled
and diffuse" with "little of the dramatic strength of mind that makes
it possible for a writer to tell a coherent, driving story in the theatre."

Percy Hammond (the New York Herald-Tribune) called Mulatto,
"a stirring story of evils redressed and insults unavenged. That it

*Used by permission of the publisher, Random House. Copyright ©
1926 by Alfred A. Knopf, Inc., and renewed by Langston Hughes
in 1954.

failed to be altogether persuasive was due to the fact that it lacked
judicial impartiality as well as knowledge of the theatre." Wilella
Waldorf (New York Post) felt Hughes thoroughly documented his
subject as truthfully as Uncle Tom's Cabin in its day but wondered,
"Whether it will do the Negroes and the Mulattoes any particular
good to plead their cause before a Northern audience rather than
in the South which should be the place for this indictment." Robert
Garland (New York World-Telegram) wrote, "Rose McClendon, one
of the great ladies of our stage, brings the accomplished artistry
to a role that pleads for it. But she is defeated in the end--the
less said about Mulatto, the better. Neither play nor propaganda,
it is a mischief maker in between."

Theatre Arts magazine concluded, "The picture is searing;
what destroys its effectiveness is Mr. Hughes's weak, amateurish
writing, and the unvarnished fact that the negro protagonist is as
ingrate and obnoxious as the villainous whites believe--Miss McClendon's rare sensitivity and beautiful voice made her scenes glow like
bright lights in shoddy surroundings." Rose McClendon left the
cast when she became ill with pneumonia. She was replaced by
Gertrude Bondhill, until Lucille La Verne assumed the role of Cora
on December 9, 1935. The supremely talented actress Rose McClendon of the "sensitive personality and bell-like voice" died on Sunday, July 12, 1936, at the age of fifty-one.

Mulatto was banned in several cities but played successfully
on the road for several years. Eventually Mulatto was performed
in those cities where nervous politicians had imposed the ban. Leon
Janney starred in the long-running Broadway production, with Mer-
cedes Gilbert as Cora; on the road, James Kirkwood headlined the
cast.

Michael Myerberg and Joel Spector produced The Barrier as
an "intellectualized operatic" version of Mulatto. The Barrier, with
book and lyrics by Langston Hughes and music by Jan Meyerowitz,
was first produced at Columbia University's Opera Workshop at
Brander Matthews Hall in January 1950 for ten performances. Directed by Doris Humphrey, the musical drama opened on Broadway
at the Broadhurst Theatre on November 2, 1950. The Barrier
starred Lawrence Tibbett as Colonel Thomas Norwood and Muriel
Rahn as Cora Lewis, with Wilton Clary as Robert. Brooks Atkinson
(the New York Times) reported, "Even in terms of opera, this is a
primitive subject that springs out of savage passions. It is also an
indigenuously American drama." But The Barrier closed after four
performances.

Edward Sheldon's theme in The Nigger was somewhat mitigated
in Samson Raphaelsons's failed drama White Man, which opened on
Broadway at the National Theatre on October 17, 1936, for seven
performances. Raphaelson's Paul Grimm (Sam Byrd) and his sister
Lucy (Patsy Ruth Miller) were born of a Negro mother and a white

father in North Carolina. Paul is warned by Lucy not to marry
Mary Nile (Louise Campbell) despite Mary's assurance that she does
not want children. When Mary becomes pregnant Paul confesses his
Negro blood, and their daughter is given to black Pansy Washington
(Sylvia Field) to raise. Paul returns to Harlem, where he is not
accepted by his black peers. Samuel Raphaelson's play was originally titled Harlem (1929). Arthur Kober dropped production plans for
the play after changing the title to White Man. Earlier, Eva Le
Gallienne had dropped her option on Harlem.

   The basic story of White Man had been far better dramatized
in Michael L. Landman's four-act play The Pride of Race, which was
based on a story by Wallace Irwin and produced on January 11,
1916, at Broadway's Maxine Elliott Theatre. Landman's play dealt
with a Yale honor man Deegan Folk (Robert Hilliard) who marries
Louise Calhoun (Kathlene MacDonell) of Alabama knowing he has
the Negro blood of the Folk family. Louise realizes the truth when
her son by Deegan is born black; she deserts her husband and his
black son. Deegan later becomes the wealthy owner of a tobacco
plantation in Cuba where his black son works as foreman and where
both men have found acceptance.

   Lillian Smith adapted her controversial novel of "the white
problem" Strange Fruit (1945) to the stage. Produced by José
Ferrer at Broadway's Royale Theatre on November 29, 1945, for
sixty performances, Strange Fruit dramatized the tragedy of the
love of Tracy Dean (played by Melchor "Mel" Ferrer who also directed) for beautiful black Nonnie Anderson (Jane White) who bears
his child in a small, prejudiced Georgia town. The theme was
further expanded in Arnaud d'Usseau and James Gow's more successful drama Deep Are the Roots, which opened at Broadway's
Fulton Theatre on September 26, 1945, and was directed by Elia
Kazan for 477 performances.

   Deep Are the Roots returned World War II hero black Lieutenant Brett Charles (Gordon Heath) to the small Southern town where
his mother Bella (Evelyn Ellis) is the housekeeper for staunchly
Southern Senator Langdon (Charles Waldron) in whose home Brett
was raised. Brett rejects the love and proposal of marriage of
Senator Landon's daughter Genevra (Barbara Bel Geddes) and dismisses her belief that they could create their own world as a wild
dream because "no man and woman can create a world apart. There
are no islands. There is no escape."

   Bernard Reines's drama Forward the Heart opened on January
28, 1949, for nineteen performances at Broadway's Forty-eighth
Street Theatre. Reines told of Boston artist David Gibbs (William
Prince), who was blinded during World War II and falls in love with
his mother's black maid Julie Evans (Mildred Joanne Smith). David's
contention that blindness knows no color and is no barrier to their
marriage is gently denied by Julie who refuses to marry him.

THE NIGGER

Prestigious professor George Pierce Baker taught English and
Drama at Harvard University where his post-graduate English 47
drama workshop each seminar consisted of twelve selected students
who became known as "Baker's Dozen." From these seminars
emerged several of America's best playwrights: Eugene O'Neill,
S. N. Behrman, Sidney Howard, George Abbott, John V. A. Weaver, Philip Barry; authors and drama critics (e.g., Heywood Broun
and John Mason Brown) also took Baker's seminars. A week after
George Pierce Baker's death, Eugene O'Neill eulogized his former
teacher in a letter to the New York Times (Sunday, January 6,
1935), "Only those of us who had the privilege in the drama class
of George Pierce Baker--can know what a profound influence Professor Baker exerted toward the encouragement and birth of modern
American drama."

The first student to attain fame in Baker's workshop and im-
pregnate modern American drama was Edward Brewster Sheldon
(class of 1907), born in Chicago, Illinois on Thursday, February
4, 1886. While in Baker's class, Sheldon, at the age of twenty-two,
wrote a full-length play specifically for actress Minnie Maddern
Fiske. The play (Salvation Nell) was a romantic drama heightened
by detailed realism and set in the slums of Manhattan's lower East
Side. It was produced on Broadway at the Hackett Theatre on
November 17, 1908, and starred Mrs. Fiske as Nell Sanders of the
Salvation Army. The immediate success of Salvation Nell established
Sheldon as America's most promising playwright; Sheldon brought a
new sense of realism and originality to American drama. Eugene
O'Neill later acknowledged his debt to Sheldon for first showing
him "the existence of a real theatre in Salvation Nell."

Sheldon's second play, called Philip Morrow, sensationally combined realism and racism. Before the play opened at New York's
The New Theatre on December 4, 1909, the title was changed to
The Nigger. Produced by Winthrop Ames and directed by George
Foster Platt, The Nigger was highly praised and highly damned because of its controversial theme and what was considered its deplorable altered title.

Sheldon's defense of his new title was as follows:

> I surely meant in no way to cast any reflection on the
> Negro. Quite the contrary, I wanted to get into the title
> of the play the attitude of the white race to the black.
> When the play is seen, I am sure that the development of
> the character will show how ironical the title is meant to
> be. When the black man is known as "the negro" there
> is no problem. In the South where he is "The Nigger"
> there is a problem. I wrote the play in a comparatively
> short period of time. I seemed to know exactly what I
> wanted to say and it all came easily.

What Sheldon had to say in The Nigger was a sad commentary on
the human condition and the old South; his commentary included an
exposure of miscegenation before only hinted at in American drama
(although Shakespeare had dramatized the subject in his first play
Titus Andronicus) and Dion Boucicault had used it in his play The
Octoroon.

        The play related the story of Philip Morrow (Guy Bates Post),
scion of a prominent Southern family and Sheriff of Westbury county, who is elected governor of the state. Morrow's aging black
mammy, Jinny (Beverly Sitgreaves), pleads with liberal plantation-
owner Morrow to protect her ne'er-do-well drunken son Joe White
(Oswald Yorke) who has been accused of raping a white woman.
Morrow's attempted protection and intervention does not save Joe
from his being lynched by an enraged mob. On the night before
his wedding to patrician Georgiana Byrd (Annie Russell), Morrow
discovers that his grandmother was a Negress. After overcoming
her initial revulsion, Georgiana agrees to marry Morrow. Threatened
by his political enemies, Jake Willis (Pedro De Cordoba) and Police
Chief Tilton (Wilfrid North), and aware he will be classified as a
"nigger," the new governor resigns his position and admits his Negro
heritage to the city's citizens who have gathered on the Capitol
steps. Morrow explains the impossibility of their marriage to Georgiana and resolves to dedicate his life working for the oppressed
people of his newly discovered race.

        The New York Dramatic Mirror reported,

>   Mr. Sheldon, author of Salvation Nell, in his second effort,
> The Nigger--has again shown that he is a dramatist of un-
> usual originality and force, and in the later play he has
> offered some things that will provoke wide discussion and
> perhaps disagreement. To attempt to handle a problem as
> potent as that which now excites those interested in the
> future of the negro in America is commendable for the pos-
> sibility of enlightenment that may result, aside from the
> vitalities of drama that may be invoked. The phase of the
> question into which Mr. Sheldon goes most fully presents
> great difficulties to the dramatist, involving as it does the
> effects on the Southern generation of today of the relations
> which historians rather unpleasantly say existed between
> white owners and slave women in the South half a century
> and more ago.

Theatre magazine added,

>   Here is a play without a purpose on a subject that is full
> of purpose. The play proved to be a melodrama, written
> with such sure and effective craftsmanship that no doubt
> can be left that its young author has a career before him--
> Of course, a play on such a serious subject must have a

purpose. This play appears to be an argument for the
physical unity of the American people with the negro.

William Randolph Hearst's New York Journal-American critic
Alan Dale sardonically slashed the play as "Repulsive, old as the
hills, and very unpleasant." The New York Times found it to be
"Very effective melodrama" and the New York Daily Tribune noted,
"It is a play of unusual power, it sounds great depths of human
feeling, it deals with a tremendous problem in the life of this na-
tion." Forty years later, in 1949, Cosmopolitan magazine called
The Nigger one of "The Ten Dramatic Shocks of the Century."

Sheldon is probably best known for his 1912 romantic drama,
Romance, which he wrote for Doris Keane, an actress he'd hoped to
marry. Romance created a career for Doris Keane; the long-running
Broadway play lasted 1,049 performances in London. A few years
after the tremendous success of Romance, Sheldon's health failed.
He developed a disease called ankylosing spondylitis, an advanced
and debilitating form of arthritis. Ultimately, his immobile body remained on a raised bed resembling a catafalque, which was covered
with a blue spread falling to the floor. Sheldon became totally blind
in 1931, and a black mask covered his sightless eyes. But nothing
obscured his indomitable spirit, wit, and intelligence that attracted
the elite of the theatre, opera, and literary worlds to bask in his
ever-pleasant personality, astute counsel and encouragement.

Edward "Ned" Sheldon's enduring friendship with John Barrymore resulted in Sheldon's persuading Barrymore to abandon light
comedy for more serious and classical roles; in these roles, the actor
became famous. For the talents of John and Lionel Barrymore, Sheldon translated Sem Benelli's play La Cena delle Beffe, retitling it
The Jest; the play opened on Broadway, April 19, 1919.

Sheldon wrote several other plays--The Boss and Princess
Zim-Zim in 1911; The High Road (for Mrs. Fiske) in 1912; and
Egypt. He translated Herman Sudermann's Der Hohe Lied as The
Song of Songs, and, in 1914, he wrote The Garden of Paradise.
During his state of paralysis, he wrote The Lonely Heart (1921)
and in 1924 collaborated with former Harvard alumnus Sidney Howard
on a play called Bewitched. With his relative through marriage,
Charles MacArthur, he wrote Lulu Belle (1926) and collaborated with
Dorothy Donnelly (1927) on the musical comedy My Princess, an
adaptation of his 1911 play, Princess Zim-Zim, music by Sigmund
Romberg. Margaret Ayer Barnes was his collaborator on two plays
--Jenny in 1929 and Dishonored Lady in 1930.

Fox Films produced The Nigger in 1915. The film starred
William Farnum as Philip Morrow. The Moving Picture World denounced the film version and called for its suppression as a

production that never should have been made. Repulsive,

harmful and void of any moral lesson worth pointing. It
presents the worst sores in American civilization without
any decency or restraint and without suggesting a remedy.
Nothing so nauseating as The Nigger has been shown on
the screen--it is a brutal appeal to the most dangerous of
human passions.

The Nigger was banned in Ohio and stormily protested
throughout the country. Police were called to quell a disturbance
at Proctor's Theatre in Elizabeth, New Jersey, and at Keith Theatre
in Portland, Maine. Fox withdrew the film and reedited several of
the more objectionable scenes. The studio rereleased The Nigger
under the title The New Governor, but the revisions failed to attract
audiences, and the motion picture was removed from distribution.

Edward Brewster Sheldon died of a coronary thrombosis (Monday, April 1, 1946) in his six-room penthouse apartment at 35 East
Eighty-fourth Street in Manhattan; he was sixty-years-old. Shortly
after Sheldon's death, Eugene O'Neill and his wife Carlotta leased
Sheldon's apartment, and it was there O'Neill completed his play
The Iceman Cometh. Anne Morrow Lindburgh wrote an article about
her friend "Ned" for Reader's Digest (1946) called "The Most Un-
forgettable Character I've Ever Met" and Edward Sheldon was that,
and more, to many, many people. Ruth Gordon, whom Sheldon
helped in her early playwright efforts, said of him, "He was the
handsomest creature that ever lived and a brilliant playwright with
charm galore." Sheldon had wisely advised Ruth Gordon, "When you
have success, enjoy it. It doesn't come often; enjoy it." His friend
Thornton Wilder observed that Sheldon's life became "an elaborate
usefulness to others." Helen Hayes on opening nights had dinner
with Sheldon, "because he steadied me and gave me strength."

Sheldon Rosen's play Ned and Jack directed by Colleen Dewhurst had ten previews but one performance at New York's Little
Theatre on November 8, 1981. John Vickery played Ned Sheldon,
and Peter Michael Goetz was John Barrymore.

THE BIRTH OF A NATION

The national outcry over The Nigger was but a whimper in
the wilderness compared to the chorus of condemnation that arose
with the opening of David Wark Griffith's incendiary motion picture
The Birth of A Nation. Griffith's classic film was based on Thomas
Dixon, Jr.'s play The Clansman, which previewed on January 1 and
2 in 1915 at Riverside, California. The film opened at William H.
Clune's 2,600-seat Auditorium in Los Angeles on February 8, 1915.
The two-a-day showings of The Clansman were preceded by an
elaborate live prologue. A full forty-piece orchestra and large choir
accompanied the 187 minute film, playing the first complete musical

score written for a motion picture; the score was composed and compiled by Joseph Carl Breil. Breil's score was based on nineteenth-century music and highlighted by repetitive themes, notably Elsie's theme, "The Sweetest Bunch of Lilacs," derived from Gaetano Braga's "Leggenda Valaccia," or "La Serenata"--called "Angel's Serenade"--which in later years became the theme song of Amos' and Andy's popular radio show and was known as "The Perfect Song."

The Reverend Thomas Dixon, Jr.'s first play, The Clansman --based on his novels The Leopard's Spots (1902) and The Clansman (1905)--dealt with the reconstruction period in the South from 1866 to 1870. The play was enthusiastically received in the South-- except in Columbia, South Carolina. Columbia's State newspaper openly challenged Reverend Dixon's cavalier compilation and distortion of historical facts and questioned his sincerity regarding his subject. A Charleston, South Carolina correspondent to the New York Evening Post on October 25, 1905, reported,

> It is now many years since the first ill-advised production of Mrs. Stowe's Uncle Tom's Cabin. Something like the tremendous wave of passion which that play wrought in the North, at a time when passion ran high, is being reproduced by The Clansman in the South at a time when passion sleeps, but sleeps restlessly. In Uncle Tom's Cabin the negro is shown at his best. In The Clansman the negro is shown at his worst.

The Governor of Alabama denounced the play as "a nightmare" comparable to "flogging a dead horse."

Prior to the Broadway opening of The Clansman, Dixon's article "Why I Wrote the Clansman" was published by Theatre magazine in January 1906. Dixon's prediction of "a civil-racial war" within fifty years and his defense of his play read in part,

> The accusation that I wrote The Clansman to appeal to prejudice or assault the negro race is, of course, the silliest nonsense. For the negro I have only the profoundest pity and the kindliest sympathy. My play is a demonstration of Abraham Lincoln's words, "There is a physical difference between the white and black races which will forever forbid them living together on terms of political and social equality"--In my play I have sought National Unity through knowledge of the truth. The Southern people vainly imagine they have solved the negro question by Jim Crow cars and Grandfather Clauses for the temporary disfranchisement of the blacks. They have overlooked the fundamental fact that this Nation is a democracy, not an aristocracy, and that equality, without one lying subterfuge --is the supreme law of our life.

What of the future! This is the question I am trying
to put to the American people North and South--reverently
and yet boldly. I believe the stage is the best medium for
placing this tremendously vital question plainly before the
whole people. My play cannot be misunderstood. In the
fierce white glare of the footlights its purpose and the lesson it conveys become clear to every man and woman in this
broad land of ours. It is, indeed, the "writing on the
wall." Will the American people heed its warning?

Thomas Dixon, Jr. was born at Shelby, North Carolina, on
Monday, January 11, 1864. A former lawyer and member of the
North Carolina legislature, Dixon became a Baptist minister in October 1886. He died at the age of eighty-two on Wednesday, April
3, 1946. The dedicaiton on Dixon's monument in the Sunset Cemetery of the Episcopal Church of the Redeemer at Shelby, North
Carolina reads:

>"Lawyer-Minister-Author
>Orator-Playwright-Actor
>A Native of Cleveland County
>And most distinguished son
>of his generation.
>He was the author of 28 books
>dealing with the Reconstruction
>Period. The most popular
>of which were The Clansman
>and The Leopard's Spots
>from which The Birth of A Nation
>was dramatized.
>Erected by His Friends.

The Clansman opened on Broadway at the Liberty Theatre on
January 8, 1906, for fifty-one performances. Produced by George
H. Brennan and directed by Frank Hatch, the controversial play
was besieged by negative editorials and general condemnation of its
subject. Dixon gave a curtain speech on the opening night during
intermission, again explaining his purpose in writing The Clansman,
"My object is to teach the North, the young North, what it has
never known--the awful suffering of the white man during the dreadful reconstruction period. I believe that Almighty God anointed the
white men of the South by their suffering during that time--to
demonstrate to the world that the white man must and shall be
supreme." Despite his holier-than-thou pronouncements, Dixon's
persistent rhetorical defense of his novels and his play served to
illuminate his racism.

The New York Dramatic Mirror echoed the general adverse
critical opinion of the drama:

It is difficult to do justice to so bad a play as The Clansman.

This statement may seem contradictory, but the fact is that
this peculiarly obnoxious melodrama contains some effective
episodes and some clever stage-management. Why at the
present day, in the dawn of a friendly understanding between the South and the North, Thomas Dixon or any other
man should consider it his duty to recall the terrors of that
horrible period immediately after the Civil War it is difficult
to comprehend. Moreover, he has distorted history so as
to make affairs seem even worse than every one knows they
actually were--It is certainly not the business of the technical critic to write historical essays, nor is it the business
of the playwright to tamper with American history for the
distinct object of reawakening section prejudices--As a piece
of constructive playwrighting The Clansman is altogether
amateurish.

The post-Broadway tour of The Clansman, with basically a
new cast, reaped much the same critical and public reaction as it
had in New York. The Philadelphia Record (May 1, 1906) reported,
"No matter what may be the views of some of the public as to the
propriety of presenting a play having to do with the clash of blacks
and whites, there can be no gainsaying the interest that Mr. Dixon's
treatment of a national problem has aroused." The Chicago Tribune
reviewed the play at McVicker's Theatre, "Mr. Dixon has not tried
in The Clansman to solve the vital problem that the South faced at
the close of the Civil War. He has contented himself with placing
it before the public, and his so doing can scarcely be taken amiss
by calm thinking, cool minded people--For Mr. Dixon has not painted
the Negro all black."

More words alternatively praising and damning D. W. Griffith's
The Birth of a Nation have been written on its filming, showing,
riots and protests, praise, attacks, counterattacks and demands for
censorship reform than are to be found in the Holy Bible and all
of Shakespeare's works. D. W. Griffith and Thomas Dixon wrote
the screenplay for The Clansman. Griffith considerably toned down
the rabid racism of Dixon's novel, which had been described as "a
hymn to hate." After six months of rehearsals, shooting started
on July 4, 1914, artistically photographed by George William (or
Gottfried Wilhelm) "Billy" Bitzer and brilliantly directed by Griffith;
production time was nine weeks. The film originally opened in Los
Angeles under the title of The Clansman. But for the Wednesday,
March 3, 1915, opening on Broadway at the Liberty Theatre where
the play had been produced, the motion picture became The Birth
of a Nation. Cast and credits are given below.

THE BIRTH OF A NATION. Produced by Epoch Producing
Company (D. W. Griffith, H. E. Aitken, Roy Aitken). Director, David Wark Griffith; Screenplay D. W. Griffith and

Frank W. Woods, based on the novel The Clansman by the
Reverend Thomas Dixon, Jr. (with additional material from
Dixon's novel The Leopard's Spots); Camera, George William
"Billy" Bitzer; Assistant cameraman, Karl Brown; Settings,
Frank Wortman; Original musical score compiled and arranged
by Joseph Carl Breil and D. W. Griffith; Costumes, Robert
Goldstein; Assistant directors, George Siegmann, W. S. Van
Dyke, Jack Conway, Robert Harron, Erich von Stroheim,
Raoul Walsh, Herbert Sutch, William Christy Cabanne, Fred
Hammer; Screenplay consultant, the Reverend Thomas Dixon,
Jr.; Editors, James Smith and Joseph Allen; Explosive ef-
fects, Walter Hoffman; Song "The Sweetest Bunch of Lilacs"
by Joseph Carl Breil; Released February 8, 1915)

Henry B. Walthall (Benjamin Cameron--"The Little Colonel");
Mae Marsh (Flora Cameron); Miriam Cooper (Margaret Cam-
eron); Josephine Crowell (Mrs. Cameron); Spottiswoode
Aitken (Dr. Cameron); George Andre Beranger (Wade Cam-
eron); Maxfield Stanley (Duke Cameron); Lillian Gish
(Elise Stoneman); Ralph Lewis (The Hon. Austin Stone-
man); Elmer Clifton (Phil Stoneman); Robert Harron (Tod
Stoneman/Blackface Spy); Mary Alden (Lydia Brown,
Stoneman's Mulatto Housekeeper); Sam De Grasse (Senator
Charles Sumner); George Siegmann (Silas Lynch); Walter
Long (Gus, the Renegade); Wallace Reid (Jeff, the Black-
smith); Joseph Henaberry (Abraham Lincoln); Alberta Lee
(Mrs. Lincoln); Donald Crisp (General Ulysses S. Grant);
Howard Gaye (General Robert E. Lee); William Freeman
(The Mooning Sentry, Federal Hospital); Olga Grey (Laura
Keene); Raoul Walsh (John Wilkes Booth); Elmo Lincoln
(Whitearm Joe/Slave Auctioneer/Piedmont Confederate Lead-
er); Tom Wilson (Stoneman's Negro Servant); Eugene Pal-
lette (Union Soldier); Mme. Madelaine Sul-te-wan* (Negro
Woman with Gypsy Shawl); William DeVaull (Nelse); Jennie
Lee (Faithful Mammy); Erich von Stroheim (Man Who Falls
from Roof); Monte Blue, John French (Soldiers)

*D. W. Griffith's close friend, black actress Madame Sul-te-
wan's first name seems to have eluded everyone, including
Lillian Gish and many others who knew her. An obscure
black press release in 1915 gives her full name. Madame
Sul-te-wan was the only one of Griffith's former players who
was at Los Angeles' Temple Hospital when Griffith died on
July 23, 1948.

Prior to the opening of the motion picture on Broadway,
D. W. Griffith showed The Birth of a Nation to President Woodrow
Wilson and invited guests in the East Room of the White House.
Wilson's critique was "This is history written with lightning, and

it's all too true." President Wilson later repudiated this statement (April 1915) to the National Association for the Advancement of Colored People, who had wildly protested the showing of the film. Race riots occurred throughout the country wherever The Birth was shown. Again, Dixon rose to the defense of his saga, "I am not attacking the Negro of today. I am recording faithfully the history of fifty years ago. I portray three Negroes misled by white scoundrels. Is it a crime to paint a bad black man, seeing we have so many white ones?"

Advertised as "The Dawn of a new Art which marks an Epoch in the theatres of the World with 18,000 People and 3,000 Horses; Cost $500,000 (actually the final cost was estimated about $91,000); founded on Thomas Dixon's Novel and Play The Clansman," The Birth opened at the Liberty Theatre (March 3, 1915) to unanimous praise. The three-hour film played twice daily, including Sundays, at 2:10 P.M. sharp and 8:05 P.M. sharp with an eight-minute intermission at each showing. The house was scaled at prices from twenty-five, fifty, seventy-five cents and one dollar to reserved seats at two dollars when other films were being shown in New York City at five and ten cents. The Birth of a Nation remained at the Liberty Theatre for forty-four weeks; a symphony orchestra of forty men played Joseph Carl Briel's symphonic score.

The Reverend Thomas B. Gregory wrote in the New York American, "Mr. Griffith comes pretty near working a miracle. By all odds the greatest thing that has ever come into New York." Burns Mantle (Daily News) enthused, "The pictures are wonderful, and there is an element of excitement that swept a sophisticated audience like a prairie fire in a high wind." Hector Turnbull (Tribune): "A decided achievement for D. W. Griffith, and is certain to appeal to every one who cares for novelty, spectacular drama and thrills piled upon thrills." Charles Darnton (Evening World): "Griffith's work is big and fine, stirring and affecting. The most dramatic events in our United States History reproduced with striking realism."

The encomiums continued with Rennold Wolf (the Morning Telegraph): "Nothing so thrilling has ever been produced by an American director." Lewis Serwin (the Globe): "Griffith's work is beyond question the most extraordinary picture that has ever been made--or seen--in America." The New York Times praised the film as "An impressive illustration of the scope of the motion picture camera."

According to Lillian Gish, D. W. Griffith--throughout the storm and fury over The Birth--maintained his belief that the Negro "had made great strides since the end of slavery, when a million white men had died to help set them free. He said that the white man had taken centuries to attain the intellectual and spiritual powers that many Negro citizens had achieved in a few decades. He believed that no other race in the history of mankind had advanced so far so quickly."

Years later, James Agee (the Nation, September 4, 1948) said that accusations calling The Birth an anti-Negro movie were "vicious nonsense" as well as unfair and that an honest depiction of "the salient facts of the so-called Reconstruction years" were carefully presented. Agee wrote,

> The Birth of a Nation is equal with Brady's photographs, Lincoln's speeches, Whitman's war poems; for all its imperfections and absurdities it is equal, in fact, to be the best work that has been done in this country. And among moving pictures it is alone, not necessarily as "the greatest"—whatever that means—but as the one great epic, tragic film.

Arthur Knight in his fine panoramic movie history, The Liveliest Art, succinctly explained the lasting effect of Griffith's film. "What makes The Birth of a Nation difficult to view today is precisely what touched off the controversy that raged about the film in 1915—the use of Negro stereotypes and its sympathetic account of the rise of the Klan." Griffith was not the first to depict the rise of the infamous Ku Klux Klan. General Film Company's three-reel drama, The Night Riders of Petersham, released on April 4, 1914, showed the Klan harassing whites in Kentucky. Other silent films featured the Klan's activities: Louis B. Mayer's One Clear Call (1922); Frank B. Coigne's The Mask of the Ku Klux Klan (1923)—also known as Knight of the Eucharist; E. M. MacMahon's The Fifth Horseman (1924); Paramount's The Mating Call (1928). Otto Preminger's 1963 film The Cardinal contains a segment in which a priest is elevated to bishop due to his courageous fight against the Klan. The Black Klansman was released by U.S. Films in 1966, and the Klan was prominently exposed in Metro-Goldwyn-Mayer's 1970 production ...Tick...Tick...Tick.

Explaining The Birth, Knight continued,

> Griffith seems to have been genuinely shocked at the charges of anti-Negro bias leveled against him on all sides when the film appeared, and not without reason. One has only to read The Clansman, on which it was based, to become aware of the pains that Griffith had taken to eliminate from his version the rabid hatred that seethes through Thomas Dixon's book—He balanced his renegade Negroes and vengeful mulattoes with happy, faithful "darkies" and thought he was being fair—But perhaps the true measure of this film is to be found in the very depth of the passions it aroused."

"ALL THE WORLD'S A STAGE--

And all the men and women merely players
They have their exits and their entrances;
And one man in his time plays many parts."

(Shakespeare: As You Like It; act 2, scene 7)

White players in blackface continued making their entrances as servants, mammys, and protagonists for many years after the diminished halcyon days of Uncle Tom's Cabin led to the inevitable final exit. Compiling a list of blackface players and their roles would be an encyclopedic task. One of the more notable roles was black Cuffee, played by Mr. Bogart in actor John Brougham's 1856 play, Life in New York; or Tom and Jerry on a Visit. Although Cuffee was a contemporary of Uncle Tom, he had more of the characteristics of a minstrel show comic.

There were other blackface players--other roles. Augustin Daly's play Norwood, based on Henry Ward Beecher's novel Legend of Norwood; or Village Life in New England, was produced at the New York Theatre on November 11, 1867, with Welsh Edwards as black Peter Sawmill. Daly's Under the Gaslight, seen at the Worrell Sisters' Theatre on August 12, 1867, had Mr. Williams as an eclectic black servant, Sam. Nat C. Goodwin played a shoeblack at Wood's Museum on April 8, 1873 in Law in New York and blacked-up with minstrels.

Dion Boucicault's drama Belle Lamar, written specifically for John McCullough and produced at Booth's Theatre on August 10, 1874, had its black Uncle Dan (J. E. Irving) offering his life for the life of his mistress-owner Belle. The Black Hand; or The Lost Will at New York's Bowery Theatre on January 9, 1875, starred Frank Jones in his own play during which he performed six roles, including Pompey Snowball, "A Color'd Swell" with Charles Foster as Sam, "an aged darkey Faithful 'till Death" and Thomas Leigh as Bill Jackson, "The Black Hand." The Dark Face; or Two Parts White with Charles Reynolds as "true blue" slave Sable and Frank Dumont's four-act "romance" Marked for Life with Skid (Sidney C. France)--"a darkey true as steel"--appeared in 1875. James Steele MacKaye's play adapted from Albion Tourgee's novel A Fool's Errand (1881) depicted the problems of freed slaves. David Belasco's May Blossom; or Between Two Loves (April 12, 1884) featured Eph (J. Nick Long) as comedy relief.

William Gillette's drama Held By the Enemy was produced at New York's Madison Square Theatre on August 16, 1886; it engaged Harry Woodson as blackface Uncle Rufus. Woodson had also played an aged Negro at the National Theatre on June 21, 1886 in Passing the Toll Gate. Gillette's 1895 drama, Secret Service, housed the faithful Negro servants Jonas (H. D. James) and Martha (Alice

Leigh). Otis Skinner made his first stage appearance in 1887 as
the Negro Old Jim in Philip Stoner's play Woodleigh; he then played
Uncle Tom in Uncle Tom's Cabin.

Charles Hale Hoyt's comedy, originally called A Case of Wine,
became the hit play, A Texas Steer, on November 19, 1890. The
comedy satirized "a colored statesman" Christopher Columbus Fishback (Will H. Bray), Minister to Dahomey of Washington, D.C.,
with Barry Maxwell as black waiter Othello Moore.* Augustus
Thomas's Negro character Decatur (Reub Fax) was a servant in
Alabama at the Madison Square Theatre on April 1, 1891. Clay M.
Greene's and Joseph R. Grismer's drama The New South was William
A. Brady's first production on January 2, 1893 at the Madison
Square Theatre and dramatized the mental anguish and quaking fear
of a Negro murderer, slave Sampson (James A. Herne, succeeded
by George Fawcett).

Charles K. French was black Neb, "an old family servant who
dates from befo' de wah," (People's Theatre on September 11, 1893)
in Charles Turner Dazey's long-running play In Old Kentucky.
French also appeared at the Madison Square Theatre (December 14,
1903) as Napoleon Lee "who worked fo' de Calverts when dey all was
rich" in the musical comedy called The Girl from Dixie. Charles
H. Sheffer played Napoleon's wife. Frank Mayo dramatized and
starred in Mark Twain's indictment against racial prejudice and slavery, Pudd'nhead Wilson (Herald Square Theatre on April 15, 1895)
with Mary Shaw (Eliza Mary Anne Trenar, the fourth wife of Thomas
S. Hamblin), who was succeeded by Eleanor Moretti as "a sixteenth
negress slave" Roxy. (This part was later enacted by Laura Hope
Crews in a 1903 revival of the play.)

James A. Herne's drama Griffith Davenport, Circuit Rider (or
The Reverend Griffith Davenport) was based on Helen H. Gardener's
novel An Unofficial Patriot. It appeared for twenty performances,
beginning January 31, 1899, at the Herald Square Theatre. Herne's
play explored the deplorable slavery condition. Half the cast required blackface. They played slaves who resented being set free
by conscience-stricken Methodist circuit-riding minister, the Reverend Griffith Davenport.

In the twentieth century the masquerade in black continued
in many plays. Jules Bledsoe (Fourteenth Street Theatre on
January 5, 1903) had Mr. Martin as Banty Tim and, in a minstrel
show scene, Master Harry Le Van as Little Breeches. George W.
Lederer's integrated "Musical Study in Black and White," The
Southerners (New York Theatre on May 23, 1904) headlined Eddie
Leonard as black Uncle Daniel, with Vinie Daly as Parthenia, Wheel-
er Earl as Sam, Walter Dixon as Aunt Matilda, and Charles Moore

_____
*Harry Fern was Fishback in 1913's musical version of A Texas
Steer (called A Trip to Washington).

as Uncle Mose. Clay Clement, John McGovern, and Jesse Edson's drama, Sam Houston (Garden Theatre on October 16, 1906) employed Hazel Brun as a Mammy, John P. Wade as Mose, and William L. Visscher as Uncle Caesar.

George Broadhurst and George V. Hobart's "racing comedy," Wildfire, starring Lillian Russell (Liberty Theatre on September 7, 1908) featured Ernest Truex as the Negro jockey Chappie Raster; Annie Buckley was colored maid Hortense Green. David Belasco's production of Eugene Walter's dramatic sensation The Easiest Way at the Belasco-Stuyvesant Theatre on January 19, 1909 cast Emma Dunn, a splendid actress, as Frances Starr's colored maid and confidante, Annie. The 1921 revival of The Easiest Way had Marion Kerby as Annie.

William Vaughn Moody's play The Faith Healer (Savoy Theatre on January 19, 1910) included Robert McWade as old Negro Uncle Abe, a part originally played by James Kirkwood in the March 15, 1909, tryout of the play in St. Louis. Through the character of the old Negro servant Uncle Abe, playwright Moody investigated the intense superstitious and religious fervor of the Negro. Edward Henry Peple's play The Littlest Rebel (Liberty Theatre on November 14, 1911) gave former minstrel man George Thatcher the role of black Uncle Billy; Lawrence Merton was Jeems-Henry, "a runaway," and Mamie Lincoln was slave Sally Ann. George Ade's comedy The County Chairman (Wallack's Theatre on November 24, 1913) had minstrel man Willis A. Sweatnam as black Sassafras Livingston. Will Rogers did a blackface imitation of Negro comedian Bert Williams (Ziegfeld Follies of 1918) and George Marion was faithful old Negro servant Uncle Toby in Toby's Bow (Comedy Theatre on February 10, 1919).

There were also white female performers who made a career portraying blacks. Aunt Chloe, the Mammy created by Mrs. Dunn in Self in 1856, spawned many future interpreters. The daughters of Chloe excelled in characterization. None was better than Mrs. Charles G. Craig, who was described as "the most celebrated 'Mammy' in the country." Rotund and jovial Mrs. Charles G. Craig first appeared in blackface as Mammy Lindy in The Southern Gentleman (1868) and continued playing colored mammys in, among other roles: We Uns of Tennessee (1869--Aunt Millie); At the Old Cross Roads (1894--Aunt Eliza); Captain Barrington (1903--Mandy); Beverly of Graustark (1904--Aunt Fanny); A Wife's Secret (1905--A Virginia Mammy); The Clansman (1906--Aunt Eve); The Warrens of Virginia (1907--Sapho); 1910's vaudeville act Mammy; The Bridal Path (1913--Aunt Kitty); When Claudia Smiles (1914--Synthia); Old Reliable (1915--Aunt Selma); Sins of the Fathers (1915--Miss Minerva); Come Out of the Kitchen (1916--Amanda); and The Melting of Molly (1918--Aunt Judy).

Alice Leigh played Mammy Lu in Clyde Fitch's sentimental

drama <u>Barbara Frietchie</u> (Criterion Theatre on October 23, 1899).
<u>Barbara Frietchie</u> was the basis for Sigmund Romberg and Dorothy
Donnelly's fine musical drama, <u>My Maryland</u>, produced at Jolson's
Theatre on September 12, 1927, for 312 performances, with Mattie
Keene as Mammy Lu. Stella Congdon was Mammy Lina in <u>Cameo</u>
<u>Kirby</u> (Hackett's Theatre, December 20, 1909), and Nellie Peck
Saunders was Mammy Sal in <u>George Washington</u> (Lyric Theatre,
March 1, 1920). Frank Craven's 1920 hit comedy, <u>The First Year</u>,
gained added laughter through Hattie, a comic black maid adept
at mixing orange juice to "blossom" with gin. Leila Bennett played
blackface Hattie for 278 performances, and, in later revivals of the
play, Harriet MacGibbon and Mary Marble "blossomed" as Hattie.

Mrs. Jacques Martin played Aunt Hepsy in Hubert Osborne's
1922 play, <u>Shore Leave</u>, which Herbert Fields adapted to the musical
stage as <u>Hit the Deck</u>, with music by Vincent Youmans and lyrics
by Leo Robins. Aunt Hepsy was renamed Lavinia and assigned the
rousing hit song "Hallelujah!" <u>Hit the Deck</u> opened at the Belasco
Theatre on April 25, 1927, to play 352 performances. For the role
of Lavinia, Vincent Youmans coaxed former stage mammy and "Coon"
singer Stella Mayhew out of retirement. She stopped the show with
her robust singing of "Hallelujah!"

Born Izetta Estelle Sadler in Waynesburg, Ohio in 1874, Stella
Mayhew has been acclaimed the greatest female delineator of black
female character roles. Stella started her long stage career at the
age of eight as Little Eva in Ober Stock Company's production of
<u>Uncle Tom's Cabin</u>. For seven years she toured the United States
as black Mammy Lindy in Stair and Havlin's production <u>On the</u>
<u>Suwanee River</u> and gave over fifteen-hundred performances singing
"My Aunt Elizaer" and "I Wonder What is That Coon Game." Stella
brightened 1904's <u>The Man from China</u> as Anastasia Giltedge singing
"Fifty-seven Ways to Catch a Man," and she was Veronica Vendigris
Jackson, a black chorus lady, in <u>The Jolly Bachelors</u> (January 6,
1910), singing "Savannah" and "Stop That Rag." Stella partnered
in blackface with Al Jolson in his first Broadway show, <u>La Belle</u>
<u>Paree, a Jumble of Jollity</u> (Winter Garden Theatre on March 20,
1911). Mayhew recorded several of her "Coon" songs for Edison
Records. They included: "I'm Looking for Something to Eat"
(1909); "Savannah" (1910); "De Devilin' Time" (1911); and "There
Are Fifty-seven Ways to Catch a Man" (1912). After her rousing
singing and strutting of "Hallelujah!" in <u>Hit the Deck</u>, Stella Mayhew's career faded. She died penniless (Wednesday, May 2, 1934)
in New York City and was buried by the National Vaudeville Association.

Several Broadway shows were built around Negro life; the
Negro roles were performed by whites in blackface. Among these
theatrical oddities were the following.

ACHILLES HAD A HEEL

Walter Hampden, having appeared on Broadway in Shakespeare's Hamlet, The Merchant of Venice, Macbeth, The Taming of the Shrew, Henry V, Richard III, Othello, Arthur Goodrich's adaptation of Robert Browning's The Ring and the Book (called Caponsacchi), and Henrik Ibsen's An Enemy of the People (between extensive and seemingly interminable engagements in the title role of Brian Hooker's adaptation of Edmund Rostand's Cyrano de Bergerac), deserted the classics to appear in a modern play in blackface. The versatile and talented Mr. Hampden dipped heavily into the burnt cork to appear as Jumbo, Keeper of the Elephant, in an allegorical play by Martin Flavin.

Flavin related the tale of an illiterate, expert crap-shooting black war hero nicknamed Jumbo (Walter Hampden), who has lost his right forearm in World War I but wins the Croix de Guerre. Jumbo returns to civilian life to become a Zoo's Keeper of the Elephant. Jumbo's former white World War I Captain, Slats (John Wray), is keeper of the zoo's monkeys. Slats is vengefully envious of the Elephant Keeper's position. Failing to kill the Elephant with the help of the machinations and incantations of a voodoo witch doctor (Howland Chamberlain), the revengeful Slats hires black prostitute Lou (Sylvia Field) to seduce the Elephant Keeper. Jumbo is demoted to the monkey house and Slats replaces him. Devoted to his former keeper, the Elephant kills Slats. The black man is reinstated as the Keeper of the Elephant. Before returning to his beloved pachyderm, Jumbo locks lascivious Lou in the monkey house.

Martin Flavin's plays Children of the Moon (1923), The Criminal Code and Broken Dishes (1929) were successful but his allegorical Achilles Had a Heel was something else. Flavin's symbolism and mystical message escaped both the audience and most of the critics, who labeled it "a strangely clumsy play" and "one of the more melancholy sins of symbolism."

Robert Garland (the New York World-Telegram) described Flavin's fable as "muddled, mediocre and mysterious" and its producer, star and director (with assistance from the playwright and Howard Lindsay) as "Smoked Virginia Hampden--whose blackface is as incredible as his dialect, an Uncle Tom whose Eva is an elephant." Richard Lockridge (the Evening Sun) felt "Mr. Flavin has missed the simplicity of allegory without achieving any particular profundity." The New York Times' Brooks Atkinson admitted, "this student of the arts must publicly confess that the meaning of Achilles Had a Heel has flown clean over his astonished head." Atkinson further recommended that anyone with an Achilles heel should wear high boots.

Lou, like Eugene O'Neill's Yank Smith (in his 1922 drama, The Hairy Ape), who was dying in the arms of a Gorilla in a Bronx Zoo

cage, might well have asked Yank's final question, "Where do I fit
in?" Mr. Hampden and Mr. Flavin may have known the meaning,
but it all remained a secret to those outside a zoo.

Walter Hampden had tested Achilles Had a Heel at Pasadena,
California's Community Theatre (April, 1935). He opened the play
on Broadway at the Forty-fourth Street Theatre (October 13, 1935)
where it completed eight performances. Among the cast members,
classified as "Monkeys and Members of Society," were Virginia Grey,
Roland Kibbee, and Mary Martin. (Martin progressed from Achilles
to become Broadway's Venus and one of the theatre's most famous
musical comedy stars.)

COME SEVEN

The first all-white blackface comedy to appear on Broadway
was Come Seven, produced by George Broadhurst (Broadhurst Theatre on July 29, 1920). The comedy ran for seventy-two performances. Come Seven was written by Octavus Roy Cohen, a Charleston, South Carolina, writer of many popular comedic stories based
on Negro life, which appeared in The Saturday Evening Post. "It
certainly is different from any other comedy you have ever seen and
frequently highly amusing. It also had the advantage of excellent
performances by the white players engaged, the whole cast being
in the varying shades of the colored race," wrote Burns Mantle
(Daily News).

Cohen's blackface fable was based on his Saturday Evening
Post stories. Black Urias Nesbit "borrows" and pawns his wife's,
Elzevir's, genuine diamond ring for seventy-five dollars to finance
the purchase of a secondhand Ford automobile, with his flashy,
colored, Casanova friend, Florian Slappey. Unfortunately Semore
Masby, the pawnbroker, loans the ring to racy, dusky, octoroon
beauty Vistar Goins who proudly displays her latest acquisition to
Mrs. Nesbit. Urias and Florian force Semore to repay them $300
for being unable to produce the ring, and they buy Mrs. Nesbit
another genuine diamond ring. Unknown to Vistar, Elzevir has
surreptitiously replaced the original diamond ring with a paste ring
substituted by her husband. Canny Elzevir becomes the proud
owner of two gen-u-wine diamond rings.

Recruited from Hollywood, Gail Kane and Earle Foxe played
Vistar and Florian; Arthur Aylesworth was Urias Nesbit. The
Evening Telegram praised the fine actress Lucille La Verne's performance as the wily and wise Elzevir, calling her "adept as a
delineator of colored types, made a pronounced hit as the wife."
Heywood Broun (Tribune) added, "the one performance in the play
which seemed to us to capture a suggestion of authenticity was that
of Lucille La Verne."

Lucille La Verne was no stranger to blackface, having played the black maid in William Gillette's comedy Clarice (New York's Garrick Theatre on October 16, 1906) and portrayed a black Mammy on the screen in Samuel Goldwyn's 1917 film Polly of the Circus. Two years later, in 1922, she would be back on Broadway at the Maxine Elliott Theatre as Magnolia the black maid in Gladys Unger's play The Goldfish and would continue to play burnt-cork women on both stage and screen.

Heywood Broun (New York Tribune) reported that Come Seven

> is a play of one dimension, with no more depth than the black smudge which lay upon the face of the actors--Scratch any character in the play and you will catch nothing more than a burnt cork comedian. Come Seven marks a step forward only in that it is written with the confident assumption that the theatrical public may be interested in a play which deals with negro characters.

Come Seven's all-white, all-blackface cast was as follows: Lucille La Verne (Elzevir Nesbit); Earle Foxe (Florian Slappey); Gail Kane (Vistar Goins); Arthur Aylesworth (Urias Nesbit); Charles W. Meyer (Semore Mashby); Harry A. Emerson (Probable Huff); Henry Hanlin (Lawyer Evans Chew); Thomas Gunn (Cass Deegers); Susanne Willis (Lithia Blevins); Eleanor Monteil (Mrs. Chew); Carrie Lowe (Mrs. Goins). The play was directed by Mrs. Lillian Trimble Bradley.

LULU BELLE

David Belasco, born in San Francisco on Monday, July 25, 1853, had appeared as Sambo in Uncle Tom's Cabin in 1873, and, on July 3, 1882, he played Uncle Tom in a San Francisco production of the famous play. One of America's legendary, flamboyant theatrical producers and playwrights, white-haired Belasco affected a sartorial eminence. He masqueraded in a black suit and an ecclesiastical collar befitting his self-appointed position as "High Priest of the Theatre." His biographer, Craig Timberlake, anointed him "The Bishop of Broadway." Brooks Atkinson called Belasco "the master of mediocrity," while Niven Busch classified him as "The Great Impersonator." Belasco was tabbed by George Jean Nathan as "the Broadway Rasputin."

For all his eccentricities and the deprecating descriptions of him, David Belasco produced, directed, wrote, and extensively altered plays that became some of the theatre's greatest hits, notable for their lavish, realistically detailed settings, brisk direction, heavily populated casts, and high-blown hokum. Belasco made Broadway

stars of David Warfield, Mrs. Leslie Carter, Blance Bates, Frances
Starr, Ina Claire and his protegée, Lenore Ulric. Disliking the
name of young actress Gladys Marie Smith, Belasco changed it (be-
fore the curtain rose on December 3, 1907, on Belasco's production
of William de Mille's play The Warrens of Virginia) to Mary Pickford.
Belasco also produced, directed, wrote--or altered--such plays as
Madame Butterfly, The Rose of the Rancho, The Girl of the Golden
West, Zaza, The Easiest Way, DuBarry, The Music Master, The Re-
turn of Peter Grimm, Laugh, Clown, Laugh, Kiki, and The Gold
Diggers; in 1926 he produced and directed Lulu Belle.

Lulu Belle was Charles MacArthur's first play. It was written
in collaboration with playwright Edward Brewster Sheldon, whose
sister Mary married MacArthur's brother Alfred. Five years prior
to his death at seventy-eight (Thursday, May 14, 1931), seventy-
three year old Belasco brilliantly staged his massive production of
MacArthur and Sheldon's four-act play, and all the while masked
the drama's shortcomings. Belasco employed 112 performers, of
whom 93 were black (including a four-member jazz band) and 19
were white (in varying shades of burnt cork).

Sexy, sultry Lenore Ulric--Belasco's Galatea--had gained
fame in his productions of Kiki and Tiger Rose. She played the
wanton, high-yellow, fulminating femme fatale Lulu, with Henry
Hull as her mulatto lover, Harlem barber George Randall. The
controversial melodrama created a sensationally, slightly scandalous
success. Under instructions from Sheldon to curtail any "improvements" Belasco made to their play, MacArthur attended rehearsals
of Lulu Belle. Despite the co-author's objections, the "master of
the drama" cut an entire scene from the script.

LULU BELLE. Opened February 9, 1926; Belasco Theatre,
New York--461 performances. Produced and directed by David
Belasco; A drama by Edward Sheldon and Charles MacArthur;
Settings by Joseph Wickes' Studio; Costumes by George Had-
den; Lighting by Louis Hartman; Miss Ulric's Gowns by Berg-
dorf & Goodman; Properties by Matthew Purcell; Song: "Lulu
Belle," Music by Richard Myers; Lyric by Leo Robins; Band
directed by Earl Bumford

Lenore Ulric (Lulu Belle); Henry Hull (George Randall);
John Harrington [succeeded by Jack Hartley] (Butch
Cooper); Jean Del Val (The Vicompte De Villars); Tam-
many Young (Shorty Noyes); Sybil Bryant (Mrs. George
Randall); Thomas Trisvan (Walter Randall); Margaret Petty
(Violet Randall); Goldye M. Stiener (Vangie Bowtelle);
Elizabeth Williams (Mrs. Bowtelle); Ollie Burgoyne (Mabel
De Witt); Lorraine Hunter (Ada May Ramsay); Marguerite
Wyatt [succeeded by Hattie Christian] (Ivy Whiteside);

Edna Thomas (Valma Custer); George Callender [succeeded
by Oswald Alvaranga] (Mt. Vernon Jackson); William Talia-
fero (Royal Williams); Edna Thrower (Mrs. Royal Williams);
Edward Thompson (Herman); James Jackson (Lew); W. S.
Bell (Roscoe); Altomay Jones (Geranium Monroe); Jean
Ward (Stella La Vergne); Mildred Bell (Lovie Bowtelle);
Nellie R. Reynolds (Mrs. Monroe); Fannie Belle DeKnight
(Mrs. Frisbie); Evelyn Preer (Ruby Lee); Smothers Ward
(Eugene Frisbie); Mattie V. Wilkes (Mrs. Jackson); Oswald
Edinborough (Elmer Jackson); Seifert Pile (Clarence De
Voe); J. Louis Johnson (Brother Staley); Virgie Winfield
(Sister Sally); Annie Rhinelander (Sister Blossom); Per-
cival Vivian (Skeeter); Lawrence Eddinger (Uncle Gustus);
Eva Benton [succeeded by Mattie V. Wilkes] (Mrs. Trum-
bull); William St. James (Dr. J. Wilberforce Walker);
Fred Miller (Duke Weaver); J. W. Jackson (Happy); Allen
Waithe (Moke); Hemsley Winfield [succeeded by William
H. Raymond] (Joe); Clarissa Blue (A Flower Girl);
Zaidee Jackson (An Entertainer); Lillian Fairley, Mayme
Riley (Bridesmaids); Samuel Bolen (A Bartender); Minnie
Brown (Coat Room Girl); Barclay Trigg (Milton); Herman
Profit (Williams); Joseph Allenton (Bunny Delano); Mildred
Wayne (Grace Wild); Utoy D'tyl (Pussy Harrison); Sidney
Elliott [succeeded by Stephen Gross] (Fred Harrison);
Edward Hannery (Policeman/Sergeant Healy); Harold Seton
(An Ambulance Doctor); Anthony Knilling (Ambulance
Driver); George Thomas (Another Patrolman); William
Boag (Wilkins); Jane Ferrell (Barton)

The plot of Lulu Belle closely paralleled Prosper Mérimée's
Carmen, which had been considerably laundered in Ludovic Halévy
and Henri Meilhac's libretto for Georges Bizet's opera in 1875. Between lovers, Lulu Belle, a Harlem harlot, sings and dances at the
Elite Grotto cabaret. Lulu seduces mulatto barber George Randall
into leaving his wife and children and becoming her lover. Lulu
has an affair with prizefighter Butch Cooper. (Interestingly, Oscar
Hammerstein, II would reincarnate toreador Escamillo into prizefighter
Husky Miller in his reworking of Bizet's opera in 1943, called Carmen Jones.) She also coerces Randall into helping her hustle passionate tricks (including black dentist Dr. J. Wilberforce Walker
from whom they remove his wallet and a detachable gold tooth).
Randall is jailed after stabbing Butch Cooper during a cabaret brawl,
and Lulu leaves for Paris with her latest conquest, millionaire Vicompte de Villars. Lulu becomes Villars' mistress and the star of a
Parisian revue. Five years later Randall is released from Sing-Sing
prison. He locates Lulu in her luxurious Paris apartment where he
strangles her to death.

The Sheldon-MacArthur play opened at Philadelphia's Broad

Street Theatre on January 26, 1926. The Evening Bulletin commented, "The negro's place in this drama is as old as Othello but
totally different from anything that has gone before." Lulu Belle
opened on Broadway at the Belasco Theatre on February 9, 1926,
to play 461 performances. Burns Mantle (Daily News) reported,
"As a play and as a production Lulu Belle proves two points I have
often made. That David Belasco is the greatest of the physical
realists of the theatre, and that Lenore Ulric is the most understanding interpreter of primitive females the stage knows."

Time magazine considered the play less than a major contribution to the literature of the theatre and suggested, "If you do not
gag at the spectacle of a Negress courtesan with a white lover,
Lulu Belle will not, after some of the lurid entertainments that have
come this way recently, seem offensive." Alexander Woollcott (New
York Herald) saw Lulu Belle as "A brutal, sardonic, vivid play,
tumultuous and crowded with life." Hearst's American scribe Alan
Dale lashed out at the sensation-mongers, "For a time, the hypo-
crites with the putrid minds were silenced. Before such magnificent
stage work everything prurient was forgotten. It was perhaps the
most notable scene that Belasco ever staged."

Following the successful Broadway run Lulu Belle took to the
road, but Boston's Mayor Nichols banned the play and informed the
manager of Boston's Colonial theatre, Thomas B. Lathian (March 23,
1928), that Lulu Belle could not parade her wares in his pristine
province. Twenty-two years later Columbia Pictures filmed Lulu
Belle. Dorothy Lamour starred as a white New Orleans chanteuse
of easy virtue. The burnt-cork element disappeared and the white-
washed 1948 screenplay by Everett Freeman, which conformed to
Hollywood's then strict code of censorship, was properly considered
"a waste of effort."

THE NO 'COUNT BOY

Paul Green's one-act play The No 'Count Boy was first published in Theatre Arts magazine. Later it was produced by The
Little Theatre Tournament, conducted, in 1925, by Walter Hartwig
in co-operation with the Manhattan Little Theatre Club. The Little
Theatre of Dallas, Texas presented Green's The No 'Count Boy as
an entry in the tournament at Wallack's Theatre (New York on May
6, 1925), where the play won the David Belasco Trophy as the
best in the series.

A young black, romantic, gentle dreamer of a boy (Ben Smith)
in rural Eastern North Carolina entrances a young black girl Pheelie
(Geraldine Knight) with his alluring and imaginative description of
the world he has never seen. He entices Pheelie to desert her lustful lover Enos (Jack F. Hyman) and roam the earth with him forever

in peace and freedom. Pheelie's realistic granny (Margaret Bentley) refuses to permit her granddaughter to leave on the mythical
tour with that no 'count boy.

Paul Green (who died at the age of eighty-seven, Monday
May 4, 1981) was born in Barnett County near Lillington, North
Carolina (Saturday, March 17, 1894). He became a professor of
philosophy at his alma mater, The University of North Carolina.
Green wrote approximately forty one-act plays depicting poor
whites or blacks. Many of the plays were written for the Carolina
Playmakers, a student group led by Professor Frederick H. Koch,
which was geared to the development of native folk drama and the
production of original, untested scripts. Professor Koch's Chapel
Hill, North Carolina seminars were similar to, but not as famous
as, those of George Pierce Baker's 47 Workshop at Harvard University.

Paul Green's brief The No 'Count Boy had a great deal of
charm; considerable acclaim was given to it. Green's first full-
length play In Abraham's Bosom won the 1927 Pulitzer Prize. The
play opened at New York's MacDougal Street's Provincetown Playhouse on December 30, 1926, and moved successfully to Broadway's
Garrick Theatre to complete 200 performances. Directed by Jasper
Deeter, In Abraham's Bosom featured an excellent cast of black
actors, including Frank Wilson, Rose McClendon, Abbie Mitchell,
and Julius (Jules) Bledsoe. The theme of the tragedy was miscegenation. Mulatto Abraham McCranie, son of a white plantation-
owner Colonel McCranie, kills his white racist brother and in turn
is shot and killed.

White players in burnt cork played all the parts in The No
'Count Boy.

THE OCTOROON

The most famous nineteenth-century play dealing with the
subject of miscegenation was Dion Boucicault's well-constructed melodrama The Octoroon, or Life in Louisiana. Boucicault loosely based
his play on Mayne Reid's 1856 novel The Quadroon; or a Lover's
Adventure in Louisiana. Cleverly balancing his characters, Boucicault won sympathy from both the North and the South. He also
reduced Reid's one-quarter Negro quadroon to an one-eighth octoroon. James Gordon Bennett's Herald published inflammatory antiabolitionist editorials that damned the play as "Negro-worshipping
mania" and noted that it was disgustingly comparable to Harriet
Beecher Stowe's Uncle Tom's Cabin. At the same time, the editorials denounced Boucicault as being "imported into this country from
the British hotbed of abolition to fan the flames of sedition."

Boucicault responded to Bennett's diatribe on December 5, 1859, with,

> I believe the drama to be a proper and very effective in-
> strument to use in the dissection of all social matters.
> The Greeks thought so, who founded it; Molière thought
> so when he wrote Tartuffe; and a very humble follower of
> theirs thinks so too. It is by such means that the drama
> can be elevated into the social importance it deserves to
> enjoy. Therefore, I have involved in The Octoroon sketches
> of slave life, truthful I know, and I hope gentle and kind.

Dionysius Lardner Boursiquot was born in Dublin, Ireland presumably on Thursday, December 26, 1822 (or in 1820). He has been registered as one of the world's most prolific playwrights, having written or adapted approximately 125 to 150 plays. Sir Arthur Sullivan called Boursiquot "The Shakespeare of Ireland." Boursiquot's first play was a disastrous affair called A Legend of Devil's Dyke; it was produced at Brighton on October 1, 1854. In the play, the precocious young author, using the name of Lee Moreton, played the part of a rat-catcher named Teddy Rodent.

Dion altered the spelling of his surname to Boucicault, and his first success in the theatre came with his play London Assurance when he was about nineteen.* The play opened at Covent Garden in London on March 4, 1841, with a sterling cast, which included Charles Mathews, William Warren, and Mme. Vestris.

Boucicault spent four years in France where he married a much older widow of a Frenchman. His first wife's death had over- tones of mystery. His wife had fallen from an Alpine cliff in Swit- zerland and Dion had descended the mountain alone. Boucicault arrived in America in 1853 with his second wife, Agnes Kelly Robert- son, who had been born in Edinburgh, Scotland, on Christmas Day, 1833, and who was the ward of Charles and Ellen (Tree) Kean. The prolific playwright, however, obviously neglected to legally marry Agnes Robertson (this knowledge surfaced in 1888 when he wed actress Louise Thorndyke). Dion and Agnes Boucicault pro- duced three children, Nina, Aubrey and Dion, all of whom gained prominence on the English stage. Because of their father's casual matrimonial misfeasance, they were all also casually illegitimate.

Philadelphian playwrights Robert Montgomery Bird (author of the 1831 drama The Gladiator, given fame by Edwin Forrest and John McCullough) and George Henry Boker (who wrote the play Francesca da Rimini in 1855) had tried but failed to have a copy- right law passed for playwrights in the United States. In 1856 Boucicault was instrumental in having the American copyright law

---

*The original title of London Assurance was Country Matches, al- tered to Out of Town.

passed, extending it to cover playwrights. The French had unsuccessfully enacted a similar copyright bill in 1791 (which had
been backed by the Comite des Auteurs and Sociéte des Auteurs).
England's Copyright Bill, or Dramatic Authors Act of 1833, provided that no play could be produced without the author's permission; this bill was equally ineffectual as well as feebly enforced.

The "Irish Shakespeare" liberally borrowed and reworked
many plays. The Sidewalks of New York (also known in 1857 as
The Poor of New York) appeared in London as The Streets of Lon-
don and in Liverpool as The Poor of Liverpool; in Ireland it ap-
peared as The Poor of Dublin and in France as The Poor of Paris.
Boucicault based his geographically adaptable The Sidewalks of
New York on Eugene Nus and Edouard Brisebarre's French play
Les Pauvres de Paris, produced in 1856 at the Ambigu Comique
Théâtre in Paris. The play was translated for the English stage
in Stirling Coyne's Fraud and its Victims and Barrett's Pride and
Poverty, both seen in London in 1857.

Boucicault's play called The Streets of New York was given
a travesty-revival by F. Douglas Hutchins at the 14th Street Spanish Theatre on April 25, 1929, and the same year Edward Everett
Horton successfully revived the old play for six weeks in California.
The Streets of New York, or Poverty is No Crime reappeared on
Broadway on October 6, 1931, at the Forty-eighth Street Theatre
with Dorothy Gish, Rollo Peters, Romney Brent, Fania Marinoff,
and Moffat Johnson playing the revival for 87 performances. A
musical version of the play, which opened on October 29, 1963, at
off-Broadway's Maidman Playhouse, recorded a remarkable 318 per-
formances. Curiously, the old drah-ma reappeared at the Westport
County Playhouse in June of 1980 with Farley Granger, Katharine
Houghton, and Orson Bean. Boucicault's original play The Poor of
New York premiered at Wallack's Theatre on December 8, 1857, with
Lester Wallack, E. H. Sothern, Mrs. J. H. Allen, and T. B.
Johnston.

From Charles Dickens' The Cricket on the Hearth and a French
play Le Marchand d'Enfants, Boucicault produced his play Dot in
1859 and returned to Dickens' Nicholas Nickleby the same year for
his play Smike. That same year Boucicault wrote a purely American
drama, The Octoroon, or Life in Louisiana, and was accused of
borrowing scenes from DeWailly and Texier's French version of
Uncle Tom's Cabin and a photographic incident from Albany Fon-
blanque's English novel The Filibuster, plus the general theme of
Shirley Brooks's play The Creole; or Love's Fetters produced in
London at the Lyceum Theatre in 1857.

The theme of miscegenation had also been dramatized in J. T.
Trowbridge's play Neighbor Jackwood, produced at the Boston Museum on March 16, 1857. Trowbridge's drama of the rescue and
protection of Camille, an octoroon, until her marriage to white Hector

Dunburg, played on the Boston stage for the next eight years.
The tragedy of mixed blood was also central to Mrs. Stowe's novel
Dred, a Tale of the Dismal Swamp, which was adapted to the stage
in several versions in 1856. But Boucicault's melodrama The Octoroon was infinitely superior in every way to any previous treatment
of the subject of miscegenation.

The usually impeccably definitive and accurate historian and
professor of dramatic literature at Columbia University, George
Odell, erroneously recorded the opening date of Boucicault's The
Octoroon as December 5, 1859. The Winter Garden Theatre "A
Conservatory of the Arts" (until October 1858 known as the Metro-
politan Theatre) announced on December 5, 1859:

> No performance. The author of the new Drama having re-
> quired special rehearsals of new machinery and scenery;
> therefore tomorrow, Tuesday, December 6, 1859 will be the
> first night of a New Play in Five Acts by Dion Boucicault,
> Esq., the author of many popular Dramatic Works. NEW
> SCENERY, APPROPRIATE COSTUMES, MR. BOUCICAULT
> as Wah-n-tee, A Lepan Indian Chief; MISS AGNES ROBERT-
> SON as ZOE, the Octoroon.

The original cast also included Joseph Jefferson as Salem
Scudder; A. H. Davenport (George Peyton); Mrs. J. H. Allen
(Dora Sunnyside); T. B. Johnston (Jacob McCloskey); George Holland (Squire Sunnyside). Mrs. Dunn was the black cook Dido,
with Miss Ione Burke as the young slave Paul. George W. Jamieson
played the faithful slave, Old Pete.

The Octoroon's drama related villainous Yankee Jacob McCloskey's swindling of half the late Judge Peyton's Terrebone Plantation
(including ownership of his slaves). To secure foreclosure of Peyton's Terrebone, McCloskey kills young black servant boy Paul from
whom he steals a letter and check (the check would have insured
Mrs. Peyton's financial stability and prevented the sale of the property). Dedicated, honest, and shrewd Yankee Salem Scudder has
been unable to rectify the late Judge's gross mismanagement of the
plantation. Terrebone is sold to Squire Sunnyside and the slaves
are auctioned off to the highest bidder. McCloskey, lusting after
Judge Peyton's beautiful octoroon daughter, Zoe, has been rebuffed
by her in his offer that she become his mistress--but, of course,
never his wife. McCloskey outbids everyone and buys Zoe for
$25,000.

An accidentally exposed photographic plate (discovered by
Salem Scudder) proves McCloskey to be the murderer of Paul. Mc-
Closkey tries to escape lynching by setting afire the cotton boat
Magnolia, but Paul's close friend the Indian Wah-no-tee tracks the
killer into the swamp and kills him. Zoe rejects George Peyton's
love for her, "Do you know who I am? There is a gulf between

us as wide as your love and as deep as my despair. That is the ineffaceable curse of Cain. Of the blood that fills my heart, one drop in eight is black--but the one black drop gives me despair, for I'm an unclean thing--forbidden by the laws--I'm an Octoroon!" Unaware that McCloskey is dead, and preferring death to becoming his slave and mistress, Zoe drinks poison and dies in George's arms.

The New York Times, on December 7, 1859, published this review:

> Mr. Boucicault's new drama of Southern life called The Octoroon--concerning which, for a fortnight past, the wildest rumors have been circulated, rumors tending to impress the public mind with a sense of something awful and "irrepressible"--was produced here on Tuesday night. The event passed off with not more excitement than was justly due to the writer of "many popular dramatic works" and the author of the new piece. Neither the civil nor the military arm was called into operation, except in the pleasant way of assisting in the general applause--Nothing in the world can be more harmless and noncomittal than Mr. Boucicault's play. It contains no superfluous appeals--no demonstrations in favor of the "down-trodden"--no silly preachings of pious negroes--no buncombe of Southern patriots--no tedious harangues of Eastern philanthropists. The Octoroon is simply and purely what it pretends to be--"a picture of Life in Louisiana."

Joseph Jefferson later recalled that The Octoroon was successful simply because "it was non-committal"; also, Boucicault's clever writing had balanced sympathies equally between the North and the South through the Yankee and Southern characters and the slaves. Jefferson added, "As a matter of act, Boucicault printed on his bills, 'Nothing extenuate, nor aught set down in malice'; also 'Tros Tyriusque mihi nullo discrimine agetur'."

Dion Boucicault and Agnes Robertson withdrew from the cast of The Octoroon on Wednesday, December 14, 1859, over a dispute with the Winter Garden Theatre management regarding salary increases. They were replaced in the cast the following evening by Mrs. J. H. Allen as Zoe and Harry Pearson as Wah-no-tee. Mrs. J. H. Stoddart took over Mrs. Allen's former part of Dora Sunnyside and Mr. Harrison succeeded Harry Pearson in the part of Captain Ratts of the cotton-boat steamer Magnolia. Agnes defensively wrote to Bennett's Herald, "I will not permit my name (or my husband's, if I can help it) to be associated with any scheme to make money out of a political excitement--especially on such a subject as slavery and at such a moment as this."

Agnes's astonishing damnation of her husband's play (which

dealt not only with slavery but with miscegenation) was but a cov-
erup for the Boucicaults' insistent financial demands. Agnes's tirade
obviously met with Dion's approval. A month later he sold the rights
to The Octoroon to the owner of the Bowery Theatre. This sudden
reversal of ingenious sentiment was pure fiction since two weeks before, Boucicault had strongly urged the Winter Garden management
"to work up the anti-slavery feeling of the community to benefit the
run of the piece." He had also vigorously opposed James Gordon
Bennett's antiabolitionist editorial in his letter to the Herald on December 5, 1859, one day prior to the opening of the play. Neither
the departure of the Boucicaults nor Agnes's published diatribe
forced The Octoroon to close. Until January 21, 1860, the drama
continued playing to capacity audiences.

Thomas Bartley Campbell (who died of paresis on July 30,
1885, at the age of forty-five at the Middletown Insane Asylum)
wrote a melodrama called The White Slave; the play opened at Haverly's Theatre on April 3, 1882. Campbell's White Slave was an innocent pure-white heroine who had been accused of being an octoroon and forced to survive the tortures of the damned, which included escaping from an exploding river steamer reminiscent of
Boucicault's blazing cotton-boat Magnolia in The Octoroon, or Life
in Louisiana. There were frequent revivals of Campbell's "stirring
melodrama." Long-suffering Liza remained on the nation's boards
for over fifteen years.

The Octoroon was played with great success and added encomiums across the nation. As he would with many plays, David
Belasco "retouched and rearranged" Boucicault's melodrama in San
Francisco's production on July 8, 1878. He did the same for Gustave
Frohman's production of The Octoroon, which opened at San Francisco's Baldwin Theatre for two weeks on June 12, 1882. Belasco's
genius for staging included augmenting the cast of The Octoroon
with the entire Callender Minstrels company. A San Francisco critic
noted, "The clever pen of Mr. Belasco had evidently elaborated the
(slave) auction scenes." Among Belasco's "re-arrangements" were
specialty numbers, dances, and songs performed by Callender Minstrels contingent and a highly effective scene of slaves. In his
biography of Belasco, William Winter describes the slaves as "making
their way homeward, at evening, through the cotton fields, singing
as they went, and the result was extraordinarily picturesque and
impressive. More than 150 persons, besides the actors of the chief
characters, participated in the performance, and the slave sale and
the burning of the river steamboat Magnolia were portrayed with
notable semblance of actuality." Mrs. F. M. Bates was Zoe--Harry
Colton (McCloskey); Edward Marble (Salem Scudder); George Osborne (Wah-no-tee); Kitty Belmour (Paul); W. T. Doyle (George
Peyton); Edward Barrett (Old Peter); the Sunnywides (R. G. Marsh
and Abbie Pierce).

Twenty years after the première performance of The Octoroon,

or Life in Louisiana, the play was revived at Broadway's Haverly's
Theatre on November 17, 1879, with Florence Elmore as Zoe, Frank
Losee as McCloskey, H. S. Duffield as Wah-no-tee, J. N. Gotthold
as Salem Scudder, Charles Mason as George Peyton, Madge Butler
as Paul, L. R. Stockwell as Uncle Pete, J. E. Kirkwood as Sunny-
side, and Rena Maeder as Dora. Numerous revivals of The Octoroon
were mounted through the years. New York's Fourteenth Street
Theatre revived the melodrama on June 12, 1905, with Laura Wall
as Zoe--Tully Marshall (Wah-no-tee); E. J. Ratcliffe (McCloskey);
John Fenton (Salem Scudder); Charles Dow Clark (Old Pete); Marion
Fairfax (Paul); J. Griffith Wray (George Peyton); Velma Berrell
(Dora); George Turner (Mr. Sunnyside); Katherine King (Dido).

The Vitagraph Company filmed Boucicault's play The Octoroon,
or Life in Louisiana under the title of Bartley Campbell's play The
White Slave. The two-reel motion picture was released on May 31,
1913, with Clara Kimball Young as Zoe, Herbert L. Barry as Wah-
no-tee; William Ranous as McCloskey; and Leo Delaney as Salem
Scudder. Earle Williams played George Peyton; Lillian Walker was
Dora Sunnyside; Kenneth Casey was the young black slave, Paul;
and William Shea was Old Pete. The same year, the Kalem Company
filmed their version of Boucicault's play in Florida under the title
of The Octoroon. Released on December 1, 1913, the three-reel
picture had Marguerite Courtot as Zoe, Robert G. Vignola as the
Indian Wah-no-tee, Benjamin Ross as McCloskey, Harry Millarde
as Salem Scudder, Guy Coombs as George Peyton, Miriam Cooper
as Dora, and Robert Patterson (blacked-up) as the young slave,
Paul.

The Octoroon, or Life in Louisiana returned to Broadway on
March 12, 1929, at Maxine Elliott's Theatre, it was produced by
John Leffler and staged by Frank Hatch. The New Yorker magazine
felt the production confirmed "Boucicault's theatrical merits" despite
"an average stock-company production," but he found the play's
rhetoric and rococo plot still highly effective and advocated that
"no one should miss The Octoroon." The 1929 revival featured Inez
Plummer as Zoe, with Herbert Corthell as Salem Scudder. David
Landau played McCloskey; William Nunn, Old Pete; Maurice Freeman,
Wah-no-tee; James Meighan, George Peyton; Margaret Bayers, Paul--
a Boy Slave; Marjorie Dille, Dora Sunnyside; John E. Henshaw, Mr.
Sunnyside. The program noted, "The present revival is in every
way similar to the original production, even to the inclusion of the
playing and singing of pre-Civil War ballads between the acts."

John W. Isham's musical revue The Octoroons (also known as
Darktown Derby) had found an audience in 1895 and the octoroon
and quadroon, both as character and as subject became popular on
the dramatic stage (though less successful when the plays they
were in were set to music). Laurence Stalling, who had co-authored
the 1924 drama What Price Glory? with Maxwell Anderson, wrote the
book and lyrics for Deep River. Franke Harling's musical score for

Deep River was a curious combination of spirituals and jazz, coun-
terpointed with overtones of Puccini. Beautifully produced and directed by Arthur Hopkins at Broadway's Imperial Theatre on October 4, 1926, as "A Native Opera With Jazz," Deep River was both
ahead of--and a failure within--its time; the musical disappeared
after thirty-two performances.

Deep River wove its tragic tale around what was described
as "a melange of whites, creoles and negroes"; the play had been
set against the background of the spring Quadroon Ball in 1835
New Orleans. The Quadroon Ball was an annual event designed to
help the rich Creole gentlemen select the most beautiful of the
quadroon debutantes for their mistresses. Older quadroon Octavie
(Rose McClendon) warns the hopeful girls that only at their first
Quadroon Ball will they find true love. The wealthy leader of the
Creole Society is temperamental and ruthlessly dangerous Brussard
(Luis Alberni), who is intent on replacing his recently discarded,
unfaithful quadroon mistress with lovely and charming young quadroon Mugette (Lottice Howell). Mugette attends the Voodoo Queen's
(Charlotte Murray) ceremony in the Place Congo for a voodoo charm
so that she might win the love of white, handsome Kentuckian Hazzard Streatfield (Roberto Ardelli). Infuriated at Colonel Streatfield's (Frederick Burton) insults, Brussard kills him in a duel.
Hazzard vengefully kills Brussard at Monsieur Hercule's (Antonio
Salerno) Quadroon Ball, but he is fatally wounded. Mugette dances
at the ball, desperately aware that Octavie's predictions will be un-
fulfilled.

Burns Mantle (Daily News) deplored Broadway's loss of such
"a lovely thing" as Deep River, but he sadly observed, "the opera
going public would not come down to it, nor could the theatre public rise to it." Brooks Atkinson (the New York Times) classified
Deep River as "more like an animated panorama than a drama" and
found the script was "Little more than an incident in its dramatic
value--clearly the libretto does not suffice to bind all the florid
details of this little fable together." Alan Dale (the American)
wrote, "Deep River skipped and jumped from grand opera to ora-
torio, and from play form to no form at all--It was all absolutely
operatic and nothing more."

John Anderson (Evening Journal) wrote "Somehow Deep River
seems to miss by a narrow but fatal margin a memorable achievement.
It stands on the stage at the Imperial merely as a fine, honest and
often beautiful attempt, lacking complete fulfillment." But Anderson
singled out one performer for unstinting praise:

> An actress who created out of a few wisps of material an
> unforgettable picture of a proudly withered woman in the
> house of quadroon girls. Hers was a faded but imperious
> beauty, the gauntly tragical grandeur of stately ruins.
> She caught a whole day and time in the swish of wide black

lace along a moonlit patio, and the lurking hurt in eyes
that had seen too much. Her name is Rose McClendon.

With the possible exception of Julie in Show Boat, the beautiful
mulatto or quadroon seldom succeeded on the musical stage.

Edna Ferber's 1941 novel, Saratoga Trunk, is an intriguing
tale of the adventures of Clio Dulaine, granddaughter of a black
woman and illegitimate daughter of a mulatto mother and an aristocratic Creole. The story is set in 1800 New Orleans. Saratoga
Trunk was boringly filmed by Warner Bros. in 1946. The movie
starred Ingrid Bergman and Gary Cooper. In 1959 Morton DaCosta
adapted the novel to the musical stage as Saratoga, which opened
at Broadway's Winter Garden Theatre on December 7, 1959. Harold
Arlen and Johnny Mercer's musical score for Saratoga was undistinguished and unmemorable. The show failed after eighty performances despite being beautifully mounted with settings and costumes
by Cecil Beaton and excellent performances by a capable cast headed
by Carol Lawrence and Howard Keel.

Brooks Atkinson (the New York Times) found Saratoga to be
"hackneyed and dull" with "lacklustre tunes" that became "increasingly innocuous." Noting the array of professional talent responsible
for the production, Atkinson added, "All the old pros are off their
form in Saratoga," and adaptor Morton DaCosta "has not been able
to sail his own scenario out of the doldrums." Gerald Bordman
(American Musical Theatre) wrote, "In proper hands there was no
reason why Edna Ferber's colorful period piece about New Orleans
and Saratoga could not have been made as rich a musical as had
her Show Boat. But the fine talents that labored on the new adaptation were distressingly uninspired."

One hundred and two years after its Broadway première,
The Octoroon, or Life in Louisiana was produced by New York's
Phoenix Theatre on January 27, 1961; its forty-five performances
were directed by Stuart Vaughn. Naturally, the play was dated
(any period piece in revival would have been), but Boucicault's
theatrical genius was still evident. Howard Taubman (the New
York Times) wrote,

> Although Boucicault's object was to score a success in the
> theatre, The Octoroon in its day stirred genuine emotions.
> Even today the auctioning of the slaves, despite the dated
> orotundity, can touch one, and so can Zoe's brooding on
> the shame of her blood. And when the slaves and Zoe
> prepare for their grim fate on the auction block as they
> sing "What Wonderous Love Is This," The Octoroon becomes
> honestly affecting.

Taubman added, "Sophisticated theatregoers will be amused by
Boucicault's flamboyance as they will be impressed by the Phoenix

faithful deadpan presentation. But they should not forget that
Boucicault's literary equals thrive in our day, too."

Juliet Randall was Zoe in the Phoenix revival--Franklin Cover
(Salem Scudder); John Heffernan (McCloskey); Robert Blackburn
(George Peyton); Ray Reinhardt (Wah-no-tee); Gerry Judd (Dora
Sunnyside); Albert Quinton (Squire Sunnyside). In the former
burnt-cork parts were black actors P. Jay Sidney as Old Pete,
Alan Weeks as Paul, Vinnette Carroll as Dido, and others.

ROSEANNE

Nan Bagby Stephens of Atlanta, Georgia, wrote a one-act play,
which, in 1923, she expanded into her first full-length play, Roseanne. Produced by Mary H. Kilpatrick, Roseanne opened on Saturday, December 29, 1923, at the Greenwich Village Theatre and was
relocated in the Punch and Judy Theatre to complete forty-one performances. The entire white cast of Roseanne appeared in burnt
cork as citizens of a rural Georgia town.

Stephens's Roseanne, a poor, middle-aged, hard-working black
laundress is enamored of pompously dictatorial Reverend Cicero
Brown, whose ego has been seriously inflated by the doting Ladies
Society of Mt. Zion Church. Devious and greedy Reverend Brown,
discontent with his exorbitant demands on his poor, black, and awed
congregation, persuades Roseanne's much younger sister Leola to
steal Roseanne's hard-earned money--money she was carefully saving
to purchase her humble home. Reverend Brown, fearful of exposure,
terrorizes innocently duped Leola into leaving town. Roseanne finds
Leola in Atlanta. Before dying, Leola reveals the perfidy of the
good Reverend. During a revival service at Mt. Zion Church, Roseanne exposes the duplicity of Reverend Brown to his adoring congregation who viciously vent their wrath on the religious faker and
plan vengefully, to lynch him with the rope from the church bell.
Ever-forgiving Roseanne shelters the minister in her home, and he
escapes unharmed during the night. Roseanne resumes her menial
work with great patience and renewed, albeit desperate, hope for
a brighter tomorrow.

Blonde and beautiful Chrystal Herne, who would gain fame as
George Kelly's Craig's Wife two years later, gave a stunning performance in the title role of Roseanne. Alexander Woollcott wrote,
"Chrystal Herne is Roseanne and hers is a superb performance,
rich and imaginative and free." The New York Times reported,
"Interesting as the play is, however, it cannot be said that it is
convincing--In the writing of the dialogue there is something less,
or more, than African. At times it is positively literary, or rather,
litteresque." The New York Telegram added, "Roseanne is a folk
play of everyday negro life in Georgia today, and is so graphic and

ROSEANNE, by Nan Bagby Stephens

Greenwich Village Theatre
Produced by Mary H. Kilpatrick
December 29, 1923--41 performances

Shubert-Riviera Theatre
Produced by Jules Hurtig
March 10, 1924--16 performances

Character	Greenwich Village cast	Shubert-Riviera cast
Roseanne	Chrystal Herne	Rose McClendon
Cicero Brown	John Harrington	Charles S. Gilpin
Leola	Kathleen Comegys	Evelyn Ellis
Sis Tempy Snow	Marie Taylor	Lillian Brown
Sis Lindy Gray	Tracy L'Engle	Margaret H. Brown
Andy Johnson	Sterling Holloway	Walter Hilliard
Son, a blind singer	Blaine Cordner	Lloyd Gibbs
Rodney	Murray Bennett	C. Edward Brown
Winnie Caldwell, the organist	Irma Caldwell	Jeanne Roberts
Alex Gray	Robert Strauss	Louis Schooler
Dacas Snow	Leslie M. Hunt	Arthur Gaines
Dot Randolph	Grace Stephens	
Selena Trail	Rosa Powell	Minnie Johnson
Bee Cummings	Mary Vandiver	Marian Laventore
Polly Satterwhite	Marguerite Harding	Armintine Latimer
Vashti Gatewood	Alice Bussey	Bessie Whitman
Pearl Pollard	Emma Gadsden	
Normal Coffee	Chappell Corey, Jr.	
Zack Toomer	Grover Burgess	Charles H. Downs
Morninglory Trimble	Conway Sawyer	Marion Taylor
Uncle Dick Landrum	Brown Bates	John W. Turner
Dootsie Stork	Frances Manning	
Al Shell	Albert Barber	Joseph Loomis
Frenchie Fowler	Elizabeth Braxton	
Elisha Holt	Robert Craik	

moves forward so clearly and dramatically in its unfolding of a simple, yet absorbing, story that it is one of the most refreshing plays
this year has shown."

E. W. Osborn (the Evening World) wrote, "Taking to old
clothes and burnt cork demanded by this unique drama is a radical
departure for Miss Herne. She makes it with the facility and the
thoroughgoing sincerity of a true artist of the theatre." Osborn
described the play as "a serious, an enlightening, an entertaining,
a well-constructed and a decidedly worth-while dramatic offering"
and extolled the emotionally exciting and well performed revival
scene: "Negro spirituals are sung by the company--with characteristic fervor, and without a trace of levity or burlesque, this act
rises to the climactic entrance of the denunciatory Roseanne."
Actress Dorothy Donnelly called Roseanne "A real achievement of
the American Theatre profoundly emotional and with an enormous
quality of spirituality."

Roseanne reappeared on March 10, 1924, at New York's
Shubert-Riviera Theatre; it was produced by Jules Hurtig with an
all-black cast. The remarkably fine black actress Rose McClendon
was Roseanne and Charles S. Gilpin (the original Brutus Jones in
Eugene O'Neill's play the Emperor Jones for 204 performances in
1920) played the part of the Reverend Cicero Brown. Alexander
Woollcott's panegyric about talented Rose McClendon read as follows:
"There were times when the flash of her performance suggested
that here was a dark Duse rising to the call of a fine role. Excellent too, was Evelyn Ellis as the erring sister." But, according to
Woollcott, as the shameless, hypocritical minister, "Mr. Gilpin was
given to fitful grimaces and all the portentuousness of the bad, bad
stock actor."

A comparison of the blacked-up white cast at the Greenwich
Village Theatre and the all-black cast of Roseanne uptown is shown
on page 335.

SCARLET SISTER MARY

The winners of the 1928-1929 Pulitzer Prize were Burton J.
Hendrick, for his biography The Training of an American: The
Earlier Life and Letters of Walter H. Page; Fred Albert Shannon,
for his history The Organization and Administration of the Union
Army--1861-1865; Stephen Vincent Benet, for his poem John Brown's
Body; Elmer Rice, for his play Street Scene--and a $1,000 award for
the best novel went to Julia Mood Peterkin for her tale of Scarlet
Sister Mary.

Julia Peterkin was born in South Carolina on Sunday, October
31, 1880, and died at Fort Motte, South Carolina, on Thursday,

August 10, 1961, at the age of eighty. She had based her novel
on the Gullah Negroes who were living on her two-thousand-acre
Lang Syne Plantation at Fort Motte, South Carolina. The Gullah
Negroes of coastal South Carolina never intermarried with other
races. They retained their own communal characteristics and were
unique in their distinctive dialect. Spoken in rhythm, the Gullah
dialect was a linguistic mixture of Huguenot French, African patois,
and native American English; Gullah syntax was often incomprehen-
sible. Mrs. Peterkin utilized her knowledge of and exposure to the
Gullahs in her later books Bright Skin (1932), Roll, Jordan Roll
(1933), and A Plantation Christmas (1934).

Scarlet Sister Mary is the tale of pregnant Sister Mary's
(called Si-May-e) marriage to her ne'er-do-well lover, July, who
deserts her for black siren Cinders. Mary, "a virtuous sinner in
a pagan world," gives birth to July's son, Unex (unexpected) and
rebels against the restrictive mores of the community by acquiring
July's twin brother, June, for her lover, by whom she has a daughter, Seraphine. Robust Mary's passionate encounter with a stranger
from Poughkeepsie produces a son named Keepsie (since Mary neglected to ask the stranger his name). After having nine children
and affirming her vigorous freedom of living ("Everybody has a self-
ness that makes the root of his life and being"), Mary confesses her
years of sinnin'; she is baptized and accepted once again by the
church that for years, had shunned and denounced her. Twenty
years later, July returns to the now-purified, eternal mother, Mary.
He asks forgiveness but she sends him away, dedicating her energies to God and her children.

Regal Ethel Barrymore, born on Friday, August 15, 1879,
in Philadelphia, Pennsylvania, became fascinated with Julia Peterkin's novel, and she commissioned Daniel Reed to dramatize the
story. Reed stopped working on a dramatization of Peterkin's first
novel Black April (written in 1927) to develop a play from Scarlet
Sister Mary; but Mary was a novel that obstinately resisted adaptation to the stage. Edward Harold Crosby wrote in the Dramatic
News (In December of 1930 prior to the play's opening in Boston),

> Those who have read the novel of Mrs. Julia Peterkin will
> wonder with me how any drama could be made out of the
> material furnished and still keep within the law. I have
> perused the book very carefully avoiding the vulgarity and
> blasphemy as much as possible and beyond a graphic dis-
> sertation of a peculiar type of Southern Negro, the customs
> and religious views, its superstitions and abnormal views on
> social matters, there is little else save to the student of
> ethnology.

Daniel Reed, director of a Columbia, South Carolina, theatre
and a personal friend of Julia Peterkin, explained the play's strange
dialectic,

The most interesting of all Negro dialects is, perhaps, the
Gullah--There are variations in the different localities, but
the root speech is the same and the Negroes in these sec-
tions seem to have preserved their African linguistic qualities more than any other class of blacks living in a white
society. They seem the least contaminated. Perhaps, most
careful and insistent upon an honest reproduction of the
black quality of speech and manners in the theatre is Miss
Ethel Barrymore, who directed her own production of Scarlet
Sister Mary, Julia Peterkin's Pulitzer Prize novel which I
made into a play. Miss Barrymore is sensitive to the strange
subtleties of Gullah dialect and in her various contacts with
the Negroes who use it she has acquired a true knowledge
of it.

Ethel Barrymore later said, "I knew the minute I read the
story that I must play the role if it were at all possible." But in
later years Miss Barrymore bitterly recalled what became the biggest
flop in her career, "I think it's mob psychology. The people got
together and said they'd not see me black. That's heartbreaking.
Why, if a play has art, if it's fine drama what difference would it
make if I were colored green?"

Scarlet Sister Mary opened at the Hartman Theatre in Columbus, Ohio on September 25, 1930. After an extensive tour in the
Midwest, where the drama received unanimous pans, Miss Barrymore
ventured to Broadway as black Sister Mary. Produced by Lee Shubert and directed by E. M. Blyth (Ethel Barrymore), with settings
by Watson Barratt and costumes by Orry Kelly, Scarlet Sister Mary
opened at the Shubert's Ethel Barrymore Theatre (the inestimable
Ethel had inaugurated the theatre on December 20, 1928 when she
portrayed another Sister--Gracia, a catholic nun--in Gregorio Mar-
tinez Sierra's 1916 drama The Kingdom of God).

Seventeen-year-old Ethel Barrymore Colt made her stage debut
as Mary's daughter Seraphine in Scarlet Sister Mary, and the Barrymore's cousin Georgie Drew Mendum joined her in blackface as Doll.
Other unaccomplished and unlikely "blacks" were Estelle Winwood
(Cinders), Beatrice Perry (Maum Hannah), Walter Gilbert (July) and
Marjorie Main (Gracey). They were backed by spirituals sung by
ten members of the Heavenly Gate Singers. For the opening of
Scarlet Sister Mary (November 25, 1930), the patrician and elegant
fifty-one-year-old Ethel Barrymore wore burnt cork, a shapeless
calico dress, and flat shoes. According to the gentlemen of the
press, the evening was not an occasion for rejoicing or dancing in
the streets, or shouting out hozannahs.

Prior to the opening of the play on Broadway, Percy Hammond
in New York's Herald Tribune on Sunday, October 12, 1930, succinctly recommended the proper approach to Miss Barrymore's blackface bacchanal,

The publishers of New York newspapers are notorious for their chivalry. They are always eager to aid pretty women in distress. So it is suggested to them that they prohibit their drama experts from going to see Miss Barrymore in Scarlet Sister Mary and describing her in terms which might not be sufficiently rhapsodic--Might it not be enough to merely publish that she appeared last night as a notable Negress in a play called Scarlet Sister Mary, supported by an [watch out for that knife!] "adequate" company and greeted by the usual Barrymore audience. Thus would the duties of journalism be approximated and an incensed artiste be soothed.

Hammond's review of the opening restricted his usual perspective and reduced his views to a statement of production credits and plot. Hammond noted, "What a jam the gutsier critics are in today! If they compliment Miss Barrymore and her play it will be said that she whipped them into subservience. And if they dare to remonstrate, they will be accused of persecution."

SCARLET SISTER MARY. Opened November 25, 1930, Ethel Barrymore Theatre, New York--24 performances.

Produced by Lee Shubert; A drama by Daniel Reed adapted from the novel by Julia Peterkin; Directed by E. M. Blyth; Settings by Watson Barratt; Costumes by Orry Kelly; Choir and Orchestra directed by Maurice Nitke; Stage manager, Edward A. McHugh

Ethel Barrymore (Sister Mary--called Si May-e); Beatrice Terry (Maum Hannah); Horace Braham (Budda Ben--Hannah's Son); Estelle Winwood (Cinder); Marjorie Main (Gracey); John Roseleigh (June); Walter Gilbert (July); Leo Kennedy (Cousin Andrew); William B. Mack (Daddy Cudjoe); Georgie Drew Mendum (Doll); Herbert Gentry (Big Boy); Anita Rothe (Mona); Ethel Barrymore Colt (Seraphine); Alan Campbell (Brunton); Marcel Dill (Thatcher); Daniel Bagnell (Brer Dee); Albert Ridge (Unex); Charles Quigley (Wade); Denise Morris (Tressie); Burke Clarke (Luke); Blanche Collins (Tussie); Wilbur Cox (Gadsen); Marcel Dill (Reverend Duncan); Theodore de Corsia (Big Boy--at age of 30); Malcolm Soltan (Unex-- at age of 20)

The Heaven Gate Singers: Sylvia Allen, Alice Cannon, Joseph Christian, Helen Dowdy, Toussaint Duers, Sam H. Gray, Frank Jackson, Bertha Powell, William Raymond, Mabel Ridley

Most of the appraisers on the aisle were clearly embarrassed by the proceedings. Richard Lockridge (the Evening Sun) carefully reported,

> Miss Barrymore, with all her brightness, shines fitfully through another mediocre play; a diffuse thing which is moderately loyal to the novel without being the novel, which is ostensibly a play without ever fully attaining drama. From Miss Barrymore's end of the cast to the other there is no actor or an actress who, for any sustained period, suggests anything more indigenous to the Negro race than good, old-fashioned blackface.

The New Yorker magazine titled their review "Mrs. Bones" and allowed that "When an actress of Ethel Barrymore's intelligence and judgement decides to black up and play Negress, she must have some good reason for it--Scarlet Sister Mary does not offer much of an evening's entertainment." Robert Garland (Evening Telegram) kindly noted that "Miss Barrymore--does what she can with a role to which she is amazingly unsuited." Forty years later Brooks Atkinson recalled, "She put on mulatto make-up to appear in a Negro play called Scarlet Sister Mary, in which white actors played Negroes in blackface. The result was embarrassing."

<u>OTHELLO</u> PERFORMANCE HISTORY

The following is a performance history of <u>Othello</u> in England and America, however, it is but a sampling of innumerable performances.

	Othello	Iago	Desdemona
1604	November 1, 1604: First performance with Richard Burbage as Othello		
1660	Nathaniel Burt	Walter Clun	
1669	Nathaniel Burt	Michael Mohun	Margaret Hughes
	Charles Hart	Michael Mohun	Mrs. Cox
1674	Nathaniel Burt	Michael Mohun	
1675	Nathaniel Burt	Michael Mohun	
1683	Thomas Betterton		
1684	Thomas Betterton		
1689	Thomas Betterton		
	Robert Wilks	Joseph Ashbury	
1691	Thomas Betterton	Samuel Sanford	Mrs. Bracegirdle
1703	Thomas Betterton	John Verbruggen	Mrs. Bracegirdle
1704	Thomas Betterton	John Verbruggen	
1705	Thomas Betterton	John Verbruggen	
1707	Thomas Betterton	John Verbruggen	Mrs. Bracegirdle
1708	John Thurmond	Theophilus Keene	
1709	Thomas Betterton	Colley Cibber	
1710	John Thurmond	Jack Shepherd	
	Barton Booth	Theophilus Keene	Mrs. Bradshaw
1711–	Barton Booth	Theophilus Keene	Mrs. Bradshaw
1718	James Quin	Lacy Ryan	Mrs. Santlow
1720	Barton Booth	Colley Cibber	Mrs. Porter
	James Quin	Lacy Ryan	Mrs. Seymour
1721	James Quin	Lacy Ryan	Mrs. Porter
	Barton Booth	Colley Cibber	Mrs. Bradshaw
1722	Charles Beckingham		
	Barton Booth	Colley Cibber	
	James Quin	Lacy Ryan	Mrs. Seymour
1723	Barton Booth	Colley Cibber	
	James Quin	Lacy Ryan	
1724	Barton Booth	Colley Cibber	
1725	James Quin	Lacy Ryan	
	Barton Booth	Colley Cibber	
1726	Barton Booth	Colley Cibber	
1727	Barton Booth	Colley Cibber	
1728	James Quin	Lacy Ryan	
	Ralph Elrington	Colley Cibber	

	Othello	Iago	Desdemona
1729	William Mills	Colley Cibber	
1730	William Paget	James Rosco	
	Henry Giffard	James Rosco	
	James Quin	Lacy Ryan	
	William Mills	Colley Cibber	
	Mr. Royer	Mr. Roberts	
1731	James Quin	Lacy Ryan	Mrs. Younger
	William Mills	Colley Cibber	
	Dennis Delane	James Rosco	
1732	James Quin	Lacy Ryan	
	Dennis Delane	James Rosco	
1733	Dennis Delane	James Rosco	
	James Quin	Lacy Ryan	
	John Mills	William Mills	
1734	Colley Cibber	A. Hallam	
	James Quin	Colley Cibber	
	Samuel Stephens	Lacy Ryan	
	Robert Drury		
1735	Dennis Delane	James Rosco	
	Mr. Freeman	Mr. Oakley	
	James Quin	Colley Cibber	
	Charles Hulett	James Rosco	
	Samuel Stephens	Lacy Ryan	
1736	James Quin	William Mills	Mrs. Cibber
1737	Dennis Delane	Lacy Ryan	Mrs. Horton
	Samuel Stephens	James Rosco	Mrs. Stevens
	James Quin	William Mills	Mrs. Cibber
1738	Dennis Delane	Lacy Ryan	Mrs. Horton
	Samuel Stephens	A. Hallam	Mrs. Vincent
	James Quin	William Mills	Mrs. Cibber
1739	James Quin	William Mills	Mrs. Giffard
	Samuel Stephens	Lacy Ryan	Mrs. Horton
1740	James Quin	William Mills	Mrs. Pritchard
	William Walker	Mr. Paget	Mrs. Giffard
1741	Dennis Delane	William Mills	Mrs. Mills
	Mr. Perry	Lacy Ryan	Mrs. Pritchard
1742	Samuel Stephens		
1743	James Quin	Lacy Ryan	Mrs. Cibber
	Spranger Barry (Dublin)	Mr. Wright	Mrs. Bailey
1744	James Quinn	Lacy Ryan	Mrs. Pritchard
	Samuel Foote	Charles Macklin	
	Samuel Foote	Henry Giffard	Mrs. Giffard
	Colley Cibber	Mr. Paget	Jenny Cibber
1745	David Garrick	Charles Macklin	Mrs. Cibber
	Dennis Delane	Charles Macklin	Miss Copin
	Thomas Sheridan (Dublin)		Mrs. Bellamy
1746	Thomas Sheridan (Dublin)	David Garrick	Mrs. Bellamy
	Mr. Cashell	Lacy Ryan	Mrs. Pritchard
	Spranger Barry	Charles Macklin	Mrs. Ridout
	John Ward (Stratford-upon-Avon)		

	Othello	Iago	Desdemona
1747			
1748	Thomas Sheridan (Dublin)	Charles Macklin	Mrs. Bellamy
1749	Thomas Sheridan (Dublin)	Henry Mossop	Mrs. Vincent
	Henry Mossop (Dublin)	Thomas Sheridan	Mrs. Mozeen
	Spranger Barry	David Garrick	
1750	Spranger Barry	David Garrick	
	Henry Mossop (Dublin)	Thomas Sheridan	
	Robert Montgomery (Dublin)	Thomas Sheridan	
	Thomas Sheridan (Dublin)	Robert Montgomery	
1751	Henry Mossop	Thomas Sheridan	
	James Quin	Lacy Ryan	Mrs. Cibber
	Spranger Barry	James Quin	
	Francis Delaval	John Laval	Lady Mexborough
	Spranger Barry	Charles Macklin	Mrs. Cibber
	Mr. Goodfellow	Lewis Hallam	Mrs. Hallam

On December 23, 1751, Othello was first produced in America at the
Nassau Street Theatre in New York City; Robert Upton played the Moor.

	ENGLAND			AMERICA
	Othello	Iago	Desdemona	Othello
1752	John Sowdon (Dublin)	Robert Montgomery	Miss Cole	
	Henry Mossop	Robert Montgomery	George Anne Bellamy	
	Spranger Barry	Charles Macklin	Mrs. Cibber	
	Mr. Goodfellow	Thomas Wignall	Mrs. Fisher	
1753	Spranger Barry	Charles Macklin	Mrs. Cibber	
	Henry Mossop	David Garrick	George Anne Bellamy	
1754	Spranger Barry	Lacy Ryan	George Anne Bellamy	
	Arthur Murphy	Lacy Ryan	George Anne Bellamy	
1755	Mr. Hackett	Colley Cibber	Miss Barton	
1756	Spranger Barry	Lacy Ryan	Miss Nossiter	
1757	Thomas Sheridan (Dublin)	John Lee	Mrs. G. Phillips	
	Tate Wilkinson (Dublin)	Thomas King	Mrs. G. Phillips	
	John Dexter (Dublin)	Robert Layfield		
	Spranger Barry	Lacy Ryan	Miss Nossiter	
	Spranger Barry	Lacy Ryan	George Anne Bellamy	
1758	Tate Wilkinson (Dublin)	Thomas King		

	ENGLAND Othello	Iago	Desdemona	AMERICA Othello
	Thomas Sheridan (Dublin)			
	David Ross	Lacy Ryan	George Anne Bellamy	
	Spranger Barry	Lacy Ryan	George Anne Bellamy	
1759	Tate Wilkinson	William Havard	Mrs. Davies	David Douglass
	David Ross	Lacy Ryan	Mrs. Ward	
1760	David Ross	Luke Sparks	Mrs. Ward	
	Spranger Barry	Henry Mossop	George Anne Bellamy	
	Ignatius Sancho			David Douglass
1761	Thomas Sheridan (Dublin)			
	Thomas Sheridan	William Havard	Mrs. Cibber	
	David Ross	Luke Sparks	George Anne Bellamy	
	William Bridges	William Havard	Mrs. Cibber	
1762	Davis Ross	Luke Sparks	Maria Macklin	
1763				David Douglass
1764	Samuel Foote	Charles Macklin		
	William Powell	William Havard	Mrs. Yates	
1765	David Ross	R. Smith	George Anne Bellamy	
	William Powell	Charles Holland	Mary Ann Yates	
1766	William Powell	Charles Holland	Mary Ann Yates	
	Spranger Barry	Mr. Lee	Mrs. Dancer	
1767	William Powell	Charles Holland	Mrs. Baddeley	
	Spranger Barry	John Sowdon	Mrs. Dancer	
	William Powell	Charles Macklin	Mary Ann Yates	
1768	Spranger Barry	Charles Holland	Mrs. Dancer (Mrs. Barry)	David Douglass
1769	Edward Phillips	John Henry	Mrs. Smith	Major Moncrieff
	Thomas Sheridan	John Sowdon	Miss Hamilton	
	Spranger Barry	Charles Holland	Mrs. Barry	
1770	Spranger Barry	Samuel Reddish	Mrs. Barry	
	Mr. Davis	Mr. Lloyd	Mrs. Dyer	
	Spranger Barry	Richard Hurst	Mrs. Barry	
1771	David Ross	Robert Bensley	Miss Miller	
1772	Spranger Barry	Samuel Reddish	Mrs. Barry	
	David Ross	Robert Bensley	Miss Miller	
	Thomas Sheridan (Dublin)	Charles Macklin		
1773	James Brown Williamson	Robert Bensley	Miss Miller	David Douglass
	Spranger Barry	John Palmer	Mrs. Barry	
	John Henderson (Bath)		Miss Mansell	Lewis Hallam
1774	Spranger Barry	Robert Bensley	Mrs. Barry	
	Spranger Barry	John Palmer	Miss Younge	
1775	Mr. Grist	Robert Bensley	Miss Younge	

	ENGLAND Othello	Iago	Desdemona	AMERICA Othello
	Mr. Wroughton (Liverpool)	Mr. Moody	Miss Mansell	
1777	Mr. Lacy	Samuel Reddish	Miss Younge	
	Mr. Peile	Charles Macklin	Mrs. Lessing- ham	
	Mr. Newton	John Henry	Miss Powell	
	David Ross	Charles Macklin	Mrs. Hartley	
1778				Major Moncrieff
1779	Mr. Daly	Robert Bensley	Mrs. Crawford	Major Lowthar Pennington
	John Henry	Robert Bensley	Miss Farren	
1780	Thomas Crawford (Bath)	Robert Bensley	Mrs. Crawford	
	William Barrymore		Mrs. Sarah Siddons	
	John Henry	Robert Bensley	Miss Farren	
	William Brereton (Liverpool)	John Henderson	Mrs. Ward	
	Richard Wrough- ton	John Henderson	Miss Younge	
1782	William Farren	Robert Bensley	Miss Farren	
1783	John Philip Kemble	John Henderson	Miss Satchell	
1784	William Farren	Robert Bensley	Mrs. Ward	
	Stephen Kemble		Miss Satchell	
	Alexander Pope	George Frederick Cooke	Miss Younge	
	William Farren	John Henderson	Miss Ranoe	
1785	John Philip Kemble	Robert Bensley	Sarah Siddons	
	Alexander Pope	John Henderson	Miss Younge	
	Mr. Lacy	Robert Bensley	Miss Woollery	
1786	Mr. Lacy	Robert Bensley	Miss Woollery	
1787	Mr. Cambray (James Fennell)	Thomas Ryder	Mrs. Pope	Owen Morris
	James Middleton (Bath)			
	John Philip Kemble	Robert Bensley	Sarah Siddons	
1788	Alexander Pope	John Ryder	Mrs. Pope	
	Mr. Middleton (Bath)			
1789	John Philip Kemble	Robert Bensley	Mrs. Powell	
	James Fennell	Mr. Harley	Mrs. M.A. Pope	
1790	James Fennell	Mr. Harley	Mrs. M.A. Pope	
1791	John Philip Kemble	Robert Bensley	Mrs. Siddons	John Henry
1792	Mr. Baker	Tate Wilkinson	Mrs. Churton	John Hodgkinson
	John Philip Kemble	Robert Bensley	Sarah Siddons	
	Alexander Pope	Mr. Harley (George Davies)	Mrs. M.A. Pope	

| ENGLAND | | | AMERICA |
Othello	Iago	Desdemona	Othello
1793 John Philip Kemble	Robert Bensley	Mrs. Powell	John Hodgkinson
Mr. Middleton (Stage name of James Magan)	George Davies	Mrs. M.A. Pope	
1794 Alexander Pope	George Davies	Mrs. M.A. Pope	John Hodgkinson
John Philip Kemble	Robert Bensley	Sarah Siddons	
Alexander Pope	George Davies	Mrs. Chapman	
1795 George Frederick Cooke (Dublin)	Mr. Daly	Miss Campion	
1796 Alexander Pope	Charles Murray	Mrs. M.A. Pope	John Hodgkinson
Henry Siddons, Jr. (Bath)		Miss Betterton	
1797 John Philip Kemble	John Palmer	Sarah Siddons	James Fennell
Robert W. Elliston (Bath)	Mr. Harley	Miss Biggs	
James Middleton	George F. Cooke		
Robert William Elliston	John Palmer	Miss DeCamp	
1798 Thomas Huddart	Charles Murray	Mrs. M.A. Pope	James Fennell
1799 Alexander Pope	Charles Murray	Mrs. M.A. Pope	Thomas Abthorpe Cooper
1800 Mr. Lacy	Mr. Cory	Mrs. Powell	James Fennell
Alexander Pope	George F. Cooke	Mrs. M.A. Pope	
1801 Alexander Pope	George F. Cooke	Mrs. M.A. Pope	Thomas Abthorpe Cooper
Henry Siddons, Jr.	George F. Cooke		James Fennell
Robert W. Elliston	George F. Cooke	Miss Daniels	
George Frederick Cooke			
1802 Henry Siddons, Jr.	George F. Cooke		
1803 Thomas A. Cooper	George F. Cooke		James Fennell
1804 John Philip Kemble	George F. Cooke	Sarah Siddons	James Fennell
Mr. Carles	George F. Cooke		Thomas A. Cooper
Mr. Meggett (Wakefield)			
1805 John Philip Kemble	George F. Cooke		Thomas A. Cooper
1806 Alexander Pope			James Fennell
			Thomas A. Cooper
1807 Charles Mayne Young	George F. Cooke		James Fennell
1808 John Philip Kemble	George F. Cooke		Thomas A. Cooper

	ENGLAND Othello	Iago	Desdemona	AMERICA Othello
	Mr. Egerton (Bath)	George F. Cooke	Miss Fisher	
	William Barry-more			James Fennell
	Charles M. Young	George F. Cooke	Miss Norton	
1809	Charles M. Young	George F. Cooke		James Fennell
1810	Charles M. Young	Mr. Elrington		Thomas A. Cooper
	Alexander Pope (Bath)		Miss Vining	James Fennell
1811	Charles M. Young	Charles Kemble	Miss Johnston	George F. Cooke
				Thomas A. Cooper

	ENGLAND Othello	Iago	AMERICA Othello	Iago
1812	Edmund Kean	Mr. Mason	Joseph George Holman	Thomas A. Cooper
1813	Mr. Sowerby	Alexander Pope	Mr. Usher	Mr. Doyle
	Edmund Kean	Mr. Mason	Thomas A. Cooper	
1814	Charles M. Young	William A. Conway		
	Alexander Pope	Edmund Kean		
	William A. Conway	Charles M. Young		
	Mr. Sowerby	Edmund Kean		
	Alexander Rae	Edmund Kean		
	Robert W. Ellis-ton	Edmund Kean		
	Edmund Kean	Alexander Pope		
	Mr. Sowerby	Mr. Egerton		
1815	Edmund Kean		Thomas A. Cooper	Thomas Hilson
	Master Betty (Bath)			
1816	William C. Mac-ready	Charles M. Young		
	William A. Con-way	Thomas A. Cooper		
	Charles M. Young	William C. Mac-ready		
	Edmund Kean			
1817	Edmund Kean	Junius B. Booth		
	Edmund Kean	Robert C. Maywood		
	Edmund Kean	Alexander Rae		
	Charles M. Young	Junius B. Booth		
	Edmund Kean	James W. Wallack		

| | ENGLAND | | AMERICA | |
	Othello	Iago	Othello	Iago
	Charles M. Young	Mr. Yates		
1818	Edmund Kean	Robert C. Maywood	Jacob Woodhull	Mr. Hawxhurst
	Robert C. Maywood	Edmund Kean	Thomas A. Cooper	Thomas Hilson
	Mr. Cleary	Edmund Kean	James W. Wallack	Thomas A. Cooper
	Edmund Kean	Mr. Cleary		
1819	Edmund Kean	Alexander Pope	Robert C. Maywood	
	William C. Macready	Mr. Yates	James W. Wallack	Thomas A. Cooper
	Edmund Kean	Mr. Rowbotham	James W. Wallack	Robert C. Maywood
			Thomas A. Cooper	James W. Wallack
1820	Edmund Kean	Junius B. Booth	H. J. Finn	Robert C. Maywood
	James W. Wallack	Thomas A. Cooper	Robert Campbell	Robert C. Maywood
	Edmund Kean	Mr. Egerton	James Pritchard	Robert C. Maywood
	Thomas A. Cooper	Junius B. Booth	Thomas A. Cooper	James W. Wallack
1821	Edmund Kean	Thomas A. Cooper	Edmund Kean	Robert C. Maywood
1822	Edmund Kean	Charles M. Young	John Jay Adams	Robert C. Maywood
	Thomas A. Cooper	Edmund Kean	Henry James Finn	Thomas A. Cooper
	William C. Macready	Charles M. Young	James Hewlett	
	Charles M. Young	William C. Macready	Junius B. Booth	
1823	Edmund Kean	Henry Wallack	John Jay Adams	Robert C. Maywood
			Isaac Starr Clason	D. Reed
			Charles Mathews	
			Edwin Forrest	
1824	Edmund Kean	John W. Calcraft	William A. Conway	Thomas A. Cooper
			Thomas A. Cooper	William A. Conway
			Junius B. Booth	Henry Wallack
			Thomas A. Cooper	Thomas Hilson
			James W. Wallack	W. Robertson
1825	Ira Aldridge		William A. Conway	Thomas A. Cooper
	Edmund Kean	Henry Wallack	Junius B. Booth	Henry Wallack

	ENGLAND		AMERICA	
	Othello	Iago	Othello	Iago
			Robert Campbell Maywood	Henry Wallack
			James H. Caldwell	Edwin Forrest
			William A. Conway	Edwin Forrest
			Edmund Kean	Edwin Forrest
			John Jay Adams	R. C. Maywood
1826	Ira Aldridge		Edwin Forrest	Henry Wallack
	William C. Macready	Charles M. Young	Junius B. Booth	R. C. Maywood
	Mr. Fitzharris	T. A. Cooper	Edwin Forrest	Jacob Woodhull
			Edwin Forrest	William Augustus Conway
	Mr. Serle	Mr. Miller	William A. Conway	Thomas A. Cooper
	Frederick Warde	Charles M. Young	Edwin Forrest	John Duff
			Thomas Sowerby Hamblin	Junius B. Booth
			Edmund Kean	John H. Clarke
			Edwin Forrest	Thomas S. Hamblin
1827	Ira Aldridge	John Vandenhoff	Edwin Forrest	Alexander Wilson
	Charles M. Young	Edmund Kean	Thomas A. Cooper	J. H. Hackett
	Charles Kemble	Charles M. Young	Edwin Forrest	Thomas Archer
			Isaac Starr Clason	Thomas Barry
			William C. Macready	Henry Placide
			Edwin Forrest	William Chapman
1828	Edmund Kean	Frederick Warde	Thomas A. Cooper	John R. Scott
			Edwin Forrest	Junius B. Booth
			Thomas A. Cooper	Edwin Forrest
			Junius B. Booth	Edwin Forrest
			Edwin Forrest	Thomas A. Cooper
			John Jay Adams	R. C. Maywood
			Edwin Forrest	Alexander Wilson
			Thomas A. Cooper	James H. Hackett
			Edwin Forrest	J. H. Hackett
1829	Charles M. Young	T. A. Cooper	John Jay Adams	Thomas Archer
	Edmund Kean	Charles M. Young	Thomas A. Cooper	Junius B. Booth
	Charles M. Young	Henry Wallack	Thomas Archer	Mr. Walton

ENGLAND Othello	Iago	AMERICA Othello	Iago
		Junius B. Booth	Thomas A. Cooper
		Thomas A. Cooper	Edwin Forrest
1830 Edmund Kean	Thomas A. Cooper	Junius B. Booth	Edwin Forrest
		Charles Kean	Thomas Barry
		Thomas S. Hamblin	Thomas A. Cooper
		Edwin Forrest	Junius B. Booth
		G. W. Hazard	Thomas A. Cooper
		Thomas S. Hamblin	A. A. Addams
		Junius B. Booth	Thomas A. Cooper
		John Jay Adams	W. R. Blake
1831 Ira Aldridge	John Vandenhoff	A. A. Addams	C. R. Thorne
Edmund Kean	James W. Wallack	Thomas S. Hamblin	Junius B. Booth
Edmund Kean	William C. Macready	Mr. Barton	H. G. Pearson
		W. H. Keppell Edwin Forrest	H. G. Pearson
1832 Thomas A. Cooper		Edwin Forrest	R. C. Maywood
Edmund Kean	William C. Macready	Mr. Harrison	Thomas Placide
		Thomas S. Hamblin	Junius B. Booth
		Edwin Forrest	Thomas A. Cooper
		Alexander Wilson	John H. Clarke
1833 Edmund Kean	Charles Kean	Thomas S. Hamblin	Junius B. Booth
Ira Aldridge	Frederick Warde	Edwin Forrest	Thomas A. Cooper
William C. Macready	John Cooper	Thomas S. Hamblin	Henry Wallack
1834 Henry Wallack		Thomas S. Hamblin	Junius B. Booth
John Vandenhoff	Frederick Warde	C. B. Parsons	David Ingersoll
Elton Denvil	John Vandenhoff	Thomas S. Hamblin	Edwin Forrest
		David Ingersoll	T. H. Palmer
		John R. Scott	Junius B. Booth
1835 Henry Wallack		Augustus A. Addams	J. H. Clarke
William C. Macready		Thomas S. Hamblin	Junius B. Booth
Charles Kemble	George Bennett	David Ingersoll	Mr. Harrison
		Charles Kemble Mas	J. H. Clarke

	ENGLAND Othello	Iago	AMERICA Othello	Iago
			Charles H. Eaton	
			Mr. Harrison	David Ingersoll
			John Reeve	Henry Placide
			Thomas S. Hamblin	Thomas A. Cooper
1836	William C. Macready	George Vandenhoff	Mrs. Henry Lewis	Mr. Harrison
	Edwin Forrest	Junius B. Booth	H. Goodenow	T. McCutcheon
	Edwin Forrest	Frederick Warde	Mr. Harrison	David Ingersoll
			H. Goodenow	J. F. Wells
			Mr. Barton	Mr. Harrison
			Mrs. Henry Lewis	George Jamieson
			John Oxley	J. H. Clarke
			John Reeve	Henry Placide
			Edwin Forrest	J. H. Clarke
			Thomas A. Cooper	Thomas S. Hamblin
			Charles Howard	Junius B. Booth
			David Ingersoll	Mr. Jackson
			Judah	Charles H. Eaton
			H. Goodenow	J. F. Wells
			Mr. Lyne	
1837	Edwin Forrest		Edwin Forrest	J. H. Clarke
	William C. Macready	Samuel Phelps	W. S. Fredericks	Charles Kemble Mason
	Samuel Phelps	William C. Macready	H. Goodenow	Charles H. Eaton
			Seth Greer, Jr.	J. H. Clarke
			James W. Wallack	John Vandenhoff
			Seth Greer, Jr.	Junius B. Booth
			John R. Scott	Junius B. Booth
			Judah	Thomas Barry
			John Vandenhoff	James W. Wallack, Jr.
			George Jones	Charles H. Eaton
			Henry Wallack	John Vandenhoff
			David Ingersoll	John R. Scott
			Charles H. Eaton	George Jamieson
			H. Goodenow	C. R. Thorne
			Mrs. Henry Lewis	Mr. Harrison
			John Vandenhoff	Henry Wallack
			William C. Macready	John Ryder
1838	William C. Macready	Samuel Phelps	Thomas S. Hamblin	Henry Wallack

Year	ENGLAND Othello	Iago	AMERICA Othello	Iago
	Samuel Phelps	William C. Macready	Edwin Forrest	W. C. Forbes
	Charles Kean	Mr. Ternan	Junius B. Booth	Henry Wallack
			John Vandenhoff	James W. Wallack
			Junius B. Booth	Mr. Jackson
			Robert Rue	John Hazard
			Seth Greer, Jr.	J. A. J. Neafie
			Henry J. Wallack	Junius B. Booth
1839	William C. Macready	Samuel Phelps	Edwin Forrest	Henry Wallack
	Samuel Phelps	William C. Macready	Charles Freer	T. McCutcheon
			N. H. Bannister	T. S. Cline
			Charles Kean	Thomas S. Hamblin
			N. C. Johnson	
			Thomas S. Hamblin	Charles Kean
			John R. Scott	Mr. Harrison
			Henry Wallack	Junius B. Booth
			Robert Rue	N. H. Bannister
1840			Edwin Forrest	Joseph Proctor
			Edwin Forrest	George Jamieson
			Lewis Fitzgerald Tasistre	Henry Wallack
			Edwin Forrest	Henry Wallack
			John R. Scott	J. H. Kirby
			Henry Wallack	John Vandenhoff
			John R. Scott	Junius B. Booth
			Edwin Forrest	Thomas S. Hamblin
			Henry Wallack	Junius B. Booth
1841	William C. Macready	Samuel Phelps	Edwin Forrest	George Jamieson
			Thomas S. Hamblin	John Vandenhoff
			Edwin Forrest	Thomas S. Hamblin
			John R. Scott	Junius B. Booth
			Junius B. Booth	John R. Scott
1842	William C. Macready	Samuel Phelps	Augustus A. Addams	John Gilbert
			Edwin Forrest	Junius B. Booth
			Thomas S. Hamblin	George Vandenhoff
			Junius B. Booth	Edwin Forrest

	ENGLAND Othello	Iago	AMERICA Othello	Iago
			Edwin Forrest	John R. Scott
			John R. Scott	J. H. Kirby
1843	Samuel Phelps	William C. Macready	James Wallack, Jr.	Junius B. Booth
	Gustavo Marenco (Italy)		Junius B. Booth	James Wallack, Jr.
	Samuel Phelps	Henry Marston	E. S. Coner	Mr. Pickering
			Junius B. Booth	John R. Scott
			Thomas S. Hamblin	John R. Scott
			William C. Macready	John Ryder
			James Wallack, Jr.	John R. Scott
			Edwin Forrest	John R. Scott
			W. C. Forbes	
1844	Samuel Phelps	Henry Marston	John Ryder	William C. Macready
	Charles Kean	Alexander Pope	William C. Macready	John Ryder
	Henry Marston	Samuel Phelps	James R. Anderson	John Dyott
1845	Edwin Forrest	Mr. Graham	Mr. Warner	Mr. Drummond
	Edwin Forrest	Gustavus V. Brooke		
	William C. Macready		George Vandenhoff	Junius B. Booth
1846	Edwin Forrest (Scotland)		Edwin Forrest	John Dyott
	William C. Macready		Edward Eddy	H. P. Grattan
1847	Gustavus Vasa Brooke		Junius B. Booth	Edwin Booth
	William C. Macready	John Cooper	James Wallack, Jr.	George Vandenhoff
			C. Webb	W. Hield
			William C. Macready	John Ryder
			Wyzeman Marshall	J. B. Roberts
			E. S. Conner	H. P. Grattan
			Thomas Duff	J. B. Roberts
			Edwin Forrest	George Jamieson
1848	Gustavus V. Brooke			
	William C. Macready	John Cooper	Edwin Forrest	James Wallack, Jr.
			Augustus A. Adams	H. P. Grattan
			Wyzeman Marshall	John Dyott
			James W. Wallack, Jr.	W. M. Fleming

	ENGLAND Othello	Iago	AMERICA Othello	Iago
			Augustus A. Addams	Junius B. Booth
1849	James W. Wallack	Charles Kean	Edwin Forrest	John Dyott
	Charles Kean	James W. Wallack	C. W. Couldock	John Dyott
			James W. Wallack, Jr.	John Gilbert
1850	J. R. Anderson	John Vandenhoff	J. B. Atwater	
	Edward L. Davenport	William C. Macready	Richard Graham	John R. Scott
	William C. Macready	E. L. Davenport	George Vandenhoff	C. K. Mason
			James W. Wallack, Jr.	Junius B. Booth
			E.H.A. Perry	Junius B. Booth
			MacKean Buchanan	John Dyott
			Mr. Lovell	N. B. Clarke
			John R. Scott	Richard Graham
			Mr. Carleton	John Hambleton
			John Hambleton	Henry Coad
1851	James W. Wallack	J. Wallack	A. Henry	
			J.A.J. Neafie	MacKean Buchanan
			MacKean Buchanan	J.A.J. Neafie
			Thomas S. Hamblin	Edward Eddy
			C. D. Pitt	W. H. Smith
			J. G. Hanley	Junius B. Booth
			Mr. Winslow	John Dyott
			N. B. Clarke	Junius B. Booth
			Edward Eddy	Mr. Lovell
			John R. Scott	Junius B. Booth
			Gustavus V. Brooke	H. Lynne
			Edwin Forrest	
			Gustavus V. Brooke	Frederick Barlett Conway
1852	Ira Aldridge	Mr. Stanton	Grattan Dawison	G. J. Arnold
	Henry Farren	S. Hawkins	Gustavus V. Brooks	H. Lynne
			Edwin Forrest	
			J.A.J. Neafie	John R. Scott
			W. G. Jones	Junius B. Booth
			N. B. Clarke	W. R. Goodall
			John R. Scott	J.A.J. Neafie
			Thomas S. Hamblin	Junius B. Booth
			Mr. Winslow	John Dyott
			Harry Watkins	
1853	E. L. Davenport	G. V. Brooke	Edwin Forrest	
	James W. Wallack	John Vandenhoff	Mr. Seymour	Mr. Connor

ENGLAND		AMERICA	
Othello	Iago	Othello	Iago
		Mr. Radcliffe	John R. Scott
		James R. Anderson	
		H. A. Perry	John R. Scott
		Wyzeman Marshall	
		John R. Scott	Harry A. Perry
1854		Edward Loomis	
		E. L. Davenport	F. B. Conway
		J. W. Wallack, Jr.	Robert Johnston
		Arnold Hacke	
		James R. Anderson	Edward Eddy
		Joseph Proctor	John R. Scott
		G. J. Arnold	
		Edward Eddy	Wyzeman Marshall
		Edwin Forrest	Charles Fisher
1855	S. Atkyns	Edwin Forrest	Charles Fisher
		E. L. Davenport	Harry A. Perry
		J. W. Wallack, Jr.	Robert Johnston
		E. L. Davenport	Charles Fisher
		Grattan Dawison	John R. Scott
		MacKean Buchanan	J. Canoll
		E. S. Connor	
1856	Tommaso Salvini (Italy)	Lorenzo Piccinini	Mr. Fletcher	Mr. Drummond
	Ernesto Rossi (Italy)		W. H. Smith	James Bennett
	Charles Dillon		Harry A. Perry	J. J. Prior
	James R. Anderson		Edward Eddy	Robert Johnston
			Edwin Booth	Charles Fisher
			James W. Wallack, Jr.	E. L. Davenport
			J. E. McDonough	
1857	V. V. Smoilov (Russia)		Edwin Forrest	H. E. Daly
	W. Chapman (Ireland)	E. Bell	J. W. Wallack, Jr.	E. L. Davenport
			Charles Fisher	Edwin Booth
			MacKean Buchanan	F. B. Conway
			E. L. Davenport	John Dolman
1858	Ira Aldridge (Russia)		Charles Verner	John Vandenhoff

	ENGLAND Othello	Iago	AMERICA Othello	Iago
	Mr. Pennington (Scotland)	J. B. Howard	James Stark	J. Canoll
	Ira Aldridge	Mr. Stuart	James Proctor	
			E. L. Davenport	Edwin Booth
			J. W. Wallack	John Dolman
			Edward Eddy	Carroll Hicks
			Henry Loraine	J. B. Roberts
			P. Warner	H. A. Howard
			J. W. Wallack, Jr.	George C. Boniface
1859	L.L. Leonidov (Russia)		J. B. Roberts	Harry Loraine
	Hermann Vezin		J. B. Howe	J. M. Craig
			John Wilkes Booth	Edwin Booth
			Barry Sullivan	L. R. Shewell
			Charles Pope	Edwin Booth
			Barry Sullivan	Mr. MacFarland
			Edward Eddy	Edwin Booth
			J. H. Allen	
			James W. Wallack	John McCullough
			James W. Wallack, Jr.	F. B. Conway
1860	T. C. King (Dublin)		Edward Eddy	Harry Seymour
	MacKean Buchanan	G. V. Brooke	Edwin Forrest	F. B. Conway
	J. H. Richards	James Johnstone	J. B. Roberts	
	George Owen	J. W. Windley	E. L. Davenport	James W. Wallack, Jr.
			John McCullough	Edwin Forrest
			John Wilkes Booth	
			Edwin Booth	Barton Hill
1861	Samuel Phelps		John McCullough	Edwin Forrest
	Charles Fechter	John Ryder	Charles Dillon	Edwin Booth
			Edwin Forrest	John McCullough
			J. W. Wallack, Jr.	Edwin Booth
			Edwin Booth	J. W. Wallack, Jr.
			Charles Fechter	John Ryder
			Edwin Booth	Barton Hill
			E. L. Davenport	J. W. Wallack, Jr.
			John Wilkes Booth	I. W. Albaugh
1862	Ira Aldridge (Russia)		John McCullough	Edwin Forrest

ENGLAND		AMERICA	
Othello	Iago	Othello	Iago
Samuel Phelps	G. V. Brooke	E. L. Davenport	J. W. Wallack, Jr.
John Ryder	Charles Fechter	Edward Eddy	George P. Farren
		Edwin Forrest	John McCullough
		Edwin Booth	F. B. Conway
		F. B. Conway	Edwin Booth
		E. L. Davenport	George C. Boniface
		Otto Hoym	Leonhard Scherer
1863 Mr. Creswick	Samuel Phelps	Joseph Proctor	J. B. Studley
Walter Montgomery		E. L. Davenport	J. W. Wallack, Jr.
		Edwin Booth	George Jamieson
		James W. Hackett	
		Daniel E. Bandmann	Otto Hoym
		C. M. Lewis	F. B. Conway
		Lawrence Barrett	John McCullough
		Otto Hoym	Leonhard Scherer
1864 Samuel Phelps	William Creswick	Edwin Booth	F. B. Conway
		John Wilkes Booth	L. R. Shewell
		Edwin Forrest	John McCullough
		Lawrence Barrett	F. B. Conway
		Charles Pope	Leonhard Scherer
		C. M. Lewis	F. B. Conway
		Walter Shelley	
1865 Ira Aldridge	Walter Montgomery	Edwin Forrest	John McCullough
		Charles Barron	Edwin Booth
		George C. Boniface	Walter Grisdale
		J. W. Wallack, Jr.	E. L. Davenport
		Walter Grisdale	George C. Boniface
		Charles Kean	J. F. Cathcart
1866		Charles Barron	J. H. Taylor
		Wilmarth Waller	McKee Rankin
		Charles Barron	J. H. Taylor
		Wilmarth Waller	McKee Rankin
		Charles Barron	Edwin Booth
		Edwin Booth	Charles Barron
		J. Newton Gotthold	Charles Barron
		Bogumil Dawison	Casar Frank
		Edwin Booth	Frank Mayo
		Bogumil Dawison	Edwin Booth
		Edwin Booth	J. B. Roberts
		Barton Hill	Edwin Booth

Year	ENGLAND Othello	Iago	AMERICA Othello	Iago
			W. H. Pope	Thomas Graham
1867			J. C. McCollom	F. B. Conway
			Bogumil Dawison	Otto Hoym
			Boothroyd Fairclough	J. Newton Gotthold
			J. Newton Gotthold	Boothroyd Fairclough
			W. H. Whalley	J. B. Studley
			Edwin Forrest	John McCullough
			E. L. Davenport	F. B. Conway
			Edwin Forrest	Barton Hill
			Edward Eddy	E. L. Tilton
			Edwin Booth	Barton Hill
1868	Daniel Bandmann	Boothroyd Fairclough	J. B. Studley	Charles Barron
			Edwin Booth	S. K. Chester
			E. L. Davenport	F. B. Conway
			Edwin Forrest	G. H. Clarke
1869	Charles Dillon	T. C. King	Neil Warner	MacKean Buchanan
	T. C. King	Charles Dillon	Edwin Booth	Edwin Adams
	Morgan Smith	H. S. Hayner	Edwin Adams	Edwin Booth
			John McCullough	Edwin Booth
			Mr. Neville	Mr. Collmer
1870	Barry Sullivan (Manchester)		Walter Montgomery	E. L. Davenport
	John Dewhurst (Bradford)	Hector MacKensie	E. L. Davenport	Lawrence Barrett
			J. B. Roberts	
			Edwin Forrest	
			Edward Eddy	
			Neil Warner	W. B. Laurens
1871	Charles Dillon (York)		Lawrence Barrett	Edwin Booth
	Barry Sullivan (Bristol)	J. F. Cathcart	Edwin Booth	Lawrence Barrett
			Walter Montgomery	
			Henry Wolfssohn	Herr Harry
			William Creswick	James Bennett
1872	Barry Sullivan (Dublin)		Edwin Forrest	William Harris
	H. J. Young		Edwin Booth	Charles Walcott
			E. L. Davenport	
			Edwin Booth	Joseph Wheelock

| ENGLAND | | AMERICA | |
Othello	Iago	Othello	Iago
1873		Neil Warner	Frank Roche
		E. L. Daven-port	
		Tommaso Salvini	Alessandro Salvini
		L. R. Shewell	Edwin Booth
		E. T. Stetson	
		Thomas C. King	Charles Wheatleigh
		Edwin Booth	Joseph Wheelock
1874		Tommaso Salvini	
		W. J. Cogswell	
		E. L. Daven-port	Louis Aldrich
		Charles Barron	H. F. Daly
1875	Tommaso Salvini	Edwin Booth	Edwin Booth	D. H. Harkins
		D. H. Harkins	Edwin Booth
		John McCullough	
		Milnes Levik	F. A. Tannehill
		Edwin Booth	Charles Walcott
		John H. Bird	Joseph Byrnes
		E. L. Daven-port	
		Edwin Booth	W. E. Sheridan
		John H. Bird	Thomas F. Clark
1876	Henry Irving	Henry Forrester	Ludwig von Ernst	Max Freeman
		Charles Barron	W. E. Sheridan
		Edwin Booth	Frederic Robinson
		Frederic Robinson	Edwin Booth
		John McCollough	Frederick Warde
1877	Henry Forrester		Archie C. Cowper	J. C. Cowper
		Albert Roberts	D. H. Hawkins
		John McCollough	Frederick Warde
		Frederic Robinson	Edwin Booth
		E. A. Sothern	W. J. Florence
		Frederick B. Warde	John McCullough
		D. H. Harkins	John W. Norton
		G. DeForrest	James O'Neill
		Henry L. Thomas	
1878	Samoilov (Russia)		John McCullough	John C. Cowper
	Ira Aldridge (Russia)		"Count Joannes"	Frank Noyes
	Neville Moritz	Hermann Vezin	Joseph Wheelock	Edwin Booth

	ENGLAND Othello	Iago	AMERICA Othello	Iago
	Henry Forrester	George S. Tith-eradge	Edwin Booth	Joseph Wheelock
	Charles Dillon	John Ryder	John McCul-lough	Edwin Booth
	Jean Mounet-Sully (France)		Lawrence Bar-rett	
			D. H. Harkins	Edwin Booth
			John J. Murray	Eugene Moore
			John McCul-lough	Frank Mayo
			W. E. Sheri-dan	Otis Skinner
			John McCul-lough	Joseph Wheelock
			Charles Pope	
			Perkins D. Fisher	Frank L. Inion
			Daniel Gilfeth-er, Jr.	Eugene Moore
1879			George Edgar	Joseph Wheelock
			John McCul-lough	Louis James
			Frederic Rob-inson	Edwin Booth
			John McCul-lough	Edwin Booth
			Edwin Booth	Frederic Robinson
			Franz Reinau	Otto Hoym
			John McCul-lough	Frederick N. Warde
			W. E. Sheridan	Thomas W. Keene
			Lawrence Bar-rett	
			Daniel E. Band-mann	
1880	Barry Sullivan (Stratford)	W. A. Hallat	Frederic Rob-inson	Edwin Booth
	Charles Warner	Hermann Vezin	Edwin Booth	J. C. McCollom
			Tommaso Sal-vini	L. R. Shewell
			J. C. McCol-lom	Edwin Booth
			W. E. Sheridan	Thomas W. Keene
			John H. Bird	Henry S. Spelman
			John McCul-lough	Frederick B. Warde
			Louis James	
			William Stafford	Frederick B. Warde
			Ernesto Rossi	Milnes Levick
1881	Henry Irving	T. Swinbourne	Tommaso Sal-vini	L. R. Shewell
	Edwin Booth	Henry Forrester	John McCul-lough	Edmund K. Collier

	ENGLAND Othello	Iago	AMERICA Othello	Iago
	Henry Forrester	Edwin Booth	Edwin Booth	Lawrence Barrett
	Henry Irving	Edwin Booth	Lawrence Bar-rett	Edwin Booth
			Edmund K. Collier	John McCullough
	Edwin Booth	Henry Irving	William Stafford	Frederick B. Warde
			Ernesto Rossi	Milnes Levick
	John McCullough	Hermann Vezin	John McCul-lough	Joseph Haworth
			George Edgar	Joseph Wheelock
			Ernesto Rossi	Milnes Levick
1882	Hermann Vezin		John H. Bird	C. S. Withington
1883			Tommaso Sal-vini	Lewis Morrison
			Thomas W. Keene	
			Edwin Booth	Eben Plympton
1884			John McCul-lough	
			John H. Bird	Robert Mantell
			Benjamin G. Ford	J. A. Arneaux
			Edwin Booth	
			Thomas W. Keene	Frederick B. Warde
1885			Charles Barron	Edwin Booth
			Tommaso Sal-vini	John A. Lane
			Edwin Booth	Charles Barron
1886	Frank R. Benson	Mr. Thalberg	Benjamin G. Ford	J. A. Arneaux
			Charles Barron	Edwin Booth
			Daniel E. Bandmann	F. Newton Gott-hold
			Tommaso Sal-vini	Edwin Booth
			Frederick B. Warde	Harry Aveling
			Louis James	F. C. Mosely
1887	Charles Char-rington	Hermann Vezin	Daniel E. Bandmann	F. Newton Gott-hold
			Louis James	F. C. Mosely
			Frederick B. Warde	
			Edwin Booth	Lawrence Barrett
			Lawrence Bar-rett	Edwin Booth
1888			J. J. Crow-ley	Adam Dove
			James Owen O'Connor	
			Louis James	F. C. Mosely
			Lawrence Bar-rett	Edwin Booth

	ENGLAND Othello	Iago	AMERICA Othello	Iago
			J. Gordon Emmons	Stanislas Stange
			Oskar Kruger	Ernst Possart
			Ludwig Barnay	Gustave Kober
			Thomas W. Keene	
1889			Tommaso Salvini	John Malone
			Edwin Booth	Lawrence Barrett
			Lawrence Barrett	Edwin Booth
			Louis James	F. C. Mosley
1890	Frank R. Benson	Charles Cartwright	Maurice Morrison	Richard Tauber
	Osmond Tearle	Edwin Lever	Tommaso Salvini	George Fawcett
			Thomas W. Keene	George Learock
			Robert Mantell	
			Frederick B. Warde	
			Lawrence Barrett	Edwin Booth
			Edwin Booth	Lawrence Barrett
1891	Lion Margrave	George Hughes	R. D. MacLean	Marie Prescott
			Edwin Booth	Lawrence Barrett
			Lawrence Barrett	Edwin Booth
			Adalbert Matkowsky	Arthur Eggeling
1892	Edmund Tearle	Charles Pond	Robert Downing	Frederick Mosely
	Frederick Scarth	Charles Pond	R. D. MacLean	Marie Prescott
	J. S. Blythe	Charles Pond	Wilson Barrett	
	Hermann Vezin	Loring Fernie	Maurice Morrison	
1893			Wilson Barrett	Franklin McLeay
			Tacatanee	Charles Fletcher
			Louis James	Barry Johnstone
			Thomas W. Keene	Frank Henning
			Creston Clarke	Russ Whytal
			Herbert Carr	
1894			John T. Malone	William Ingersoll
			Wilson Barrett	Franklin McLeay
			Thomas W. Keene	
			Robert Mantell	
1895			Wilson Barrett	Franklin McLeay
			Henry Jewett	George Milne
1896	Charles Pond	Hermann Vezin		
	Constantin Stanislavsky (Russia)			

	ENGLAND Othello	Iago	AMERICA Othello	Iago
1897	Frank R. Benson	Frank Rodney		
	Mrs. Charles Whitley	John H. Manley		
	Wilson Barrett	Franklin McLeay		
	Johnston Forbes-Robertson			
1898	Frank Cooper	Lewis Calvert	Richard Buhler	
			Louis James	Frederick B. Warde
			Charles B. Hanford	Frank Henning
1899	Wilson Barrett	J. Carter Edwards	R. D. MacLean	Charles B. Hanford
	Jean Mounet-Sully (France)			
1900	Hermann Vezin	Frank Rodney	Charles B. Hanford	Joseph S. Haworth
	Oscar Asche	Herbert Grimwood	Robert Mantell	Mark Price
			Daniel E. Bandmann	William Bramell
1901			Robert Mantell	
1902	Frank R. Benson	Frank Rodney	Robert Mantell	Francis McGinn
	Johnston Forbes-Robertson	Herbert Waring	Creston Clarke	Edwin Holt
1903	Ermete Novelli (France)		Edwin Holt	Creston Clarke
	Otjiro Kawakami (Japan)		John Craig	John Sainpolis
1904	Edmund Tearle	Cyril Este	Thomas E. Shea	
	F. J. Nettleford	Gilbert Hudson	Robert B. Mantell	Russ Whytal
1905	Hubert Carter	J. H. Barnes	Robert B. Mantell	Harry Leighton
	Frank R. Benson	Arthur Whitely		
1906	Lewis Waller	Henry Irving	Robert B. Mantell	Francis McGinn
	Whitford Kane		Francis McGinn	Robert B. Mantell
			Ermente Novelli	L. Ferrati
1907	Matheson Lang		Augustus Phillips	Hal Clarendon
	Lewis Waller	Lyall E. Swete	Robert B. Mantell	Francis McGinn
	Oscar Asche	Herbert Grimwood	Francis McGinn	Robert B. Mantell
	Oscar Asche	Alfred Brydone	Thomas E. Shea	John E. Gilbert
1908			Maurice Morrison	Maurice Schwartz
1909			Robert Mantell	
1910	Giovanni Grasso			
1911	Oscar Asche	Herbert Grimwood	Robert B. Mantell	Fritz Leiber

	ENGLAND		AMERICA	
	Othello	Iago	Othello	Iago
			Fritz Leiber	Robert B. Mantell
1912	Frank R. Benson	Henry Herbert		
	Herbert Beerbohm-Tree	Laurence Irving		
1913	Sir Johnston Forbes-Robertson	J. H. Barnes	Johnston Forbes-Robertson	S. A. Cookson
1914	Philip Ben Greet		R. D. MacLean	William Faversham
	Frank R. Benson	F. Randle Ayrtem	James K. Hackett	
1915	Philip Ben Greet		Robert B. Mantell	
1916	Jerrold Robertshaw	Robert Atkins	Edward Sterling Wright	John H. Ramsey
	Philip Ben Greet			
1917	Philip Ben Greet		Maurice Morrison	E. Rothstein
1918			Robert B. Mantell	Fritz Leiber
1919	E. Stuart Vinden	Frank Moore		
	F. J. Nettleford	H. A. Saintsbury		
1920	Matheson Lang	Arthur Bourchier		
1921	Godfrey Tearle	Basil Rathbone	Giovanni Grasso	
1922	William Stack	Baliol Holloway	Walter Hampden	
	James Hackett	Baliol Holloway	Robert B. Mantell	
	Fritz Kortner (Germany)	Rudolf Forster		
1923	Wilfrid Walter	George Hayes		
1924	Baliol Holloway	Eric Maxon		
	Ion Swinley	George Hayes		
1925	Godfrey Tearle	Cedric Hardwicke	Walter Hampden	Baliol Holloway
1926				
1927	Baliol Holloway	Neil Porter	Louis Leon Hall	Fritz Leiber
	Robert Loraine	Ion Swinley		
1928				
1929	Scott Sunderland	Julian d'Albie	Ben Zvi Baratoff	Maurice Schwartz
	Paul Wegener (Germany)			
1930	Wilfrid Walter	George Hayes	Gilmor Brown	Morris Ankrum
	Paul Robeson	Maurice Browne	Fritz Leiber	
	Leonid Leonidov (Russia)			
1931	Emund Willard	Gerald Cooper		
1932	Wilfrid Walter	Ralph Richardson		
	Ernest Milton	Henry Oscar		
1933	Camille Pilotto (Italy)	Filippe Scelzo	Curtis Cooksey	Richard Maibaum
1934			Walter Huston	Kenneth MacKenna

	ENGLAND		AMERICA	
	Othello	Iago	Othello	Iago
1935	Abraham Sofaer	Maurice Evans	Philip Merivale	Kenneth MacKenna
	Wilfrid Walter		William Thornton	Sydney Head
1936	Frederick Volk	Alec Clunes	Walter Huston	Brian Aherne
1937	Frederick Volk			
1938	Ralph Richardson	Laurence Olivier		
1939	John Laurie	Alec Clunes		
1940	Donald Wolfit	Donald Layne-Smith	John C. Webb	
			Burton Bowen	Paul Tripp
1941	Anew McMaster	Ronald Ibbs		
	Donald Wolfit	H. Worrall Thompson		
1942	Frederick Volk	Bernard Miles	Paul Robeson	Jose Ferrer
1943	Baliol Holloway	Abraham Sofaer	Paul Robeson	Jose Ferrer
	Abraham Sofaer	Baliol Holloway	John Carradine	Alfred Allegro
1944	Donald Wolfit	Eugene Wellesley	Canada Lee	John Ireland
1945	George Skillan	Anthony Eustrel	Paul Robeson	Jose Ferrer
1946	Donald Wolfit	Eugene Wellesley		
	Frederick Volk	Donald Wolfit		
1947	Jack Hawkins	Anthony Quayle		
	Frederick Volk	Donald Wolfit		
1948	Godfrey Tearle	Anthony Quayle		
1949	Godfrey Tearle	John Slater		
	Michael Aldridge	George Hagen		
1950	Alme Clariond (France)	Jean Debucourt		
1951	Douglas Campbell (Scotland)	Paul Rogers		
	Orson Welles	Peter Finch		
	Douglas Campbell	Paul Rogers		
1952	Anthony Quayle	Leo McKern		
1953			Earle Hyman	William Thornton
1954	Anthony Quayle	Raymond Westwell		
1955				
1956	Frederick Volk (Canada)	Murray David	William Marshall	Jerome Kilty
	Richard Burton	John Neville		
	John Neville	Richard Burton		
	Harry Andrews	Emlyn Williams		
	Walter Richter (Switzerland)	Gustav Knuth		
	Vittorio Gassman (Italy)	Osvaldo Ruggieri		
	Salvo Randone (Italy)	Osvaldo Ruggieri		
1957			Earle Hyman	Alfred Drake
1958			William Marshall	Robert Geiringer
1959	Paul Robeson (Stratford)	Sam Wanamaker		
	Douglas Campbell (Canada)	Douglas Rain		
1960				
1961	John Gielgud	Ian Bannen		

	ENGLAND Othello	Iago	AMERICA Othello	Iago
1962				
1963	Errol John	Leo McKern	Brock Peters	
	Rolf Boysen (Germany)		David Sabine	
	Laurence Olivier	Frank Finlay		
1964	Laurence Olivier	Frank Finlay	James Earl Jones	Mitchell Ryan
1965	Laurence Olivier	Frank Finlay		
1966				
1967	Earle Hyman (Norway)	Felke Hjort		
	Robert Ryan	John Neville		
1968				
1969			Earle Hyman	
1970			James Earl Jones	
			Moses Gunn	Lee Richardson
1971	Brewster Mason	Emrys James		
	Bruce Purchase	Bernard Miles		
1972	Brewster Mason	Emrys James	Ernie Stewart	Laird Williamson
1973	Nachum Buchman (Canada)	Douglas Rain	Manu Tupou	John Devil
	Russ Costen	Gus Fleming	Ernie Stewart	Laird Williamson
1974	Paul Rogers	Gerald Harper		
1975	David Burke	Michael Kitchen	George Collins	Lou Lippa
	Chaim Topol	Keith Michell		
1976	Robert Stephens	Edward Fox	John Hancock	
	Simon Chilver (Australia)	Philip Hinton	William Marshall	
1977			Ron O'Neal	Patrick Farrelly
			Haskell V. Anderson III	
			Jonathan Lutz	
1978	Keith Michell (Australia)		Sidney Hibbert	Philip Pleasants
	Alan Scarfe (Canada)	Nicholas Pennell	Earle Hyman	Nicholas Kepros
			Joseph Blankenship	
			Ray Aranha	
			Paul Winfield	
1979	Donald Sinden	Bob Peck	Fred Neuman	George Bartenieff
			Maurice Woods	Bill Roberts
			Paul Winfield	Richard Dreyfuss
			Alan Scarfe	Nicholas Pennell
			Raul Julia	Richard Dreyfuss
1980	Paul Scofield	Michael Bryant	Paul Winfield	
1981			James Earl Jones	Christopher Plummer
			Clayton Corbin	
1982	Kenneth Haigh	George Sewell	James Earl Jones	Christopher Plummer
1983			Morgan Freeman	

	ENGLAND		AMERICA	
	Othello	Iago	Othello	Iago
1984	Joseph Marcell	Philip Whitchurch		
	Stephen Hartford	David Calder		

OTELLO (VERDI)

Summary of The Metropolitan Opera productions of Otello compiled from Metropolitan Opera Annals by William H. Seltsam (New York: H. W. Wilson Company, 1947).

	Otello	Iago	Desdemona
1890 (March 24)	Francesco Tamagno	Giuseppe de Puente	Emma Albani
1892 (January 11)	Jean de Rezke	Eduardo Camera	Emma Albani
1894 (December 3)	Francesco Tamagno	Victor Maurel	Emma Eames
1902 (January 31)	Albert Alvarez	Antonio Scotti	Emma Eames
(November 24)	(Same as above)		
1909 (November 17)	Leo Slezak	Antonio Scotti	Frances Alda
(November 26)	(Same as above)		
(December 4)	Leo Slezak	Pasquale Amato	Frances Alda
(December 13)	(Same as above)		
1913 (January 6)	Leo Slezak	Pasquale Amato	Frances Alda
1937 (December 22)	Giovanni Martinelli	Lawrence Tibbett	Elizabeth Rethberg
(December 30)	"	"	Irene Jessner
1938 (January 15)	(Same as above)		
(January 28)	"	"	Elizabeth Rethberg
(March 20)	"	"	(Silver Jubilee Testimonial)
	to Giovanni Martinelli--Duet, Act II Martinelli and Tibbett		
(November 21)	Giovanni Martinelli	Lawrence Tibbett	Maria Caniglia
(December 31)	"	Richard Bonelli	Helen Jepson
1939 (February 9)	"	Carlo Tagliabue	Irene Jessner
1940 (January 18)	"	John Brownlee	Elizabeth Rethberg
(February 3)	"	Carlo Morelli	"
(February 24)	"	Lawrence Tibbett	"
1941 (January 18)	"	"	Stella Roman
(February 3)	"	"	Elizabeth Rethberg
(December 4)	"	"	Stella Roman
1942 (January 2)	"	Alexander Sved	"
(January 28)	"	"	"
1946 (February 23)	Torsten Ralf	Leonard Warren	"
(March 29)	"	"	"
(November 16)	"	"	"
(November 22)	"	"	"
(December 9)	Ramon Vinay	"	"
1947 (January 9)	Torsten Ralf	Lawrence Tibbett	"
(February 22)	"	"	Florence Quartarare
(March 12)	Ramon Vinay	"	Daniza Ilitsch

	Otello	Iago	Desdemona
1948 (November 29)	Ramon Vinay	Leonard Warren	Licia Albanese
(December 9)	"	"	"
1949 (January 5)	"	"	"
(March 12)	"	"	Stella Roman
1952 (February 9)	"	"	Eleanor Steber
(February 15)	Mario Del Monaco	"	"
(February 20)	"	"	"
(March 3)	"	"	"
(March 13)	"	Paolo Silveri	Delia Regal
1955 (January 31)	"	Leonard Warren	Renata Tebaldi
(February 11)	"	"	"
(March 1)	"	"	"
(March 5)	"	"	"
(March 12)	"	"	"
(March 17)	Set Svanholm	"	Lucine Amara
1958 (February 27)	Mario Del Monaco	"	Victoria De Los Angeles
(March 8)	"	"	"
(March 17)	"	"	Zinka Milanov
(March 28)			Victoria De Los Angeles
(April 9)	"	"	
(November 15)	"	"	Renata Tebaldi
(November 24)	"	"	"
(December 9)	"	"	"
(December 20)	"	Tito Gobbi	"
(December 28)	"	Leonard Warren	"
1959 (January 24)	Dimiter Uzunov	"	Zinka Milanov
1963 (March 10)	James McCracken	Robert Merrill	Gabriella Tucci
(March 13)	"	"	"
(March 23)	"	"	"
(March 30)	"	"	"
(April 4)	"	"	Zinka Milanov
(April 9)	"	Anselmo Colzani	"
1964 (February 8)	"	Robert Merrill	Leonie Rysanek
(February 12)	"	"	"
(February 15)	"	Anselmo Colzani	"
(February 18)	"	"	Zinka Milanov
(February 25)	Arturo Sergi	Robert Merrill	"
(February 28)	James McCracken	"	Leonie Rysanek
(March 9)	"	"	Zinka Milanov
(March 18)	Arturo Sergi	Anselmo Colzani	"
(March 21)	James McCracken	Robert Merrill	"
(April 4)	"	Anselmo Colzani	Renata Tebaldi
(April 9)	"	"	"
(April 30)	"	Robert Merrill	"
(May 9)	"	Anselmo Colzani	"
(November 7)	Dmiter Uzunov	Cornell MacNeil	Raina Kabaivanska
(November 21)	"	"	Zinka Milanov
(November 28)	"	"	Raina Kabaivanska
(December 4)	James McCracken	"	Zinka Milanov

	Otello	Iago	Desdemona
1964 (December 23)	Dimiter Uzunov	Robert Merrill	Renata Tebaldi
(December 29)	"	"	"
1965 (April 15)	"	Cornell MacNeil	Zinka Milanov

(Based on Metropolitan Opera Annals (1966-1976) compiled by Mary Ellis Peltz and Gerald Fitzgerald (Clifton, N.J.: James T. White & Company, 1978).

	Otello	Iago	Desdemona
1967 (February 27)	James McCracken	Tito Gobbi	Montserret Caballo
(March 7)	"	"	"
(March 11)	"	"	"
(March 15)	"	"	"
(April 3)	Jon Vickers	Gabriel Bacquier	Gabriella Tucci
(April 14)	"	"	"
(April 22)	James McCracken	Tito Gobbi	"
(April 29)	"	"	"
(May 6)	"	"	"
(May 20)	"	"	"
(May 27)	"	"	"
(June 1)	"	"	"
(August 25)	Jon Vickers	"	Renata Tebaldi
1974 (February 9)	"	Thomas Stewart	Kiri Te Kanawa
(February 12)	"	"	Teresa Stratas
(February 15)	"	"	"
(February 21)	"	"	"
(March 7)	James McCracken	Cornell MacNeil	Kiri Te Kanawa
(March 25)	"	"	"
(April 13)	"	"	"
1975-1976 --			
1976-1977 --			
1978 (January 30)	Jon Vickers	Cornell MacNeil	Katia Ricciarelli
(February 4)	"	"	"
(February 8)	"	"	"
(February 11)	"	"	"
(February 17)	"	"	"
(February 20)	"	"	"
1978-1979 --			
1979 (September 24)	Placido Domingo	Sherrill Milnes	Gilda Cruz-Romo
1980-1981 --			
1981-1982 --			
1982-1983 --			
1983-1984 --			

WHITES IN BLACKFACE--FILMS

The following listing is but a small sampling of the many whites who appeared in blackface in the long history of motion pictures.

Abbey, May	Grand Opera in Rubeville (Edison 1914) Sapphria
Alba, Orpha	Heart of Maryland, The (Warner Bros. 1927) Mammy
Alexander, Edward	In Slavery Days (Universal 1913) Caspar Robinson Crusoe (Universal 1913) Friday
Anderson, William	Bar Sinister, The (Edgar Lewis 1917) Sam Davis, Negro
Ashbrook, Florence	A Fair Rebel (Biograph 1916) Old Mammy
Asher, Max	Ladder Jinx, The (Vitagraph 1922) Sam, Negro Porter
Astor, Camille	A Cure for Carelessness (Selig 1913) Dinah, Negro Washerwoman
Austin, Jere	Uncle Tom's Cabin (Paramount 1918) George Harris
Bates, Tom	Her Father's Son (Paramount 1916) Mose
Belasco, Walter	Grip of Jealousy, The (Universal 1916) Uncle Jeff
Blackwell, Jim	Witching Hour, The (Paramount 1921) Harvey Desperate Youth (Universal 1921) Sam Traveling Salesman, The (Paramount 1921) Julius Abraham Lincoln (First National 1924) Tom, Negro Servant Dancing Cheat, The (Universal 1924) Mose Barbara Frietchie (PDC 1924) Rufus Love's Wilderness (First National 1924) Jubilo
Balkemore, Henry D.	In the Diplomatic Service (Metro 1916) Negro Butler
Blanchard, Eleanor	A Soldier of Peace (Lubin 1914) Mammy Grip of the Past, The (Lubin 1914) Mammy
Bonner, Jerry	Old Oak's Secret, The (Vitagraph 1914) Moses, an old Slave
Boss, Yale	Sally Castleton, Southerner (Edison 1915) Negro George

Brooke, Myra

Lovely Mary (Columbia-Metro 1916) Mammy
A Daughter of Maryland (Mutual 1917) Mandy
Liar, The (Fox 1918) Mammy Lou
A Daughter of the Old South (Paramount 1918)
Black Housekeeper

Broussard, Walter

Voice of Conscience, The (Metro 1917) Crazy Pete

Brower, Robert

Held by the Enemy (Paramount 1920) Uncle Rufus

Bryson, Arthur

Wildfire (Vitagraph 1923) Jockey Chappie Raster

Burton, J. W.

Ghost Breaker, The (Paramount, 1914) Rusty

Burton, S. J.

A Daughter of Maryland (Mutual 1917) Neb, faithful
Negro servant

Byrd, Anthony

Voice of Conscience, The (Metro 1917) Uncle Mose
Pals First (Metro 1919) Uncle Alex

Caldwell, Goldie

Adventures of Kathlyn, The (Selig 1914) Pundita

Carpenter, Florence

Uncle Tom's Cabin (Paramount 1918) Eliza

Carter, Douglas

Love Is an Awful Thing (Selznick 1922) Porter
Modern Matrimony (Selznick 1923) Rastus
Hold Your Breath (Christie 1924) Negro Boy

Chamberlain, Ray

Bar Sinister, The (Edgar Lewis 1917) Moe

Chandler, Chick

Swanee River (20th Century-Fox 1939) Bones

Clark, Jack J.

Missionaries in Darkest Africa (Kalem 1912) Native
Chief

Clarke, Harvey

Honor Thy Name (Triangle 1916) Uncle Toby

Cogley, Nick

Boys Will Be Boys (Goldwyn 1921) Aunt Mandy
Coward, The (Triangle 1915) Negro Servant
Crinoline and Romance (Metro 1923) Uncle Mose
Heart of Maryland, The (Warner Bros. 1927) Negro
Butler
In Old Kentucky (Metro-Goldwyn-Mayer 1927) Uncle
Bible
Marriage Clause, The (American Releasing Corp.
1922) Uncle Remus
One Clear Call (Mayer-First National 1922) Toby
Restless Souls (Vitagraph 1922) Uncle Ben
Toby's Bow (Goldwyn 1919) Uncle Toby
An Unwilling Hero (Goldwyn 1921) Negro Servant

Cowles, Jules

Bar Sinister, The (Edgar Lewis 1917) Buck Moe
Service Star, The (Goldwyn 1918) Jefferson, Negro
Servant
Ne'er Do Well, The (Paramount 1923) Allen Allan--
Negro Soldier of Fortune

	Lost World, The (First National 1925) Zambo Money to Burn (Gotham Productions 1926) Black Giant
Crain, Jeanne	Pinky (20th Century-Fox 1949) Mulatto Nurse Pinky
Curry, John	In Old Kentucky (Mayer-First National 1919) Uncle Neb Faith Healer, The (Paramount 1921) Uncle Abe Day of Faith, The (Goldwyn 1923) Isaac
Dailey, Dan	You're My Everything (20th Century-Fox 1949) Song & dance man in blackface
Davis, Lizzie	A Soul in Trust (Triangle 1916) Mammy Judy
De Brulier, Nigel	Golden Dawn (Warner Bros. 1930) Hasmali
Dempsey, Pauline	Voice of Conscience, The (Metro 1917) Aunt Jennie Pals First (Metro 1918) Aunt Caroline Youthful Folly (Selznick 1920) Mammy Women Men Love (Bradley Feature Films 1921) Mammy Chloe Good-Bad Wife, The (McCord Productions 1921) Mirandy Destiny's Isle (American Releasing Corp. 1922) Mammy Broadway Rose (Tiffany 1922) Negro Maid Modern Marriage (American Releasing Corp. 1923) Mammy
De Vaull, William	An Innocent Magdalene (Triangle 1916) Old Negro Joe Kentucky Days (Fox 1923) Scipio White Shoulders (Preferred Pictures 1922) Uncle Enoch Tea-With a Kick (Associated Exhibitors 1923) Napoleon
Dove, Billie	Love Mart, The (First National 1927) sold as "An Octoroon"
Dresser, Louise	Not Quite Decent (Fox 1929) Mame
Ellsworth, Zula	Service Star, The (Paramount 1918) Martha, Negro servant
Elmer, Billy	Circus Man, The (Paramount 1914) Isaac Perry, Negro Lawyer
Ferrer, Mel	Lost Boundaries (Film Classics 1948) Mulatto Scott Carter
Fitzroy, Louis	Around the World (Cub 1916) Cannibal

Foreman, Grant

Vain Justice (Essanay 1915) Aged Negro

Forrest, Marguerite

Renaissance at Charleroi (General Film Co.
    1917) Quadroon

George, George

Around the World (Cub 1916) Cannibal Chief

Godowsky, Dagmar

Hitchin' Posts (Universal 1920) An Octoroon

Grant, Frances Nellie

Mating, The (Vitagraph 1918) Mammy
Come Out of the Kitchen (Paramount 1919)
    Mammy Jackson
Cousin Kate (Vitagraph 1920) Jane
In Walked Mary (Pathé 1920) Mammy
Sisters (American Releasing Corp. 1922)
    Mammy
Counterfeit Love (Playgoers Pictures 1923)
    Mandy
Leavenworth Case, The (Vitagraph 1923)
    Dinah
Warrens of Virginia, The (Fox Film Corp.
    1924) Mammy
Dancer of Paris, The (First National 1926)
    Mammy
Her Unborn Child (Windsor Pictures 1930)
    Mandy

Grauer, Ben

Idol Dancer, The (First National 1920) Native
    Boy

Greene, May

Cause for Thanksgiving (Vitagraph 1914)
    Black girl

Gross, William J.

Bar Sinister, The (Edgar Lewis 1917) Uncle
    Jimmy

Harris, Leona

Stainless Barrier, The (Triangle 1917)
    Mammy

Harris, Lucretia C.

A Kentucky Cinderella (Universal 1917) Aunt
    Chlorindy
Captain of His Soul (Triangle 1918) Mammy
A Mother's Secret (Universal 1918) Mammy
Last Rebel, The (Triangle 1918) Mammy
Desperate Youth (Universal 1921) Aunt
    Chlorindy
Nobody's Fool (Universal 1921) Melinda
Human Hearts (Universal) Carolina
Forgotten Law, The (Metro 1922) Mammy Cely

Harrison, Irma

One Exciting Night (United Artists 1922)
    Agnes, Black maid

Hazelton, Joseph

Suwanee River, The (Selig 1913) Uncle Abe,
    old Negro servant

Herman, Al   Swanee River (20th Century-Fox 1939) Tambo

Hiers, Walter   Ghost Breaker, The (Paramount 1922) Rusty Snow
                              Excuse Me (Metro-Goldwyn-Mayer 1925) Negro
                                  Porter

Hines, Johnny   Lincoln the Lover (Vitagraph 1914) Old Negro
                                  Servant

Hoffman, Ruby   Uncle Tom's Cabin (Paramount 1918) Cassie

Hopkins, William   In Old Virginia (Lubin 1914) Old Tom

Houseman, Arthur   A Clean Sweep (Edison 1915) Blackfaced Chimney
                                  Sweep

Hunt, Mrs. Jay   Bride of Hate, The (Triangle 1917) Mammy Lou

Ivans, Elaine   Littlest Rebel, The (Photoplay Productions 1914)
                                  Slave Sally Ann

James, Walter   Idol Dancer, The (First National 1920) Black Chief
                                  Wando

Jamieson, Bud   Texas Steer, A (First National 1927) Othello

Jeffrey, James   Wildfire (World 1915) Jockey Chappie Raster

Jenkins, J. Wesley   His Father's Wife (World 1919) Mose
                              Good-Bad Wife, The (McCord Productions 1921)
                                  Scipio

Jenkins, William   Counterfeit Love (Playgoers Pictures 1923) Mose

Jonasson, Frank   Fighting Coward, The (Paramount 1914) Rumbo

Keaton, Buster   College (United Artists, Sept. 10, 1927) The Boy

Kelly, Paul   A Juvenile Love Affair (Vitagraph 1912) Old Negro's
                                  Son

Kennedy, Mary   Wife for Wife (World 1919) A mulatto

Kennedy, Tom   Ham and Eggs at the Front (Warner Bros. 1927)
                                  Lazarus

Kerrigan, J. Warren   One Dollar Bid (Paralta 1918) Questionable white
                                  origin--sold for $1 in Kentucky

Kingston, Natalie   River of Romance (Paramount 1929) An Octoroon

Kohner, Susan   Imitation of Life (Universal 1959) Mulatto

Lambert, Clara   Her Husband's Wife (Paramount 1913) Aunt Delia

La Pearl, Harry   Black and White (MinA 1915) Black Clown

La Varnie, Laura   Butterflies and Orange Blossoms (Biograph 1914)
                               Mammy

La Verne, Lucille   White Rose, The (United Artists 1923) Auntie Easter

Lee, Dick   Seventeen (Paramount 1916) Genesis

Lee, Jennie   An Innocent Magdalene (Triangle 1916) Mammy
                           A Woman's Awakening (Triangle 1917) Mammy

Leighton, Lillian   Secret Service (Paramount 1919) Martha
                           Louisiana (Paramount 1919) Aunt Cassandry
                           Red Hot Romance (First National 1922) Mammy
                           Crinoline and Romance (Metro 1923) Abigail
                           Bedroom Window, The (Paramount 1924) Mammy

Lewis, Mitchell   Bar Sinister, The (Edgar Lewis 1917) Negro Ben
                               Swift

Lewis, Sheldon   River Woman, The (Gotham Productions, 1928)
                               Mulatto Mike

Loy, Myrna   Across the Pacific (Warner Bros. 1926) Roma, a
                               half-caste
                           Heart of Maryland, The (Warner Bros. 1927) A
                               Mulatto
                           (Myrna Loy played many exotic roles--including
                               a Black woman in Ham and Eggs at the Front.)
                           Crimson City, The (Warner Bros. 1928) Chinese
                           Noah's Ark (Warner Bros. 1929) Slave Girl
                           Black Watch, The (Fox 1929) Yasmani (Hindu)
                           Desert Song, The (Warner Bros. 1929) Azuri
                           Evidence (Warner Bros. 1929) Native Girl
                           Squall, The (First National 1929) Gypsy Nubi
                           Great Divide, The (First National 1930) Manuella--
                               half-breed
                           Isle of Escape, The (Warner Bros. 1930) Moira,
                               Native Girl
                           Mask of Fu Manchu, The (Metro-Goldwyn-Mayer
                               1932) Fu Manchu's Daughter

Lucas, Wilfred   His Trust (Biograph 1911) Negro Slave
                           His Trust Fulfilled (Biograph 911) Negro Slave

McCord, Mrs. Lewis   Warrens of Virginia, The (Paramount 1914) Sapho

Mackin, John E.   Wife for Wife (Kalem 1915) Mulatto George

Maison, Edna   In Slavery Days (Universal 1913) An Octoroon

Marion, George, Sr.   Excuse Me (H. W. Savage Productions 1915) Negro
                               Porter
                           Texas Steer, A (First National 1927) Fishback

Marsh, George   Southern Justice (Universal 1917) Uncle Zeke

Martin, J.	A Fair Rebel (Biograph 1916) Nelse
Mattox, Martha	Scarlet Drop, The (Universal 1918) Mammy
Miller, Ella	Fog Bound (Paramount 1923) Mammy
Miller, Frances	Adventures of Carol, The (World 1917) Mammy Bondage of Fear (World 1917) Mammy Diamonds and Pearls (World 1917) Mammy Troublemakers (Fox Film Corp. 1917) Mammy
Miller, Fred	Sisters (American Releasing Corp. 1922) Negro Servant
Miller, Liza	In the Diplomatic Service (Metro 1916) Mammy
Montague, Monte	Tip-Off, The (Universal 1929) Negro
Moran, Polly	Hunt, The (Keystone 1915) Black gal By Stork Delivery (Keystone 1916) Janitor's Wife
Nesbitt, Miriam	Lena (Edison 1913) posing as Negro maid "Lena"
Nova, Hedda	Bar Sinister, The (Edgar Lewis 1917) Belle Davis--raised as Negro
Oliver, Guy	Secret Service (Paramount 1919) Jonas
Osborne, Jefferson	Around the World (Cub 1916) Cannibal
O'Shea, James	Jim Bludsoe (Triangle 1917) Negro Banty Tim
Pearson, Beatrice	Lost Boundaries (Film Classics 1948) Mulatto Marcia Carter
Peterson, Jerry	Janice Meredith (Metro-Goldwyn 1924) Cato
Phillips, Carmen	Fighting Coward, The (Paramount 1924) Mexico--an octoroon
Pitts, ZaSu	Pretty Ladies (Metro-Goldwyn-Mayer 1925) Blackface disguise
Pixley, Gus	Saved from the Vampire (Biograph 1915) Jumbo Bridge Across, The (Biograph 1915) Uncle Pompey Mystery of Henri Villard, The (Biograph 1915) Negro
Powell, Russell	Carnivals and Cannibals (L-Ko 1917) Cannibal Chief No Place to Go (First National 1927) Cannibal Chief
Price, Kate	A Juvenile Love Affair (Vitagraph 1912) Old Mammy
Prouty, Jed	Her Second Choice (Vitagraph 1926) Black Stable Boy

Reagan, Martin   Littlest Rebel, The (Photoplay Productions 1914)
                        Uncle Billy

Rice, Josephine   Big Tremaine (Metro 1916) Mammy

Richardson, Jack   Free and Equal (Woods-Ince 1915 & 1925) Alexander
                        Marshall, Negro

Robson, Mrs. Stuart   At the Old Cross Roads (Select 1914) Old Mammy

Roccardi, Albert   Liar, The (Fox 1918) Sam Harris--Negro

Sadler, Josie   John Tobin's Sweetheart (Vitagraph 1913) Black
                        Princess

St. Leonard, Florence   Bar Sinister, The (Edgar Lewis 1917) Lindy Davis,
                        Mammy

Schumann, Milton   Varmint, The (Paramount 1917) The Coffee Colored
                        Angel

Shea, William   Doctor Polly (Vitagraph 1914) Zeb

Shepard, Iva   In Slavery Days (Universal 1913) Mammy Sue

Short, Florence   Idol Dancer, The (First National 1920) Black Pansy

Smith, Clara   Rose of Sharon, The (Essanay 1913) Mammy
                        Tit for Tat (Essanay 1913) Negro Woman

Smith, J. S.   Out of the Jaws of Death (Kalem 1913) George, faith-
                        ful slave

Sparks, Frances   A Romance of Happy Valley (Paramount 1919) Topsy

Stevens, Jessie   Girl of the Gypsy Camp (Edison 1915) Mammy

Strong, Porter   A Romance of Happy Valley (Paramount 1919) Negro
                        farmhand
                        Idol Dancer, The (First National 1920) Black minister
                        Peter
                        Dream Street (United Artists 1921) Samuel Jones
                        One Exciting Night (United Artists 1922) Romeo
                        Washington
                        White Rose, The (United Artists 1923) Apollo

Sweatnam, Willis   County Chairman, The (Paramount 1914) Sassafras
                        Livingston

Sydmeth, Louise   A Queen for a Day (Edison 1912) Negro Maid

Tincher, Fay   Excitement (Universal 1924) Mammy

Von Meter, Harry   The Lost Sermon (American 1914) The Negro

Wadsworth, William   A Clean Sweep (Edison 1915) Blackface chimney
                       sweep

Walker, Robert   Dear Old Girl (Essanay 1913) Jim, faithful old Negro

Ward, Carrie Clark   Conqueror, The (Fox 1917) Mammy

Ward, Lucille   Her Father's Son (Paramount 1916) Mammy Chloe

Warde, Francesca   Mice and Men (Paramount 1916) Mammy

West, George   Human Hearts (Universal 1922) Old Mose
                       The Tar Heel Warrior (Triangle 1917) Uncle Tobe

William, John J.   Marse Covington (Metro 1915) Uncle Dan

Willis, Susanne   Uncle Tom's Cabin (Paramount 1918) Aunt Chloe

Wilson, Hal   A Juvenile Love Affair (Vitagraph 1912) The Old
                       Negro

Wilson, Tom   Americano, The (Triangle 1917) Negro Tom
                       Greatest Question, The (Paramount 1919) Uncle Zeke
                       Sink or Swim (Fox 1920) George Washington Brown
                       Red Hot Romance (First National 1922) Thomas Snow
                       Alias Julius Caesar (First National 1922) Mose
                       Minnie (First National 1922) Janitor
                       Reported Missing (Selznick 1922) Negro Sam
                       Soft Boiled (Fox 1923) Negro Butler
                       Fools in the Dark (FBO 1924) Diploma
                       His Darker Self (Hodkinson 1924) Bill Jackson
                       Secrets of the Night (Universal 1925) Old Tom Jeffer-
                       son White
                       American Pluck (Charwick 1925) Jefferson Lee
                       Manhattan Madness (Fine Arts Pictures 1925) Porter
                       Best-Bad Man, The (Fox 1925) Sambo
                       California Straight Ahead (Universal 1925) Sambo
                       Madame Behave (Christie 1925) Creosote
                       Rainmaker, The (Paramount 1926) Chocolate
                       Across the Pacific (Warner Bros. 1926) Tom--Negro
                       servant
                       No Control (PDC 1927) Asthma

Wolff, Jane   Pudd'nhead Wilson (Paramount 1916) Roxy

BIBLIOGRAPHY

Addenbrooke, David. The Royal Shakespeare Company (William Kimber, London, 1974)

Allen, Percy. The Stage Life of Mrs. Stirling (E. P. Dutton & Co., 1924)

Allen, Shirley S. Samuel Phelps and Sadler's Wells Theatre (Wesleyan University Press, 1970)

Arandell, Dennis. The Story of Sadler's Wells (Hamish Hamilton, London, 1965)

Asche, Oscar. Oscar Asche by Himself (Hurst & Blackett, Ltd., London, 1929)

Atkinson, Brooks. Broadway (The Macmillan Company, New York, 1970)

Avery, Emmett L. The London Stage (1700-1729) (Southern Illinois Press, 1960)

Baker, Henry Barton. English Actors (Henry Holt & Co., New York, 1879)

Baker, Herschell. John Philip Kemble (Greenwood Press, 1942)

Baldick, Robert. The Life and Times of Frédérick Lemaître (Hamish Hamilton, London, 1959)

Ball, Robert Hamilton. Shakespeare on Silent Film (Theatre Arts Books, New York, 1968)

Barnes, Eric Wollencott. The Man Who Lived Twice (Charles Scribner & Sons, New York, 1956)

Barry, Faith. Langston Hughes: Before and After Harlem (Lawrence Hill & Co., 1983)

Barrymore, Ethel. Memories (Harper Bros., New York, 1955)

Barton, Margaret. Garrick (The Macmillan Company, 1949)

Behn, Aphra. Oroonoko; or The Royal Slave, A True Story (London, 1688)

Benson, Frank R. My Memoirs (Ernest Benn, Ltd., London, 1930)

Bingham, Madelene. Henry Irving, The Greatest Victorian Actor (Stein & Day, New York, 1978)

Birdoff, Harry. The World's Greatest Hit--Uncle Tom's Cabin (S. F. Vanni, 1947)

Bradley, A. C. Shakespearean Tragedy (Macmillan-St. Martin's Press, 1904)

Brady, William A. Showman (E. P. Dutton & Co., Inc., 1937)

Bordman, Gerald. American Musical Theatre (Oxford University Press, 1978)

_____. Jerome Kern (Oxford University Press, 1980)

_____. Oxford Companion to American Theatre (Oxford University Press, 1984)

Bowdler, Thomas. Family Editon of Shakespeare (1818)

Brook, Donald. A Pageant of English Actors (Rockliff, London, 1950)

Brooke, Dinah. Les Enfants du Paradis (Lorrimer, London, 1968)

Brown, Karl. Adventures with D. W. Griffith (Farrar, Straus and Giroux, New York, 1973)

Brown, T. Allston. A History of the New York Stage (Benjamin Blom, 3 vols., 1903)

_____. Early History of Negro Minstrelsy (New York Clipper, 1912)

Bullough, Geoffrey. Narrative and Dramatic Sources of Shakespeare (Routledge and Paul, London, 1957)

Campbell, Oscar James, and Quinn, Edward G. Readers Encyclopedia of Shakespeare (Thomas Y. Crowell Company, New York, 1966)

Carlson, Marvin A. Theatre of the Revolution (Cornell University Press, 1966)

_____. The German Stage in the 19th Century (Scarecrow Press, 1972)

_____. The French Stage (Scarecrow Press, 1972)

Chute, Marchette. Shakespeare of London (E. P. Dutton & Co., 1949)

Cinthio (Giovanni Battista Giraldi). Gli Degli Hecatomimithi (1565)

Clapp, William W., Jr. Record of the Boston Stage (James Munroe & Co., 1853)

Collins, Herbert F. L. Talma: A Biography of an Actor (Hill & Wang, New York, 1964)

Condee, James. Thespian Dictionary (Publishers, 1805)

Cuttrell, John. Laurence Olivier (Prentice-Hall, 1975)

Davies, Thomas. Memoir of the Life of David Garrick (London, 1780)

Doran, Dr. Their Majesties Servants (W. H. Allen & Co., 2 vols., London, 1864)

_____. Annals of the English Stage (6 vols., London, 1938)

Downer, Alan S. William Charles Macready: The Eminent Tragedian (Harvard University Press, 1966)

Duncan, Barry. The St. James Theatre: Its Strange and Complete History (Barrie & Rockliff, London, 1964)

Dunlap, William. Memoirs of George Frederick Cooke (Henry Colburn, London, 1813)

_____. History of the American Theatre (Richard Bentley, London, 1833)

Dunning, John. Tune in Yesterday (Prentice-Hall, 1976)

Durham, Frank. DuBose Heyward: The Man Who Wrote Porgy (University of South Carolina Press, 1954)

Eaton, Walter Pritchard. Plays and Players (Stewart & Kidd, Cincinnati, 1916)

Echert, Charles W. Focus on Shakespearean Films (Prentice-Hall, Inc., 1972)

Elsom, John, and Tomalin, Nicholas. The History of the National Theatre (Jonathan Cape, London, 1978)

Engle, Gary D. This Grotesque Essence (Louisiana State University Press, 1978)

Field, Kate. Charles Albert Fechter (Benjamin Blom, London, 1882)

Findlater, Richard. Lilian Baylis: The Lady of the Old Vic (Allen Lane, London, 1975)

Fitzgerald, Percy. The Kembles (Savell, Edwards & Co., London) (Tinsley Brothers, 1871)

Fitzsimons, Raymond. Edmund Kean: Fire from Heaven (The Dial Press, 1976)

Fleahy, Frederick Gard. A Chronicle History of the Life and Work of William Shakespeare (London, 1886)

Foner, Philip S. Paul Robeson Speaks (Brunner & Mazel, New York, 1978)

Forbes, Bryan. That Despicable Race (Elm Tree Books, London, 1980)

Forbes-Robertson, Sir Johnstone. A Player Under Three Reigns (Little Brown & Co., 1925)

Fordin, Hugh. Getting to Know Him (Random House, New York, 1977)

Foster, Charles H. The Rungless Ladder (Duke University Press, 1954)

Foy, Eddie, and Harlow, Alvin F. Clowning Through Life (E. P. Dutton & Co., 1928)

France, Richard. The Theatre of Orson Welles (Associated University Press, 1977)

Francisco, Charles. The Radio City Music Hall (E. P. Dutton & Co., 1979)

Freedley, George, and Reeves, John A. A History of the Theatre (Crown Publishers, New York, 1941)

Frohman, Daniel. Encore (Lee Furman, New York, 1939)

Gagey, Edmund M. The San Francisco Stage: A History (Greenwood Press, 1950)

Genest, John. The English Stage (1660-1830) (H. E. Carrington, 10 vols., London, 1832)

Gielgud, John; Miller, John; Powell, John. Gielgud: An Actor and His Time (Clarkson N. Potter, Inc., New York, 1979)

Gilliam, Dorothy Butler. Paul Robeson (New Republic Book Co., Inc., Washington, D.C., 1976)

Gish, Lillian. The Movies, Mr. Griffith and Me (Prentice-Hall, 1969)

Goreau, Angeline. Reconstructing Aphra (Dial Press, New York, 1980)

Hawkins, F. W. The Life of Edmund Kean (Tinsley Bros., London, 1869)

Hayman, Ronald. John Gielgud (Random House, 1971)

Hillebrand, Harold Newcomb. Edmund Kean (AMS Press, New York, 1966)

Hodge, Francis. Yankee Theatre (University of Texas Press, 1964)

Hoyt, Edwin P. Paul Robeson: The American Othello (World Publishing Co., 1967)

Hughes, Alan. Henry Irving, Shakespearean (Cambridge University Press, 1981)

Hughes, Langston. I Wonder as I Wander (Hill & Wang, 1956)

Hunter, G. K. Dramatic Identities and Cultural Tradition (Liverpool University Press, 1978)

Ireland, Joseph Norton. A Memoir of the Professional Life of Thomas Abthorpe Cooper (Burt Franklin, New York, 1888)

Irving, Laurence. Henry Irving, the Actor and His World (Faber & Faber, London, 1951)

Jefferson, Joseph. The Autobiography of Joseph Jefferson (The Century Company, 1889)

Jones, Emrys. The Origins of Shakespeare (Oxford Clarendon Press, 1977)

Jorgens, Jack J. Shakespeare on Film (Indiana University Press, 1977)

Joseph, Bertram. The Tragic Actor (Routledge & Kegan Paul, London, 1959)

Kahn, E. J., Jr. The Merry Partners (Random House, 1955)

Kelly, Linda. The Kemble Era (Random House, 1980)

Kimmel, Stanley. The Mad Booths of Maryland (Dover Publications, New York, 1940)

Kirkham, E. Bruce. The Building of Uncle Tom's Cabin (University of Tennessee Press, 1977)

Knight, Arthur. The Liveliest Art (The Macmillan Company, 1957)

Langner, Lawrence. The Magic Curtain (E. P. Dutton Co., Inc., 1950)

Laurie, Joe, Jr. Vaudeville (Henry Holt & Co., New York, 1953)

Leavitt, M. B. Fifty Years of Theatrical Management (Broadway Publishing Co., 1912)

Lennep, William Van. The London Stage (1660-1800) (12 vols., Southern Illinois University Press, 1958)

Leonard, Eddie. What a Life: I'm Telling You (Leonard, 1935)

Lockridge, Richard. Darling of Misfortune (The Century Company, 1932)

McBride, Joseph. Orson Welles (The Viking Press, 1972)

Macliammóir, Michéal. All for Hecuba (Methuen & Co., 1946)

_____. Put Money in Thy Purse (Methuen & Co., 1952)

MacQueen-Pope, W. The Footlights Flickered (Herbert Jenkins, London, 1959)

_____. Ladies First (W. H. Allen, London, 1952)

_____. Haymarket: Theatre of Perfection (W. H. Allen, London, 1948)

Magarshack, David. Stanislavsky (Greenwood Press, 1950)

Manvell, Roger. Shakespeare and the Film (A. S. Barnes, 1979)

_____. Sarah Siddons (G. P. Putnam, 1970)

Marshall, Herbert, and Stack, Mildred. Ira Aldridge, the Negro Tragedian (Macmillan & Co., 1958)

Mathews, Brander, and Hutton, Laurence. Macready, Forrest and Their Contemporaries (L. C. Page & Co., Boston, 1886)

Meltzer, Milton. Langston Hughes (Thomas Y. Crowell Co., 1968)

Mitchell, Lofton. Black Drama (Hawthorn Books, Inc., New York, 1967)

Moody, Richard. The Astor Place Riot (Indiana University Press, 1958)

_____. Edwin Forrest (Alfred A. Knopf, New York, 1960)

_____. America Takes the Stage (Indiana University Press, 1955)

Morehouse, Ward. Prince of the American Theatre (J. P. Lippincott, Philadelphia, 1943)

Morris, Clara. Life on the Stage (McClure, Phillips & Co., 1901)

Morris, Lloyd. Curtain Time (Random House, 1953)

Moses, Montrose, J., and Brown, John Mason. The American Theatre As Seen by Its Critics, 1752-1934 (Cooper Square, rept. of 1934 ed.)

Nagler, A. M. A Source Book in Theatrical History (Dover Publications, Inc., New York, 1952)

Nathan, Hans. Dan Emmett and the Rise of Negro Minstrelsy (University of Oklahoma Press, 1962)

Noble, Peter. The Negro in Film (Hutchinson, London, 1948)

Novak, Maxmillian E., and Rodes, David Stuart. Thomas Southerne: Oroonoko (University of Nebraska Press, 1976)

O'Connor, Garry. Ralph Richardson--An Actor's Life (Atheneum, New York, 1982)

Odell, George C. D. Annals of the New York Stage (15 vols., Columbia University Press, 1949)

Olivier, Laurence. Confessions of an Actor (Simon and Schuster, New York, 1982)

Parish, James Robert, and Leonard, William T. The Funsters (Arlington House, 1979)

Paskman, Dailey. Gentlemen, Be Seated! (Clarkson N. Potter, Inc., 1976)

Pemberton, J. Edgar. The Kendalls (Dodd, Mead & Co., 1900)

Quinn, Arthur Hobson. A History of American Drama (Appleton-Century-Crofts, New York, 1927, 1936, 1955)

Rankin, Hugh F. The Theatre in Colonial America (University of North Carolina Press, 1960)

Rhode, Eric. A History of Cinema from Its Origins to 1970 (Hill & Wang, New York, 1976)

Rossi, Alfred. Astonish Us in the Morning: Tyrone Guthrie Remembered (Hutchinson, London, 1979)

Ruggles, Eleanor. The Prince of Players (W. W. Norton & Co., 1953)

Rust, Brian (with DeBus, Allen G.). The Complete Entertainment Discography (Arlington House, 1973)

Saintsbury, H. A., and Palmer, Cecil. We Saw Him Act: A Symposium of the Art of Sir Henry Irving (Benjamin Blom, 1939)

Salgado, Gamini. Eyewitnesses to Shakespeare (Barnes & Noble, 1975)

Salvini, Tommaso. Leaves from the Autobiography of Tommaso Salvini (The Century Company, New York, 1893)

Samples, Gordon. Lust for Fame (McFarland & Co., 1982)

Sampson, Henry T. Blacks in Blackface (Scarecrow Press, Inc., 1980)

Sann, Paul. The Lawless Decade (Crown Publications, 1957)

Seilhamer, George A. History of the American Theatre (3 vols., Globe Printing House, 1891)

Shattuck, Charles H. Shakespeare on the American Stage (Folger Shakespeare Library, 1976)

Sheehan, Vincent. Oscar Hammerstein I (Simon and Schuster, New York, 1956)

Sheldon, Esther K. Thomas Sheridan of Smock Alley (Princeton University Press, 1967)

Skinner, Otis. Footlights and Spotlights (Bobbs Merrill Co., 1923)

_____. The Last Tragedian (Dodd, Mead Co., 1939)

Speaight, Robert. Shakespeare on the Stage (Little, Brown & Co., 1973)

Spewack, Bernard. Shakespeare and the Allegory of Evil (Columbia University Press, 1958)

Stanislavski, Constantin. My Life in Art (Theatre Art Books, 1924)

Stoker, Bram. Personal Reminiscences (The Macmillan Company, 1906)

Stone, Fred. Rolling Stones (Whittesley House, New York, 1945)

Stone, George Washington, Jr., and Kahal, George M. David Garrick: A
    Critical Biography (Southern Illinois University Press, 1979)

Taylor, John Edward. Comparison of Cinthio's Tale and Shakespeare's
    Tragedy (Chapman and Hall, London, 1855)

Terry, Ellen. The Story of My Life (McClure & Co., New York, 1908)

Timberlake, Craig. The Bishop of Broadway (Library Publications, 1954)

Toll, Robert C. Blacking Up (Oxford University Press, 1974)

Toynbee, William. The Diaries of William Charles Macready (Benjamin Blom,
    2 vols., London, 1912)

Trewin, J. C. Benson and the Bensonians (Barrie & Rockcliff, London,
    1960)

_____. Shakespeare on the English Stage (Barrie & Rockcliff, London,
    1964)

Tynan, Kenneth. Curtains (Antheneum Press, 1961)

_____. Olivier: Actor and the Moor (Rupert Hart-Davis, London, 1966)

Watermeier, Daniel J. Between Actor and Critic (Princeton University Press,
    1971)

Williamson, Audrey. Old Vic Drama (Rockcliff, London, 1948)

_____ (with Landstone, Charles). The Bristol Old Vic (J. Garnett Miller,
    Ltd., 1957)

Wilson, Arthur Herman. A History of the Philadlephia Theatre (Greenwood
    Press, 1968)

Wilson, Forrest. Crusader in Crinoline (J. B. Lippincott Co., Philadelphia,
    1941)

Winter, William. In Memory of John McCullough (DeVinne Press, 1889)

_____. Life and Art of Edwin Booth (Macmillan Company, 1893)

_____. Other Days (Moffat, Yard & Co., 1908)

_____. The Wallet of Time (Moffat, Yard & Co., 1913)

Wilmoth, Don B. George Frederick Cooke: Machiavel of the Stage (Green-
    wood Press, 1980)

Wittke, Carl. Tambo and Bones (Duke University Press, 1930)

Wright, Richardson. Revels in Jamaica (Dodd, Mead & Co., 1937)

Young, Dr. Edward. The Revenge (Longman, Hurst, Pees and Orme, London, 1816)

Index 413